Scorched

Sands

of the

Kalahari

TREVOR FROST

Author's note

Brought up in a poor neighbourhood in Salisbury (now Harare), not only have I experienced hard times, but through circumstances, lived an extremely unique and challenging life.

Monica, my eldest sister, is abundantly blessed with a talent for writing. She successfully ran her own publishing company for a few years and is completely responsible for my becoming an author. She has written many published articles for various magazines and having a good idea of my unique bush experiences, never let up on persuading me to put them down on paper before they were lost forever.

Eventually I buckled to her pressure and self-published my first book *"Drilling Where Leopards Cough"* in February 2012. The book has been successful with minimal marketing apart from making it available on Amazon.com in paperback and Kindle format. Due to the odd negative comments over the last year regarding the word "Drilling" I have since changed the title to simply *"Where Leopards Cough"*.

Monica once again pressurised me into writing a sequel as she felt readers would now want to know what happened after we left Zimbabwe and immigrated to South Africa and ultimately on to Botswana.

"Scorched Sands of the Kalahari" is the result of this, but I feel the reader should read the first publication to fully appreciate my new book.

I trust you will enjoy the read either way.

With best wishes,

Trevor Frost

Contact detail:
E-mail: majortrevor.frost@gmail.com
Phone: 0027-46-6241803
Cell:0027-829415866

Review on Trevor Frost's first book:
"Drilling Where Leopards Cough"
Now marketed as:
"Where Leopards Cough"

I believe that *everyone* should write their autobiography, not necessarily for publication, but for their grandchildren and their children. This is what Trevor Frost has done and the result is a book full of adventure, set in the African bush and written well enough to appeal to all not just his family. His love of the African bush and the wild animals is apparent all the way through and his description of drilling procedures certainly breaks new ground for me.

It depicts a wonderful life for a young man who loves living in the great outdoors surrounded by the bush, the wild animals and the peace and quiet of a time long gone. At his side is his best friend, a dog named Major and between the two of them they get into a lot of trouble, mostly through Trevor's lack of foresight or fear. One can only assume that Trevor's guardian angel eventually retired completely worn out! He used up more lives than a cat!

Written in short chapters and certainly a page-turner the book will appeal to anyone who loves the bush or the animals of Africa and will certainly make those people who have to live in the city want to head for the closest game reserve as soon as possible.

Trevor,
I loved the book and wish you lots of sales and look forward to the sequel.
Wilma Jugensen

Foreword
By Penny Mitrovic

Shortly after retiring, then moving to and settling in Port Alfred five years ago, my husband and I met Trevor. Immediately we were drawn to his relaxed, friendly manner and sense of humour. The common ground was bowls and I assumed his healthy tanned look was due to the amount of bowls he played, but through subsequent discussions came to realise he'd spent most of his life outdoors, in work and play!

On meeting Trevor one initially doesn't have a hint of the formidably competitive spirit, extraordinary stamina and steely determination of the man or his ability to see opportunities where others only see impossible challenges. Furthermore, he has a really empathetic side, mostly evident with regard to animals! Before Trevor even hinted about publishing a book I was enthralled by how remarkably he could recall and regale one with isolated incidents from his life experiences.

I consider myself fortunate and privileged to have been involved in a small way in assisting Trevor in the publishing of this book and can assure any reader of an amazing journey during which insight into an abnormal lifestyle and new cultures will be experienced, a mixture of emotions experienced and, at times, tears shed and gasps uttered! In the end the reader will be left feeling the great sense of achievement of the author and perhaps ponder on their own life experiences and a possible new approach going forward.

Acknowledgements

Editor

Penny Mitrovic

Sub-Editor

Jennifer Frost

Proofreading and Typesetting

Daryl-Anne Leveton

Chapter 1

Silently I sat watching from the driver's seat of our 1958 Ford Fairlane with the 302 V-8 engine purring like a kitten as the countryside flashed by. All our worldly possessions had been crammed into the vehicle utilising every available space with only the driver's seat left open for me.

Les, my wife, and our two infant children stayed behind with her parents and would be joining me some time later once settled. Dion, our second child, was only a couple of months old at the time. As much as we hated the idea of being apart, we both felt he was too young for a trip like this considering we were heading off into the unknown.

Emigrating from Rhodesia (now known as Zimbabwe) to South Africa was not only stressful, but also extremely heartbreaking. Were we making the right decision? We had both spent all our lives in that wonderful country and would now be leaving behind our immediate family and friends.

I had been successful in my application for the post of a diamond driller at the Messina Copper Mine situated in the North Eastern corner of South Africa, fifteen kilometres from the Beitbridge Border Post that spans the Limpopo River, the international boundary separating Rhodesia and South Africa. For the first time since our family became complete with our two sons Darrin and Dion, we were going to be living in a house, albeit a mine house, we could kind of call our own. We could make it as comfortable as possible, not withstanding our desperate money constraints at the time. One of the main reasons for me resigning from my employment in Rhodesia was that we would no longer need to share a house with anyone or live in a tiny caravan.

The passage through the passport and customs controls at Beitbridge is always a time consuming exercise and this was no exception. One hour after my arrival on the Rhodesian side, I drove off leaving the Border Post behind, now legally in South Africa. Fortunately, prior to my leaving Rhodesia we had applied for permanent residence in South

1

Africa, having all the relevant documentation to produce to the immigration officials was a huge help.

On my arrival at the mine in Messina, as instructed, I reported to the Mine office. I was briefed on the location of our new accommodation together with being issued my portfolio outlining the requirements expected of me work wise. Once all the documentation requiring my signature was disposed of I left with one of the office assistants to find what was to be our new house.

The dwelling or possibly more accurately the shack was extremely small, adjoined on either side by the same type shack, for lack of a better word. In our row there were five such houses split only by the fence running between each in the front and back garden. There was a similar row of houses opposite and the same again joining our two blocks together in the shape of a U.

In the back garden, there was only room for a single washing line with the front not being that much larger. I was pleased to see ours had a small swing, the type with a tyre cut in half used as the seat. I felt sure our two boys would enjoy that, once old enough. Parking was in the open space in front of each house outside of the fence line. It felt impersonal parking there, more like parking at a shopping centre than at your home.

Eventually after unpacking the car and almost filling the house in the process due to the lack of interior space, I drove off to the Post Office to use the pay phone to let Les know I had arrived safely. She was excited to hear from me and after discussing my trip asked about the house.

"Well.... I managed to squash all our belongings from the car inside and the rest I will leave as a surprise for you when you arrive," I answered. "However I must stress that when you do come down, please pack lightly!"

I could immediately hear the concern in her voice, "From that I have to assume the house is tiny?"

"Well to give you the good news, it is a touch bigger than the caravan we were offered in Filabusi!" I said with a laugh.

"I'm not sure I see the funny side!" she exclaimed. "Are you telling me we have made this huge decision to move out of Rhodesia due to accommodation issues and yet will be moving into some insignificant little shack in South Africa?" She really did not sound happy. "So what other good news do have for me?" she asked sarcastically.

"Well I haven't been here long enough to find any more, so hopefully will have something else for you in a couple of days." Once again, I

2

laughed when saying it. The humorous side of that seemed to ease the tension a little.

I then went on to tell her about the shift work and the various shafts I would be working in underground. Initially I was to supervise five underground diamond drills. The operators were all black South Africans. Once the regular underground supervisors returned from leave in a few weeks time I would move out from underground to operate one of the five surface rigs on the mine.

Chapter 2

The town of Messina is the most northerly settlement in South Africa and lies fifteen kilometres south of the Limpopo River, which forms the border of Zimbabwe and Botswana. Ancient indigenous African tribes discovered the copper deposits centuries ago. Many stone hammers, soapstone artefacts and iron tools were discovered in the area. On the high ridges within twenty kilometres of Messina, ancient smelting sites are still plainly visible. Tales of this nature led Lt.-Colonel J.P. Grenfell to explore the area and eventually form a mining company in 1905. By 1914, Messina was exporting high-grade matte to Welsh refineries. Between 1938 and 1940, Messina was producing 10,000 tonnes of copper annually.

From inception of mining operations, forty million tonnes of ore yielded approximately 700,000 tonnes of copper. Copper, which occurs in the primary sulphide minerals chalcopyrite, bornite and chalcocite, is the only economic metal from these ore bodies. The chalcopyrite is present along the peripheries of ore bodies and is gradually replaced by bornite, chalcocite and native copper towards the centre and downward. There are five separate mines: the Artonvilla, Spence, Messina, Harper and the Western Campbell mine. These mines show slight variation in their local geology and mineralization. In 1992, the last mine (Messina - No. 5 Shaft) stopped production and was closed down. This ended 88 years of copper mining in this region. Messina became famous for its quartz crystals. It is by far the most abundant and attractive mineral from a collector's standpoint because of the habits and varieties of size and groups, together with several colourful secondary mineral inclusions. The Messina Mine (No. 5 Shaft) is famous for its wealth in beautiful quartz crystals ranging from microscopic to a metre in size. Almost all of the larger crystals are zoned internally and one can find over a dozen phantom layers in some crystals. The presence of flaky specula hematite gives a striking sparkle to the well-formed clear crystals. A feature of the quartz crystals is that many are doubly terminated, the

4

large crystal in a group is sometimes encircled by a peripheral halo of small crystals. The colour of the calcite ranges from bright yellow or orange to white. Also found in the Messina Mines are large groups of calcite.

Chapter 3

I was up at 6am on my first day of work to report at Spence Mine shaft at 7.45am. There we changed into our overalls and mine safety boots with steel toecaps. Then on route to the mineshaft, collect, sign for and attach the heavy battery to our belts giving power via an electric cable to our underground light firmly clipped to our hard hats. We were now ready for our decent via the cable car to our relevant stations at various levels down the shaft. All instructions to the hoist driver were through a coded ringing mechanism that worked safely and efficiently.

The first few days were to some extent a learning curve for me as I had worked on surface diamond drilling rigs only. Air produced by large high-pressure compressors was used to drive the pneumatically driven rigs. This is delivered to the drill sites through endless pipelines winding through the drives like never ending serpents. The machines gave off a high-pitched, almost deafening sound. When more than one machine was in operation in the same section the sound resonating from the machines was quite something. They were functional and to all intents and purposes reliable. The rate of progress required was in the region of six metres per shift per machine to qualify for the production bonus. Generally, this was not a problem, but required your constant close attention. Any delays required attention immediately to maintain the production throughout the month.

Often the rigs were not all on the same level, which entailed an enormous amount of ladder climbing. I managed in a short time to become extremely ladder fit. I say ladder fit because when rugby training started at the mine club I thought it would be a breeze. Well ladder fit and running fit are two entirely different things. Within one lap of the field, I was breathing heavily. Just goes to prove how using separate muscle groups affect your fitness levels.

Essentially the rigs operated around the clock Monday to Friday, running on three shifts per day; morning 8am to 4pm, afternoon 4pm to 12pm and night 12pm to 8am. We were all issued with our shift schedules, with everyone at some stage doing the dreaded 12pm to 8am.

I found it difficult adjusting to the shift work after years of operating surface rigs from sun up to sun down. Yet it had its advantages, especially over the weekends when running the morning shift. Once you came out the shaft at 4pm, you were off for the whole weekend through to Monday afternoon to start the 4pm shift. This gave us a long weekend every three weeks.

On one of my day shifts, we were working close to the face of an old deserted drive. The main drive was approximately 500 metres long from the shaft. Ten metres before the end of the main drive there were crosscuts off to the left and right. I was to have two machines drilling in each. Recent development work to extend the main drive had begun in earnest. Each day the jumper drill crews moved in and drilled the pattern of holes clearly marked out with paint by the miner for the charging of explosives. It never always worked out this way, but the plan was to drill and charge all the holes by 3.30pm each day as 4pm was the standardised blasting time throughout the mine. Once the air was free of fumes the night shift would then come in to clear the development end of the blast material ready for further development the following day.

A qualified miner with a valid blasting licence had to go in and 'make safe' our area as such before we could move in. He would check for loose hanging wall and ensure there were no live explosives or for that matter any dangerous substance or loose material. Once receiving the duly signed certificate of safety, we moved in and set up our rigs.

This involved placing the drilling bar in an upright position. Once correctly set up and adjusted we drove wooden wedges tightly between the top of the bar and the hanging wall of the drive. When stable, with the use of a crow bar and screw jack attached to the base of the bar, we jacked it tightly into the hanging wall wedges.

The screw feed machine was then attached via a clamping system to the bar in the precise direction and angle required. Connections to air and water lines completed the rigging exercise and drilling would commence. It must have taken in the region of an hour to set all the rigs up and start operations for the day.

I floated between the rigs in both left and right crosscuts checking both production and safety wise all was in order. The noise from the rigs together with the jumper drills going full tilt in the main drive was deafening. We were all in possession of earplugs and kept them firmly in place the entire shift. Ear damage without this protection was a certainty.

With only a few minor problems, the shift had gone well with reasonable production. It was eerily quiet with none of the rigs running due to pulling rods for core removal. After the resonating scream of the air motors, I felt like I would be able to hear a pin drop. I was about to walk over to the left crosscut to check the core. As I turned, I noticed three lights go by in the main drive fifty metres away heading towards the shaft. Initially I thought nothing of it, but for some reason checked my wristwatch for the time.

A cold chill ran down my back! It was blasting time and the shift boss responsible should have cleared us from the crosscuts some thirty minutes ago. I immediately assumed they must have charged the explosives, ignited the fuse and were heading back to the safety of the main shaft to catch the cage to surface! In total panic, I immediately shut the two rigs down in our working area and shouted for the men to run to the shaft. I then went tearing off waving my light in an attempt to warn the crews drilling on the rigs in the opposite crosscut of our disastrous predicament!

As I burst out into the main drive I looked to the right and to my shock and total disbelief the tell-tale sparkle of the lit fuse was confirmation the explosives could go off anytime! Running in total panic and shouting at the same time to try and get the attention of my guys on the other rig, my foot caught a rock and I went crashing down onto the rough floor. I had hardly hit the ground when I was up and running again. By this stage the crews realised what the problem was, had shut their machines off and were running along the crosscut as fast as their legs could carry them.

The ironic thing was, from their working area, we had to run back towards the danger to get to the main drive then turn right towards the shaft. As the nine of us were running at full speed around a sweeping left hand bend some three hundred metres from the blast face, there was suddenly the loudest explosion you could imagine. To be honest I was not sure if I heard or felt it. The resulting blast of air knocked all of us flat onto the ground with hard hats and lights flying in all directions. I am sure not one of us believed we were going to survive! How we would ever manage to get through the vent doors before the fumes overwhelmed us was beyond comprehension. We had been warned repeatedly just how lethal the post blast fumes were.

Scratching around to retrieve our hats and lights from the initial blast, we struggled to our feet, stumbling, and running as fast as we could eventually arrived at the vent door. It felt like a lifetime since the drama started when in effect it was only a few minutes. Construction of the ventilation door is manufactured from conveyer belt rubber material being held in place either side through a heavy weight attached to a chain. As luck would have it, trying to pull the door open too hastily the chain on the shaft side caught one of the bolts on the railway line and held fast.

Through sheer panic, we put all our energy into pulling at it, but to no avail. How could this happen to us? How is it possible the shift boss responsible for clearing the end could have forgotten about us? What would the outcome have been if I had not looked down the crosscut at just the right time to see the lights? Had I not checked my watch and seen the time we would already be dead! I shouted at the crew, pushed them away from the door, and in so doing released the tension on the chain. It came loose and we managed to open it and get through into a safety area.

The shift boss's face turned an opaque white colour when seeing us all running out the drive towards the shaft. He had totally forgotten his briefing of us moving into the two crosscuts. For the last month, there had only been the drilling crew on the face and the miners working that area. He moved toward us on shaky legs looking like he had just seen a ghost while enquiring if there was anybody left behind. The relief on his face after we had made our head count was immense.

After some heated discussion before catching the cage back to the surface we agreed that due to the incredible amount of paper work, investigation and the high probability of dismissals of those responsible we would not say anything. Hey, we are all human and make mistakes. However, he owed us *'BIG TIME'* and made sure he paid his due in drinks and cigarettes to my operators and helpers. Often something good comes from bad, but only if you are prepared to look hard enough. If nothing else, the almost tragic disaster certainly tightened up safety procedures on our level and all went smoothly thereafter.

Another particularly interesting shift was at No 5 shaft. I was working the night shift with all five rigs running like a dream. I had seen a light approaching our position and wondered who it could be. As he came closer, I was surprised to see it was my good friend John, the Mine Captain.

"Hi Trevor, how is the drilling going down here?" he asked. I gave him the run down on the shift telling him things were running smoothly.

'Well as you have some time on your hands I want you to come and see something on the section above us." He sounded excited.

I was surprised at his request. "What's happening up there? I certainly don't have any rigs working on that level."

"It's your lucky day so don't ask questions, come with me, I promise you'll be amazed at what you are about to see and will be privileged to be only the second person in the world to see it!" John would not tell me, as he did not want to spoil the surprise. Intrigued off we went to the main shaft and climbed the ladders to the level above us. Once up we walked for about thirty minutes before reaching the end of the main drive.

"Okay, so what is so unusual about a development end with loose fly rock everywhere after the blast?" I asked still completely puzzled as to what could have excited John to such an extent.

"Follow me," John said and crouched down low to squeeze his way through the smallest opening you could imagine. Following like a little puppy, I crouched down and pushed my way through. As I stood up, I was speechless being in total awe of my surroundings. I cast my light all around me and to my amazement I was standing in a crystal palace, well that was the first thought that went through my mind. There were crystals of every size and length surrounding me. The cavity was approximately three metres by two metres wide and four metres high. Being in total darkness our light made the crystals sparkle. There was no visible rock whatsoever, only an astonishing array of beautiful crystals with a clear pool of water in one corner to finish it off.

"Wow John, I have never seen anything quite as spectacular in my life!" I said excitedly having eventually found my voice after the initial surprise.

"Yes, I thought you would enjoy it and we are the only two people in the universe to have seen it!" He really had this look of total accomplishment due to his unusual discovery. Before giving the all clear for the night shift to go in to clean up, he had gone through checking the end for safety after the blast. Luckily he noticed a tiny opening on the one side of the resulting rubble and with some effort he managed to open it up enough to squeeze through into a once in a lifetime discovery.

I thanked him and felt honoured that he had taken the time to come down and call me. After having sealed off the opening to the crystal palace, he shut that section down. He then issued strict instruction to the night shift to clean up the rubble from the blast, but to stay well clear of the exciting discovery. He went on to tell them that once cleaned up of loose material, the drive was to be closed until further notice.

Thereafter the crystal palace remained as a unique attraction for any special visitors who came underground. Development of the drive was continued, but with a wide diversion around the priceless find. It made me wonder as to just how many people at any stage of their lives are ever lucky enough to be one of the first to witness such magnificent and natural beauty.

Chapter 4

Surprisingly, I was summoned to a meeting at the drilling superintendent's office after only three weeks on the mine. Some surface drilling was required in the Prieska area in North West Cape. There were four surface drill holes required, with further work dependant on results. Accommodation initially would be a caravan and he enquired if I would be interested.

To me the opportunity of drilling on surface exploration again was a huge incentive. I have and always will enjoy being outside in the open bush away from the hustle and bustle of city life. I was not worried in any way about working underground apart from the episode of almost been blown to pieces. However, I certainly cannot say I enjoyed it. Disappearing down a dark and oppressive mine shaft each day was not my idea of fun.

I readily agreed to go there, the thought of being out there soaking up the sun every day really sounded attractive. Added to the excitement I had never visited the north-west part of South Africa. One major concern however, speaking or understanding Afrikaans was not one of my strong points. All the labour in the area had a similar problem with English and only spoke Afrikaans. I nonetheless assured the superintendent I would get through it even if it meant just using hand signals.

Leaving his office, I set off immediately for the Post Office to phone and inform Les of the new arrangement. Although shocked at first she settled down to the idea. I explained it would only be for a few months and we would move back to Messina and our house as soon as the contract was completed. I packed the few belongings I owned and set off the following day heading for Prieska.

I met the company geologist in Prieska, a small Karoo town seemingly in the middle of nowhere. From there we set off to Marydale some sixty kilometres out of town. There I was introduced to the field officer I would be working with at the drill site. After spending a pleasant evening in the camp and meeting with some of the field staff I set off at first light the following morning for the drill site.

The previous drill operator had set the rig up on site prior to packing his bags and disappearing off to who knows where. Sadly, drillers have a reputation for this, to some loyalty to your company only goes as far as the next best offer. My caravan was seriously small and immediately I thought to myself how I had left Rhodesia for exactly that reason. The caravan offered us up there with our two young children was of similar size. However, I would be moving back to the Marydale camp to a small, but comfortable cottage as soon as the current hole was completed. I was informed that the results from the first two holes were extremely disappointing, therefore these would be the last to be drilled in the area. Considering I was on my own, I had no problem being out there.

I set about thoroughly checking all the drilling equipment to ensure there was oil in the engines and gearboxes. I checked the condition of the fan belts together with the cleanliness of the air filters. My full crew were on site and as expected, none of them could speak a word of English. Anyway, between my broken Afrikaans and hand signals we somehow managed to get the rig up and running. At the end of the shift I soaked myself in my tin tub bath and eventually climbed into bed by 8pm, I was desperately in need of a good night's rest. With an extremely long drive through from Messina to Prieska, I was tired to say the least.

All went well until the early hours of the following morning. I woke around 4am feeling freezing cold! Hey, this was not supposed to happen! This is a known hot part of the South Africa. No matter what I put on, I just could not warm up. Eventually daybreak arrived. I climbed out of bed, pulled on two pairs of long socks, denims and shirt, a full set of overalls, a thick jersey and a jacket. When I ventured out of the caravan, I could not believe my eyes. The drill rig was completely white under a layer of snow. So was everything else for as far as the eye could see.

That accounted for the extreme cold during the night and although the sun was trying to show its head, it was certainly chilly. I later discovered this was the first snow in the area for forty years! Why oh why did it have to pick now while I was out here in a caravan?

Ten days later I had completed the drill hole and as there were no more in that area, took the rig down, loaded everything onto the trucks and headed back to Marydale. Thereafter days came and went with no more drill holes marked out. I spent all my time doing maintenance repairs on the vehicles and generator sets around the camp. It kept me busy, but I needed to get back to drilling. Trying to survive on the basic wage was difficult, I needed to drill and make production bonuses.

The message came through on the Monday that Les and my two boys, Darrin our firstborn and Dion all of twelve weeks old at the time, were to fly to Kimberley, the closest commercial airport to our position, on that Wednesday. I was most excited about their arrival. The plane landed on time and it was such a thrill to see my family again. It felt like I had been on my own for months, but in reality was only six weeks. We talked non-stop on our way back to Marydale about all that had happened since last seeing each other.

Arriving at the cottage in the Marydale camp Les was quite taken aback to see just how small our cottage was. Generally, it had been used as single status accommodation, however, as the rest of the camp was full we had to make do.

Once again the dreary days passed by with no prospects of any drilling. I really was not happy with the situation and complained bitterly. I could not believe I was earning a salary for not doing anything apart from the odd maintenance job. The site geologist informed me that the likelihood of any further drilling for the next few weeks was extremely slim.

Our pride and joy, a1958 Ford Fairlane had served us well, however, it had started burning a significant amount of oil. What can you expect after having a few hundred thousand kilometres on the clock? I decided to head off into Prieska and order new rings and bearings for the old bus. I had purchased the car from a onetime owner who had informed me the engine was stock standard and never opened. This knowledge helped tremendously as I could confidently order standard rings and bearings. The garage owner really sounded like he knew what he was doing and said he would order them from his contact in Kimberley and should have them within a few days.

Once the spares arrived, I pulled the engine from the vehicle with the use of a tick-tok and stripped it down to check for the cause of the excessive burning of oil. Amazingly, there was little wear with only a slight ridge showing on the cylinders. I was relieved as it saved me the expense of a re-bore and new pistons, something financially I could ill afford.

Checking all the components carefully I found the only obvious problem being a broken oil ring on number 2 cylinder. Placing and old ring on top of a new one clearly indicated minor wear on all. With the use of a ridge cutter and honing machine loaned to me from my friend at the garage, I removed the ridge and glaze from the cylinders. This is essential to help the new rings bed-in and work efficiently.

I carefully fitted the new rings and bearings with the utmost care on cleanliness. As the old engine mountings were cracked and worn out through wear and tear over the years, I replaced them prior to reinstalling the motor. Once everything was complete, I cranked the engine a few times until the fuel reached the carburettor and surprisingly she fired into life with the unique V8 rumble, the sound of which almost made the hair on my arms stand up. I was confident we now had a car that would last us for many years to come.

Chapter 5

By this stage, I was at my wits end and complained bitterly to the site geologist due to not only the lack of work, but also our pathetic accommodation. I felt sorry for Les and the kids and believed I had let them down badly! Essentially I gave him three options, either sort it out, or if there were to be no more drill sites in the area, send us back to Messina or I would quit. Enough is enough and believe me I had certainly reached that point!

Miraculously the following day the geologist told me there was some drilling required in the Vosburg area southwest of Prieska. Before agreeing to go there, I asked the most important question, "Where are we going to live?" He replied saying we would have a cottage all to ourselves located on a farm many kilometres from anywhere. Apparently, it contained basic furniture, a gas stove and fridge. This sounded wonderful and by the following morning, we had packed and were heading off to a new adventure.

On arrival at the cottage, or possibly more accurately described as a small dwelling, we were pleasantly surprised. From outside it looked neat with a dry stream running behind the house and, surprisingly, a medium sized green tree in the front garden. I say garden, yet the only growth of any kind was the tree. There was not a blade of grass to be seen anywhere in the arid terrain.

Hey, things could be worse I thought to myself! Even Les managed to muster a smile at the sight. Amazing how when you have nothing any improvements, regardless how insignificant, are greatly appreciated.

The farmer eventually arrived and introduced himself. It was plain to see he came from farming stock and was an extremely nice old man. He had that sun ravaged look about him with a nice firm handshake and extremely calloused hands from years of hard work. He was most apologetic, but non-specific when explaining that we could possibly encounter a few problems with the cottage as it had not been lived in for fifteen years.

However, he stressed they had cleaned it up as best they could for our arrival. After going through the house with us he explained how everything worked, including the gas heater for hot water. Eventually, after wishing us a pleasant stay, he left, handing a sketch map to me showing the location of the main farmhouse, insisting we could come for help anytime. We bade him farewell and set about sorting ourselves out in the quaint little cottage.

The old wooden floorboards creaked as we walked through the lounge/dining room to the only bedroom. On our first night a series of scuttles throughout the house made sleep difficult, we figured it could only be rats, big ones! If ever Les had a pet hate it was most definitely with rats, she was far more relaxed confronted by a snake. To get to the toilet from our bedroom involved walking through the rat infested lounge area into the kitchen, then down a short passageway.

For Les this was going to be a nightmare in the dark knowing there were all these revolting critters running around. Anyway, we all slept pretty well and morning dawned with chickens clucking away whilst scratching around outside our window for food. They had wondered over from the small kraal on the opposite bank of the stream where some of the farm staff lived. Also in a small stockade were a couple of horses used for patrols of this section of the farm.

The geologist arrived around 8am and joined us for a cup of coffee prior to taking me out to the proposed drill site. We travelled approximately ten kilometres south on the secondary dirt road running past the front of our new abode, turned east through a concertina gate on a small farm road and then travelled a further eight kilometres of totally barren, flat land before arriving at the site. He walked around the area for a while before deciding the exact location of the exploration hole. With the use of a hammer, he knocked a peg into the ground marking the spot for me to set the rig up on and to drill at an angle of 45 degrees.

Puzzled that he had not inserted a line peg, I asked him in what direction I should set the rig. He shrugged his shoulders, vaguely looked around the surrounding landscape and told me to drill toward the left edge of a far off hill. Bewildered, I insisted we set the line pegs so there would be no comeback as to drilling in the wrong direction. This was prepared in an extremely haphazard manner, but in the general direction of the hill.

Seeing the look of total disbelief on my face, he explained it was a new geophysical generated drill target unlike the standard geological targets generally used. Essentially the hole was more for exploratory purposes to prove the worth of the extremely expensive geophysical

17

equipment recently acquired by the company. Being a geologist from the old traditional stock, he openly told me he had little to no faith in the system, but the instruction from head office was to drill so we were to go ahead with the hole regardless.

We set off again for roughly five kilometres on a vaguely discernible track across open ground and arrived at the borehole that I would be carting water from for drilling purposes. Constructed adjacent to the borehole was a sizeable water reservoir constantly fed via a windmill. I tasted the water and found it to be quite sweet and the geologist confirmed tests had been undertaken that the water was safe to drink.

Satisfied we left, heading back to the cottage where I could arrange for the rig to move onto site. On arrival, I was surprised to see Les and the kids standing outside in the shade of the tree. She had a concerned look on her face. I ran over to them and was staggered when informed of a beehive under the flooring in our bedroom. Les said that the movement in the abandoned house had obviously disturbed them and they had started flying into the room through the openings in the floorboards. Terrified the bees would attack the children she pushed them in their prams to our lone tree in the yard. She then shouted for the supervisor at the kraal to please come and help. Thankfully, he ran across to the cottage and immediately understood the problem through sign language from Les.

First off, using a medium sized tin, he brought some coals in from the fire. Then adding an unknown substance looking much like dry ground- up horse dung to the hot coals he miraculously made lots of smoke. He blew this smoke through the floorboards continuously. By this stage there were bees flying around everywhere. We all kept well clear of the action, terrified of being stung by the masses, yet the bees looking most lethargic never seemed to bother him in any way.

While they buzzed around him with many landing on his arms and face he looked calm and totally in control of the situation. With the use of a crowbar, he prised open a few floorboards. To our total shock attached to these was a massive beehive complete with honeycomb. Slowly he lifted these boards and carried them, bees and all outside. It seemed impossible that he was not stung, as they were everywhere. In his bid not to upset them any more than necessary, he steadily wandered off into the veld with his lethal parcel and disappeared in a cloud of bees. For some reason it reminded me of the Pied Piper and his rats. Sadly, however, the resident vermin remained hiding inside.

Our room was full of smoke from his concoction in the tin and although there were a few bees around, they were totally lethargic and uninterested in us. It was quite something to see a gaping hole where our bed had been. We had slept peacefully the previous night completely oblivious of being right over a huge swarm of bees!

I joked with Les saying, "If there was ever proof of the house being vacant for years, this had to be it!" Shame, she was not sure whether to laugh or cry. I could just imagine her thinking 'Are our housing problems ever going to end? Where on earth has he brought us to this time?' I often wondered what thoughts regarding our accommodation had to have gone through her mind after marrying me. She had lived such a sheltered life with her parents in a lovely house in the city and then 'bang' her whole life turned upside down. Instead of improving things, living quarters being the reason for our dramatic move from Zimbabwe to South Africa, all I had achieved was quite the opposite! After the excitement was over, thanks to the local supervisor who showed no fear and extreme bravery in my book, I managed to get all the equipment to site, rigged the machine and started drilling. I was happy and enjoyed being out in the open with the sun beating down while watching the chuck spin. Once again, each metre produced extra cash in the pay packet at the end of the month. Believe me, with the amount I was being paid at the time there was plenty of room in the packet to house the extra cash. All ran smoothly apart from Les being terrified of the rats in the house, which we discovered were many. I managed to get some poison called ratex from the farmer and spread this all over the house. More than to kill them I just wanted to chase them away. Surely they could go and live happily elsewhere then move back once we completed the contract?

Chapter 6

Time literally flew by with my leaving before sun up and returning in the dark every day. There was little for Les to do apart from looking after and keeping the kids happy and out of trouble. However, she accepted the situation and made the best of it, to be honest life at that stage was not bad and we were happy.

Then suddenly out of nowhere, she started having the weirdest dreams. They were so incredibly clear and vivid that she wasn't sure if they were dreams or the real thing? She dreamed that when she got up at night to go through to the loo on the opposite side of the house she would meet up with twelve children ranging in age from five to twelve years old. When asking them what they were doing here they told her they had lived in the house for the past fifteen years. As we had now moved in, they were scared and would go into the roof during the day and only come out at night once we were asleep. She told them not to be scared and as it was more their house than ours to make themselves at home. However, they insisted that as long as we were there they would keep out of our way and would only come out at night.

These reoccurring dreams were so vivid she honestly felt she was there with them. Each time it was the same children with the eldest being their representative. First off, she experienced large rats, then bees under our bed and now the dreams! The settled feeling Les started enjoying disappeared instantly. She really was not happy with our new situation nor should she have been. We had made this earth shattering decision to pack up and move to South Africa from our homeland Rhodesia to improve our living conditions yet we were worse off! However, there was no going back, so we had to buckle down and see our way forward one way or the other. If nothing else I joked with Les saying that since marrying me, she most certainly never had the opportunity of becoming bored with life.

A couple of days later I was surprised when the farmer arrived at my drill-rig. He had come to see how we were getting on and apologised profusely about the bees and rats in the house causing concern. To try to compensate in some way for our recent inconvenience he invited us to a Sunday lunch the coming weekend, which I accepted gratefully.

The meal was special. Not only was his good wife a lovely person, but also one hell of a cook. We all talked non-stop through the meal and had a wonderful afternoon. During these discussions Les happened to mention her strange dreams of the ghost children living in our cottage.

They both showed immediate surprise and gave each other a strange look, almost as if there were some major significance to the dreams. They quickly changed the subject and so the day went on with us leaving at around 4pm.

As we were about to drive off they asked if we had seen the cemetery across the stream from the cottage. When telling them we had not, they suggested we do so immediately when we arrived home as it could possibly offer an explanation to Les's dreams.

Both puzzled and intrigued by them mentioning the cemetery we drove off in a cloud of dust, waving out the windows. After settling the kids in the house, we wondered through the stream to some scraggly bushes that had hidden the view of the cemetery from the cottage.

Their consternation at the mention of Les's dreams was instantly realised when seeing the engraved scripts on the tombstones. There were twelve small tombstones, all of children ranging between the ages of five to twelve years old! This made the hairs on our necks stand rigid. How could that be possible? There had to be a connection, the coincidence was just too great. It was incredible, but from that day forward the dreams disappeared completely. Certainly makes you think.

Chapter 7

Eventually we returned to Messina after completion of the contract in the Northwest Cape. On our return, I was extremely disappointed to hear I was once again required underground for an indefinite period.

My salary was pathetic to say the least, hardly covering our day-to-day living requirements. On the positive side, we had been given a larger mine house, but, I had no money to provide Les with the home comforts she truly deserved. Due to this and being placed on permanent day shift from 7am to 3pm each day allowed me to apply for the position of barman at the Mine Club when advertised. The bar opened at 4pm and closed at 10pm each day, thus giving me a full hour to get home after my shift, shower, change and get to the club to open up. I was thrilled to receive the news of my application being successful.

Again, the salary was nothing to write home about, but as a supplement to my monthly drilling wage made a tremendous difference. I believed what had possibly helped in making my application successful over all the others was due to my indicating I drank no alcohol whatsoever.

Once I got into the swing of things, I really enjoyed my evening occupation. Yes, it certainly made for long hours with little time to spend with the family during the week. However, I was underground from Monday to Friday, so during the day over weekends was free to do as I pleased. As in all mine bars many fights broke out. Numerous times I had to jump over the bar counter to separate the fighters. Once I had managed to settle them down, they generally shook hands and continued drinking together.

It is common for men with a few beers under the belt to feel far stronger than they really are! Often the one that started the fight came off second best for just that reason. If they continued to be unruly, it was my responsibility to throw them out the pub. In so doing, I received verbal abuse and threats that they would be back to sort me out. I always told them not to bother about coming all the way back, but to go ahead and give it their best shot there and then. Not once did they take me up on my offer. They all came back to drink the following night as if nothing had happened.

I felt privileged to be in a position to meet many interesting people. One unfortunate, but extremely reliable and regular customer was at the door at opening time every day without fail. Sadly, for reasons unbeknown to me, he allowed his wife total domination of his life. She essentially controlled his every move including his drinking activities. Despite knowing he desperately needed his daily booze fix, under no circumstance would she allow him to sit and drink with the boys as was the norm. Instead, she would drive him to the club everyday and have him there punctually just before opening time.

Prior to opening the doors, I made his nightly cocktail of three triple vodkas and two beers already opened and poured into a glass. The beers were the chasers and he would have all the drinks downed within five minutes. He always had the exact amount of money ready to pay before leaving. He would thank me, say good-bye and jump back into the passenger seat so the wife could drive him home. I enquired often as to what happened once he arrived home, but he was reluctant to discuss it so eventually I gave up. I used to wonder about the possible damage that abuse to his liver would have in a few years time. Not to mention the damage a wife like his could cause to their marriage. However, there are always two sides to a story.

Although financially better off thanks to my second career as barman, our lounge was still in desperate need of curtains as there simply weren't any. The only solution we could find was to use old newspapers glued together, an embarrassing situation when you have friends around! Financially things were extremely tough even with me working sixteen hours a day and the strain was beginning to show. I felt terribly guilty for not being able to adequately provide for the family and this was becoming an increasingly difficult issue for me to handle. However I truly believed somehow, somewhere, it had to change.... it was only a matter of time.

Chapter 8

Les and I talked late into the night, should we, shouldn't we? Eventually deciding there was nothing to lose in applying, I wrote a letter that night giving full details of my experience in surface drilling. I knew if successful, I would need to operate one of the most powerful deep-hole drilling rigs ever designed in South Africa, the Sullivan 50. It was designed especially for the gold fields and capable of drilling to depths of five thousand metres. I had no experience on the rig or for that matter even seen one in operation. This I mentioned in my application, because as a youngster learned the truth always pays. However, I also added that I had a limited amount of experience on the slightly smaller Sullivan 45 and felt that would be of some small advantage.

Fortunately, Les had a few stamps available at home allowing me to go into town to post the application that evening. I held onto the envelope for a few seconds before letting it drop into the box. I was fully aware it could change our lives forever, but wasn't sure if it would be for the better? I honestly felt if it were possible to suck it back up into my hand for further consideration, I would have done so. It felt so final letting it slip from my fingers, all I could do now was wait. I kept asking myself, "Could this be the break I'm looking for?"'

Ten days later the reply came through and to my surprise was positive. The job was mine, all I needed to do was phone the contact number provided to confirm acceptance. This I did and within two weeks we were on site halfway between Welkom and Virginia in the Free State. Once again, as far as accommodation was concerned we had gone backwards. Our bedroom was a small round tin shack as was our combined kitchen, bathroom and storeroom. There was no insulation whatsoever on the walls and being winter turned into a fridge at night, I had never been so cold in all my life.

I was cross shifting with a driller called Andy who was the charge hand and apart from Sundays, our shifts ran from 5am to 5pm on day shift and 5pm to 5am on night shift. Each week we alternated from day to night shift. I had no problem running the new rig as it is like changing from a small to medium car to driving a bigger car. Although not drilling on Sundays, we still worked in that we performed a complete service on all the equipment to ensure continuous operation for the following week.

By this stage the hole was drilled to a depth of over two thousand five hundred metres. It was progressing well, yet considering the solid formation drilled, I felt we could increase the production considerably. I spoke to Andy regarding ordering from the head office a set of four three-metre single tube core barrels that joined together allowing for a twelve metre run instead of the six-metre double-tube currently in operation. Andy said it would not be allowed as the contract stipulated unconditionally that it had to be double-tube and you could not get one over six metres long. He of course was quite correct. However, I was young, confident and cocky so believed that under certain circumstances some rules were made to be broken. There was most definitely merit in what the client wanted and in certain fractured formations I agree a double-tube is essential. .

The following day our drill supervisor came to site to see how things were progressing. He was pleased with the performance and was surprised when I made the same request to him that I had spoken to Andy about. After checking the core samples, he agreed there should not be any problems with grinding of the core with a single tube and radioed through to head office in Johannesburg to send out the equipment. He stressed, however, to be exceptionally careful and that if the client were to find out it would be on my shoulders. Two days later the equipment arrived and production increased dramatically with no detrimental effect to the core samples. Instead of pulling all the drill rods from the hole every six metres to remove core, we were now able to drill twelve metres at a time. However to keep it *'legal'* we marked the core in six metre sections in the core trays.

All went well, even our drill crew were excited about being given more time to relax between pulls. Pulling one hundred and forty lengths of eighteen metre rods from the hole, removing the core and lowering them all back again was no easy job on the machine, the men, or us, the operators. Whenever life in any form becomes easy, you have to know something will go wrong, especially in the drilling game.

The rig was housed within a drill shack so vision from within was restricted. I was running the day shift and had not seen the vehicle arrive, also, due to the excessive sound emanating from the rig whilst drilling, never heard it. Suddenly three well-dressed people walked into the drill shack immediately going over to our stick-up board.

This consisted of a large permanently marked board with information required for working out the exact depth of the hole. Using a piece of chalk, we filled in the total number of eighteen-metre length drill rods. To this, the quill rod and any odd rods in the string less than eighteen-metres in length are included, together with the length of core barrel producing a total figure. From this figure is subtracted what is called the stick-up, being the length of quill rod sticking up out of the hole, ultimately assuming your arithmetic was correct this gives you the exact depth of the hole.

Immediately I knew I was in trouble as the board clearly displayed that my core barrel was twelve metres long instead of the mandatory six metres. From where I was standing, I could see and study the board. Luckily, for me, and by sheer coincidence, although my core barrel showed as just over twelve metres my stick-up showed as just over six metres. Pretending I had not noticed them come in and standing with my back to them, I concentrated on operating the drilling controls getting ready to start drilling a new run. Suddenly I felt this heavy tap on my shoulder from one of my learned friends.

"Stop the rig now and come over to the board!" Shit! I thought, surely he could have at least said 'hi' before talking to me like something he had just scraped off his shoe! However, they were quite obviously the client so obediently I obliged.

"Hi, Trevor Frost," I said as I walked over extending my greasy hand in what I felt to be a gesture of politeness.

In a disgruntled voice the smart arse that had come over to call me said, "To be honest we don't care who you are, but are extremely concerned with what we find on the stick-up board! You have stated here that your core barrel is twelve metres long." Looking at the board with as confused a look on my face as I could muster, I threw my hands up onto my head and said, "Hell, I'm sorry I see I have the stick-up and the core barrel the wrong way around. I'm sure you are well aware you cannot get a double-tube barrel longer than six metres." I have never been good at telling lies and felt sure they could see it.

"Funny, but I find that really difficult to believe, why on earth would you make such a silly mistake and not notice? We think you are drilling with a twelve metre single-tube core barrel and if this is the case there are going to be serious repercussions!" "I am also sorry and don't mean to be presumptuous, but have you checked the core recoveries. I feel quite sure you are well aware achieving such solid sticks of core with a single-tube core barrel is nearly impossible, even for an experienced and reputable drilling company as ours!" Although I know I was stretching the truth to its limit, it annoyed me immensely that some self-proclaimed important wimp called me a liar! "Further more, I'm really not used to being called a liar so for safety reasons I must ask you all to please move out of my drill shack whilst I pull the rod string. That is the only way to show you firsthand what length the core barrel is. Doing so is going to severely affect our production for the day as we have just completed lowering the rods, hence the smoke coming from the break bands and we are ready to start drilling so there will be no core." With that I turned and called my guys together, telling them we were going to pull again and the disappointment on their faces was clearly visible to all.

At that point, one of the other well-dressed clients came over and apologized to me, but added due to the error on the board, needed to ask the question. He agreed core presentation was excellent and they were most impressed with our production, so to please continue drilling as we were.

Our drill supervisor who had accompanied the three to site knew I was really treading on extremely thin ice. For fear of being forced to tell the truth, he stood back and stayed completely out of the conversation. However, when leaving with the distinguished guests he turned, giving me a funny look, knowing that somehow I had miraculously averted an extremely serious situation. He shook his head and with a smile walked off. Later that day he returned telling me to go back to the double-tube barrel when I next pull rods, he said his heart would not take another episode like that again. I laughed and said I agreed it was a little tense there for a minute and that I would revert to the double-tube.

Chapter 9

For safety reasons when pulling or lowering drill rods from the hole extreme care is required at all times. The labourers operating the foot clamp, wrench spanners or top boy controlling what happens eighteen metres up in the drill mast during this essential part of the drilling operation can, through a lapse in concentration, cause horrendous accidents to man and machine. The operator himself, through a split second loss of concentration, could just as easily be the culprit of expensive mistakes and possibly worse, cause serious injury. Not having a water return on our current hole due to underground fissures caused many problems. One being the lack of cushioning effect of water in the rare case the drill rods accidentally or carelessly drop down the hole. Added to this, excessive greasing of the rods is essential for lubrication as rotation at speed in a dry hole causes tremendous friction. With full water circulation (obviously not available to us) water is continuously pumped and re-cycled under high pressure through the drill bit, up the annulus between drill rod and side wall of the hole allowing for special drilling muds to be used. The flow is recycled through a surface-dug water sump providing the required lubrication together with transportation of the drill cuttings ultimately resulting in a cleaner hole with improved penetration rates.

At 4am a short burst of engine power woke me with a start. Any abnormal sounds emanating from the rig got my attention immediately due to our tin shack location, a mere two hundred metres away. Under normal drilling conditions, sleep is possible as the sounds are constant. I sat up listening and it was obvious to me that Andy was pulling three metres at a time. Disaster bells started ringing in my head, wondering what was going on. Climbing quietly out of bed trying not to disturb Les, I pulled my overalls on more in an attempt to stave off the freezing night air than as a requirement. Then slipping my safety boots on I   wandered off to find out what had happened on the site. The chill of the night air had a real winter bite to it, which regularly left us in trouble with solidly iced pipelines. Anti-freeze was an essential ingredient in all water-cooled machinery on site, including the vehicles. I covered the distance between our bedroom and the rig as quickly as possible to get to the warmth of the drill shack. At night we continuously burned wood in a drum with holes punched in the sides. It helped tremendously as a heater and certainly the drill shack proved the warmest place to be after dark.

Andy having lowered the complete rod string connected the quill rod and started the water pump being almost ready to start drilling. Instead of using the hydraulic chuck and cylinders for safety, he tried the quick and dangerous route. With the use of the break lever controlling the hoist cable attached to the quill rod he slowly lowered down the drill bit to the stick-up mark when somehow he accidentally released the break and the rods dropped the remaining two metres and crashed bit first into the bottom of the hole! Dropping two metres sounds unimportant, but when it involves the dead weight (tons) of two thousand six hundred metres of drill rods it is a serious problem!

Once the bit comes crashing down to a dead stop the remaining rods' momentum and incredible weight continued their downward motion. To give a hypothetical example: had these been hanging from a tall skyscraper and dropped two metres the lower rods, due to the weight of the rods above, would buckle and break. Being free of any restriction they would spew off in all directions leaving a pile of smashed up drill rods.

In our case however, the rod string is contained in a hole drilled with an internal diameter (ID) of 60mm through solid rock for thousands of metres. Essentially, apart from minimal movement in the annulus between outside diameter (OD) of drill rod and ID of drilled hole, the rods have nowhere to go so effectively are forced into a spiral (corkscrew). At best with a hole as deep as ours you could safely count on a minimum loss of the lower half of the rod string being rendered permanently unusable causing an enormous expense, taking into account replacement costs. Secondly, and possibly a more expensive scenario, due to the excessive spiralling your rods can become permanently jammed in the hole. This being the case, not only are you liable for rod replacement, but also for the re-drill to whatever depth you last invoiced the hole out at!! Trying to absorb these kinds of exorbitant costs could easily force the drilling company into bankruptcy.

Fortunately, although proving to be tight, Andy had managed to remove a few three-metre lengths of drill rod from the hole. Being an experienced operator, he pulled through the quill and hydraulic rod chuck. This method was insurance in case the rods became completely stuck. It would then be possible to tighten the chuck and utilizing hydraulic power from the two massive cylinders pull up or push down the rods depending on the situation. Strange as it may sound, but, more often than not, assuming your drill bit is off bottom, pushing down often brings success in loosening the obstruction allowing the rods to free themselves. If panic sets in and continuous upward force exerted through the hydraulics, the chances are you will reach the point of no return as the harder you force the rods up, so you extenuate the problem.

It was now 4.45am, nearing the official starting time of my day shift. After discussing the problem at length, coupled with remedial action required I took over the controls. Although proving to be a long and slow operation I managed to keep the rods coming out one by one. As long as there was movement, albeit extremely slow, there was hope of saving the hole. Twelve hours later at the end of my shift, I had only removed 60% of the total lengths of rods. We worked non-stop and at last were making headway with the rods coming out more easily. I was managing to pull nine-metre lengths at a time. Once each length came loose, the rod was run out through the gap in the shack we had opened specifically for this purpose. Looking out from the drill shack at all those bent and buckled rods it was hard to believe. The financial loss to the company was going to be enormous and all through Andy trying to short cut the standard tried and tested procedures. We are all human and somehow manage to have these lapses from time to time. It was a full week before we started drilling again. First off, only once the total number of rods requiring replacement had been calculated, could we send our order through to head office. Eventually these arrived and then started the tedious process of joining the three-metre lengths together into eighteen-metre lengths. These kind of in-hole risks are always a distinct possibility, but realistically we had come off reasonably lightly as we were eventually able to go back into a clean hole and start drilling again.

Chapter 10

There was a non-smoking zone within the drill shack. Reason being there was a strong presence of methane gas emanating from the drill hole. It is extremely flammable and set alight by the smallest spark. We prominently displayed the warning signs both inside and outside the shack. It had become so much the norm for all who smoked to move to a safe distance before lighting up, so the initial concerns of fire faded into insignificance. Sadly, however, in life there is no such thing as never!

I was running the night shift that week and having filled the core barrel we were ready to pull the rods to remove the core and possibly do a bit change as the current one was nearing its end. Perhaps we could have drilled one maybe even two more runs with it, but at this depth, it was not worth taking the chance. Once I had pulled and loosened the quill rod from the main string, I engaged the rod chuck to hold it in place. I then racked the machine back off the hole with the use of the strong-arm hydraulic cylinder to allow space for pulling the rods.

After successfully stacking the first five lengths, I commenced pulling the sixth one. I almost had it out when I was shocked to see fire shooting up the outside of the rod. I immediately engaged the break as the clamp operator successfully completed a back flip urgently getting away from the fire. I ran to the high-pressure water pump and directed a full blast of water at the annulus of the drill rod and casing through the by-pass hose. It made no impression, the flames stayed constant. How could this be? We had just been through the disaster of dropping the rods and now here I was trying to set the whole machine alight!

In desperation I wet one of the hessian sacks laying to one side in the shack and ran back carrying it across to the fire. I called for Meshack the clamp operator to come and help. In a bid to smother the flames, I was trying to force the sack between the rod and casing with the use of a long screwdriver. The heat from the flames was intense and I could feel it singeing the hairs on my arms. I had to save the machine. How was I going to explain to the supervisor how I had burnt the rig to a black melted shell? I kept working as fast as I could and was making headway. As the remaining gap in the annulus became smaller, so the flames died down. Finally, I jammed the sack into the final opening and the flames stopped almost as suddenly as they had started. The panic was over, the machine safe and to be honest, after all the drama, it felt like an anti-climax. The fire was there and now it had gone, I had effectively starved the flames of oxygen.

Meshack was standing off to one side a few metres away from me and was clearly shaking, seemingly in a trance. "What's wrong with you? I called for your help and you just stood there shaking like a leaf! What the hell happened here, did you start the fire?"

"I'm truly sorry my baas (boss), I cannot tell you why, but as I leaned forward in preparation to set the clamp I lit a cigarette. I know very well the dangers of smoking, but still without thinking for some reason just went ahead and lit up!" He sat down on the floor holding his head in his hands. I was surprised and extremely pissed off at what he had done. He had always performed his duties efficiently and proved to be the best clamp operator I had ever worked with, clearly, I could see it was purely accidental. "Have you any idea how much shit you almost caused, have you any clue as to the replacement value of one of these rigs, not to mention had the rig gone up in flames, the possible damage to the drill mast?"

Shaking his head from side to side he replied, "I have said I'm sorry baas and all I know is the replacement cost of the machine would be far more than I could earn in my whole life! I don't know why I did such a stupid thing... it just happened without thought." I stood there hands on hips wondering what to do next as I had mixed feelings. Do I tell him to get out of here and never come back, not even to collect his pay as he had breached an important safety regulation, which could have proved disastrous for all of us? Deep down I knew it was not just carelessness, or that he was intentionally trying to cause any damage. Plainly, I felt it was simply an innocent and uncontrolled reaction at just the wrong time.

I made my decision there and then, now that we had seen firsthand how dangerous the gas could be, we needed to tighten up on our smoking rule. By this stage, my complete crew were all standing there expecting the worst.

"Guys, you have all seen how easily a small mistake can turn into a disaster. Due to what has just happened I am going to be placing a box outside the drill shack. All cigarettes, matches and lighters of any kind have to be placed in the box on arrival for your shift. I will be doing spot checks and anyone found with either in their possession will be in serious trouble. When you need to smoke, you will have no option, but to go outside. Okay that is it, now let us leave this problem behind and get on with completing the hole without anymore such mishaps.

Eventually we did manage to complete the hole and we were preparing to move the rig to the new site only one kilometre away. A second rig had become available and brought in to increase the production. Andy had been moved over to take over as charge hand and would be running a cross shift with an operator transferred in from another contract. I, on the other hand, was unofficially given the nod to take over my rig as charge hand. My monthly wages were to be substantially increased, helping Les and I to hopefully be in a position to get back on our feet.

Our supervisor arrived the following day and was clearly uncomfortable whilst discussing how things had gone with the move. I have always had a problem with people not coming to the point so asked him directly what was bothering him.

"Trevor, I know how much it means to you to take over as charge hand and also know you are more than qualified and deserve it." He was really struggling with this.

"Why is it that I can clearly see there is a 'but' coming?" I asked starting to become agitated.

"Despite my protesting, the powers that be will send someone down from head office as charge hand on this rig and said you would cross shift with him as you had done with Andy. They said to tell you they were going to increase both your salary and bonus seeing you had handled the last hole so efficiently." I was speechless and just stood there staring at him wondering how he could do this to me.

What was I going to tell Les? She hated living in these atrocious conditions especially in the middle of winter. She hated the kids waking at night screaming because their hands were frozen stiff and having to sit there rubbing constantly to thaw them out. She hated having baths in the little tin tub in the little tin shack and twice having a labourer wondering in to collect a drill bit whilst she was actually in the bath! She hated never seeing or meeting any other people barring those on the rigs. For her to hear that we were going to be staying on under much the same conditions indefinitely would be devastating for her.

"Listen Trevor, I really don't know what to say, but hey I almost forgot, a letter arrived for you, I have it here in my pocket." He pulled it out and handed it to me. Surprisingly, neatly typed out on a MTD letterhead they were offering me the position as supervisor on the surface rigs on the mine. Housing was to be dramatically up-graded as was my salary; however, management required my answer urgently. I just stood there with open letter in hand smiling. "Okay, so what is so amusing?" he asked.

"Well Johan, after hearing what head office have lined up for me, it gives me great pleasure to ask you to please inform the powers that be, that I have just resigned with immediate effect and will be returning to Messina. I'll stay on and complete my shift today as Les will need time to pack our things!" A little shocked at my spontaneous response after reading the letter he asked if I would not mind staying on until the end of the week to give the new operator time to get here. I really liked Johan and he had always given me his full support so readily agreed. However, I said I would need an hour or so off to let Les know what had transpired and go into town and telephonically confirm my acceptance of the offer.

I was required on my way through to Messina to stop off at the head office in Johannesburg to collect my pay. When telling the receptionist why I was there she took me through to the Managing Director's office. He offered me the world to stay on saying they had big plans for me down the road and I should really re-consider. Not wanting to burn my bridges, I said I appreciated his offer and told him I was sorry. However, for the sake of my family, I had made up my mind and the decision was irreversible. Eventually we shook hands, I collected my cheque and left their offices never to return.

Returning to Messina felt good, with decent accommodation, undeniably a huge improvement on our tin shack or for that matter, the little house originally allocated on our arrival from Rhodesia!

I was much happier at work as were Les and the kids in their new environment. The take home money had improved, but clearly, we were not going to become wealthy there. I was relieved to have the full support and respect of the drill operators. This in turn helped us all run the surface drilling operation as efficiently as possible.

Within the following six months, we made some good friends. I felt privileged to be in a position to become involved in the cricket, rugby and golf clubs all of which I thoroughly enjoyed. I say privileged as during our married life living out of town on drill sites we had none of these amenities available to us. There were many parties and organized braai's where fun and good eating was guaranteed and enjoyed by all. Messina was starting to feel like home, to feel like we belonged and were at last settled. Strange how often as I reached this stage in my life, the stage where you think that you have at last made it, something or someone, somehow, somewhere leaps up and bites you. This was no exception as once again our lives took a further life-changing and dramatic turn.

Chapter 11

Unexpectedly a telegram arrived for me from a Mr. Alan Longstaff. Prior to moving to South Africa I had worked for his father in Rhodesia and highly respected him as one would his own father. I had never met Alan who at that time was not involved in drilling.

I was astonished when reading the telegram that he was offering me the position as Managing Director of their Botswana drilling operations. The current manager up there was leaving shortly and they were desperate to find a replacement. For personal reasons neither Les nor I was interested. However, the telegrams kept coming and eventually I relented and agreed to go through to Botswana to assess the situation and meet with the outgoing Manager.

Les was not excited in any way with the prospect of moving there. Nevertheless, the offer on the table was three times what I was earning with the mine so she reluctantly agreed that possibly I should go and check it out. She had good reason for being unenthusiastic about the idea. The effects of the Rhodesian war were still evident, especially in the north east from where we would be operating. We had heard of a few nasty incidents directed at the Whites at roadblocks and yet I had also heard to the contrary and that life generally was fine. I told Les if I don't go through and see for myself I would never know and it might worry me for the rest of my life.

Les's other concern was our furniture, how would we get it there? Was there somewhere to put it once there and so on? Worrying about furniture had never been an issue in our lives, simply put, we had never owned any. When eventually taking the plunge to go out and buy, it was a huge decision for us to take and purchasing the furniture on credit was a revelation.

We had a hard and fast rule, if we cannot afford it don't buy it, so our endless lack of funds ensured we purchased little. However, we were at last in a liveable house, settled and in a great place to raise children. With no intentions of going anywhere in the near future, we decided to go through to Pietersburg on a shopping spree. It meant a drive of one and a half hours west of Messina, but most certainly afforded you far more choice than at home.

On arrival, we entered one of the larger well-known furniture stores. We were most impressed to see them stocked with every conceivable household item available at the time. I said to Les that it was obvious as to why they were one of the more popular furniture stores around. Within an hour, after much deliberation, more concerning finance or lack of than product quality, we settled on the lounge/bedroom suites, fridge and stove we liked and felt we could afford. Proudly I called for the manager to discuss the special six-month credit plan they were advertising.

Once disposed of the normal niceties between manager and customer I asked if we could please sort out the paper work. He handed us the standard credit application forms that we duly completed and felt confident the granting of the application would be a breeze. We clearly showed on the form we had no other accounts and felt this had to be a huge bonus. We handed the signed form back to him and that is where the problem started. "Oh dear, you haven't completed the form correctly, see there you haven't included any references of past credit!" he said pointing to the relevant section and handed the forms back to me.

"Well, yes that is just the thing, we have never had credit before so our only monthly payment would be to yourselves so we can certainly afford these instalments. I'm sure you don't have too many customers with that luxury." I sat back with my special smug look, thinking to myself, 'Haven't we managed our finance situation well in the past, if that doesn't seal the deal nothing will?' The manager wiped that look off my face in an instant saying,

"In that case I'm terribly sorry, but I cannot help you, with no references there is absolutely no chance of offering you credit facilities." This time the look on my face turned to utter astonishment. "Are you telling me that because I don't have to pay a bunch of other accounts on top of yours every month you cannot approve the application?" Not only was I astonished, but also to be frank was becoming totally pissed off!

"I'm really sorry and would love to help you, but rules are rules!" I thought to myself what a pompous ass he turned out to be. "Okay, then explain to me how the hell do I arrange credit references when I cannot get credit due to not having references, I mean what comes first the chicken or the egg?" With that, I turned to Les saying, "Come on doll, let's get out of here and buy the furniture elsewhere, I certainly didn't drive all the way here to listen to this crap!" I was angry and generally not a nice person when I get to that stage.

With that, I tore the application form into little pieces in front of him and we walked out the shop. We had not walked more than one block when the store manager arrived, huffing and puffing like a steam train from running to catch us.

"Listen, I'm terribly sorry, once I thought about what you had said about the chicken and the egg it made a lot of sense to me. Please accept my most humble apology. I'm more than willing to offer you the special credit deal and will even deliver free of charge to Messina." It was incredible how he had turned from a pompous old fart to a slick sales clerk in an instant. We really liked the furniture and the prices, so as much as I wanted in principal to tell him to go to hell, agreed to go back to his shop. Accordingly, with all arrangements and relevant papers signed, the deal was sealed. A week later, our new furniture arrived at our modest home in Messina and to celebrate, we immediately invited a few good friends for dinner to show it off. Buying furniture was to most people a normal and necessary evil. To us, this was a massive step forward, being the first time in our married life we owned any furniture, or certainly owned the deposited part of it as we still had to pay off the rest over a six month period.

Chapter 12

At dawn on 15th September 1973, I left the house for a couple of days travel bound for Martins Drift, the Botswana Border Post some two and a half hours drive from Messina. I arrived there just after eight o'clock in the morning and after the normal customs procedures I climbed into my car heading for Palapye one hundred kilometres north into Botswana. The road was gravelled, there was no sign of tar, but in certain areas cattle droppings completely sealed the surface. I could clearly appreciate why beef at that time rated as Botswana's largest export. There were literally hundreds of cattle along the way.

I eventually arrived in a little village called Palapye and fortunately managed to fill my car with petrol. From there I continued onto Serule and then turned east heading for Selebi-Phikwe sixty kilometres away and my final destination. There was not much there at all. A couple of houses in the village, one small filling station, a Co-op for your shopping needs and an open-pit mine was about all I could see. Having a map of the area and directions of how to find the bush camp I headed off in a southerly direction. All roads were gravel and I wondered what it would be like if there were to be heavy rains. I took a few wrong turns down little sandy tracks before eventually finding the road out to the Selebi Mine shaft. The map showed it to be twelve kilometres out and to the south of the open-pit. I headed off feeling some excitement in the pit of my stomach. How was Les going to feel about being so isolated with precious little of anything for kilometres? We had been in similar circumstances living in a caravan whilst drilling in Rhodesia, however this felt different, possibly as it was a country neither of us truly knew anything about. Eventually arriving at the camp feeling bewildered and yet relieved at the same time, I pulled up in front of what I figured to be the main house. There was a sense of self-achievement in being successful in finding it considering the remoteness, coupled with an excited tingle through my veins that this could possibly be our new home for the foreseeable future. On the other hand, was it trepidation of what Les might think of our new abode? Alan, the current manager and his good wife with

39

warm and friendly handshakes, met me. Two wonderful people who had lived there under trying conditions for a couple of years and had decided the time had come for them to move back to South Africa and civilisation again.

After a welcome cup of tea, a grand tour of the house was organised. The complete structure was a cement floor with gum poles strategically placed in an upright position demarcating the various rooms. In order to separate the various rooms throughout the house hessian sacking was utilised. Effectively it is attached and pulled tightly to the inside of these wooden poles, similarly also pulled up the length then held in place with nails. This construction technique continued throughout the house. The same process continued around the outside of the poles effectively producing a double-layered wall.

A slush cement mix was applied by brush, both inside and outside the taut hessian and left to dry for a couple of days, then finished off with white wash. The gum poles were all but hidden from view, effectively giving off the impression of a concrete wall. The roof was constructed of wooden beams covered with corrugated iron sheets. To be honest I was not at all happy with the pitch as I felt it was far too flat and would result in a leaking roof with any significant rain. However, I was not there to criticize, more to acquaint myself with pros and cons regarding our possible move.

There were two bedrooms, a lounge-dining room combined, with an outside bathroom and toilet. Hot water reliably supplied via a Rhodesian boiler worked amazingly well. This consisted of a forty-four gallon drum lying on its side approximately two metres above the ground, bricked in all round, barring an opening left in the front.
A fire lit through this opening beneath the drum produced the heat required. There was an abundance of wood considering hundreds of square kilometres of the ever tough and extremely hard red-centred Mopani tree surrounded the camp. As far as successful braai wood is concerned, it has to rate right up there with the best.

With water reaching boiling point at times, there was a necessity for the installation of a blow- off point. To achieve this entails removing and replacing the small screw in plug at the top of the drum with a ninety-degree elbow facing upwards. Connected to this elbow was a 20mm-galvanised pipe tightly screwed in place. A sturdy tank stand was then erected about four metres above the drum. A five-thousand-litre tank mounted on top of the stand and plumbed into the tank, kitchen and bathroom completed the operation. As a final touch a six-metre blow- off pipe was stabilised to the top of the stand with clamps. This was a system successfully utilised throughout Southern

Africa. The only possible constraint to the system would be the availability of wood in your area to fuel the fire each day.

Constructed in the same manner as the house, the workshop was located some one hundred metres away. This contained a small workbench complete with a medium size vice, petrol driven welding machine, steel toolbox and a set of gas cutting bottles. I felt, the ramp built from bricks close to the workshop and designed to drive up onto as opposed to a sunken pit, would be useful. This was a cheap, but effective method for checking the undercarriage of a vehicle when servicing or general repair work required to exhaust, suspension and braking systems.

Neatly tucked away beneath one of the shady trees was a real antiquated homemade mechanism for breaking the bead from a wheel rim to enable the repair of a puncture or to fit new tyres. Although roughly manufactured from bits of old cut-off steel, Alan assured me it worked like a dream. Working in such an environment, you have no option but to learn to improvise.

I was excited at what I had seen, sure there was hardly anything to get excited about and yet had a good feel to it. Almost felt like someone telling me this is an opportunity of a lifetime. I really liked the camp and looked forward to the challenges of working in such a harsh environment. Once back in the house, over another cup of tea, we discussed where the rigs were operating and for which mining houses and all the aspects of how the company was managed. I went through the accounting system, which we discussed at length. Then again with the wage system, how the bonuses worked, when in the month they were paid. When asking how things were at the bank, I was shocked to see the financial state in which the company found itself. There was not enough money to pay the wages at the end of the month. The bank had only authorised a minimal overdraft facility, so to all intents and purposes the Company was in serious financial difficulties. This fuelled my urge to take on the challenge, I felt sure that with a lot a hard work, blood, sweat and tears, combined with a little good luck and management thrown in, the situation could be turned around in the positive. The following morning I was up at first light ready to familiarize myself with the rigs working in that area. Alan eventually came through from his room and after a cup of coffee and some two hours after I'd climbed out of bed, we headed out in the old Company Series 3 Land Rover. There were only two rigs working in the area and neither was more than thirty minutes drive from the camp. Both were Sullivan 22's with the standard shear legs manufactured from 150mm heavy-duty steam piping.

The first rig we arrived at was standing waiting for an NXC diamond bit ordered on the Friday. I could not believe the rig was standing for something so trivial. I suggested to Alan we go back to camp and get one, but he replied saying it really was not a problem and would send one out after visiting both machines. Taken aback by this, I clearly saw the need for new management. I knew for a fact Alan was an extremely competent drill operator as I had worked with him some years before at Gokwe in Rhodesia. Essentially, at that time I was still wet behind the ears as far as drilling was concerned and learned a huge amount from him. I was also aware that over the past two years he had managed the Company in Botswana extremely well.

However, for the last six months he had been anxious to get out and go back south. He really felt he had done his bit and openly admitted his heart was no longer in it. This had obviously affected his interest in the operations and clearly showed in the state of the rigs, tractors, vehicles, D800 Ford truck and of course the all-important financial situation. To be honest I felt he had good reason to feel that way. It made me wonder just how long I would last managing a drilling company here. Eventually arriving back at the base camp I asked Alan if it were possible to phone Les. Firstly to let her know I had arrived safely, but also possibly more importantly, to dispel some of her concerns. Although only having been there for one day I felt safe. The local Motswana blacks were all cheerful, polite and helpful, somehow, everything just felt right. Crazy as it may sound, I knew, there and then, that this only comes around once in a lifetime and I was ready to embrace the opportunity with everything I had.

Alan just burst out laughing. "You can go and try at the Post Office, but to be honest, assuming the phone even works, which is extremely doubtful, it is quicker to drive to South Africa than get through on the phone!" I thought he was joking, but as I would later discover this most certainly was the case. I was eager to get back home to Messina, give notice to the Company there, pack up and get back here as soon as possible. Alan and his good wife were also excited with the knowledge that I would be taking on the challenge. They could now start organising their lives for their permanent move down to South Africa. I thanked them for everything and set off soon after lunch. Alan had provided me with a map of a much shorter route home via the Zanzibar Border post only one hundred and five kilometres from the camp on a reasonable gravel road. Immigration and customs procedures were straightforward and handled in a friendly manner by the officials. Once leaving the Botswana Border post I drove parallel with the Limpopo River, crossed an extremely narrow bridge over a tributary leading to the main river and weaved my way through impressive and enormous Apple Ring Trees. Although the area was extremely dry I marvelled at the beauty and tried to imagine just how incredible it would be in full growth after the rains. Somewhere in the back of my mind I said to myself that I would not mind owning a piece of this one day......

An impossible pipedream maybe, but if you don't dream you don't get, who knows down the road, what life may bring? The Limpopo River itself required careful navigation via a low-level narrow, rough and pot-holed causeway, then up the bank arriving at the South African Border Post. There was no question this route cut a huge chunk off the total trip. I eventually arrived back home in Messina early evening to a warm welcome from Les and the kids. I had only been away a few days, but having travelled to a new country, together with all I had learned, it felt far longer. We sat up late into the night discussing our way forward. Les eventually conceded to us moving up there on condition it was for a maximum of a two-year contract. She was adamant that was the longest she was prepared to go up for, it was non-negotiable!

Chapter 13

Having accepted the position in Botswana, Alan Longstaff, my new boss, arranged for a truck to come down and collect the meagre furniture we had accumulated whilst in Messina.

It was late September 1973, we drove through to Grobler's Bridge, the Botswana Border post, headed once again to a new country and unknown life... Once again, customs and immigration officials were friendly and most helpful. Within the hour, we left the border post in convoy, eventually arriving at camp in Selebi-Phikwe, hot and tired, but thrilled to be there with no major mishaps whatsoever. Creating a fair amount of dust driving in on the dry dirt road, essentially being our driveway of sorts, we parked in front of our new house. With a slight breeze having followed us in, the dust wafted past us and for a moment our little hessian house was obscured. Slowly through the haze, the depth of vision improved. Les just sat in the car for a few minutes shaking her head from side to side with her eyes going from the house back to me. All she could say was *'you have got to be joking'* and remained steadfast sitting in the car. Eventually with a little help from the kids, we managed to coax her out of the old Ford into the house. Alan and his wife had left the day before for South Africa, which left the house or, as Les more accurately called it, the shack, empty and clean for us to move our belongings inside. The remainder of that day was spent sorting ourselves out and trying to get Les's head around the fact that we were actually here, it was not a figment of her imagination. This was it, we were going to be living here indefinitely.

Once we had off-loaded everything and unpacked our clothes I drove her and the kids into Phikwe village in the hope of lifting her spirits, I managed to achieve quite the opposite. She was sure we had not yet arrived as there was so little there.

"Are you trying to tell me this is the closest civilised town to camp?" she demanded with total disbelief on her face. "Well yes it is, but I was informed that there's a far bigger town only one hundred and fifty kilometres north west of here named Francistown." Surely, that had to make her feel a little more relaxed. "Oh great, so if we need something urgently for the kids or a pint of milk we can just pop up there and buy it assuming they have stock!" Shame, she was not impressed and failed miserably to see the excitement I felt surging through my veins. I gave them a quick tour of all the places of interest, quick being the operative word. There was the Post Office and Co-Op grocery store in which the only thing Les could find to purchase was their last loaf of bread and believe me it was not very fresh. There was also a fly infested butchery of sorts that certainly didn't smell all that good and had precious little meat in stock. Eventually we drove back to camp, had a bath, dinner and all trundled off to bed. The kids had been so excited and amazingly good throughout the day and settled down well in their new room. To them this had been a great new adventure, to Les, however, a catastrophe! Alan Longstaff had driven through from Salisbury early that morning and spent the night in Francistown, planning to be with us first thing the following morning. I was up early in anticipation of his arrival. We would spend the rest of the week going around the mines primarily to introduce me to the Chief Geologist at each site. As we were drilling on their projects, I would obviously be working closely with them.

I was shocked at the attitude of these guys when we first met. Yet when giving it a little thought afterwards, here is Alan introducing a twenty- three year old longhaired youngster as the new Managing Director. The company had failed miserably over the last year so I could just imagine them wondering how this new little whippersnapper would in any way resolve or improve on the spiralling problem. Obviously, and not requiring a crystal ball for confirmation, the general feeling and confidence in our company was non-existent at best! The client's negative attitude strengthened my resolve to turn this to a positive in as short a time as possible. With all the confidence I could muster, I assured everyone concerned things would change. They were all nice people, but had that look of, '*sure we have heard that one before*'. I mentally vowed to prove them wrong.

Chapter 14

We had settled down in our new environment within the first few weeks. I was on the go twelve hours a day seven days a week. I had to float between our fleet of four drill rigs, two within eight kilometres from the camp, one at Bushman Mine, some two hundred and thirty kilometres away and our last rig being up at Orapa Mine close on four hundred kilometres away.

I spent many hours behind the steering wheel of my old Company Series 3 Land Rover. It was certainly not the fastest or most comfortable vehicle on four wheels, but in most cases reliably got me to where I needed to be safely. The normal quirks, as in the need to install the mandatory tennis ball over the low- range gear level to quieten the vibration when cruising was most certainly required. As was the case with most Series 3 Land Rovers, the third gear required holding in place when accelerating or it would jump out.

I soon learned to take a lunchbox with me on all my trips. The roads generally could only be described as bad to extremely bad and the Land Rover itself, old to extremely old, not a great combination. Furthermore there were few places on any route travelled where a meal could be found or for that matter where a decent take-away could be sourced. Canned Bully Beef, bread and Cokes/water were essential when travelling.

It is strange, but on many occasions driving from Selebi-Phikwe to Francistown I would drive on the right-hand side of the road. Not because I was intoxicated, but due to what I felt was the better side taking into consideration corrugations and exposed rocks etcetera. Often approaching from the opposite direction would be a vehicle also travelling on the wrong side of the road. There would be no flashing of lights or waving of hands in frustration by either party. We simply passed by each other without even thinking of it, the only reaction possibly being a little wave to say hi. To all intents and purposes, it was just part of life back then.

A concern for travellers in the mid 70's was theft. Not that you would be held up at gun point and robbed, but vehicles involved in an accident or just broken down and left unattended whilst the driver went off seeking help were stripped in no time at all. Miraculously by the following day the engine, gearbox, suspension, axels and anything else of value was stripped from the vehicle! Sadly, this occurred on many occasions leaving the roads strewn with body shells of all makes of vehicles. I honestly believed there had to be an organised syndicate combing the roads looking for such an opportunity!

The Company's equipment generally through lack of maintenance was desperately in need of repair. To get all the equipment back into mechanically sound condition required a huge amount of effort and time. One example was the six and a half metre load body of the eight-ton Ford truck. It was cracking up badly from front to back, being my only truck I set one Sunday aside to methodically go about welding the whole thing back together.

Initially on the bad sections of the underside of the body, I welded scrap pieces of metal I found lying around the workshop area for supports. Due to essentially requiring overhead welding, definitely not for the faint-hearted, combined with having chassis, prop shaft and axel hindering my movements. The area's I repaired were held together more through good luck than good welding! Not to mention all the burns suffered from red-hot flux and sparks constantly raining down on you. It most certainly confirmed the fact I would not make the grade as a coded welder.

Once complete with the under body I started from the front on the top flat section. This was turning into a far bigger job than anticipated. The actual welding was far easier as I could run the end of the welding rod along the cracks from the top, but the physical effort squatting on my haunches for hours whilst welding was exhausting. The temperature in the direct sunlight had to be well into the forties. To say it was hot there in my shorts with the electrode continually burning between my knees would be an understatement of note and a lesson well learned.

Les kindly brought out an ice cold Coke at regular intervals for me get some liquid into my system, this disappeared down my throat without touching sides. It was slow hard work, from time to time having to add pieces of metal to close some of the larger openings, which were far too wide for normal welding. The hours went by with the sweat pouring off me; many times, I seriously considered leaving it for another day. However, I knew all that would achieve is delaying the inevitable and possibly causing the repaired cracks to reopen having not being welded and strengthened accordingly. I pressed on with only half an hour lunch break and eventually completed the repair work to my satisfaction by 4pm. I felt sure had we employed a qualified welder at journeyman rates it would most probably have been cheaper to purchase a complete new body!

Well if I thought that was the end of it, boy oh boy was I wrong! I came into the house, stripped off and jumped into a cold shower to cool off. When I came out and dried myself the inside of my legs felt tender. Pulling my shorts on I walked through to the lounge to sit and enjoy my umpteenth Coke for the day.

Les with a shocked look on her face, pointing to my legs, asked what I had done in the shower. I looked down and the inside of both legs from the shorts line high on the leg to sock line just above the ankle had turned to a glowing red colour. The hours spent squatting with the welding electrode sparking and spitting between my legs had burned me far worse than the sun ever could have. I really suffered for days and had trouble walking, looking as if I was carrying the proverbial carrot around stuck up where it should not be! It was an extremely painful and embarrassing lesson learned and a mistake never repeated.

My predecessor causing major production loss had left basic repairs unattended for weeks. On my first visit to the Sullivan 22 drill rig working in the Selebi area, I checked it over thoroughly looking for obvious repairs required whilst White Koonyatse, my local Botswana operator, continued drilling to fill the three-meter core barrel with 'BX' size core. Once full, the 'B' rods were pulled from the hole by winch to enable removal of the core barrel containing the rock core samples. These cores are cut utilising industrial surface set diamond drill bits, hydraulic pressure or if a deeper hole, rod weight.

Prior to pulling the rod string, the quill rod requires extracting through the quill shaft and lowered onto the rod stand. Thereafter the drilling machine is retracted by a hydraulic ram generally known as a 'strong arm' for ease of the rod pulling operation. In this case, however, after retraction of the quill rod two labourers with the use of an old drill rod for leverage struggled to move the rig off the hole. Not only was it hard physical work, but also time consuming. When asking White as to why he didn't use the strong arm, he pointed under the machine to where the brackets securing the cylinder where broken off. "When did that happen?" I asked him in Fanagolo, as he could not speak English. "About two months ago, Sir" was his reply in the same language, I was shocked! Immediately I drove back to the camp. With the help of my store-man named Madala ('Old Man') we loaded the diesel powered welding machine together with an angle grinder and set off back to the drill rig. Within thirty minutes I had removed the broken brackets, cleaned them up with the use of the grinder and welded them securely back in place. For the first time in months, the strong arm worked like a dream. All the staff on the rig were most impressed and yet it was such a simple repair job, neglected due only to complete lack of interest. There were many similar repairs needed and slowly, but methodically I worked my way through them. In the first three months, I worked seven days a week from sun up to sun down and the results were starting to show. Production had increased by around forty percent together with far more enthusiasm from my staff. Constantly summoned to the labour office to face charges of ill treatment had begun to wear a little thin with me. For some reason a select few wanted me out of Botswana, yet if I left so would their jobs be gone. There was no one to replace me. Gus Von Platen, a major shareholder and pioneer of the Company, had told me that if I could not turn the Company around in six months they would have no option but to cut their losses and close down. All the equipment had been brought into Botswana from Rhodesia on a clearance heading of *'To be returned on completion of contract'*. Therefore, if this were to happen all the equipment would be returned to that country. Nevertheless, not only had production increased, so had their pay packets. All my staff including drivers received a basic salary plus a production bonus. Needless to say with the improved production and extra cash in their pockets through all my efforts, slowly, but surely, I was gaining their respect. Yet there are always those few troublemakers who continued to push their luck, to try to show the majority that they ruled supreme.

Chapter 15

Two of my drivers arrived late for work at around 10am one Monday morning after month-end pay weekend. Both were carrying the distinctly strong odour of booze coupled with bloodshot eyes and a cocky attitude. I never drank alcohol back then, not even at a function. I had made it quite plain to all my staff I would not tolerate drunkenness at any level during working hours and it would be cause for immediate dismissal.

"Well I can see why you two are late, you are both so drunk I'm surprised you can even stand up!" I said as they approached me in the workshop. Immediately in an aggressive tone, fuelled by the excessive booze oozing from their pores they shouted back at me in slurred voices.

"You are not a Botswana and who do you think you are to tell us we are drunk when we are not!" Taken aback slightly and before I could say anything, they continued. "Also you just come here to our country from South Africa and think you can make us work from six to six everyday!" By this stage, I was struggling to control my temper as I have always had a short fuse, particularly as far as drinking is concerned, yet I surprised myself by calmly replying,

"If you have a problem working those hours, understand that we all work from six to six, including myself. So go home, bring your monthly contract form back for me to sign and you are welcome to go." For a moment, they just stood there looking at me through eyes that by the law of physics should not have been able to see anything at all. "Trust me, there are many local drivers that come and see me daily crying out for your jobs. Replacing you won't be a problem, it will be a pleasure."

"You white bastard you cannot just tell us to leave the job, we will show you what we think of it by giving you a really good Mopani hiding." Various stories abounded as to the origins of this practice, but I will refrain from going into it too deeply. There had been a few nasty instances where whites were dealt the full treatment. Basically, the Motswana's had been informed by whoever that if they were treated badly by a white man, they were to break off branches from the Mopani tree that God had given them and thrash him with them!

I was now way beyond angry. If I were to print some of the language that erupted from my mouth, I feel sure this book would be banned from the shelves. Five other local Motswana's happened to be standing close by witnessing our little altercation, one being Madala Toteng, my faithful and trusted store man.

"Well go and get your bloody sticks, but believe me, when we are finished not only will you both be in hospital, but also fired from your employment with immediate effect! I will clearly indicate this on your contract form to ensure you never secure another job of any description around here again. Now piss off!"

They staggered off down the driveway waving their arms in the air muttering all sorts of abuse in the local language that I could not understand. I then continued working on the water pump, desperately needed on one of the rigs. It must have taken about an hour for me to complete the repairs and still there was no sign of the two drunken and disorderly drivers.

With the help of the five staff, I loaded the pump onto the back of my Land Rover. Prior to leaving for the rig, I called to Madala whom I not only trusted fully, but also respected. He was a hard worker and nice man. Without fail, he was up at 5am every morning making the fire on the Rhodesian boiler to ensure we had hot water. "Madala please, you have seen the problem today and I want you to ensure those two don't come anywhere near the house, the madam or the kids. Do you understand?"

"Yes boss, you mustn't worry, we don't want them here either."

I went to the house to inform Les of what had taken place and warn her to keep a look out for them. All I had to do was drive to the drill rig not more than five kilometres from camp, drop the pump off and ensure it was operating properly then head back to camp. I told her I would not be away for more than half an hour. As the two drunkards had not come back yet, I felt sure they had decided to sleep off the hangover or had passed out somewhere and would only come back the following day.

It turned out exactly that way except only one of the drunkards arrived at around ten on the Tuesday morning. He came up to me empty handed with neither the Mopani stick nor his card. Trying to be a big deal in front of my guys he pulled a letter from his pocket and handed it to me, then spoke in the surliest voice he could muster.

"That letter is instructing you that the Labour Officer wants to see you right now!" I was surprised at this. "Where's your fighting partner

51

and what happened to the sticks you were bragging about yesterday?" Pushed beyond my limits by the drunken gang leaders I rather looked forward to a good punch-up "No, we decided to take the problem to the Labour Officer instead so we should go now, he is waiting for us. With my blood boiling, I told him to get into the back of my Land Rover, which he did. Once again, I went to tell Les of the new arrangement and for her not to worry, as I would be back shortly.

We were ushered in on arrival and instructed to stand in front of the Labour Officer's large desk while he sat, arms folded, in his plush chair. He was a large man who obviously enjoyed his food. Since my arrival, I had become well accustomed to his office answering to allegations of some sort or the other about labour problems.

"Okay, so tell me what the problem is this time?" He said, and leaned back in his chair. As I attempted to speak, he put his hand up to stop me from speaking he wanted to hear the story from the driver first. Thereafter, he would allow me the opportunity to reply.

The driver commenced giving his version of what had taken place. Well I was astounded and could not believe my ears. He made all sorts of allegations about how badly I mistreated my staff. Then continued stating he and his accomplice made a special effort to come to work early the previous day, as they wanted to speak to me about the hours of work, going on to say I had then threatened to beat them up.

Each time I attempted to intervene wanting to tell the big guy what had really taken place he just pointed his finger at me and told me straight, "You must just shut up!" This had happened now three times and I was being pushed way beyond my controllable limits. Here was a driver who firstly arrived late for work, secondly, was drunk to the extent of staggering when trying to walk and thirdly, threatened me with a Mopani hiding. He then turned everything around which the Labour Officer accepted without any input from me and that was about as much as I could take.

Eventually the Labour Officer held up his hand to tell the driver he had heard enough.

"Mr. Frost, I have lost count as to how many such problems have been reported to this office about your treatment toward our citizens." Once again, I tried to tell my side, however, received the same instruction to 'shut up'. "This episode has convinced me you are a huge problem and I believe our beautiful country would be far better off without you. I am giving you twenty-four hours to leave and never to return. If you are not out of the country by then you will be arrested and thrown in jail until such time as your case will be heard by the courts." It was plain to see the satisfaction he derived from doing this to a white man in front of the black complainant. "Do I make myself abundantly clear?"

"Oh yes, extremely clear," I said. "Now seeing I'm being kicked out anyway I would like to make myself abundantly clear too. It will be my pleasure to get out of the country." He had his hand held up again, but I was not about to stop this time so continued by holding my hand up in the same fashion he had to keep me quiet. "I believe this is, or certainly should be classed as a dispute, meaning two or more people have to be involved. I also believe in your work portfolio it must state you as the labour officer and arbitrator of such a dispute should listen to both parties." Now in full cry I continued, "I fully realise my skin is white and I'm working in a black-governed country so as far as you are concerned I have no say. Well let me tell you something, I'll most certainly be out of the country in twenty-four hours not because you ordered it, but because I want to leave." I paused for a few seconds to allow it to sink in. Clearly, he had now become equally as angry and glared at me with hostility written all over his face.

"Why on earth would I want to work under these conditions? I am here in an all out effort to improve the mineral wealth of this, your precious country. This in turn provides massive financial benefits to your government together with employment for the locals in whatever area of Botswana we are contracted to work." Once again, I paused for a second or two for him to register. "Now please understand one thing very clearly, when I go, so does my Company and therefore all those employed by me will join the vast ranks of the unemployed. Don't think for a minute I won't tell them all as to who is responsible for their future suffering!" By this stage, his facial expression had marginally changed from anger to concern. "However, before I leave, I have witnesses at my camp as to exactly what transpired. They are not here on restricted work and resident permits as I am. They don't have the disposition of white skin in your country as I have. They are all black Motswanas with the same freedom of speech as you. Surely you would therefore have no option but to listen to them as opposed to rudely telling them to 'shut up' as you have done with me."

My driver attempted to say something and I immediately snapped back telling them I wasn't willing to speak to either of them and with that turned and walked out of the office. I drove back to camp, collected the staff and returned to his office. I fully expected to be arrested on my return, but purely on principal, I was determined, regardless of the consequences, that he would get to hear the true version of the dispute! Hell, if I had to go I would go fighting!

I was relieved and bewildered at the same time to find there was no evidence of police waiting for me. The Labour Officer was noticeably calmer and afforded Madala the freedom to speak. Despite a thorough grilling, with endless questions trying to get him to change his story, he consistently stuck to the truth.

He then continued, informing the now totally confused Labour Officer of how many ways I had made a difference in their lives. Housing had improved, food rations increased, as had the wages and as long as they performed their duties and kept off the booze, they were being extremely well looked after. He concluded confirming that not only they, but also all my staff, were more than happy to continue working for me. Confirmation of this came via the other four staff I had brought in nodding their heads in agreement. The silence in the room could be cut with a knife.

Firstly, he turned to me and to my absolute surprise and astonishment apologised most sincerely for his hasty and uncalled for actions. He continued to tell me that if ever I had such labour issues again to inform him immediately and he would handle it. Then turning to the driver told him clearly that he would be dealing with them after we had left. Thanking me for my patience and shaking my hand, we bade farewell and to this day, there has been no sign of either driver.

News travels fast by bush telegraph and in no time my staff spread everywhere throughout Botswana had full knowledge of the outcome. Thereafter, apart from a few minor hiccups sorted out immediately by the Labour Department, all went well for quite some time. Tested to the limit by the Labour Department and through sheer determination I had not backed down, the respect shown by my staff was incredible from that point on with close working relationships formed.

Chapter 16

Whilst I spent my time running around the drill rigs, at times being away for up to ten days, Les was stuck at home with our two young boys. In our first three months of isolation, she only met two other white people. The only white staff member I had at that time was a drill supervisor at Orapa Mine.

Our bottle store in town was unique in that it consisted of Mr. Mac Nickels' vehicle, a Chevrolet Elcomino. He drove to Pietersburg once a week and filled the back to the brim of his canopy with booze. On his return he then sold directly from the vehicle. You had to be there at the right time and the right day, generally a Thursday, to buy your booze. His small beginning selling from his bakkie eventually turned into a large bottle store. He was a well-respected member of the Selebi-Phikwe community and in his own right became a wealthy man who was always willing to participate in the form of sponsorship of various sports. In golf, The Mac Nickel floating trophy became one of the most popular events of the year. His success was hard earned and he most certainly deserved all he had.

Les kept herself busy with the kids whose only toys were old tractors, discarded drill bits together with whatever else they could find. They were too young to know any better having never being exposed to children's toys or for that matter white children at all. Madala had a young son of similar age who through circumstances was in the same position and was their only friend. The three of them would happily play together for hours.

Initially Les was a nervous wreck due to the number of scorpions and spiders freely running around. However she had managed to catch a few of these dangerous creatures, showed them to the three kids and told them to leave them be as their sting was terribly painful and in some cases a scorpion could be deadly to a young child.

She taught them to call her, or any of the staff nearby, immediately if they ever came across any. It was a relief to see how terrified they were of these little critters and would call out loudly in unison the instant they saw one. Growing up is always a learning curve to life, possibly never ending through to death. This was just one of the many lessons learned by the three youngsters.

Torrential rains chose that year, 1973, to arrive not only early, but to continue unabated and abnormally heavy for weeks. The road into town was impassable in a car, this rendered our Ford Fairlane useless. In some places along the route even a 4x4 experienced difficulties getting through.

The main road to Francistown was totally blocked as truck after truck became bogged down to the axles in the mud. As each new truck, many carrying perishable goods arrived and tried to negotiate around the blockage, they, as all before them, ultimately succumbed to the treacherous black cotton soil in that area. Some drivers in desperation attempted disconnecting the fifth wheel from the trailer in an attempt to drive off with the horse. All they achieved was once again sinking deeply into the quagmire and a separation of three to six metres from their trailer. Eventually there were approximately fifteen large horse and trailer trucks spread over the area in sticky black mud.

The sixty kilometre rail link joining Selebi-Phikwe to Serule had a section washed away, completely disabling that means of travel, and the airport was totally under water and obviously closed to all air traffic. Nothing came in or went out of the town for three weeks. The supplies dried up and life started becoming desperate. It reminded me much of when working in Ruangwa Valley when we had run out of supplies, living only on sudza and peas for weeks.

Here we were in the same situation caused solely by the inclement weather. Les was amazing and took everything in her stride. Her main concern being what would happen if the kids were sick or injured and needed medical help? How would we solve that problem with all the roads closed? I assured her that in the unlikely event of that happening I would get help one way or another, yet, to be honest, at the time I had no idea quite how. Shortly prior to these heavy rains, I had been away at Bushman Mine trying to get an important hole completed. Drilling conditions were challenging to say the least and the formation was terrible as far as drilling was concerned. There was an enormous amount of graphite with quartz/chert pebbles imbedded throughout the zone. Whilst being a prerequisite, drill rod rotation and high water pressure pumped into the hole proved also to be an extremely destructive combination under those conditions. The soft graphite formation washed away which ultimately left you with a hole full of loose and extremely hard abrasive pebbles.

This caused endless problems not to mention extremely high bit costs. The only method I found to be successful was to drill three metres BX size and then ream three metres of BX casing. This practice of drill and case to keep safe was continued throughout the hole to completion, thus being both extremely time consuming and costly. I had no communication with Les at all during this period and had been away for a full ten days. It was by far the longest period I had left her on her own with the kids in the bush. Shame, I felt sure she would be as concerned for me as I certainly was for them.

As I arrived home, having been through some heavy rain on the way, I was shocked to see all our furniture outside in the sun. It was mid-afternoon and my immediate thought was Les had had enough of all the hardships and my being away for extended periods, she was obviously packed and ready to move out. I had a pang of guilt come over me having talked her into coming here in the first place. She really had not been keen on the idea, yet I left her for all that time on her own. I could not blame her for wanting to go.

On my side I was having endless staff problems, not to mention not having a life being completely absorbed in my work seven days a week in an all out bid to keep the Company solvent. 'Surely the family are far more important than the Company or their drill rigs? If she has decided enough is enough, then let's go' I thought. It is incredible how the brain conjures up the wildest imaginable sequences even when you have no idea what is truly going on.

Leaping out the car I ran inside. Les and the kids were happy to see me back safe. They all ran up and gave me big hugs.

"Hell, I'm sorry for being away so long, but we had to complete that hole and there was no means of communication. What on earth is going on here, we cannot just pack up and leave, the least I could do is wait for a replacement to be sent down assuming they can find one?" I felt so guilty and completely responsible for their discomfort. Les just stood there with a blank look on her face, while I was ranting and raving about us leaving Botswana. Then she burst out laughing and the kids joined in, I on the other hand totally failed to see the humour. "So you have packed up ready to go without any family discussion and you guys think it's really funny?" I had convinced myself of the imminent and spontaneous idea on her part to move, yet again for reasons way beyond my wildest imagination this made them laugh even more! "Okay I give up! What is so funny about such a serious and stupid decision? I go away working my butt off for ten days to come home to this nonsense?"

Les, still laughing said, "Well to be honest, you are the funny part. We haven't even thought about moving. The reason all our belongings are out there is because as you can see there was a huge downpour at lunchtime and the roof leaked so badly that everything inside was drenched! Thankfully the sun came out again, so it's all out there on the lawn to hopefully dry off a bit!" I now joined in the laughter at my own irrational thinking and felt sorry for Les having had to sort out the problem on her own.

Fortunately, we had some large tarpaulins stashed away in the stores. Taking note of the worst areas and with help from a couple of my staff and the ever-faithful Madala, we covered the roof as best we could. We placed rocks strategically on top to hold them in position for the night. This was a temporary fix, as we really needed new sheets of corrugated iron. I managed to organize these the following day through my good friend Rob Watt who had contacts in the Mine Store.

There is merit when saying everything happens for a reason as without this repair to the roof we would have been in serious trouble with the deluge of rain that followed for weeks. Madala's smaller but similarly constructed house was located on the far side of the workshops and storeroom. I told him to cover his roof with the tarpaulins. I felt sure these would adequately provide cover, making it as leak proof as possible. Every little stream had turned into a raging torrent, the Motloutse River almost burst its banks. Massive rapids formed as the flooding waters, frothing and churning up all in its path, raced down over rocky outcrops to the already flooded Limpopo. I assumed, Botswana, essentially covered in Kalahari Desert, experienced low annual rainfall. Late November 1973 totally dispelled this theory from my mind.

Chapter 17

I used two separate routes to Orapa Mine depending on how I planned the trip. If going direct, I turned west five kilometres north of Francistown off the Nata road. From there, I travelled a further two hundred and forty kilometres to the main gate at the mine, once again on gravel roads, as were all the roads in Botswana in the early 70's. This road was different in that there were tons of calcrete successfully used on route for compaction, the calcrete gave a lovely finish to the surface. Generally, not withstanding all the cattle on route, you could count on a smooth, fast drive most of the way. However, where there is a plus, somewhere along the way there has to be a minus.

Botswana Road Services had the contract to deliver fuel and supplies to the mine from Francistown. Their trucks travelled up and down on a regular basis, coming up behind one of these always turned into a nightmare. The calcrete was a reliable and extremely efficient producer of powder white dust, believe me it never failed billowing up into the skies behind you. You are heading out into the Kalahari so the countryside is flat; therefore, the tell-tale sign of a massive cloud of white dust billowing up behind these trucks was clearly visible from kilometres away.

Your only chance of passing a truck on the way up was having a northerly wind blowing and coming back the opposite, a southerly wind blowing, this was required to clear the dust from your vision. Sadly, due to this there were quite a few fatal head-on accidents. I could understand why as after travelling for thirty minutes behind a truck swallowing mouthfuls of fine white dust without a single vehicle passing in the opposite direction, impatience replaces logic and you take a chance through the blinding dust. I know this, because travelling up there every week there were times I had done just that, luck being the only reason for avoiding a head-on crash.

Our drilling taking place was at one of the DeBeers projects called BK9. Although a soft formation and in some cases good competent kimberlite, it generally presented all sorts of drilling challenges. The texture has a soapy feel to it and in areas is almost like clay, causing the drill bit to mud up and block, thus necessitating not only a time consuming operation pulling rods from the hole, but also the suction generated through the rods being extracted at speed caused degeneration of the side walls and imminent hole collapse. When in drilling mode, seeing excess kimberlite cuttings being pumped from the hole over and above the norm indicates the hole is being whipped out. If not closely monitored the risk of having the string of casing *'run away'* down the hole was a constant threat. In one of the holes, the casing disappeared a full sixty metres from surface. In that particular instance, I was fortunate enough firstly to re-couple using a casing tap and secondly to find the complete string intact.

There were times when the hole whipped out below and up around the bottom few lengths of casing. Drilling with rotation in a clockwise direction would cause the right-hand thread casing to back off and unscrew, thus sending just that section down the drill hole to stop at whatever point of the hole had remained standard hole size being drilled. The only remedial action being all the upper section having to be pulled from the hole, assuming there had been no swelling of formation onto the sidewalls resulting in the casing becoming stuck. Once the problem of removing the top section from the hole is complete, the fishing for the lost sections is initiated.

On several occasions prior to the operator realising there was a problem with a few three-metre lengths that had loosened off individually and separated from the casing, thus necessitating the laborious fishing for the individual sections one at a time. Fishing and re-casing to make a drill hole safe again could well take a full week. Not only were there the obvious losses in production, but possibly worse, the geological results required from that hole would be delayed. Jim Gibson, the chief geologist and one of the pioneers of the Orapa Mine exploration project, was an extremely well organised man. Operating with a complimentary staff of qualified geologists, field assistants and other qualified staff, he was highly respected by all. If there was anyone fully acquainted with the local geology of the area it was Jim.

However, and rightfully so, he insisted on efficiency from his staff and understandably even more so from us, the drilling contractor. Delays were not tolerated and he made it very plain that either we become organized regarding our drilling methods or he would look for another contractor. Our bad reputation over the past year was still evident and we had a long way to go to prove otherwise.

I had ordered three hundred metres of new left-hand thread casing. Once delivered and installed the problems were greatly reduced, giving higher production, keeping Jim happy and more importantly, my bank manager was far more relaxed with the increase in our monthly turnover.

Gradually through months of hard and dedicated work, not to mention the constant isolation from my family, there was a small light just peeping through at the end of the tunnel. During this period, I received tremendous back up and support from the owners of the company, Mr. Bob Longstaff, his son Alan and son-in-law Gus Von Platen. They all lived and worked in our neighbouring country Rhodesia where they managed a successful drilling company called R.A. Longstaff (Pvt) Ltd. I had worked for the company from 1968 - 1972 and knew and greatly respected both Mr. Longstaff and Gus. Alan, however was not involved at the time and only joined his father's business shortly after I left.

Initially Alan and I had serious issues. Never having worked together, he had possibly been informed of the work I had done with the Rhodesian Company, but for some reason possessed this obsessive attitude of *'I'm the big boss and you will do exactly as I tell you to!'* Essentially, he was my boss and so had the right to go that route. However, solely due to being new in the drilling game, he was still inexperienced and had a lot to learn, not only regarding the drilling game, but also even more importantly about me.

Experience in any profession can't be bought, neither with money nor through premature elevation to a position in management. I knew I was good at my job and gave the company 100% of my time and energy in my bid to resurrect what was a defunct drilling company. From the day I arrived, I ran it with the same passion as if it was my own and the resulting turnaround for the positive, not only gave me more confidence, but also a feeling of achievement, not just for the Company, but for my family.

Chapter 18

One of the other concerns on site was my white drill foreman. He managed to do a fair job when sober and actually was operating the rig. However, Letlhakane village and the nightlife provided therein, including available young local girls, were far too much a temptation and way beyond his self-control. One of my top drill operators on site called Tips Koketso was an honest, hard working, reliable nice guy. If he made a mistake on the rig, he openly admitted to his failure in whatever had gone wrong and always told me the truth. This helped tremendously in my making the correct decision to rectify the problem.

Well, this was a drilling problem alien to the norm. "I'm sorry my Boss, but I have something I must tell you," he said nervously. "Problem is I'm not sure how to explain it without offending you in any way?" Clearly, it really worried him.

"Tips, we have always been able to talk, why would this be any different, come on tell me what's going on?" I felt for him, he was trying to hold back, but also knew he must get whatever was bothering him off his chest.

"Well Sir, our white foreman is the problem. When he is on site and aware you won't be back for a few days he drinks *too* much," he said quietly, then continued, "The bigger problem, Sir, is he does more drilling at night with the local girls in the village than on site with the drill rig!" I had my suspicions of his after working hours activities, but to have it put across that way by my black drill operator was hilarious and I burst out laughing.

Surprised by my reaction he continued telling me the story possibly thinking that I never understood him correctly. "We tried to help him by telling him of the dreaded VD disease he would pick up from these girls!" No longer being as surprised at my laughter he went on to say, "You know Boss, we also told him when he goes drilling in the village he has to pay the girls for it, here on site he gets paid to drill, which is the better option". Well by this stage, we were both laughing at his unique way with words.

"Tips, thank you," I said with a bemused look on my face. "I've had my concerns about him for some time, but must confess have never thought of it in the way you describe it and somehow believe I'll never forget it!"

Johnny, the accused as such, was returning to site from Letlhakane with the weekly rations. I had opened accounts with the local butchery and small supermarket for this purpose. It alleviated the need for me to leave bundles of cash on site, knowing the temptation to use it where it should not be used was quite possible.

He drove to the campsite, dropped off the rations and then returned to the rig. "Hi Trevor, sorry I'm a bit late, but I had a puncture, I was worried you might have left already and I'd miss you." I, being a non- drinker, could smell immediately that he already had a few. I also casually checked the back of his vehicle and could see the spare wheel had not been touched!

"Well as you see I'm still here and was about to come and look for you." My previous bemused look, or the reason for it, had long gone and I felt quite sure there had not been a puncture at all. "I'm glad you're back so now I can leave. I have a few problems to sort out in Phikwe so will not see you for a good few days. Please keep everything going until I get back next week." I was setting up a plan I had hastily devised in my mind. Looking relieved he said, "Thank you for coming and have a good trip back, I'll try to get a message through to you if there is anything we need on your next trip." I bade farewell to all and as I walked past Tips, he gave me a puzzled look, obviously confused at my taking no action based on what he had told me. I just gave him a wink, climbed into the Land Rover and left, waving out the window.

Firstly, I drove to the butchery and supermarket to settle our accounts, then onto the geological camp to report to Jim on how the drilling was progressing. By the time we concluded our meeting it was going into late afternoon. There was a spare caravan in the camp as one of the field assistants was away on leave. Jim kindly offered this to me saying it was too dangerous driving into the night. I was thankful for this and gladly accepted his offer.

No sooner had we all sat down to relax with a drink when there was a blood-curdling scream. A second drilling contractor who was also operating for Jim; their work was contained around the main camp some eight kilometres southeast of Letlhakane village. One of their rigs was set up on a rise not two hundred metres from where we sat. To our absolute horror, the drill operator was attempting to commit suicide by hanging himself.

At the end of shift, the crew had knocked off and gone back to their tents. The black South African operator then returned to the machine. Each rig contains a winch for pulling drill rods from the hole. A standard 5/8" non-spin steel hoist cable is wound around the winch and then run up through a sheave wheel at the top of the tripod and returned back down to the ground. To this end was attached a 'D' shackle. This made changing over between the water swivel and the hoisting plug fast and safe. It was a case of remove the bolt, slip the 'D' part of the shackle over the clevis eye of whichever was required, and re-insert the bolt, job done.

He had effectively made a hangman's knot utilising the cable and 'D' shackle. This he placed over his head onto his shoulders. He then started the engine on the drill rig, engaged first gear, locked the clutch lever in place to rotate the winch. As the slack of the cable reduced, so it tightened the noose around his neck. His feet left the ground, and ever so slowly he was being winched up towards the sheave wheel!

He obviously decided that possibly this was not a great idea after all. Holding onto the cable with both hands, legs flaying from side to side trying to get out of the ever-tightening slipknot, he managed a terrifying gurgled scream, a scream for help. He was beyond the point of no return, to free himself from the cable or stop the winch were both impossible tasks. If no immediate help was forthcoming his attempt to kill himself would be a certainty, he was going to die!

I leaped out of my chair and ran as fast as my legs could carry me to try to stop the winch and lower him down. However, even though he was rising up in almost slow motion I knew I would never make it. Whilst running I had visions of his head severed from his body as the slipknot entered the sheave wheel!

Luckily, before I had even covered half the distance, one of the crew, hearing the scream, ran the short distance from his tent to the machine and released the clutch. The suicide victim was about half a metre from the sheave wheel; another few seconds and it would have been too late. Slowly and carefully, he started lowering him back to terra firma taking care not to jolt the brake lever and snap his neck! By this stage his blood- curdling screams had diminished to a choking sound through being throttled by the noose around his neck.

As his feet touched ground, I grabbed him and pulled on the cable to get some slack to remove the slipknot. Immediately, I removed the cable, he collapsed to the ground in a bundle. He was so limp I felt sure he was dead; he just lay there not moving, with eyes bulging to an impossible size, quite how they remained in their sockets was beyond me. Then there was a slight movement, a groan and suddenly uncontrollable coughing and spluttering as he tried to sit up.

Thrilled to see him alive we asked him to please just lay still until checked over by a medic from the DeBeers camp. His recovery was miraculous and the apparent reason for his foolhardy attempt at suicide came to the surface after some grilling by his manager. He had received mail from home informing him that his wife had apparently left him and moved in with another guy. The manager decided to send him back to South Africa to sort things out before returning to Botswana. It was awful to witness firsthand such an act by a desperately disturbed human being, yet thankfully, somehow he had managed to survive the terrible ordeal. As to the outcome on his arrival home, we will never know, he never returned to site, or to my knowledge was ever heard from again.

Chapter 19

The following morning before dawn I set off for the drilling site. Tips, who was busy going through the pre-start procedures on the rig was startled to see me,

"Morning Sir, we were sure you had gone back to Phikwe. Please can I send for a cup of coffee for you from the caravan?" He was that kind of guy, he seemed to know what to do and when to do it.

"Morning Tips, thanks I could kill for a cup of coffee. I don't see Johnny's vehicle here?" I had expected this and it looked like the plan might fall into place.

"No Sir, within thirty minutes of your leaving site he went back to his caravan, had a bath, changed and left. We haven't seen him since." I could see he and the crew had had quite enough of young Johnny. In no time Tips had arranged for my coffee and together we set about starting the days drilling operations.

Being so involved with getting the hole up and drilling, I never gave Johnny another thought. Our daily production and penetration rates had increased tenfold due to the use of the Bentonite mud mix in our water producing a far cleaner hole, not to mention stabilisation of the sidewalls. We were pulling our second full run of core from the hole at around ten o'clock in the morning when Johnny pitched up in his Land Rover.

After pulling to a stop he stumbled out of the vehicle and stood swaying from side to side with a priceless dumbfounded look on his face. I walked over to him finding it difficult to control myself.

"Good afternoon, Johnny, it is so good of you to join us," I said sarcastically. Speechless for a minute or two he eventually stammered,

"Why are you here, you told me yesterday you were going back to Phikwe?" His breath stank of booze and to be honest smelled like he had been pulled through a brothel backwards and most probably had been! He was an absolute wreck, eyes bloodshot, hair dishevelled and sticking up in every direction and so drunk he could hardly stand.

"Well Johnny, I suppose for the same reason you told me you never drank alcohol when I interviewed you for the position, we're both guilty of blatantly lying to each other!" Hell, I so badly wanted to punch him in the face. Fortunately, sanity prevailed and instead I grabbed him by the scruff of the neck, taking a handful of his shirt just below the chin and roughly hauled him over to the caravan. "Now listen to me, you little shit, and listen nicely, because this time I'm not lying. Have your bags packed in fifteen minutes, I'm taking you to Francistown, putting you on the next train to South Africa and trust me, *don't ever come back here or for that matter anywhere in Botswana again!*" I shoved him backwards towards the door of the caravan, he stumbled and tripped on the step and fell on his butt with legs sticking in the air. For some reason beyond my comprehension, he reminded me of a dead chicken.

I walked back to the rig and explained to Tips as to what our now redundant drunk foreman's plans were for the future. I was embarrassed at his behaviour as not only had I put him there to ensure the drilling ran smoothly, but to train the local black staff on drilling techniques and how to conduct themselves, supposedly leading by example himself. Not to mention being our liaison officer with the client, DeBeers Mining, who ultimately became Debswana.

I had really erred badly bringing him here and giving him that responsibility. Not that it made me feel much better, but at least I was mature enough to apologise to my staff for my blatant shortcoming in this regard! I then explained to Tips and the crew that as of now Tips was the new foreman and our promising learner operator Cotton, who was a local from the Letlhakane area, would officially be the new operator. The reaction was a mixture of excitement and surprise. Never in their wildest dreams did they believe I could make a black man their foreman.

By this stage Johnny had staggered his way to the Land Rover and dumped his bags in the back. I am not sure if he was too drunk or too embarrassed, but he never came over to the guys to say good-bye. I shook Tip's hand, congratulating him on his deserved promotion and left the site relieved at knowing it was at last in good and responsible hands.

There was absolute silence for the first fifty kilometres, neither of us saying a word; there was nothing to say as far as I was concerned. Johnny then attempted speaking to me saying he was sorry and if I could just give him another chance. I was way beyond being a nice guy. I told him clearly to shut up and if he spoke again I would dump him there and then in the Kalahari, dish out a hiding he'd never forget and leave him to his own devises.

He had pulled the wool over my eyes for long enough, it was now over and finished. I felt pleased I had fired him as I had sent out a clear message. Previously I had fired a few of my black staff when found drunk on site. For them to have seen Johnny my white foreman in that state and I not respond would most certainly have them lose respect for me as their manager, not to mention the obvious racist connotations that would go with it.

Almost three hours later on arrival in Francistown, I took him straight to the railway station, off-loaded his bags onto the pavement, bought him a one-way ticket to South Africa and paid him R500. I then shook his hand, wished him luck, climbed into my vehicle and without another word from either of us drove off to Phikwe. Thankfully, I never saw or heard from him again.

Chapter 20

We were now into December, it had been a tough two months, but was worthwhile, as business had turned around significantly for the better. The contracts were going well with new enquiries coming in on a regular basis. To a certain extent life in Botswana had settled down for us. Les was doing a great job on the admin side, which was a huge help. Regardless how well the production advances on site, without constant and efficient bookkeeping you would not survive as a drilling company. The kids really didn't know any better, there was nothing for them to compare their new environment with. They carried on day to day with their little lives and for the most part appeared happy.

Due to extra work imminently becoming available, certainly within the next few months, Alan, Gus and I agreed the purchase of another rig was not only necessary but also essential. Peter Gordon the chief geologist informed us that drilling would continue through 1974 at a similar pace, but more importantly, in a recent management meeting a large budget for exploration to commence early 1975 was authorised. He went on to warn us drilling would become progressively deeper and advised considering this prior to the purchase of any new equipment. We eventually decided the Sullivan 36 would be the way to go. Firstly, we liked the idea of the rig being manufactured and designed in South Africa for South African conditions. Secondly, the availability of spares should not pose a problem and thirdly, for a drill rig with the required specs, was extremely well priced.

Currently we were operating the smaller Sullivan 22's and Boyle's10. Taking conditions into account they had performed exceptionally well, but unfortunately were grossly underpowered in all departments for the drilling of holes to plus minus one thousand metres. Obviously, without the bigger more powerful rigs, bidding for the future proposed work in the Phikwe area would be futile and effectively fraudulent in that we were nowhere near adequately equipped.

Within our current financial budget we were only able to purchase one new rig. Our plan of action if successful in our bid for the work would be to initially have all three drilling machines operating. Once a smaller rig attained its maximum depth I would pull it off the hole and move the big rig there to complete the work. In so doing we would still be in a position to achieve maximum production.

The following morning I drove into town to phone my order in for the new rig through a company named Joy Manufacturing in Johannesburg. It felt satisfying and exciting knowing this kind of cash outlay was now possible and affordable for us. Having failed to connect through to South Africa on the phone at the Post Office I set off with order book and passport in hand to personally hand the order to the supplier in Johannesburg. To say I was excited would be a gross understatement. Such a cash outlay two months ago would have been completely out of the question. Yet here we were actually carrying it out.

The feeling of accomplishment was huge; it made all the long hours worthwhile and most certainly gave me the urge and absolute determination to push the Company to far greater heights. Suddenly the impossible became possible to the extent that on my long drive down I had already started contemplating the possible purchase of a second new rig. If successful with a signed and sealed two-year contract on the mine, I felt sure our bank manager could be amenable to discussing a lease agreement for a second rig.

Within two weeks, I had driven down in our Ford D800 truck and loaded the bright new orange machine. I had no option but to drive the truck myself as never had a driver been capable of driving in Johannesburg. Not only were tar roads scarce in the extreme in Botswana in the early seventies, but there were also no robots, not one anywhere in the country!

I needed a load of casing brought up from Johannesburg some time prior to this. I had my new driver, Piet, follow me down in the truck. He was proving to be an excellent heavy-duty driver, so I never gave a thought to possible problems on the trip. Driving through the town called Nylstroom in South Africa the fun started. As I approached the first robot, it changed to orange as I crossed the line. Not wanting to lose Piet while he sat at the red robot, I pulled over to wait for him.

Well, I need not have bothered. Without a care in the world he sailed through the red light! I could not believe my eyes and urgently signalled for him to pull over.

"Piet, what the hell do you think you're doing?" I am sure I was more shocked than angry. There was a total look of surprise on his face clearly showing he had no idea of what I was referring to.

"I'm sorry Sir, I'm just following you as you asked me to do."
"Well you have just driven straight through a red robot; you could easily have killed someone! I cannot believe you never saw it!" I was pointing back down the road. Climbing out the truck he stared back in that direction and maintaining the confused look said,

"Sorry Sir, but what is a robot?" I was astounded, he was not joking, he honestly had no idea what I was ranting and raving about. I pointed out the lights to him and had him watch as they turned from green to orange and then red. "Once again Sir, I'm sorry, but have never seen such a thing." It then struck me it was the first time he had ever crossed the border. There were not any robots for him to learn from throughout Botswana, thus being the obvious reason for our current dilemma.

Now in a quandary as what to do next I decided we could not continue the way we were, we still had to contend with the hectic traffic in Johannesburg!

"Piet, until I can teach you how to drive down here, you must please take my Land Rover and go back to Botswana. I will continue in the truck and collect the casing!" Relieved, but at the same time disappointed, he climbed into my vehicle and drove off. It just so happened that as he approached the robot it turned red and my heart jumped into my throat. To my relief and surprise he stopped, climbed out the vehicle, turned to face me and gave the thumbs up sign showing off a full set of white teeth with his ever-widening grin. He had that look of a little child saying, "Just look what a clever fellow I am." I stood there shaking my head while laughing aloud, waited for the lights to turn green and then watched him drive away with his arm waving madly out the window. He was a nice guy and I knew he would turn into a top driver. Shaking my head in wonder I climbed into the truck and drove off on my way to Johannesburg.

Chapter 21

On a separate trip in the old Ford truck to collect a full load of casing my family joined me with all sitting squashed up on the front seat. Having never been on a long trip in such a large vehicle the two boys were most excited.

The reason for them joining me was that I had purchased a CJ5 4x4 Jeep and needed Les to drive it back for me. All went well and we left Johannesburg in convoy with Les following me. Although slow with my full load of casing the truck ran like a dream. Whilst driving on the tarred road, keeping close watch on Les following with Darrin in the passenger seat and Dion with me in the truck was no problem.

Things changed considerably once we hit the dirt roads some one hundred kilometres from Martins Drift, the border post separating Botswana and South Africa. About thirty minutes onto the dirt road I was struggling to see if Les was following due to the huge dust clouds billowing up behind my truck. I eventually pulled over, stopped and after climbing out, lifted Dion down so he could relieve himself. I then walked around the truck checking tyres and the latches on the loading bay and was pleased to see all were in order. Within a few minutes the Jeep appeared over a small rise, drove up and parked behind the truck.

Dion ran over to say hi to Mom and Darrin. Taking one look through the side window he just burst out laughing. Puzzled I walked over to see what was so funny. It turned out that depending on which side you were on it was extremely funny. The only colour showing on either their face or whole body for that matter was grey dust.

The Jeep was a full open body from the windscreen to the tailgate. To this a steel frame was fitted covered with a custom-made canvas pulled tight and, at intervals, fastened to the body with efficient small catches at a spacing of approximately two hundred millimetres apart. Neither of us had given this a thought as far as dust proofing was concerned, but when it comes to vacuum cleaners this design was right up there with the best, everything was covered in a thick layer of dust. When I joked saying, 'Well at least it was an efficient umbrella for the sun' it somehow failed to find Les's funny spot. Shame, I felt sorry for the two of them, changed from squeaky clean to grey ghosts in a matter of half an hour!

After fifteen minutes of dusting themselves off followed by rinsing their mouths to clear their throats before taking a long drink, we made the decision. Les, although not a qualified heavy-duty driver, would take over the responsibility of driving the truck and I would follow in the dust bucket! Well, she handled the fully loaded vehicle like a duck to water. Both tired from a strenuous trip we eventually arrived safely at our campsite in Selebi-Phikwe. Strange, but when offering Les the job as our new truck driver she turned and walked into the house shaking her dust covered head.

Chapter 22

The source of the Shashe River is northwest of Francistown and flows into the Limpopo River where Botswana, Zimbabwe and South Africa meet at the site of the Shalimpo Trans-frontier Conservation Area. Effectively the surface riverbed is dry for possibly eighty percent of the year. Only once the rains come late in the year does it flow. Yet below the sand, the water remains, giving life to the fish that abound. To see the dry riverbed month after month, then miraculously as the rains arrive and pools start forming the fish appear, immediately gives faith to the wonders of nature. It is believed through scientific research that around two million years ago the great Zambezi River ran through the Makgadikgadi Pan on to the Shashe River and ultimately joining the Limpopo River. Over the millenniums this course has dramatically changed and the Zambezi today flows into Kariba Lake onto Cahora Bassa Lake.

In the early 70's through positive results of extensive feasibility studies undertaken in the catchment area of the Shashe River, selection of a dam wall site was approved approximately twenty-five kilometres south of Francistown, close to a small village called Tonota. Construction work started in earnest and by 1972, the wall was completed. For the average person, building a dam wall across a dry riverbed made no economical sense whatsoever. The majority felt it was a complete waste of money, as the dam would never fill.

How wrong we all were, from the first rains the dam not only filled, but freely released water down the Shashe River via the spillway. This had been a major part of the study as one important question asked was 'How would the people below the dam benefit and get water once the wall was built?' It turned out to be a huge success story, filling year after year to become the sole water supply at that time to Francistown and the Bamangwato Concessions Limited (BCL), a new copper/nickel mine in Selebi-Phikwe some eighty kilometres southeast. For this a large pipeline was constructed.

The service road for this construction became known as the pipeline road and was extensively utilised for many years by all as the fastest route driving from Phikwe to Francistown. However a 4x4 was essential, as you were required to cross the soft sand of the Motloutsi River. There was no bridge at the time so when the river was in flood you were forced to travel the alternative route through Serule village.

Water Utilities Corporation (WUC) efficiently managed, maintained and controlled the water purification plant, pump stations and pipeline. This proved effective and continued supplying fresh, clean water for years to come.

Chapter 23

Norbert Webster, a surveyor and certainly one of the pioneers of the Selebi-Phikwe BCL Mine, was responsible in conjunction with the geological department for the precise positioning of the drill holes. He had installed survey beacons on top of various granite kopjes that abound in the area around the mining concession. A special guy, Norbet was extremely down to earth with no airs and graces, loved the bush, was a great family man, an expert in his profession and a keen and talented sportsman. Due to our regular association both at work and on the sports field we became good friends.

Knowing our rather difficult living conditions especially considering our young family, he arrived at our camp early one morning with some exciting news. BCL had built five houses in the Tonota area some years back to house their staff working on an exploration and testing pilot plant. It was no longer being utilised to its full potential and had only the laboratory run by a Howard Maxwell, better known as Max.

He and his good wife Trina occupied one house and his assistant and his family lived in another, leaving three vacant. Norbert wanted to know if we would be interested in moving up there, he knew the contact person who could arrange this and believed our chances were good. Certainly, we were interested and decided there and then to drive through and see firsthand what was available. On arrival, we were thrilled to see the house. As Norbert had explained it was old yet neat, right on the corner closest to a lovely swimming pool some fifty paces over the road. It was a small house, as were all the rooms, and consisted of three bedrooms, a bathroom with toilet, a lounge/dining room and kitchen.

Electricity was supplied through a large generator and our hot water system through the ever-reliable Rhodesian boiler. We felt like two kids, the excitement was immense. I then drove down to the laboratory to meet Max. He was a nice, friendly and helpful guy. He showed us around the old plant and seeing an old tin shed standing empty I asked if I would be able to turn it into a workshop. Max, only too pleased to know he would be getting new neighbours, told us as long as he wasn't disturbed in the lab to go right ahead and do whatever we saw fit for our operation. Once the tour was complete he took us back to his house where we met his good wife Trina. Instantly we all seemed to get on well, cementing our positive intentions of the move up.

On our return to Phikwe I immediately went to see Norbert to confirm our interest and to ask his contact if possible could he please sort something out for us? The following day he drove out to our camp again with the wonderful news that our application for the house had been successful. We could move in whenever it suited us at the nominal fee of R100.00 per month. This covered the rental of the house, workshops and stores plus the use of the pool 24/7. I told Norbert I would love to take him and his good wife Jenny out for a meal, but were restricted as there were no restaurants within one hundred kilometres. We settled on a braai out at our camp and included a few of the geologists on the invite list.

All our drilling suppliers closed for the Christmas period so after consultation with the client we followed suit. Depending on work commitments and current completion state of the drill holes we planned to close on 20 December and start up again the first Monday after New Year's Day. As with most contractors this was our shutdown period, the time the Company took leave.

I had ordered a new Toyota Land Cruiser as my old Land Rover was needed on one of the sites in Orapa. Also with the extensive travel required to service all the sites a more reliable vehicle was required which fortunately arrived a week before going on leave. The owner of Continental Motors in Francistown, Mr. Guido De Fillipo a hot-blooded Italian, supplied the vehicle and conducted the mandatory pre-delivery service. We had dealt with him for some time and to all intents and purposes become a friend. He had given us a very good deal on the vehicle and managed to organise all the paper work within a couple of days.

Timing was perfect as this allowed us the use of it when driving through to Rhodesia where we spent our Christmas break with family. It was the first time Les or I had ever travelled in a brand new vehicle of any make and it felt special.

Chapter 24

On our return from Rhodesia in early January 1974, we packed and moved everything from our camp in Selebi-Phikwe to Shashe. The move went smoothly and within a week the camp was empty. Leaving a local Motswana as caretaker, we drove out with our last load on the Land Cruiser.

We had a beautiful eighteen-month-old Great Dane dog named Jema. Initially, we bought her as protection for Les and the kids when I spent time away from camp on the drill sites. However, as with all the animals we have owned in the past, Jema became part of the family. She had the most wonderful nature and was not only tolerant of the kids romping over her and trying to ride her like a horse, but also appeared to enjoy it immensely. There was no question we had become extremely attached to her.

With some effort, we managed to squeeze her onto the back of the vehicle in the only space available. On weekends when going down to the river for a braai she made sure we never left her behind by jumping up onto the load box, so was well accustomed to riding in the back.

With the dirt road being in desperate need of repair after the heavy rains, coupled with our load, we travelled slowly with care towards Serule trying to avoid having bits and pieces falling off the back. Approximately thirty kilometres out there was a loud agonising squeal from behind. The only reason we heard it was because of the oppressive heat bordering on 40deg Celsius and no air conditioner, I drove with both windows wide open.

Immediately I pulled up, leapt out the vehicle and was shocked to see Jema lying on the road trying to lift herself up with her front legs. Running back I could instantly see she had a broken hip! Why she jumped off I will never know, but had obviously landed awkwardly causing the injury to her hip.

Shame, obviously in excruciating pain she was whining with a pleading look in her eyes for me to help her. It felt far worse than a nightmare, how could such a thing happen to our dog and best friend? Les came up also in a shocked state, sat down and held her head on her lap whilst I tried to rearrange the load to give her more space. Once satisfied together we lifted her as gently as possible and placed her on a blanket in the back. She was so brave, seemingly knowing we were trying to help her, she never struggled.

The closest vet was in Francistown, a two-hour drive at the slow speed we were forced to travel. I wanted to drive much faster, but it wasn't an option given the circumstances. Every half hour I pulled over and gave her some water to drink and to see the pain reflected in her eyes was too terrible for words. I totally blamed myself for the accident, why oh why did I not put her lead on and tie it to the roll bar. The mind conjures up all kinds of things that should or should not have been done. Everything in hindsight is easy and appears so incredibly obvious; however, in reality it doesn't always work that way.

Eventually we arrived in Francistown and I headed immediately to the Government vet. Alas, the day's drama only worsened as he had gone out into the field, something to do with cattle inoculations and would only be back in a few days. At a loss of what to do next knowing full well Jema could not go on for a few more days, I spoke to Les and we made the decision to end her suffering as we both felt even had the vet been there little could be done. I drove off heading for the police station when coincidently Andy Du Toit, a good friend of mine, happened to pass us and waved. I signalled for him to stop. He was a local white citizen of Botswana, an enormous and physically powerful man. He had long curly blond hair, loved by all who knew him and a true gentle giant.

"Hi Andy, sorry to pull you over, but I'm desperate for your help," I said with my mind racing.

"Hi Trevor to you and your good lady, what's the problem pal?" he said with his infectious smile. Les having been stuck in camp in Phikwe all this time knew few people and had certainly not met Andy.

"Firstly, I would like you to meet my wife Les and two boys, Darrin and Dion; we are in the process of moving into a house at the old BCL Pilot Plant in Shashe so will be up in this neck of the woods a lot more."

"Good to meet you Les, Trevor has spoken of you often, but must say we began to wonder if it was just a story!" Laughing he stuck his huge arm through the open window to shake her hand then ruffled the kids' hair. I then went on to tell him of our misfortune with Jema. Being a farmer and working with animals on a daily basis he quickly checked her over and without saying a word stepped back and with a grave look on his face just shook his head. Instantly Les grasped his meaning and burst into tears. It was all I could do to control mine; it felt like the worst day of my life.

He indicated for me to come around to the other side of his vehicle. What he had to say would certainly not have eased Les's emotional state.

"I'm sorry Boet, but her hip is so badly smashed you really only have one option!" After a short silent pause as I was unable to speak he continued, "The Government vet is away, I can help you if we could go out to my farm. It will be quick and there would be no pain, I promise you."

He suggested I took Les and the kids to stay with a friend of his in town and we then go out to the farm together. This we did and although there was a protest from Les, I explained it would be better for all to do it this way. I dropped them off and before leaving, she and the kids came up and gave Jema a huge hug to say good-bye for the last time. By that stage, we all had tears running freely down our faces.

Once at the farm Andy called for two of his farm labourers and took them a little way through an open field to a clump of trees. There he marked out a spot showing them how deep he needed the hole and came back to the house. I am sure it sounds crazy as the inevitable was about to happen, but none the less I took some water for Jema in her bowl and shame, she drank it down in noisy thirsty gulps.

In a short time the grave had been dug and rather than carry her I drove over to save putting her through any more pain than she was already suffering. Gently we lifted her off the vehicle and laid her as close as possible facing the newly dug grave. I then spread her blanket over the hole, knelt down next to her and hugging her around the neck tried to tell her how sorry I was, with tears now pouring down my face.

Andy waited patiently with shotgun in hand, eventually I sat up, lifted her head facing away from him. Levelling the twelve bore shotgun inches from the back of her head, he looked me straight in the eye and as I closed my eyes and nodded, gently he squeezed the trigger.

From such close range, the sound of the shot was enormous not to mention the impact which almost jerked Jema from my hands. I just sat there stunned and not wanting to look. When I did eventually open my eyes there was definite evidence that she never felt a thing!

We lowered her down onto the blanket and wrapped it over her completely covering her body, using the blanket as a coffin. I then shovelled all the dirt back into the hole and neatly rounded the excess off in a heap above her. She was no longer in pain, which was most comforting, and knowing this to some extent relieved me of some of my pain and terrible guilt. With heavy hearts and there being nothing more we could do for her we walked back to the car. I turned to Andy and still with bloodshot eyes said, "Andy, I know of your love for animals and can just imagine how you felt having to do that, but thank you so much, we both know it was the right thing, I really owe you one." He put his huge muscled arm around my shoulder and said, "Hey bud, what are good friends for?" He was a special guy.

We drove back into Francistown, I collected Les and the kids from his friend's house and with a wave more of gratitude than good-bye we headed off back to Shashe, sadly with one less passenger.

Chapter 25

Les was obviously far more proficient at sorting out the house than I would ever be. If anything, I felt I was in the way so left her to it. Within a few weeks, she had thoroughly scrubbed the house from top to bottom with the help of a maid we had employed from the area. The curtains were up, furniture nicely arranged around the house, a couple of cheap carpets bought in Francistown laid in the lounge and our bedroom. We were only able to use a tiny carpet in the bedroom due to restricted space. The kitchen cupboards were in an awful state. These she scraped down and re-painted. Suddenly we were in a house of our dreams; it was small, but comfortable and we loved it. The positioning was also good as apart from the other houses at the plant we were isolated from the Tonota village by at least five kilometres of Mopani bush.

Our maid suggested we keep chickens for both food and of course their eggs. She was clever in that she just happened to have some for sale from the cattle post she lived in close by. This time, with the help of our garden boy, Les arranged to have a chicken run sorted out. In the one corner she built a pen made by stacking two loose cement blocks on top of each other in a configuration of two sets one and a half metres apart at the end, two sets in the middle and then another two sets on the other side in straight lines. The height was perfect to allow access for the chickens under the corrugated tin roof placed on top of the six piles.

Inside on the floor she placed a lot of dry grass for both resting and nesting purposes. The chickens gave their approval of their new house by settling in quickly and in no time started laying eggs. Although harvesting some of the eggs, Les felt sorry for the mothers and left them to sit and see if we would be lucky and get any baby chicks out of the deal. The rooster, obviously virile, knew what to do as within a few months we had baby chickens running around everywhere.

The pen became too small so we left them to roam freely around the garden. They knew where their food came from so never strayed too far from home. We were able to supply all the houses in the plant from our never-ending supply of chickens and their eggs to enjoy for breakfast or cooking. We often joked that whilst I managed the drilling business, Les in turn managed her chicken farm.

I spent any spare time sorting out my workshop and stores. There was little money available for this purpose so I had to make do with what was available at the site. Max had given me the go ahead to use anything from what effectively was the old scrap yard for the Pilot Plant.

There were old corrugated sheets I used for extending the workshop, loads of cut off timbers of all lengths which also came in handy and by the time I was finished the old RST (Rhodesian Selection Trust) scrap yard looked a whole lot tidier. Fortunately for me, three old gas fridges that were obviously irreparable had been tossed away onto the rubbish heap; I found these most useful as cupboards for drill bits and other in-hole drilling spares in my new makeshift store. Living in these isolated areas resourcefulness was an important part of life.

Also on site was an old ramp system for driving small vehicles onto for servicing the undercarriage and braking system. This I strengthened utilising old bricks lying strewn all over the area. I built it up to the height of the back of our eight-ton truck. This was certainly going to make the loading and off-loading of drill rigs and equipment far easier and safer. Max let me have a roll of shade cloth that had been lying around for as long as he could remember. This I erected over the area where I would spend a lot of my time repairing equipment when not out on site. Botswana is a hot country; extreme care is required wherever possible to keep out of the sun.

There are pros and cons to whatever we do in life, our move from Phikwe to Shashe certainly favoured the positives.

One, we were only twenty-five kilometres from Francistown as opposed to one hundred and fifty! Shopping became a pleasure, as most day-to-day requirements were available there.

Two, it was far more central to our drill sites. By this stage we had rigs at Orapa, Bushman, Matsitama and Selebi-Phikwe Mines.

Three, we were ten minutes drive from Shashe Dam where the fishing for both bream and the catfish (barbell) was excellent. Between the chickens and fish we were never going to die of starvation. *Four*, there were two families within shouting distance from the house if help was required for whatever reason; this being a huge confidence booster for Les when I was away.

Five, having the luxury of the life saving and well maintained swimming pool not more than eighty paces from our front door permanently at our disposal. Not only did we take full advantage of this on weekends, but also most evenings to cool off from the never-ending oppressive heat. We felt safe, free, settled and happy. The inhibitions Les had before moving up from South Africa faded fast. For the first time since being married we starting feeling like this is what home should feel like.

Chapter 26

Living within ten minutes drive from a dam was wonderful. Forever the averred fisherman I spent much of my spare time near the dam wall catching bream. It was remarkable just how many there were. There was nothing big, all being in the range of 1/2 to 1kg in size. Using a light fishing rod and reel and line rigged with small lead weights and two hooks baited with earthworm you were almost guaranteed two bream each cast. Being a freshwater dam they were tasty, fun to catch and to all intents and purposes free so they became quite a staple diet for us.

Gus was down on one of his monthly trips from Rhodesia and around five in the afternoon I suggested we go down and catch a few bream. He was keen so immediately after loading the rods, fishing box and worms in the back of the Land Cruiser we headed off down to the dam. Late afternoons were special, with the sun slowly changing from a blinding white light to an orange colour spreading to the sky and clouds as it settled down over the lake. I must have seen thousands of sunsets having spent most of my life in the bush, yet each one had its own unique beauty.

We baited up and cast into the dam. Normally within minutes there would be a bite and the fun would start. This time however it was quiet for the first fifteen minutes or so.

"I thought you said there were lots of fish in the dam?" said Gus with a smile on his face, also enjoying what had now become a stunning sunset. The water as far as the eye could see had changed to the golden, orange and yellow colour of the sky. It was most certainly one of those amazingly beautiful spectacles, where you cursed yourself for not having your camera with you.

"Well, maybe they're not used to you being here and are hiding!" I replied jokingly. Then almost as if on cue, Gus's rod jerked violently. What happened next was hilariously funny. So taken unawares by the strike he spun around on his heels and holding the rod over his shoulder with his right hand and cold beer in the left hand went running up the bank away from the water. He never stopped until the poor bream in absolute shock was dragged up onto the bank. I, doubled over in the mean time was laughing so much I was experiencing stomach cramps.

"Hey Gus, if you are trying to break the one hundred yard sprint record it really was a great effort, however if you care to turn that little handle on the reel you will find it does the same job with you remaining stationary! " I said sarcastically and by this stage we were both in hysterics.

"Oh you are so funny!" he said laughing heartedly, possibly more through embarrassment than from the humorous episode. He continued, "Standing there in awe of the surroundings with the sun setting, the cooler still air and cold beer in my hand and the feeling of peace, I got such I fright when the rod pulled in my hand I just took off!"

"Well not sure it means much, but I have never seen anyone land a fish that way! I was just thinking, thank heavens we weren't fishing from the top of the dam wall, you would have run yourself right off the far edge." This brought on even more laughter from both of us. The sight of him disappearing up the bank dragging a hapless fish behind him will stay with me for all time.

On another occasion Ralph Ward, a friend and top man in the Government Department of Water Utilities and in charge of all management of the Shashe Dam, came to see me one afternoon.

"Hi Trevor, I need take the boat for a run to check out a few things on the dam. Thought you might like to join me and we can use the opportunity to catch some barbel at the point the Shashe River flows into the dam?" He sounded genuinely excited at the prospect of a little fishing trip. It is known as mixing a little pleasure with work, something frequently done by most people one way or another.

"Hi Ralph, yes thanks, I would love to join you, please help yourself to a drink from the fridge while I get my fishing gear," I replied eagerly.

It was government policy that there would be no motorboats used for recreational purposes on any non-private dams in the country. The added expense for the required filtration plant to cope with oil left in the water from the boat motors was the reason given. This was always controversial in that dams all over the world allow boats for recreational purposes and they don't appear to cause excessive oil pollution problems. Secondly, oil being lighter than water always floats on the top of water, therefore would not be sucked up through the pumps. Thirdly, with the excessive heat in Botswana I imagined a thin film of oil covering the surface could possibly reduce the incredible evaporation rate to some extent. I feel, more accurately, the real reason was some time back two people were caught poaching ducks at the Gaborone Dam using a motorboat. Whatever, the reason for banning motorboats made my choice easy to take Ralph up on his offer.

Off we went to the shed at the Water Utilities, hitched up the little boat behind his Land Rover, drove around the north eastern side of the wall and launched. I only knew the dam from the shore, the beauty of it whilst going across in a boat was special. To some extent, it reminded me of Kariba, certainly not in size, but in seeing hundreds of Mopani trees, half submerged in the flooded waters.

The only thing Ralph checked that day on the dam was how well the engine on the boat performed together with ensuring we tied up to the correct tree at his favourite fishing spot. Within minutes we were baited with chopped up pieces of ox-heart and cast into what he called his barbel spot. I bent over to open the cool box to get a drink for the two of us when he stopped me saying,

"Trevor, don't bother, you won't have time to drink it, we'll have one on the way home." His words had only just left his mouth when his rod jerked in his hand and line peeled from the reel. Barbel are not the fastest fighters in the fish world, but on light tackle give a good account of themselves. I always felt they were much like a vacuum cleaner drifting along the floor of lakes and rivers sucking up and scavenging any food they can get. When they pick your bait up they don't stop to chew the food, just continue on their merry way looking for more. Then as soon as the tension of the fishing line is felt they start their run. Many of the smaller ones between the ranges of one to two kilograms will actually break water and jump clear of the surface in an attempt to free the hook from their mouth. Due to their strength and slow sluggish pull compared to many other fish, it can take quite some time to land them. Sitting in the boat with light rod and tackle, knowing the fish has just as much chance of escaping as you have landing it is a thrilling experience and certainly for me this novelty will never wear off. If anything the adrenaline rush gets better with each hook-up.

Ralph certainly was right and the catfish hungrily kept on eating the ox-heart. In the short time we were there we caught eighteen and he insisted we kept all the fish as he gave it as special rations to his local employees. To the Motswana this was a delicacy, far preferred to the bream if given the choice. Essentially it can be compared to a freshwater kingklip and it is believed in many restaurants to be sold as such. Kingklip is one of the most popular fish dishes served and yet due to the slimy feel of the skin on the barbel few will eat it. The only difference being, eating at a restaurant the fish has been caught, skinned, filleted, prepared and cooked so you don't see the original fish with slimy skin and whiskers!

The sun by this stage was all but set so we untied from the tree, took a drink each from the cool box and headed off towards the dam wall. There wasn't a breath of wind so the dam was like a millpond, our wake causing the only disturbance on the surface spreading in an ever widening 'V' as the two sides parted and drifted towards opposite banks. We were heading due east so the sun was setting directly behind us. Watching the waves work themselves through the golden/orange water makes one aware of the beauty and many wonders of nature. The peace and tranquillity of Africa came to the fore that evening and brought back once again the alluring and special beauty of Botswana.

By the time we had loaded the boat back onto the trailer, returned it to the shed and eventually arrived home it was dark. Les had heard our vehicle coming and was waiting outside anxious to view our catch. We pulled up in front of her in the driveway and when seeing the two full sacks of wriggling catfish in the back of the Land Rover, she just stood there with her mouth open, totally dumbfounded not knowing what to say, but eventually managed to get the words out.

"Did you guys use fishing rods or fishing nets?", she enquired with a smile. "What on earth are you going to do with so many fish, gee I just cannot believe it, and you have only been gone a few hours?"

"Ralph here found a magic spot, not to mention our obvious extreme talent as fishermen." We were all laughing by this stage and reflecting on the short but action filled fishing trip.

For Les, the boys and myself I kept *one* fish, then another for Max and his good wife Trina and three big ones for my Motswana staff to eat. The last thing I felt like was cleaning the fish. I carried our old tin bath from the side of the house which was no longer used by us, poured some water into it and released the five fish.

"They will be happy in there for the night and tomorrow we can get the guys to clean them," I said feeling quite satisfied with our short, but successful fishing trip.

This was met by delighted squeals from our two boys; to them this was really exciting and fun. Dion the youngest kept prodding the fish with his finger while Darrin stood back being a little weary of them. They would both jump back with shrieks of laughter as the fish wriggled. Certainly, these made unusual toys for boys of two and three years of age, but there was no doubt they were having tremendous fun and enjoying watching the fish. Living out here in the bush essentially away from civilisation, they were none the wiser as to how some of the city children lived with all their fancy toys. Even at that young age, they seemed to enjoy the unique freedom our life presented.

Ralph said he needed to get on home and would see us sometime. I thanked him and we stood at the gate watching his tail lights disappear into the surrounding bush. Being windless, the dust hung in the air almost as if in suspension. We went back into the house and immediately I was instructed to go and have a bath before I even thought about having a drink or eating the dinner Les had prepared.

As usual, I was up at dawn and wandered outside to see how the fish were doing. To my absolute shock and surprise, apart from the water the tin bath was empty. My immediate thought was who would come and steal them? Who even knew they were there apart from us and of course Ralph?

Then I saw movement some twenty metres away and walked over to find one of the fish slowly trying to make its way back to the dam, or so I assumed as where else would it be going! I picked it up and carried it back to the bath. I then continued to search the area until I had found all five and returned them to the bathtub. All were headed directly towards the dam, was this coincidence or had nature supplied them with a homing device of some sorts similar to a pigeon? Later that day I arranged to have them cleaned and skinned and we all enjoyed a tasty meal.

Chapter 27

Exploration for copper in the Matsitama schist belt had increased. We placed two more rigs there and although not drilling around the clock, ran full twelve-hour shifts. There were many ancient workings in the area as there were in many other places within a hundred kilometre circle of Francistown. The topography was flat, but blessed with many trees. After the rains, the foliage turned from dry leafless stalks to lush green leaves virtually overnight. We would jokingly say that you could stand and watch the leaves growing.

In an attempt to discover the elusive rich copper ore body, RST who owned the mining concession were going full steam ahead with an extensive exploration project. It was a well-known fact that copper was present in the area, however it never deemed financially economical for mining purposes. The site geologist directed us to an old mineshaft he felt contained sufficient water to warrant the installation of a pump. Our primary concern prior to quoting for any work was the availability of water, without which we could not drill.

The depth of the shaft was unknown; however, the water level looked to be in the region of six to eight metres. Scattered around the mouth of the shaft were boulders of all sizes with many dark nooks and crannies were evident. Guarding the mouth of one of these was an extremely large black scorpion! Their sting is excruciatingly painful and although unlikely, can be fatal, certainly to a young child. Just the appearance of the creature makes the hairs on your neck stand up coupled with a cold chill running down your spine. Enjoying the sun, he never felt threatened in any way as could clearly be seen by his tail laying flat on the hot rock with the sting protruding upwards.

It is said that the smaller the pinchers and the larger the tail the more potent the venom. This critter had unnaturally small pinchers and an extraordinarily large tail so there was no question he ranked high on the list of dangerous species. Joseph, my drill operator, picked up a stone and threw it at him. We believed the vile looking creature was fast asleep; this certainly proved not to be the case. Before the rock reached him, he disappeared into the opening of what could possibly have been his house. Looking at all the rock strewn around I felt quite sure there were many more such creatures keeping a close eye on us. "Joseph, you must tell the tractor driver to be careful when he comes for water!" I said seriously. "Hey my boss, that thing, she is biting very sore, we are all scared of it!" he said quite obviously not happy. The geologist made matters worse by warning us that two abnormally large black mamba snakes, frequently spotted in the area appeared to have taken up permanent residence amongst all the rocks.

Averaging around two and a half metres and known to grow to just over four metres, a black mamba is the longest venomous snake in Africa and the second longest in the world. Only the King Cobra grows to greater lengths. The body skin pigmentation varies from olive, brownish, dull yellowish-green to a gunmetal grey. The name *Black* Mamba is derived from the dark coloration inside its mouth, which is displayed with gusto when it is in an aggressive mood.

A black mamba bite can potentially kill a human within twenty minutes if anti-venom is not at hand, but death usually occurs within the hour, sometimes taking up to three hours. If bitten, common symptoms to watch for are the rapid onset of an erratic heartbeat, difficulty breathing, coughing or dizziness. Death is due to suffocation resulting from paralysis of the respiratory muscles.

The black mamba is regarded as one of the most dangerous and feared snakes in Africa. Nevertheless, attacks on humans are rare. Unlike other snake species, they are seldom seen in highly populated areas, generally trying at all costs to avoid confrontation.

We operated in the area for a few years on and off and drilling results, although generally showing promising mineralisation weren't quite what the mining house was looking for. The ever-elusive mother lode remained as such, hidden. Strangely, in all this time the two mambas were only seen on a few occasions, unlike the scorpions, making themselves visible sunbathing on a regular basis showing off their impressive, but lethal tails.

Chapter 28

Drilling is an incredibly high-risk business and increases dramatically with depth. This has in the past proved one of the main reasons why many companies do not make it. A wrong decision here or there can cost thousands on loss of in-hole equipment not to mention the possible complete re-drill or wedging off, starting a new hole from the mother hole above the problem area.

On deep holes this could mean drilling hundreds of metres back to the depth where the problem first occurred at your own cost. Back then Alan, due solely to being new in the drilling game and would often come up with ridiculous ideas that would quite obviously not work and in many cases drastically compound the problem.

Not known to mince my words, I have always said what I think, not what I feel the boss wants to hear and he was not happy with this at all. In most cases, I wasn't trying to be smart, my only concern was for the problem to be solved as quickly and economically as possible. I certainly was not prepared to go along with any suggestion that effectively could adversely affect the drill hole, Company and my life. As managing director I was held fully responsible for all decisions and actions in this regard and would be required to clean up the mess after the boss had left!

For some weird reason I possessed a unique talent of mentally picturing, almost as in photographic form, the exact unknown problem some eight hundred metres down the hole. I had been tremendously successful in fishing out broken or split drill rods, broken off drill bits and many similar problems. From what my brain had pictured so perfectly I would design and manufacture a fishing tool in my workshop. Prior to lowering the fishing tool down the hole I had visualised, as in video form, the fishing tool entering the top of the broken rod or object being fished. I had had many such problems arising and felt I was well experienced in my handling of them.

To all intents and purposes Alan and I were stuck in this strained working relationship, he having this attitude of 'I'm the boss and you do as you are told' while I on the other hand was grateful to have been giving the opportunity and responsibility of running the Company.

However, I was not prepared to buckle down to be a 'yes sir' 'no sir' man; it simply wasn't in my character to do so. His lack of experience on site was evident and on many occasions had I followed his instructions we would have been in serious trouble.

At the time I thought to myself that it was through no fault of his own not knowing enough about the practical side of drilling as it takes many years to learn. It has been proved that experience is the one thing in life you cannot buy regardless of how wealthy you are. He had joined the Company late in life and had been thrown into the deep end too quickly. Yet as a financial manager, he was brilliant, undoubtedly far above me in this department and proved to be tremendously helpful in all aspects of running the office efficiently with correct filing and bookkeeping procedures. We could both learn so much from each other for the betterment of the Company without the attitude problem due to self-importance.

Inevitably our strained relationship had to come to a head and eventually did on site in Orapa. Alan had sent a message through that he was driving down from Rhodesia and planned to arrive in Francistown late the following afternoon and would spend the night there and come through to us in the morning. I was in Phikwe at the time struggling to remove stuck drill rods in one of the holes. To add to my problems one of the drill rigs at Orapa Mine some four hundred kilometres north west of Phikwe also had an in-hole problem requiring urgent attention so I was under extreme pressure at the time. It was one of those cases where I could desperately do with a helping hand. However, being practical in-hole drilling problems I thought to myself Alan would not provide the help required.

I had no means of contacting him so worked on late into the night desperate to sort the problem out before leaving. The following day I continued battling with the fishing job and fortunately by mid-afternoon started making progress. To give my drilling crew their due they never complained about the overtime hours and it was eleven o'clock that night before I managed to clear the hole.

Still left with a one and a half hour drive through to my home in Shashe, I eventually climbed into bed in the early hours of the morning after a good bath as I was covered in grease and dust from head to toe from working on site all day. The thought crossed my mind that had I looked like this when Les and I first met, never mind marry me, she most probably would not have even considered going out with me!

Early the following morning our ever-reliable alarm clock rudely woke me. The roosters were merely crowing as loudly as possible and the mother hens and their chicks were clucking contentedly and scratching around for food outside our bedroom window. I felt tired and understandably so after the few days of hard work in Phikwe. Even so the feeling of relief having successfully fished out all the rods helped tremendously. I knew today would be another long hard slog.

After a great cup of coffee Les had made for me and a few deep drags of my Gunston cigarette, I left for the workshop at 6.30am. We often joked that the only good thing about smoking plain non-filtered cigarettes was that they were guaranteed to kill you before you had cancer! I started sorting out the equipment I felt could be required for the fishing job on site in Orapa. Alan drove into the workshop at around 07.30am and I was pleased he had arrived safely. After the pleasantries were concluded we drove up to the house for him to offload his bags.

Unlike the relationship Alan and I had, Les got on well with him, respected his financial managerial qualities and was grateful for all the help he offered her in the office. Having heard his vehicle come in on his way to the workshops she switched the kettle on for coffee and made breakfast for us. We were fortunate in that eggs were freely available from our ever-increasing production line in the chicken run. It always amazed me as to just how many eggs they could lay!

During breakfast, I asked Alan as to what his plans were and went on to explain the urgent problems in Orapa.

"Well, my first port of call due to appointments already arranged is with the bookkeepers and bank manager this morning," Alan said with finality.

He had been here for less than an hour and already my blood pressure was going up. His obsession to know how much money we had in the bank far outweighed the long hours and hard work actually required to get it there in the first place! "Well in that case I'll shoot off to Orapa in my Land Cruiser and start working on the problem. We are just starting to make headway with regards to our name as a drilling contractor and I'm not going to blow it just because you are so desperate to see how much money is in the bank! Les has the latest statement giving you all the facts anyway. You will have to go through to your appointments in Francistown in your vehicle. I'll try to get a message through regarding my progress with the stuck rods as and when I find both the time and a phone."

"No, please I'll need you to be present at the meetings; there could be matters to discuss that you will be in a better position to answer. We can go in your vehicle and then continue on up to Orapa, I'm sure a couple of hours aren't going to make a big difference." I could see there was no point in trying to argue this one. He had made his mind up that he wanted to see these guys and at the end of the day he was the boss. We each threw a small bag of clothes into the vehicle not knowing how many days we would be away.

Sadly once again I had to bid farewell to Les and the kids; we left for Francistown assuring her I would be back as soon as possible. Although not happy about it she was amazing in her understanding and acceptance of all my travel due to the immense spread of contracts throughout the country. She was certainly brave in staying on her own and seldom complained. I was really fortunate to have found someone like her as feel there are few women in the world that would be prepared to buckle down to living her life.

By 10.00am we were through with all the financials and Alan asked if we could pop into Haskins, a large hardware store in Francistown, there were a few things he needed to buy to take back to Rhodesia when he leaves. We had already wasted half the morning and I was starting to feel agitated. Managing the Company, I knew what our standings were with the bank and there were no surprises in our meetings. I could also imagine how my crews felt on site, not to mention the reaction I was to receive from my friend Jim, the chief geologist, for the delays. I possessed an obsessive compulsion to keep the rigs drilling at all times and was prepared to do whatever it took to achieve this goal. Yet here we were going around seeing people just for the sake of it and then throwing in a little shopping for good measure!

"Sorry Alan, you have to be joking, there is simply no time for that. It's going to be a long day and we should buy some ham, cheese, tomatoes, bread and a few cokes and you can make us sarmie's (sandwiches) on the way to keep the hunger pains at bay later."

"Trevor, why is it that you can never relax, have you any idea what it's like making food in the front of the vehicle whilst you are driving us flat-out over these corrugated and bumpy dirt roads?" Alan replied with an almost appalled look on his face.

"Alan, I succumbed to your wasting a few hours of our time meeting with the bookkeepers and bank manager, now we either leave for Orapa immediately, together, or I go on my own leaving you here to do as you please. Hey it's your call, makes no difference to me."

We bought the food, filled my Land Cruiser with fuel and were out on the road within thirty minutes of our last meeting heading directly for Orapa. Watching Alan's culinary skills trying to cut the tomatoes and cheese provided good entertainment. Then in his bid to spread butter on the bread, after dropping the butter knife a few times, add the filling, closely followed by a couple of slices of tomato, was quite amusing. When noticing the smile on my face he snapped,

"I'm glad you find this so funny, I cannot for the life of me understand why we aren't sitting comfortably in the dining-room of the Grand Hotel enjoying a good old fashioned Botswana steak!"

"Don't worry, Alan, after all your efforts I'm sure it is going to taste just as good as a piece of steak!" Two and a half hours later with dust billowing up behind us all the way, we eventually arrived on site at BK9.

Chapter 29

My drilling operator on the site was a local Motswana named Cotton, from Letlhakane village. His home consisted of a small cattle post of mud huts and was only about fifteen kilometres from the drill site, which was convenient for all concerned. He was definitely showing signs of becoming one of my top operators and a most pleasant guy. "Cotton, what is going on here and why are you all looking so disgruntled?" I asked. "Hey my boss," he said scratching his head, "we have been waiting for you for some days now and wondered if you were coming at all as you usually come immediately!"

"Yes Cotton I'm sorry, but Joseph had stuck rods on his hole in Phikwe that I needed to sort out which obviously delayed me for a few days," I said.

"Mr. Gibson the surveyor was here yesterday afternoon," he said. For some reason my staff always called a geologist a surveyor. He then continued saying, "He was too very angry and said you were to go and see him as soon as you arrived!" I had expected this so asked the drilling crew to offload all the equipment from my truck, which included five bags of bentonite.

After discussing in full Cotton's in-hole problems I was pleased to hear there was some movement on the rods, but when attempting to pull up further they kept sticking in the same place. I felt confident this could be sorted out with the first remedial action required being a good bentonite mud mix going in the water sump.

"Alan, please can you supervise the mixing of the bentonite?" then continued saying, "I need to shoot off and see Jim, he is most certainly not happy with me so I'll have some serious explaining to do. I should not be long and feel confident once we circulate the bentonite mix we should be able to work the rods up and down until they come loose. It really doesn't sound like a big problem."

"Should I not come with you?" asked Alan.

"No Alan, there is no point in both of us going to see him, I would be far happier if you get things going here and I can honestly tell Jim we are busy with the problem." Ultimately, it was my responsibility and I knew Jim would want to see me. He just shrugged his shoulders so I went on telling him that under no circumstances do anything but mix the bentonite and wait for my return. I went through the mixing procedure with Alan and Cotton, then left to go and meet with Jim. Rightfully so, on my arrival he was extremely upset with me regarding Cotton's problem and the time delay in my responding to it. After I had apologised and explained the situation, he settled down and asked what I was going to do about removing the rods and start drilling again. I explained that bentonite was being mixed as we spoke and I had brought all other equipment required to site. I assured him that by tomorrow morning at the latest, the hole should be up and running again.

"My standing here being crapped on by you is the only delaying facture in the operation at the moment," I joked and Jim being the great guy he was, laughed telling me to bugger off back to site and stop wasting his time standing around the office.

After shaking hands, I left for site and on arrival my heart sank. Seeing the look on Cotton's face I knew there was something seriously wrong. Alan was sitting on a twenty-litre oil tin some distance away from the rig. I leaped out the vehicle and walked briskly over to the machine.

"Cotton, what the hell is going on? Obviously something has happened now talk to me."

"Sorry my boss, but Mr. Alan was shouting too much. He did not want to listen to us and was trying to do things he should not. He has made the small Matata (problem) into a big Matata. The wrench jaws on the 24" are buggered and so he was trying to use the 18" wrench spanner with a long pipe to turn the stuck rods. The hook jaw broke off and fell into the hole. We now have the rods stuck and a hook jaw down the hole!"

"I specifically told you to just mix the bentonite and wait for me, why were you trying to turn the rods with a spanner anyway?" Cotton explained the rods became tighter and tighter as he pulled up firstly on the winch and then the hydraulics. To make matters worse Alan instructed him to increase the engine speed for more power, resulting in the rods becoming even tighter in the hole!

"Cotton, how many bloody times do I have to tell you that if the rods become tight in the hole, yet there is still movement no matter how small, you must work them up and down continuously? Never, and I mean never, just keep pulling up, all you are doing is jamming them even more!" I could not believe he could do such a thing, as he was one of my more experienced operators.

"I only pulled them with the winch while trying to turn them, but then Mr. Alan shouted at me saying I must tighten the chuck and pull up with the hydraulics and now they are completely stuck, cannot turn or move up or down. That is why Mr. Alan was trying to turn the rods with a small spanner and big pipe!" Just at that time Alan walked over and enquired how things had gone with my meeting?

"Well all I can say is that it went a shit load better than what you have cocked up here, why is it that you never bloody listen! For some unknown reason you think you are a whiz-kid driller and yet you haven't got a clue what you are doing!"

I was seriously angry and continued sarcastically saying,

"Shit Alan, if the drill rig could fit into the hole you probably would have dropped that in there as well as the hook jaw! Now please, I have a lot to sort out here so do me a favour and keep out of my hair by going to stand over there by the vehicle!" He gave me a funny look as if to say who the hell do you think you are speaking to, but before he could respond I once again told him I was deadly serious and way beyond being pissed off so to please just stay away from me.

Immediately I turned back to Cotton and together with the crew and the use of a jar to smash the rods down we eventually managed to get some movement. Slowly, but surely, with pumping the bentonite mix and continuously working the rods up and down they eventually became loose enough to be able to turn slowly with the chuck. I was surprised that the broken jaw in the hole was not causing major problems. It was lodged somewhere in the annulus of the 'B' drill rod and the NX casing. I simply had no way of knowing just how far it had gone down.

After an hour, I started making ground past the point clearly marked on the drill rod of where the rods were initially stuck. Each time the rods jammed some more I tightened the chuck and ever so slowly using 1st gear turned and pushed down with the hydraulics. Steadily one by one I managed to retract and remove them all from the hole. More by luck rather than good judgement, the head of the core barrel being significantly larger than the drill rods acted as a lifting device and brought the broken jaw to surface. The odds of this taking place were extremely high in the negative, yet to the loud whoops of joy from the guys the hole was clean and safe. I carefully discussed with Cotton once more the importance of the mud mix required to keep the hole clean and safe right through to completion.

By 3pm I was ready to leave for home feeling extremely satisfied with the week's work knowing everything was up and running again on all our drill rigs. Having been through months of personality problems with Alan I was not prepared to let this ride. When he approached to climb into the vehicle he said,

"Well, Trevor, you have done well and what a relief to know the hole is now safe." He then opened the passenger door to climb into the passenger seat.

Although relieved the problem on the drill hole was sorted out I was still angry regarding his total disregard for my instructions to leave things as they were. His ordering poor old Cotton to keep pulling back on the hydraulics against his will completely jamming the rods and then dropping the broken spanner head down the hole was sheer negligence. The feeling of anger and disappointment with his attitude towards me was not going away, if anything had increased. After a week of hell, with little sleep due to Joseph's problems in Phikwe, I was tired, extremely irritable and to be honest had reached my limits with our working relationship. There was no chance I was prepared to have him in the front with me.

"What the hell are you doing? If you think I am going to let you sit in front with me after your stuff up today you must be crazy. Thanks to you we almost lost the complete hole, our reputation and a good few thousand out of your precious bank balance!" My blood was at boiling point by this time. Completely amazed at my attitude he asked, "So let me get this straight, are you telling me that I must sit in the open back all the way to Shashe?"

"Well done Alan, that is the only thing you have managed to get right the whole day! Now either climb in the back or stay here, to me it's immaterial. I'm really tired, have spent precious little time with my family this week due to all the problems and have a long way to travel. Now please whatever you choose to do please do so now, because I'm leaving!"

"Shit, Trevor, I cannot believe what you are telling me and if you are serious then when we get back to Shashe you can start packing, because you are fired!" "Oh dear Alan, what a shame, you are a little late for that, I have just quit. Now get in or stay here." With that, he climbed into the back shaking his head from side to side. I looked over towards the machine to wave good-bye only to see a full set of snow-white teeth showing on Cotton's face, he was smiling from ear to ear and giving the thumbs up sign. There was no question after the hard time he had been through he thoroughly enjoyed the outcome.

After three long, tiring and extremely dusty hours, I arrived home and as always Les, hearing my vehicle approaching, was in the driveway with the kids waiting to meet us. She was shocked to see Alan sitting in the back of the Land Cruiser, but knowing my problems with Alan and seeing the expression on my face knew the final crunch had come. As I climbed out, she just stood there with her hand over her mouth too astonished to say anything. The kids ran up to say hi to me as Alan climbed off the back and started dusting himself down having been covered in white greyish dust; he kind of looked a little like a spook in the gloomy dusk as the sun settled in the west. After Les had served up a great meal of crispy roast chicken, chips and salads, and the kids had gone off to bed, we all sat up late into the night discussing a possible way forward. I had roughly told her of the day's events. To give him his due he proved man enough to admit and accept the fact he had made an unforgivable mistake and apologised for this.

He went on saying he had seen firsthand just how useful I could be on site and how passionate I was about my work and apologised for our previous problems. He suggested we write off the past to experience and start again. I stood up, apologised for my irrational over-reaction to the day's events, shook hands confirming it was now over and for the sake of the Company agreed we should put the past behind us.

From that time on, we worked incredibly well together and over time became close friends. I learned a great deal regarding managerial and financial skills from him. He in turn learned a great deal regarding the practical and mechanical side of drilling from me. Finally, we had become a team, a good solid productive team, together we successfully helped build the Company from strength to strength.

Chapter 30

It was Thursday the 4th April 1974, I was returning home from Matsitama after a long week and looking forward to the weekend when approximately ten kilometres out of Francistown, I noticed thick black smoke billowing up into the sky. I assumed it had to be a building on fire in town. The closer I came the more obvious it was that it was actually on my side of town and not too far from the airport. Due to the smoke being so intense, it had to be something major. Could a fuel tanker have caught fire on the main road through to Nata?

I pushed on intrigued to see what had happened. Shortly before Francistown there were people streaming out of town towards the smoke. Seeing a small dirt road heading off in that general direction I turned onto it and drove straight towards the smoke, which had miraculously died down considerably by that time.

On arrival, I was horrified to see a large aircraft had crashed and burst into flames. The fire engines were there dousing the smouldering wreckage. It really was a horrific experience witnessing the carnage close-up. Clearly, the aircraft had ploughed into a tree snapping the left wing off completely. This resulted in slewing the plane off, smashing the cockpit into some more trees and catching fire. It was devastation beyond words, the fire had been so intense it spared nothing, not the passengers or any part of the plane; everything was burned to a cinder.

To see completely charred bodies sitting in seats with only metal frames remaining, their hands seemingly welded into the steel bar of the seat in front of them. Obviously the result from trying to protect themselves from the impact was a tragic spectacle to witness firsthand that will stay with me for all time, The most horrendous smell, a mixture of burnt flesh, plastic and metal permeated the air. Reinforcements of police, army and medical personnel arrived pushing us all back, away from the crash site and cordoned off the area completely.

The crash investigation concluded the accident was engine failure caused through fuel contamination. Delivering fuel to the airport the supplier inadvertently pumped Jet A1-fuel into the Av-gas underground tank resulting in a 30% to 40% fuel mix contamination. Thereafter the contaminated fuel was pumped into the aircraft's tanks with tragic consequences. Soon after take-off the engine's temperatures climbed rapidly and started backfiring badly.

Immediately the pilot, in a bid to come in and land back on the runway, initiated an emergency left hand circuit. Sadly, with the plane losing altitude constantly due to lack of engine thrust it crashed some three hundred metres short; essentially a further thirty seconds in the air would have saved them!

The aircraft was a Douglas DC-4 and owned by Wenela Air contracted to transport Malawian mine workers. On this particular flight, there were eighty-four people on board, four of which were crew. Seventy-eight lives were tragically and needlessly lost simply due to carelessness. Only six people survived by jumping from the aircraft before it hit the tree and burst into flames. The aircraft was so badly damaged it was written off and scrapped after intensive investigations of the accident were concluded.

It was a sad day for Wenela Air, which due to the accident closed its doors and has not flown since. It was also a sad day for Botswana in that the needless disaster happened in that country. This, however, pales into insignificance when taking into account all the people from Malawi who lost loved ones and trying to imagine the shock and pain felt by them not only losing family and friends, but for many their only breadwinner.

Chapter 31

My good friend Max had two old, dilapidated go-carts lying around the back of his house. They looked in a mess with drive chains rusted, tyres all flat and it was difficult to tell what make the engines were due to all the dust and leaves covering them from lying abandoned for months. When speaking to him about them, he said they used to run well and he had been meaning to try and get them going again, but for whatever reason had just not done so.

"Well, I would also love to get them up and running and it would give us something to do over the weekends" I said enthusiastically.

"Well you are more than welcome, would be great if you can get the old things going again," he replied with a look of excitement in his eyes. It was a Saturday morning and so I immediately loaded and dropped them off at my workshop.

In a bid to de-rust, I removed the chains, placed them in a small tin container and poured diesel over them. After cleaning the engines, I made sure they had not seized by turning the crankshaft over. I then changed the engine oil, removed, checked, cleaned and re-set the gaps on the spark plugs. The air cleaner elements were of the paper type covered with a foam outer filter. Like the rest of the engine were completely clogged up with sand and dust. I removed these and washed the foam outer filter with petrol and once dry soaked it in oil and then squeezed out as much as possible. This ensured there was a complete protective layer of oil, but just a film and not saturated.

I blew the paper element out working from the inside using compressed air. Clouds of dust came billowing out. It made me wonder how much pushed through into the intake manifold. Madala in the mean time was busy pumping up all the tyres. He was quite sure I had gone crazy to even consider not only the repair work, but for us to try to drive such silly little cars once I had them going. "You have such a nice 4x4 why do you want to drive this skadonko (piece of scrap), even the donkey cart she is far much better than this," he said, shaking his head from side to side like it was the most ridiculous thing he had ever seen in his life. To him it most probably was!

By Saturday night, we had both go-carts up and running ready for some serious racing the following morning. Max had marked out an interesting track and soon after breakfast, we fuelled the cars and sat on the line ready to go when Les dropped the starting flag.

Not only were our black staff there, but they had put the word out and a small crowd turned up to watch the spectacle of the two of us tearing around the bush in the little go-carts. The thin bases of the hard plastic seats attached directly to the chassis together with the tiny wheels had us almost sitting on the floor.

The flag dropped and off we went accelerating into the distance, engines screaming and tyres sliding through the corners with steering at full opposite lock. Like naughty little school kids we were shouting with glee and having the time of our lives. Max's cart was slightly faster on the straights, but I managed to outbreak him in the corners, not due to being clever or a better driver, but more accurately because my brakes were nowhere near as good as his, almost non-existent and I just could not stop if I wanted to.

Somehow, although going far too fast, I managed by sheer luck rather than good judgement to slide, bounce and wiggle my way through the corners with wheels all but touching. From my tyres dust, sand, rocks and grass flew everywhere including all over Max and his cart, but I was back in the lead. The closely fought contest continued for a few more laps, but ended abruptly when Max by this stage really living on the edge, totally lost control. To the hilarious delight of our onlookers he careered off disappearing into a thick bush, not to be seen again for a few minutes whilst he untangled himself.

This was the beginning of things to come. We raced every Sunday morning assuming I was not required to be out on one of the drill sites. I enjoyed the cart, but always felt like going one-step further. Life is like that or certainly has been in my case; as soon as the novelty wears off on a new fad, you look for something else to replace it with to get the adrenaline rush going again. Then miraculously an advert for a Honda 185 motorcycle for sale in Francistown changed my life.

My motto has always been work and play hard. You must have fun, live life, enjoy it to the fullest, because believe me, regardless of who you are you are not going to get a second bite at the cherry. With this in mind, I purchased the Honda. I knew of other people with bikes in both Francistown and Shashe and planned on getting them involved. I had ridden many road bikes before, but never tried my hand at off-road riding. Furthermore, the old go-carts were now at the end of their productive life from the hammering we had dealt out. Constantly they broke down so we spent more time repairing them than racing them. The time had arrived to pension them off and start afresh with something new. With some persuasion, we managed to talk Max's wife into allowing him to go the same route.

Chapter 32

Whenever we had the chance, Max and I would go on long fast rides into the surrounding bush. Our confidence steadily grew stronger each time out. Going over one little hump in particular, not too far from the house, I was convinced even my back wheel left the ground. To confirm this I had Les out there almost lying flat on the floor trying to get a photo of this momentous occasion when the bike became airborne. Eventually after a few attempts there it was, clear as daylight, both wheels, albeit only a few inches, were off the ground at the same time! None the less, the bug had bitten and now I was ready to race.

I canvassed as many riders as I could in the area, even some of the American Peace Core guys joined in, and we started a small off-road bike club. I built a racetrack half way between the workshops and our house. Incorporated in the track were ditches and built up jumps. Within a few race meetings, we were flying through the air for metres then sliding the bikes through the next corner. Slowly the club grew in strength, producing some talented riders.

Even Les had started racing on a Yamaha DT 250 I had bought for her. The locals in the area loved it and would stand four deep all the way around the track. The shouting and cheering from the crowds never ceased until the dust settled after each race. Although not always knowing who the riders were they all had their favourite racing number. These were easily identifiable, displayed clearly on the front and sides of each bike. When one of their riders overtook another bike they went into a frenzy jumping up and down, shouting and screaming at the top of their voice. It became even louder if one of the riders inadvertently went flying over the handlebars or came to an abrupt and dusty stop crashing into one of the ditches with the bike coming out the other side on its own leaving its mount lying behind in pain. Somebody else's misfortune always appeals hugely to the crowds, not only here in Botswana, but all over the world. People love racing, not just for the fast bikes or cars, but possibly even more so for the crashes and visual excitement it brings.

As in all motor sport one always wants to go faster, reach greater heights and to achieve these ideals we bought faster bikes. I had purchased the latest Honda Elsinore 250 and to say I loved the bike would be a gross understatement. The suspension had more travel, the power was smooth with magic handling abilities and I felt immediately at home on the machine. It was now drawing close to the end of the year; dates of our shutdown period allowed me time to race in my first national race across the border in my home country, Rhodesia.

Derrick Backer, an old friend and involved in a big way with Moto-X, talked me into going up to race in the Boxing Day Scrambles out at the airport track in Salisbury. It was the last of the Rhodesian national race meetings of 1975. Filling in the entry form and sending it off felt good, almost had the feeling of applying to race in a world championship event. From the level we had been racing in Shashe, believe me this was a huge step up in my racing career at the time.

On arrival in Salisbury late Saturday afternoon with trailer in tow carrying my Honda Elsinore, I contacted my good friend Derrick.

"Hi Derrick, we have just arrived so there is no chance of me making it to the track for a practice, so will see you there first thing tomorrow morning." We were tired after the long drive through from Botswana and the last thing on my mind was going for a practice ride.

"Glad you made it," he said and then continued, "however I won't be riding with you tomorrow."

Surprised to say the least I asked, "What are you going on about; it was you that talked me into coming up in the first place and you now say you're not riding?"

"Yes, well I know that, I'm sorry, but this afternoon at practice Clive Berry, certainly one of the top riders here challenged me saying I would never get through the top left-hand sweep flat out in 5th gear." This sounded like double Dutch to me and I replied, "Well big deal, but what on earth has that got to do with not riding tomorrow?"

"Well you see the problem is it turns out he was quite right. When I tried it just to prove him wrong I had one hell of a crash and broke my leg badly in two places!" Shocked I didn't know what to say. "The medics were there with an ambulance and everything. It was quite funny, when they wanted to cut my leathers away with a pair of scissors to enable them to get to the problem area on my leg I told them they had better bring their chequebooks first. Shit, nobody just cuts my leathers, these guys have no idea how much these things cost!" Even with the seriousness of his injury, I was amused; it was exactly the reaction expected of him.

"Hell I'm so sorry to hear that," I said still chuckling, "only you could make a joke out of something so serious! What is the prognosis, how long before you can ride again?"

"They say it will be a good few months before I even think of it." Then added, "They went on to say it would be far better for my health if I were never to think about riding again!" and laughed. "Anyway, I'll be there tomorrow to cheer you on, but I'm in plaster from my toes all the way to my crotch, so will be on crutches!"

The following morning I was up early, eager to get going, this to me at the time was a huge thing and I was excited to get to the track. Whilst the family were showering and getting dressed I was down at the trailer checking the bike for the umpteenth time. I knew it had to go through scrutinising and wanted to ensure all was in order. Les's Mom had cooked a good breakfast of bacon and eggs for us saying,

"I'm not at all happy with you racing, but as you will do it anyway I won't have you racing that dangerous bike of yours on an empty stomach!"

We arrived at the track at eight-thirty, just as the registration and scrutinising opened. Everything went through without a hitch and I was surprised at how quickly they checked the bike over. Practice sessions started at 10am and we were organised and sent out in our respective classes. There had been a huge rainstorm on the Saturday afternoon rendering the track almost under water in places. Coming from Botswana, riding in the mud was a new experience for me.

I was following Clive Berry, the person responsible for poor old Derrick's broken leg, during the practice session, my reasoning being to learn from him, as he was one of the top riders in the country. He should know all the right lines around the tremendously demanding circuit.

Soon after coming out of a tight left-hander at the end of the main straight there was a high jump immediately followed by a deeply rutted and slippery mud bath. Clive took off over the jump and somehow lost it on landing and went down face first into the mud. I, following closely, possibly should have tried to take corrective action. Instead, due to my lack of experience at the time, I froze and continued on my line, unfortunately riding clean over the back of Clive's helmet. This significantly exaggerated his problem pushing his face even further into the mud!

It was incredible how when my rear wheel went over his head it kicked my bike out of shape, almost sending me face first into the mud. More by good luck than good riding, I somehow managed to stay on the saddle. With both legs stretching out independently depending on which way the bike slipped and slid all over the place, I eventually gained control, stopped and ran back to help him. I could just imagine how the crowds were laughing at me performing a totally out of control circus act through the mud bath. Feeling terribly embarrassed by the whole affair I wished the mud could just swallow me up and I would stay there until everyone had left! Why did this have to happen to me in my first National Race meeting? Not only had I ridden over the head of a competitor, but chose to pick out the top rider during practice of all times.

Clive in the mean time was desperately trying to extract himself from the sticky mess he now found himself in. I was surprised that he was conscious, or for that matter even alive! By the time I reached him, he was on his hands and knees shaking his head from side to side with the eyes being the only identifiable part of his face. With the back of one clean glove, he had managed to wipe most of the mud from his goggles. The rest was just a dark brown to black smear of sticky mud about 30mm thick. His bright yellow racing shirt was now black in the front and black spotted yellow on the back. I told him it looked quite cool, but he could not see the humour in it.

From behind, I gripped him firmly under his armpits and managed with great difficulty to pull him to his feet. His knees had to be a foot under the mud and made a suction sound as they eventually popped out. I cannot tell you what a mess he was in or how sorry I felt not only for stupidly riding over him, but also for actually riding over his head. By this stage, some of the marshals had joined me to help get him to dry land.

Ultimately he was cleaned up, checked out by the medics and was set to race again, there was no question he was some tough guy. I walked over to him to apologise with my hand outstretched. "Hey Clive, I'm so sorry, trust me I just never had time to avoid you. Your falling on the racing line wasn't a great idea for either of us." He looked me up and down as if I had come from Mars, called me a few choice names that brought back memories of my army days and then burst out laughing. Then shaking my hand said, "Just remember one thing rookie, don't ever fall down in front of me, because I owe you one *big time* and would be more than happy to reciprocate and use you for traction. I might even throw in a bit of interest with it!" I duly complied by finishing second to him in all three events in our *Street Scramblers Class*. I must add this had nothing to do with his threat. I gave it my all and then some, but he was just that much faster than I was. Something I was particularly proud of was having the current world speedway champion finishing third one place behind me in each race; albeit a different form of racing, it gave me a lot of confidence. All participants had a great day and more importantly, the adrenaline of racing dirt bikes was now flowing freely through my veins and would continue to do so for many more years.

Chapter 33

I was thrilled at being successful in my bid to undertake the extensive drilling project for BCL Mine. This was great news for the Company, however for us personally, especially Les, it was a concern as we were required to move from our comfortable home in Shashe. Selebi-Phikwe was to become our new home for the near future, with our major concern being accommodation. Development at the time had been minimal in the small mining town making housing an extremely scarce commodity.

Over the past two weeks, I had spent every spare moment available in re-building one of our best drill rigs to ensure all ran smoothly at the commencement of the contract. Within a week of the final order being issued, I had all the equipment on site.

The late Peter Gordon, chief geologist at the time, met me at the first proposed drill site. He was a tall man in his forties, highly proficient in his field and always made a point of personally checking the accurate placement of the hole surveyed in by my good friend Norbet. He was fanatical to the extreme on the rigging of the machine. I had firsthand experience of this on the initial hole. Written instructions issued gave me details that the hole was to be drilled vertically to a depth of four-hundred and fifty metres. If given a choice, a drilling company will always opt for vertical holes. One of the many advantages was not being restricted to rigging the machine in any set direction as in an angle hole. It afforded you the opportunity to rig the machine so that the operator would not need to look directly into the sun whilst pulling drill rods.

Once rigging was complete, I checked and re-checked the levels of the machine base with the use of a clinometer rule that operates with a floating bubble in a liquid that needs to be centralised. Utilising the same method I ensured the quill shaft was vertical both on the side and in the front. Eventually, satisfied all was in order to commence drilling I drove to the mine to inform Peter I was ready for his final inspection.

On arrival at the site he climbed out of his vehicle and immediately threw his hands in the air.

"Oh no, you've rigged in the wrong direction completely and will need to re-rig!" Then in an extremely agitated manner pointed out in what direction the machine should be. Puzzled and to some extent bemused I replied, "Peter, if it were April the 1st I would accept this as an April fool's joke." I paused, waiting for his amused response, which quite obviously was not to be forthcoming. "Come on, you have got to be joking, regardless at whatever direction the rig is facing the drill head remains vertical with rotation always in a clockwise direction!" He gave me an annoyed glare showing clearly he was not impressed with my response.

"You bloody drillers think you are so clever sometimes. Surely you are fully aware due to formational pull on the drill bits in the area all the holes consistently deflected on an easterly bearing?" He paused for a few seconds for this to sink into my incredibly confused brain then continued. "Rigging as you have done with the drill head facing to the east and the rear of the machine to the west will tend to exaggerate the problem due to clockwise rotation of the drill string." With a further pause as my confusion increased and sense of humour waned, he continued, "To help towards alleviating this problem the machine needs to be re-rigged at ninety degrees to its present position." Quite obviously, beyond reason climbed into his vehicle shouted for me to call him when ready and drove off in a cloud of dust whilst my staff and I stood there dumbfounded.

Unhappy with the situation, we lowered the shear legs, pulled out the dead-man bolts from the timbers and some three hours later with our sense of humour non-existent were once again set up and ready to go. To my surprise Peter, on his return, apologised and admitted he had erred badly and was completely wrong. With the use of a pencil held vertically on his desk top and then moving a matchbox at all angles around the vertical pencil he understood my argument. I accepted his apology, shook hands, had a good laugh and got on with the job at hand.

Now that I had the machine up and running on the first hole, I could focus on moving the family and our belongings down to Phikwe. Les was not impressed, or possibly more accurately described as being disgusted, when I took her to the only accommodation available to us. It was a tiny little prefabricated building with one bedroom, a lounge, come dining-room, come kitchen, come bedroom for the kids, a bathroom and separate outside toilet. There were two rows of similar shacks around us with no yard whatsoever. I promised it would only be a temporary situation until I could make other arrangements. As to what these could possibly be, I had absolutely no idea at the time.

Although living in a shack we were actually fortunate in that we had a roof over our heads, what I desperately needed was a workshop. Mine management arranged and allocated a temporary industrial area for contractors. Fortunately, for me the sites allocated were along a little dirt road that ran north south past the mine dumps. It was the ideal location for my needs, finding a more central area for servicing my rigs was not possible. I set about building immediately.

Once again, all building construction was required to be of a temporary nature. I used hessian attached to wooden gum poles splashed with cement for the walls and finished it off with whitewash. For the roof, standard corrugated iron sheets were securely nailed to the wooden beams. The completed structure consisted of a small office, a four by four metre storeroom, a workshop of approximately thirty square metres and a loading ramp.

A good friend, Rob Watt, employed by the Mine, advised me to look in the scrap yard for old fencing. This I did and to my surprise found rolls of new fencing! I purchased all the rolls at a ridiculously low price and fenced off the little piece of land allocated for my workshop. I then set about constructing a substantially sturdy main gate by cutting and welding together some old drill rods. The old fridges used in Shashe formed an integral part of my storeroom as secure cupboards for drill spares. Added to this I had managed to pick up some old wooden planks from the same scrap yard to use as shelving, everything was starting to fall into place.

Even though Bob Jones the Mine geologist found it terribly amusing due to the simple, but functional design, I was extremely proud of our workshop. I now needed to focus on accommodation; if we were going to live here indefinitely, it was imperative I had to improve our living conditions for the sake of my family. Les handled the situation extremely well, but I knew she was not happy, nor was it easy for the kids.

Chapter 34

After spending our first two difficult months in the shack, I coincidently came across someone that had purchased a three by three metre wooden garden shed. Immediately a thought jumped to mind. When enquiring from him where he had bought it and the price, he informed me it was from a company in Bulawayo some eighty kilometres from the Plum Tree Border Post in Rhodesia. The purchase price was R750.00 plus transport. I thanked him and rushed off home.

"Hi doll, I have the perfect plan to solve our accommodation problem," I told her excitedly immediately on entering our little shack.

Her eyes lit up as she enquired,

"Well I sincerely hope that means we're moving back to our house in Shashe?"

"No, you know there is no chance of that happening as the contract here can only get bigger, the geologist has already asked for two more drill rigs to be mobilised to site. We need to sort out accommodation and accept the fact that we're going to settle down here in Phikwe." The disappointment clearly showed on her face.

"I honestly believe I could make things far more comfortable for us. My plan is to drive through to Bulawayo in the Ford truck and purchase five wooden garden sheds." Les had no idea as to what I was talking about and replied,

"Why on earth would you do that when we don't even have a garden, where would we put them and why five?"

"Well I figured if I can speak to the geologist on the mine and secure a small piece of land I could use the sheds to build a house for us." Just from her expression, I could see she thought I had possibly gone mad! "I would have one shed as our bedroom, one as a bathroom, one a kitchen and the other two would be bedrooms for the kids or guests." I thought I detected a slight sparkle in her eyes. Living under our current conditions, I guess anything would sound reasonable. "These would basically be built in the shape of an inverted 'U' with our bedroom at the top. Then with the use of old drill rods and timbers I'd construct a corrugated roof over everything, giving us a closed in dining/lounge area between the wooden shacks. I would build the front wall with cemented hessian and white wash with a window and front door." I paused for my idea to sink in.

"Sounds complicated, but promising," she replied.

The Mine had been most accommodating in offering us an area not far from our little shack, with the stipulation that the dwelling be a temporary structure. I was most thankful to them for their help and within a month of our discussions, our new house was complete. At last we were truly happy and had loads of room. Due to the large centre portion between the wooden sheds we regularly held wild parties, and believe me there were many.

In a way, the garden-shed house became quite a talking point. Although I managed to cover the complete structure with a corrugated roof the pitch was nowhere near spec, much too flat. When it rained, we placed buckets all around the house as the water poured in like mini waterfalls. Jokingly couples would arrive at the house for a party with an umbrella saying they were concerned it might rain! We spent the following two years in the wooden house and it became a special time in our lives. We even had hedgehogs as pets. They were cute and so tame, religiously arriving each evening for the meal Les would leave out for them; as was the case with our two massive Great Dane dogs, they blended in becoming part of the family.

Chapter 35

I was extremely busy at work. As anticipated the contract for the BCL Mine had grown with five rigs drilling continuously; this together with other contracts scattered around Botswana demanded a huge amount of my time. I spent far more time on the drill rigs than at home with my family.

Life was simply flying by and before I knew it, the kids were growing up and getting closer to school going age. Living in Phikwe there was no confusion regarding which school to send them to as there was only one! The Mine had fortunately built and opened a Junior School called Kapano. Although new, it had a good reputation with some excellent teachers.

Brought up in the wilds of Africa Darrin and Dion were independent and always able to find something with which to amuse themselves. They both had long blonde hair, which needed to be cut short for school much to their disgust. Nonetheless, both were most excited about the new prospect. We were extremely relieved to have them both settled in, happy and enjoying school. They would get to meet many other children and make friends, as is the norm. Slowly but surely our lives were coming together. With the kids off to school every day, it freed up more time for Les to help on the admin side of running the business whilst I was away in the bush. Yet between all my work commitments together with the help of others, especially Jim Patterson, owner of the Nata Quarries, somehow found time to open the Phikwe Motor Sports Club. Jim generously made available his grader and front-end loader to help speed up the construction of a motocross and flat track circuit a few kilometres out of town in close proximity to the cemetery. There were those who jokingly asked if the ulterior motive for the positioning of the venue was the short distance required to take the bodies after the accidents!

Racing can certainly be dangerous, but so can walking down the street. Although visually spectacular racing is far safer than it appears to be. Generally, the people who participate have some idea of how to handle whatever it may be that they are racing. Secondly, I believe the more important safety factor is that you are all going in the same

direction. The club proved enormously popular in a short time. People
went out and bought off-road bikes, others built up old cars found in
scrap yards converting them with high performance motors and some
form of roll bar protection. I personally built up an old smashed Ford
Escort 1600 I had picked up for next to nothing through a panel beater
friend of mine.

The vehicle had rolled and the roof got badly damage. There was
also a fair amount of superficial damage to the bodywork, but
generally the chassis, engine, gearbox and wheels were fine. After
fitting roll bars, a free-flow exhaust system, a full tune-up of the
engine and a slap of red paint to the dented bodywork, I had an
extremely fast, but cheap race car. Nonetheless, I might add it
certainly would not have featured if entered in a beauty contest.

The car track was tight with the start taking place at the beginning
of the one hundred and fifty metre long main straight which then
swept into a fairly tight left-hand bend immediately followed by a
tight and tricky 'S' bend. Assuming you managed to negotiate this
successfully seeing the cars were bunched up at this stage jostling for
position, you joined the back straight ultimately swinging into a fast,
but continually tightening left-hand sweep. In a full opposite lock
power drift through the last section of the corner, you had to flick the
car back into a right-hander leading you back onto the main straight. It
was great fun, vehicles racing all out in power slides with lots of
bumping and nudging causing cars to go spinning off in huge clouds
of dust had the local Motswana crowds crying out for more.

Likewise, the motocross track was spectacular; I had designed the
jumps to allow the bikes to launch themselves high through the air.
On landing, they'd immediately be thrown over sideways to enter the
following tight turn with gravel, rocks and dust spraying out from the
rear wheel. The first two events were scratch races where all
participants started in a straight line, thus giving the timekeepers
accurate lap times for each competitor. A handicap system for both
cars and bikes produced incredibly close racing in the remaining
events for that day. This was not only exciting for the people racing,
but possibly even more so for the hundreds of spectators. Usually I
won the first two scratch races in both the cars and the bikes. This
ensuring that from that point on I spent the rest of the day eating dust
working my way through the field, having to start from the back in the
handicap events. The day produced non-stop racing for the screaming
fans, alternating between cars and bikes. Thus, the competitors had
no time to think of work and the stress it caused, a wonderful means
of totally de-stressing. The only break came at lunchtime when we all

had a desperately needed hour off to relax and have a bite to eat and drink as much fluids as possible. Hydration was extremely important to combat not only the physical exertion required whilst racing, but also the excessive heat.

I organised regular race meetings generally held on the last Sunday of each month that attracted an average up to fourteen bikes, eight cars and every able body for kilometres around. The spectators would come in droves and stand up to four deep all the way around the circuit. The locals clambering for vantage points transformed massive granite boulders into grandstands.

Even the important soccer matches held at the town stadium never came close to our crowd attendance. It was new, exciting and with the added attraction of the locals having free entrance to the outskirts of the circuit. Spectators thoroughly enjoyed the entertainment throughout the day with non-stop and exciting racing.

The more I raced the stronger the urge to continue racing became. A few of us would travel through to Zimbabwe on a regular basis to participate in their motocross racing in Bulawayo, Gwelo and Salisbury. Shortly after purchasing the latest Suzuki RM 370 full race machine, I entered and won the Rhodesian Flat Track Championship in Bulawayo with Colin Oakley finishing a close second half a bike length behind me. Although obviously thrilled at winning the title I am not sure it would have been the outcome had Zack Koekemoer's chain not broken half way through the race whilst leading. When it came to flat track racing, there was no doubt he was one of the top riders around. Colin and I kept pace with him lap after lap with the three of us sliding sideways through the corners together, but he managed to keep a wheel ahead and would need to have made a mistake for me to get by! Certainly rates as one of the most exciting and closely contested races I had ever experienced.

Chapter 36

In 1977, my racing career took an enormous step forward. Bill Urdley, a good friend, asked if I would not be interested in long distance off-road racing. He mentioned that entry forms were out for the '*Roof of Africa*' held in September that year in Lesotho and felt I was riding well enough give it a go. With gross ignorance not knowing what to expect, yet bubbling with confidence I agreed to enter. Unbeknown to me at the time I had entered one of the most difficult and physically demanding off-road races in the world.

Recently I had purchased a four-stroke Yamaha TT500. A powerful and fast bike I figured would be perfect for such an event, scary how wrong one can be. The epic off-road event took place in Lesotho starting in Maseru.

Initially, after successfully completing scrutinising etcetera, you were required to compete what is fondly known as '*race around the houses*'. This consists of five laps around a six-kilometre circuit, all on tar. From these results, you obtain a grid position for the main event starting at 6am the following day. The atmosphere in the pit area is electric with all shapes and sizes of cars and bikes. Colourful flags are flying everywhere giving the various sponsors mileage together with loads of beautiful woman wherever you looked. 'Hey, this really is a lot of fun' I thought to myself. Each competitor was required to attach to their racing machines ,in the relevant places, advertising stickers and racing numbers. There were people selling all sorts of aids as in leather tool-kits, small hand held high-pressure canisters for pumping wheels, plus many different makes of puncture repair kits as in small manageable tyre levers. Then there were various liquids designed to squirt into your tubes to prevent air leaking from the tyres if punctured and many other interesting accessories for such racing.

Being very green behind the ears, I was fascinated and excited by this and it gave me an adrenaline rush of note. I had previously organised a small bag I could attach to my handlebars in which I would carry my selected spanners and spares for the race. This was prior to the tool bag salesman confronting me skilfully marketing his products in the pit area. Seeing my obvious in-experience, he talked me into fitting his bag behind my seat and on top of the mudguard, telling me this was a proven method universally used by top riders. Although a little dubious I mistakenly took his advice and discarded my bag for his. He was right in that the spares all fitted in and it was neat, tidy and out of the way. My parents brought us up to trust everyone, but have found this in many cases to be a disadvantage and this was no exception.

I managed a great run in the 'race around the houses' especially considering I was a complete nobody all the way from Botswana, genuinely not expecting to be in the top fifty having seen all the top teams so professionally organised with back-up crews, mechanics and trailers filled with bike spares including complete front and rear wheels with new tyres. The only spares I carried, with no back up crews anywhere, throughout the race were contained in my little leather bag on the mudguard! The colour of their bikes hardly discernible due to the array of advertising stickers attached and similarly brightly splashed all over the racing shirts. I had to wonder just how much money sponsors had invested, but felt sure it had to be a massive amount.

This was a revelation for me in a big way and to be honest I started feeling like a fish out of water, out of my depth and much like a real country bumpkin. I seriously began to wonder if I had not leaped head first into something I was not yet ready to attempt. Yet when the results were pinned to the notice board in the hotel, I was thrilled to see my time was fifteenth fastest out of well over one hundred bikes. 'Wow, come on you can do this' I thought to myself.

The following morning we were up at 04.30 am to allow enough time to ensure everything would be in order for the start. Les and the kids were excited, but also nervous. The race covers two days of fast, rough, slow and often dangerous racing sections. Completing racing section one consisted of a tough six hundred kilometres of racing through the mountains of Lesotho to Ramatseliso's Gate where we entered South Africa. Assuming you complete racing section one, a stamped time card is issued to you by the marshal. You are required to have your bike in impound in Matatiele by a set time, providing little opportunity to work on it. Matatiele was a small town nestled some twenty kilometres from the border post separating the two countries. The following day we had to race the same route, but this time in reverse direction to the first day. Effectively to the select few capable of completing the race, a total race distance of twelve-hundred kilometres over the two days has to be endured! To try to explain the severe physical punishment dealt out to anyone who has not competed in the race is impossible and would be difficult for them to fully appreciated.

Starting time had arrived; tension amongst the riders was high knowing what lay ahead. All competitors lined up on the starting grid as per their results attained from the "race around the houses." The experienced chief starter and his helpers, all of whom had been involved over the past few years, efficiently controlled this. Each competitor then received starting orders in their relevant time slots. The sound of the engines, four strokes mixed with two stokes accelerating into what was now a thick cloud of dust made the hairs on my arms stand up.

The first race section to Butha-Butha was on reasonably flat and really fast dirt road surfaces. My 500 was running like a dream and by the time we turned off onto a small track I had passed six bikes and was currently enjoying holding 9th place overall. Being so engrossed in going as fast as possible, I chose to ignore the rubbing sound from my rear wheel each time I hit a bad bump. Eventually common sense prevailed over the adrenaline rush and I pulled over to check on the problem. To my horror the expensive leather bag, the so-called answer to my tool-carrying problem, had broken the rear mudguard off completely. Thereafter each time the rear wheel hit a bump the tyre made contact with the bag ripping it open! I had lost everything, the bag was empty! Here I was not forty kilometres into the first day of a twelve hundred-kilometre race without a single emergency spare or tool available to me!

My disappointment was immense, and I realised I would need to backtrack to look for whatever spares I could find. This I did and being the only bike going in the opposite direction was positively nerve-racking. Luckily, I eventually arrived at the spot the bag had been ripped open. My spares were scattered all over the road. Tearing around trying to pick them up was like running the gauntlet with bike after bike screaming past me on both sides.

How in that thick dust I survived by not being run over by one of them was incredible, I was on a suicide mission in my rush to pick everything up that sanity certainly did not prevail. Once satisfied I had recouped the majority of the lost spares I was in a predicament with no means to safely carry them. In hindsight, I could kick myself for not leaving my original bag strapped to the handlebars in case such a problem arose. Just how stupid could I be I thought to myself. The only option was to stuff everything, including screwdrivers, into the large side pockets of my racing jacket, the danger of which was extreme if I were to fall on one of them sticking up the wrong way!

From the time it happened to the time I managed to continue again could only have been around fifteen minutes. Yet when finally arriving at the first checkpoint in Butha-Butha my overall position had dropped to forty-third place! Where is my clever leather-bag salesman now that I desperately need him? However, as we can't turn the clock back there wasn't anything I could do, but buckle down and try making up as many places as possible. I kept reminding myself to stay in race mode notwithstanding the fact that there was a long way to go and to ride with my head and not the throttle hand.

Soon after leaving Butha-Butha, the terrain changed dramatically and we started climbing up into the Drakensberg Mountains. To explain the beauty of the area is impossible, to be fully appreciated it needs to be personally experienced. Yet with the road conditions and severe mountain passes to negotiate at speed there was no time to admire the breathtaking views.

There were times I was convinced I had to be lost. The terrain I was racing over never resembled a track of any sort, yet alone a road! The relief on seeing the little red markers indicating otherwise gave me the confidence to continue. On some descents the gradients were so steep, dismounting and sliding down dragging the bike with me was the only way down! It was fast becoming evident my choice of bike was not a clever one. Essentially, it proved a real handful being far too big and heavy. I seriously began wondering if I would reach the overnight stop in Matatiele let alone be able to complete the full race.

I had caught up to another rider named Gary coincidentally riding the same machine as mine and having similar thoughts. We made a pact to ride together all the way to help and encourage each other. High up into the mountains we came across many clear freshwater streams. We drank from them, possibly looking similar to giraffes drinking, but who cared, the water was sweet and gave us the energy needed to continue.

The route took us up and down the most beautiful mountain passes, the temperature variation between the valley and the top of the pass was hard to believe. Slowly we managed to find our second wind and rode on faster and faster. Riding together had made all the difference. We were able to push each other to the limit picking off many other riders on our way to the overnight stop, officially arriving in positions twenty-third and twenty-fourth respectively.

Chapter 37

The sense of achievement having made it this far was immense and filled us with confidence for the long and hard day to follow doing it all over again with the goal of arriving in Maseru hopefully well before the cut-off time.

Six o'clock in the morning heralded the start of our race home with the fastest rider from the previous day rightfully sent off first. Our turn eventually arrived and with the beautiful roar from our exhausts of four-stroke power, we set off together on another day of torture. Both Gary and I were stiff and sore from the exertion, not to mention the falls we had suffered, on the previous day's ride.

I had picked up a serious problem in that my right hand lost all feeling in the thumb, fore- and middle fingers. Racing with your hand in this state was not easy or sensible, but rarely did I do anything that pertained to sensibility. Being the throttle hand, this was especially uncomfortable. All I had to hold on with and control the throttle were my last two fingers and palm.

This resulted in a huge blood blister right across the palm, which was excruciatingly painful, however with Gary's encouragement we continued racing. The sheer drop-offs whilst racing through the passes were seemingly bottomless. Full concentration was required at all times. I thought to myself in the event of my making a mistake and going off the side of the mountain into the unknown below, the chances of ever being found had to be slim at best! Instantly I dismissed this negative thought from my brain and focussed once more on the race.

Arriving at what was aptly called the 'God Help Me Pass', notoriously dangerous, proved extraordinarily difficult when tackling it from the bottom up. There were boulders of all sizes strewn everywhere on the unbelievably steep gradient. Quite incredibly, there was little groundcover at all. After each of us had fallen on three attempts due to the loose boulders we decided the only way to succeed would be to walk the bike up whilst using gentle throttle control.

Walking up the pass without the bike would have been difficult, doing so whilst keeping your bike upright was close to impossible.

Again we cursed our heavy cumbersome machines and vowed if ever stupid enough to consider attempting the race again it would be on a far lighter two-stroke bike. Eventually, after exerting enormous energy and time, we reached the summit, both exhausted, grumpy, but none the less thrilled to have succeeded. We achieved what seemed an impossible feat with far more damage to our energy levels than to the machines. I said to Gary that the only positive thought that entered my mind was the bikes behind us had to come up the same pass!

After a short rest and a drink of water, we set off again. Apart from the intense concentration and energy drained from every muscle in our bodies by the physically demanding conditions, the rest of the section was essentially uneventful. Eventually, complete elation reaching the finishing line exhausted, sore and feeling we had gone ten rounds with Cassius Clay. Gary laughed saying I looked like I had gone the full fifteen rounds! However, for both of us the sense of achievement was enormous, completely outweighing everything else.

Experienced riders in the pits informed me prior to the race that possibly 10% of the riders entered to win, the remaining 90% aimed to complete the race and have the honour of being presented with the Roof of Africa star presented to all those who succeeded. Of the one hundred and forty-six bikes entered only thirty-two finished. Gary and I tied for fifteenth place, but it felt like we had just won the world championships. Strange, but having really struggled throughout the race I told Gary I would be giving it a miss the following year. On our way home the next day I was talking to Les and the kids about what bike I would be racing in the same event the following year! It is quite incredible how the human mind retains all the good and blanks out as much bad as possible.

Chapter 38

The following year, 1978, I did race in the 'Roof of Africa' again, but not on a bike. My good friend John Sweet talked me into racing a vehicle instead. We built up a Ford F100 housing a 302-V8 motor coupled to four speed manual gearbox with a limited slip diff on the rear drive. The suspension had an upgrade in that we manufactured and welded in place new brackets to enable installation of twin Bilstine gas shock absorbers on all four wheels. Also on advice from a friend, I filled the inner section of coil springs with new tennis balls to help the shocks over the tough sections ahead of us. As luck would have it, due to intense work commitments on both sides we left final preparations to the last minute. Despite working late night after night, much to my consternation by the Tuesday evening prior to the event starting on Friday the car was still not ready! Essentially a two-day trip to get there we arrived at the decision for Les and the kids together with Mavis (John's wife) to leave early on the Wednesday morning. We would follow as soon as possible thereafter once we felt the car was race ready.

Working non-stop throughout Wednesday, continuing through the night to 4am on Thursday morning had us believing the car was as ready as it was going to be. Two hours later after a brief shut-eye, we left and drove the car all the way through to Lesotho. Although we both looked and felt exhausted, our families were pleased to see us arrive safely on the Thursday evening. We had booked into the Holiday Inn Hotel in Maseru as did the majority of entrants in what was well known to be one of the most prestigious, tough and extremely energy sapping off-road races held anywhere in the world. We all enjoyed a great meal in the restaurant then retired to our rooms where we slept soundly.

Friday was spent going through scrutinising and competing in the 'round the houses race'. The day was successful and I managed to put up a reasonably fast time. The car performed well with no hiccups needing attention, unlike many of the other competitors who worked late into the night. All that remained was to enjoy a good meal together and sound sleep to be fresh for what was coming.

We were up before sunlight and shortly after 6am, the starting official sent us on our way in order of times attained in around the houses. This was no longer a dream, it was real and at last, we were on our way racing through the beautiful mountainous region of Lesotho to Matatiele some six hundred kilometres away. The vehicle performed like a dream with minimal problems apart from fuel starvation. I had been concerned that in a race of this distance through mountain passes at full throttle wherever possible, we could have fuel pump problems.

In a bid to alleviate this concern, I went to the expense of purchasing two expensive top of the range fuel pumps. These I neatly mounted laying flat next to each other in the engine compartment on the bulkhead above the left wheel. They were well away from the heat of the engine and I felt quite satisfied with the installation. However, I am guilty, and have always been, in only reading the installation instruction pamphlet once all else has failed. This time was no exception, certainly to my detriment.

To our utter surprise throughout the race, the pumps constantly stopped running. Each time John had to unbuckle himself, jump out, open the huge heavy bonnet and soundly tap each pump to get them working again.

This obviously lost us much time throughout the day, but we still managed to arrive at the overnight stop in second place in our class. All vehicles and bikes were impounded for the night only to be released one hour before starting time the following morning. I said to John that regardless of losing a little time and possibly starting a little late, we had to re-route the fuel pipe and mount the pumps on the dashboard. Once installation was complete, I had the pumps standing in an upright position within easy reach for John without even having to unbuckle his safety belt, to give them a tap each time they failed.

On race section two, the route was the exact reversal of the previous day; to our surprise, the pumps never missed a beat. This enabled us to gain ground on the leading car and eventually get past with some two hundred kilometres to go.

The locals in the area within walking distance from their village, stand three deep on sections that look dangerous, of which there are many. It really is a highlight in their year and they wave and shout as each vehicle comes through. With approximately fifty kilometres of the race remaining, I was approaching a cut-away at a speed of close to one hundred and fifty kilometres an hour. People lined the two raised sections on either side shouting and waving their arms egging us to go faster. Almost to our peril the previous day we learned this generally meant danger and to take caution.

Fortunately, I slowed down to some extent; a tight left-hand bend immediately followed the cut-away. Going wide would have us rolling down into a gulley full of rocks. As I set the car up for the turn, a large rock came flying through the air from somewhere in the crowd. More than seeing it, we heard it explode through the windscreen, thudding between our two seats and covering us in glass shrapnel. Quite how I managed to control the car through the bend seconds, I will never know! Everything happened so fast my focus on driving never had time to waver. I shouted to John asking if he was okay and with confirmation believed there was no point in stopping so continued racing with the rock wedged between our seats and no windscreen!

Eventually we crossed the finish line and to our utter amazement and relief we not only completed the race, but were also declared the winners of class 'D'! To say we were excited would not even come close to how we felt. After prize giving and a hot shower, we talked at length about the race at the dinner table. One important point brought up for future events being that we needed to be ready a good few weeks prior to the event and put the vehicle through full race conditions. This should be the norm and had it been the case for this event we would have discovered the diff ratio was far too high for racing through mountain passes!

With a correct gear ratio, our times would have been much faster climbing the many endless steep passes. Going into a race of this stature having only completed the car on the day we left for the race was crazy to the extreme. Yet thinking about it, so was I back then and feel sure many of my friends today feel this state of mind never changed over the years. Anyway, thrilled as we were with our class win it was made even more exciting for me when being informed at the time that as far as records were concerned I was the first person ever to finish and win my class in consecutive years on a bike and then in a car.

Some years later Malcolm Smith from America, star of the famous motorbike racing film titled " *On Any Sunday"*, came to South Africa and won overall on a bike and the following year won overall again, this time in a full race Sandmaster pipe car. His achievement dramatically made my consecutive class wins pale into insignificance. I have watched his film five times and there is no question that if I were to nominate an idol in off-road racing it would unquestionably be Malcolm.

At our celebratory party back in Botswana John told all concerned that he felt I was the best driver he had ever known and would join me in the left-hand seat as navigator in any off-road race. Nonetheless, this came with a condition that never again, regardless of what I offered him, would he ever do the *'Roof of Africa'* with me or anyone else again! He openly admitted he was terrified at times racing through some of the dangerous passes in Lesotho. To his full credit, he never let on at the time, helping me to drive as I saw fit in the belief he was relaxed.

Chapter 39

Driving through town heading out to one of the drill sites I noticed a friend, a local building contractor Dave Brown, working on a new house that was just over foundation level. Interested in what he was up to and wanting to say hi, I pulled over. Walking in I said, "Hi Dave, how are you doing these days? I haven't seen you around for a while." He stood up from his crouched position having been working with something on the ground.

"Morning Trevor, yes you're right I have been away in Jwaneng. I have picked up a great contract down there and joined up with Johnny the Greek. How are things your side, from what I hear work is really picking up for you?" We talked for a while and just before leaving, I asked,

"Who is the house for?" "Well you won't believe it, but the guy who contracted me to build this house went under and skipped town over night," then paused as one of his staff came up to discuss something with him.

Once out of earshot he continued. "Not being too happy with the situation as he owes big bucks I had a friend of mine in the know look into the history of this plot. It turns out that he had never fulfilled any of the conditions regarding the purchase of the land and asked if I would be interested in buying it." He paused once again whilst we both lit a cigarette. "Basically, to cut a long story short, I agreed to the asking price of the land and now here I am building my own house on spec, I say spec as I have no idea what I'll do with it once completed!" Something about it, including its location, told me in the back of my mind I needed the house, something saying 'buy me, please buy me'.

"Purely as a matter of interest what would you sell it for?" I asked.

"Well, I haven't worked out the exact price, but it would be in the ball park of around R30, 000." Seeing the obvious surprised look on my face, he continued, "You must understand it is on a double plot, will have four bedrooms, two bathrooms, large lounge/dining room and double garage." The reason for my surprise was not that I felt it was too expensive, but quite the opposite. "Well I'm interested, can you please give me first option and I'll come back to you in a few days?" He agreed to this, we shook hands and with that I raced off home to speak to Les. Right there and then a trip around the rigs was far less important than passing this news onto Les. Alan drove through two days later to view the property and agreed we should go for it. It was great coming in on the ground floor so to speak as were able to discuss the design and make changes to suite our personal needs. One of the changes was to have a sunken lounge with a stone built fireplace; although unbearably hot in the summer months, winter could be extremely cold. Being in a position to pay half the money up front helped to get the project into full production. Proudly, within three months of first speaking to Dave, I was able to move Les, the kids and our meagre belongings into our new house purchased for the sum of R28, 750.00. Primarily I had left Rhodesia five years earlier in the hope of having my family live in a real house and had at last fully achieved that goal. To us the house was like a palace and the roof wetting party was certainly something to be remembered.

With all the new contracts, our workload and Company in general had outgrown our workshop and office space in the contractor's industrial area. We were at last showing reasonable annual profits, all our accounts were up to date and thankfully, although retaining it for just in case, no longer had a need for the overdraft facility with the bank. Our reputation as an efficient drilling company had grown considerably and I felt the time had arrived to look for a larger and more permanent property. Miraculously the perfect workshop became available in the new industrial sites near the railway station. The plot was extraordinarily large, with a workshop, office and storerooms. Compared to what I had this was like comparing our little town with Johannesburg! After some serious negotiating with the owner, we purchased the property for R35, 500. I felt as a drilling company in Botswana we had at last come of age and planned to continue to improve our reliability and services in the exploration field throughout the country.

Chapter 40

Without doubt, one of the major tourist attractions in Botswana has to be the amazing Okavango Delta. It is located in the north-west of the country and the largest wetlands (swamps) in Africa and covers an area of two hundred and fifty kilometres in length and one hundred and fifty kilometres in width. (+- 35,000 square kilometres)

Water replenishment for the Delta is through seasonal rains in Angola on the west coast of Africa. Angola's rainfall season is December to February and a large percentage of the highlands catchment area runs off into the Okavango River. Ultimately, this flows 1,200 kilometres south-east and feeds the Delta. The water generally arrives in March and the flood plains swell up to three times the average size, peaking in July.

Evaporation due to the massive extent of shallow water spread over the Kalahari Dessert combined with extremely high temperatures in the area would be close to forty percent. Any excess water not swallowed up by the thirsty scorched sands surrounding the Delta flows via the Boteti River into Lake Ngami and finally ending the journey in the famous Lake Makgadikgadi Salt Pans.

Millions of years ago these pans included the delta and were likened to an inland sea and covered an area of approximately 80,000 square kilometres and fed by the great Okavango, Zambezi and Chobe rivers and the out flowing water fed the Limpopo River, eventually draining out into the sea in Mozambique.

Over thousands of years, through formational faulting, these rivers were diverted and in time, the saltpans slowly silted and dried up. Ambient temperatures in the area are extremely high causing major evaporation and ultimately end the flow of the river. Today the saltpans main feed of water flows in on the northern side through the Nata River that originates in Zimbabwe.

Due to the extensive water coverage in the Delta wild life have been drawn to it from many kilometres away and today boasts being one of the largest concentration of game in Africa in the July peak season. There is a massive diversion of species of game from the big five (elephant, rhino, leopard, lion and buffalo) all the way through to the smallest creatures imaginable. Bird life is also prolific throughout, including the elusive, beautiful and much sought after Palls Eagle Owl.

Understandably, this is a major attraction for international tourists, not only for game viewing, but also due to the extremely favourable exchange rate, especially for the US dollar and the English pound. It really made the delta and the available lodges spread throughout, most affordable to those with these resources. Every country in the world requires foreign exchange for imports etcetera, not cashing in when blessed with these amazing and unique facilities would be a travesty to any government. On the other hand, the majority of mere residents in Southern Africa paying in local currencies find these tariffs completely out of reach.

Most of the camps are highly exclusive and unique in that mostly they are serviced by air. The most popular aircraft utilised throughout the Delta being the Cessna 206 single engine aircraft. However, there are dozens of aircrafts involved including the Cessna Caravan, possibly one of the best 'bush' singles ever manufactured. Clients would board at Maun airport and be flown to camps spread throughout the region. Not only was this a quick and safe method of transport, but also viewing the swamps from 1,000' above ground level (AGL) is something quite special.

You get full views of the lagoons and islands of which there are many. Clearly visible are the little channels winding their way back and forth through papyrus grass. Hippo formed many of these channels through constant movement of their massive bodies over the same routes. In many cases these are quite large enough to navigate by motor boat and often used as access to the main channel from the various bush camps that abound throughout.

To add to this beauty there are the huge herds of elephants, zebra, wildebeest, buffalo and giraffe. Whilst the passengers enjoy the amazing views, the pilot has to concentrate on his flying. Temperatures can soar well into the 40 degree C range. Turbulence experienced in the aircraft due to the up drafts coming from the scorched sands below can be daunting for the unsuspecting passengers. Another distinct concern for the pilot is the constant possibility of encountering an eagle or vulture strike. There are literally hundreds of these birds soaring effortlessly on the heat thermals searching for a food source. Flying into one of these would most certainly result in disaster; the pilot required utmost care and vigilance at all times.

Generally, within the hour from take-off, the pilot would have the relevant airstrip in sight. Amazing how silent the passengers became once it was pointed out to them. These strips are extremely narrow and short with the gravel surface often far from smooth. On many such 'bush' airstrips your finals on landing are over lagoons and the same applies for take-off. Effectively you would go for an unplanned swim with the crocodiles and hippos if you either under-shot or through excessive landing speed, over-shot the airfield! The costs of these flights are normally included in the overall package offered.

Daily tariffs at the lodges vary from high to extremely expensive, but include luxury-tented accommodation. They are spacious and provide on suite shower/ toilet and basin adjoining the rear. Many of the camps ensure the bathrooms are efficiently ventilated through nature as they are open roofed.

The tariffs are generally all inclusive, covering all meals/drinks, game drives, game walks and boat trips, for either fishing or the ever-popular booze cruise. Due to the hot weather, evening meals are generally served in the open around a fire whilst listening to the beautiful night sounds of the bush all around you, thus enhancing a wonderful atmosphere when in the wilds of Africa. Also on offer are the popular Makoro trips. These are canoes carved from large trees and designed to accommodate two people plus the punter who propels the craft by use of a long punting pole from the rear.

This affords the opportunity to glide silently over the shallow bays covered in the most beautiful lily pads and other brightly coloured water vegetation. The waters are crystal clear which brings out the many shades of green, orange, reds and yellows. Being silent, you are able to drift in really close to the amazing bird life, which abounds throughout. For the enthusiastic photographer this is a paradise. Overall, although the package to us Southern Africans is exorbitantly expensive, the guests that can afford it, feel welcomed, comfortable and extremely well looked after.

Chapter 41

Having been brought up from a young child with a fishing rod in my hand and obviously well informed of the fantastic fishing available, particularly tiger fish and bream, my ambition was to one day be in a position financially to spend some time in the Delta. Yet at the time, with our financial constraints, I did manage to achieve possibly the second best choice.

A good friend told me of excellent bream fishing in the Motopi area, a village situated on the banks of the Boteti River approximately forty-five kilometres from Maun Village south-east of the delta and basically the gate way to the swamps. I figured if I cannot afford the camps in the Delta I could at least camp privately in the bush alongside the Boteti River and fish in the out-flowing waters.

On an extended month-end weekend, we decided to drive up and try this fishing spot. Excitedly we loaded the meagre camping equipment I had available at home. This consisted of two small tents, neither large enough to take more than two people. Next and most importantly I organised enough fishing equipment for all of us. My boys were of an age where they were quite capable of handling a fishing rod and Les although not a fishing fanatic, as in my case, also enjoyed catching fish utilising light tackle.

Then there were the basic cooking utensils required for our three-day camping/fishing trip as in a braai (barbeque) grid and tongs, all of which fitted into a medium size cardboard box. As there were no facilities whatsoever in the area we had to ensure we took all that was required. We were up early in the morning and just prior to our planned departure time at 4am, we packed some meat and drinks into a large cooler box and filled it with ice in the hope of returning home with fish fillets. Anglers always seem to be eternal optimists.

The trip up went well with the two boys sleeping comfortably on the back seat in my Nissan Safari 4x4 station wagon. First leg was to Francistown (150km) then on up north heading for Zambia where we would turn off to the left at Nata Village (180km). There we set off for Maun on a reasonably well maintained dirt road to the Makalamabedi Quarantine Gate (350km). The directions given were to turnoff left four kilometres short of the gate on a small track heading off to the river.

Arriving at the river around 11am, we set up camp under the most magnificent trees lining the banks. They were huge and well covered with leaves, giving shade all day. The river itself was disappointing in that it was more a case of being pools than running water. I was not sure if this was due to the time of year or if this was the norm. By 1pm I had the campsite sorted out, the fishing rods made up and fishing began in earnest.

As we never owned a boat, our only option was walking the banks constantly spinning into the pools using the ever-popular Mepps3. When eventually hooking my first fish it was a beauty and gave a wonderful fight as bream do on light tackle. Finally I had the fish in the shallows ready to be plucked out the water when I realised I had left the landing net in the back of the car. Desperate not to lose my prize fish I slowly dragged it out of the water on its side with the use of the rod.

Les was standing next to me also excited by the size of the fish. Suddenly the lure came loose from its mouth and with the line taught it shot up into my left eye. Holding my hand over the eye, I shouted for Les to not worry about me, but catch the fish before it wriggled back to the water. It was our first decent fish, who knows possibly the last we might catch, and I was not going to let it go. She managed to get the fish up onto the bank and being extremely concerned I had lost my eye came to check the damage.

With the two lids tightly held together by the hooks, I was blind in that eye. Being a three-prong hook, as the first barb stuck in the flesh below the eye the other two barbs spun over into the top eyelid efficiently clamping it closed! Ever so gently she removed the hooks. Fortunately having only the sharp points entering the flesh and not the holding barbs I had been extremely lucky. She was elated to see it was just the lids that were involved and not the eye itself. At the end of the day, ensuring the landing of our first fish regardless of my injury proved unnecessary. That afternoon between the four of us we hooked and landed fifteen nice sized three-spot bream, all caught with the Mepps3-spinner lure.

After our amazing success I cut a few of the bream fillets into small slices and made up barbel rods for the boys to attempt night fishing and then set about making a fire. The area was stunning and you felt like you were the only humans for miles around. Politics, work problems or any other issues never entered our minds; the peace and quiet tranquillity was special and medicinal. Eventually completing what had been a magnificent day the cumulous clouds in the western skies changed to varying shades of orange as the sun set. I do not believe I am unique in these thoughts, not being really sure what heaven is like. However, I was certain this had to be close.

Having been under a lot of pressure work wise, I could not have wished for a more relaxing environment. As darkness descended the fishing reels began screaming with constant barbel runs. Darrin and Dion were in their element and I had my hands full removing fish from their hooks, releasing them back to the river, re-baiting and casting in again. Dion hooked into an enormous one and after some fight started complaining of sore and tired arms trying to land the fish. I told him under no circumstance would anyone of us help him if this was to be classed as his fish, he needed to land it on his own. After a lengthy period, he at last achieved success with the barbel safely landed. Holding the head and tail with each hand as high as he could, the body of the fish was still on the ground. We managed to take a picture of him showing it off in this manner. He really did well landing it, even with a few gripes about how painful his arms were.

With no artificial light for miles in any direction, gazing up into the heavens the stars looked twice their normal size and sparkled like priceless diamonds. Incredible how clear they were, almost giving the feeling of looking through a telescope, quite magnificent.

Finally, dinner was ready and so deciding we had had enough excitement for one day, we all sat down to a wonderful meal of fresh bream fillets as a starter. Prime Botswana steak off the braai complete with sudza expertly made by Les and covered in tomato and onion sauce made up the main course. With bellies bulging we all retired to our little tents. I had set them up close together in case there was a problem with the kids during the hours of darkness.

Once snuggled into our sleeping bags in the wilds of the Kalahari, complete calm descended upon our campsite. Laying there listening to the beautiful night sound of crickets, mingled with the owls hooting from the trees above us with silver backed jackals calling from all around was beyond words. On the other hand, I maintained full awareness of the distinct possibility of visits from lion, hyena, aardvark and many other nocturnal animals in the area. It felt surreal, as if we had ejected ourselves into another world, a beautiful world of where we were truly interacting with Mother Nature.

In the early hours the following morning, the loud constant slapping sounds coming from the water woke me with a start. Intrigued, with torch in hand I stumbled out the tent casting the light into the river. I was astonished to see hundreds of barbel slapping the top of the water with their tails and moving slowly in an ever-decreasing semi-circle towards the shore. Instantaneously I woke Les and the kids to come and witness something seldom seen, barbel hunting in their masses. Once close to the shallows of the shoreline the quiet water began to froth and boil with thousands of small fish rounded up in front of the advancing predator fish. Almost as if given the signal all hell broke loose with the barbel attacking and devouring the small fish; within minutes all was quiet and the barbel had efficiently satisfied their hunger pains. I felt proud to be in a position to bring my children up in a manner that allowed them to witness the wonders of nature, much the same way my Dad did for me as a child. We crawled back into our tents with a feeling of complete calm and bewilderment after experiencing the amazing spectacle and slept soundly through to 6am.

After boiling water on our small gas bottle and making coffee, we eventually started fishing again. I was surprised how quiet the fish activity had become and felt that it possibly had something to do with the barbel massacre a few hours earlier. Suddenly at 8.30am, Dion squealed with sheer delight with the first strike of the day. Somehow, this set the trend for the morning with regular strikes through to 10am when Les called us for a full English breakfast that she had on the go. Time had passed quickly with all the activity and another eighteen bream were safely in the keep net. The aroma coming from the bacon and eggs certainly changed our priorities from fishing to eating and the three of us were happy to put our rods down for a while.

After breakfast, the boys continued in their quest to catch more and bigger fish than each other, always, as is normal with youngsters of that age, the competitive spirit existed between the two of them. I on the other hand was busy filleting the fish, packing them into plastic bags four at a time and then straight into the icebox. This is a tedious and time-consuming exercise and although an essential part of a fishing trip, certainly not the most enjoyable. Already I was mentally making plans for future trips to this beautiful part of Botswana. High on the list was to bring one of my local staff with us to look after the camp whilst we were out fishing and secondly to fillet the fish. We could relax and not have to worry about the camp or having to stop fishing early to allow for filleting time. I felt sure Jacob, the person I had in mind, would love to join us on such a trip.

Chapter 42

John Sweet's sister Joan and her husband Peter lived on the Zambian copper belt in a town called Ndola. Whenever possible he and Mavis would go through to visit them. On one of their trips, we joined them, as we were to go for a ten day fishing trip on Lake Tanganyika. Peter had kindly offered to supply us with two boats on trailers in Ndola that we could tow up to the lake. This was a huge incentive enticing all of us to commit and make a final decision to go. Often we had spoken of going up as we all enjoyed and looked forward to the lure of catching Nile perch, but the thought of towing boats for an approximately six thousand kilometre round trip outweighed the thrill of catching these mighty fish. The Nile perch originate in the Nile River. The introduction of this popular eating and angling fish has taken place in many lakes in Africa including Lake Tanganyika. The adult fish flourish in any habitat that supports sufficient oxygen concentrations. Juveniles however are restricted to shallow or near shore environments. They are fierce predators that dominate their surroundings, feeding on fish (including their own species), insects and crustaceans. They gather in shoals as a mechanism to protect themselves from other predators.

The species is of great commercial importance as a fish food. The Nile perch is also popular with sport anglers, as it attacks artificial fishing lures. There is always tremendous excitement and anticipation waiting for the strike. A great fight is always guaranteed regardless of the size of these mighty fish. Amazingly, they are known to peak at around the two hundred kg mark!

Lake Tanganyika, well known as one of the Great Lakes of Africa, is estimated to be the second largest freshwater lake in the world, by volume and the second deepest, in both cases, after Lake Baikal in Siberia. We packed and left in mid-December 1982 during our shutdown period. Our first stop-off was Kasane where we spent a couple of days fishing. With an extremely long trip ahead, we decided to break it up this way. Not that I ever needed an excuse to go fishing in the Chobe which I rated as some of the best fishing waters in Southern Africa. With some nice bream and tiger caught, we all enjoyed a wonderful few days. Something that was evident was the oppressive heat always experienced up there at this time of year. None the less, it seemed to be excessive on this visit. The locals that we spoke to felt it was the forerunner to heavy rains. I hoped this would be the case as they had been through a terrible drought. The Chobe National Park has one of the largest concentrations of game in Africa, for their sake rain to re-fill all the water holes and bring on growth, was desperately needed.

We were all up early anxious to head off for Ndola. Fortunately, once through with Botswana immigration and customs, we managed to be one of the first to have our two vehicles loaded onto the ferry to cross the mighty Zambezi River into Zambia (previously Northern Rhodesia). On leaving the border post our long trek began, heading for Lusaka, the capital city of Zambia and then on to Ndola, where we arrived late afternoon.

The following day we spent our time sorting out the two boats and checking, re-greasing and fitting new wheel bearings. Bearings have notoriously been a problem on trailers and I have often wondered why this happens as regularly as it does. Could it be that they are generally under-designed for the load carried? When you think about it standard vehicle wheel bearings seldom give problems and yet are effectively of the same configuration. The old bearings, after cleaning and re-greasing, were stowed away in the boats essentially as insurance in the unlikely event we encountered a problem with the new ones. We had a trip of one thousand, two hundred kilometres ahead of us with little chance of finding spares of any description.

The next morning we were up before the chickens and waving good-bye to Peter and Joan, headed off. Both vehicles carried long-range fuel tanks. Added to this we loaded as many full twenty-litre fuel containers as possible onto our vehicles and into the boats. There was no guarantee fuel could be sourced along the way. The first day we pushed on right through to Kasama where we spent the night in a small lodge with extremely basic facilities. Being tired we were more than happy to have a place to stay. The beds were clean and there was hot water in the bathroom. What more is required after a long, hot day in the vehicles? Towing the boats made the trip slow and it felt like the road would never end. At each stop along the way we took the opportunity to check the wheel bearings. We had obviously set them well as on both trailers they behaved themselves and remained cool or more accurately slightly warm to the touch. Early the following morning we were all refreshed and excited about what the day ahead might bring. We only had another three hundred kilometres to drive before reaching Ndoli Bay on the south western shore of Lake Tanganyika. The trip went well and seeing the magnificent lake stretching out before you, had all your fatigue simply melt away. Thankfully, we had arrived safely without any major hitches along the way. The lake was stunning with a magnificent view from the lodge. Beautiful blue clear waters stretched out as far as the eye could see. John pointed far out to the east where Kasaba Bay was located. He had fished there on a few occasions and said it the most popular fishing area on the lake.

Off to the left of our lodge was a small local harbour for mooring Kapenta rigs. The Kapenta are a small fish that breed and shoal in the millions out in the lake and are a staple diet for the masses. The Kapenta rigs (boats) go out at night into the deeper waters. With the use of extremely bright mercury lights, driven off inboard generators, shining down into the water, these little fish, attracted to the light, shoal in their thousands. A large net is lowered anywhere between twenty to forty metres into the clear waters. Once winched back to surface it is bursting with these small fish then emptied into the boat's holds. The same process takes place continuously until daylight with literally tons of fish caught daily.

You have to wonder how they manage to sustain themselves and yet seem to be living proof of their prolific breeding habits. Still, over the years their numbers have decreased marginally. In a bid to rectify this, many countries have banned Kapenta fishing in less than twenty metres of water, as they tend to breed in the shallows.

That afternoon we launched our boats and checked to ensure they both ran well. My boat had an inboard-mounted four-cylinder Chevy motor that ran beautifully with good performance. We then checked and made ready our fishing tackle, this being the most important equipment as essentially we were here to spend the following ten days fishing these beautiful waters.

Chapter 43

The next day at dusk, we set off with full fuel tanks, fishing gear, food and drinks for Kasaba Bay, a thirty-minute ride over amazingly blue waters. To our relief both boats performed well with a great time had by all. Yet as for the fishing, it was extremely disappointing. Trying everything we knew, both trawling with deep and shallow dive lures to spinning into gullies produced little success.

Fishing in the shallower water closer to the shoreline gave a more accurate impression of the clarity of the water. We could clearly see right to the bottom of the lake and if not for the shimmer of sunlight on the surface, it gave one the feeling of floating in mid air. A lure could be seen a long way out when reeling it in, giving a good impression of the action of each type used. Seldom did we see a fish following; it almost gave the impression of sitting in a beautiful swimming pool. By the end of the day we only managed to catch a few fish, but nothing of any significance and released them back into the lake.

What was significant were the number and incredible size of the crocodiles sunbathing along the sand beaches. They were massive and, as always, to all intents and purposes, looked fast asleep. Being fully aware of how dangerous they were we felt they could stay that way. A few days later, we discovered that all of them weren't asleep and just how treacherous these creepy monsters are.

John eventually stopped our fishing and said we should set off back to Ndoli Bay. Approximately half way across the lake on our return trip the engine started misfiring badly and eventually cut out. Firstly, I checked the fuel tank thinking possibly a leak had developed and we had run out of fuel. However, it was over half full. I continued methodically going through the standard checks of blocked fuel line, plugs, points and loose wire connections on the coil yet everything checked out.

When eventually stripping the carburettor I discovered a unique problem or most certainly one I had never come across before. The actual float controlling the fuel level in the carburettor, at some stage, developed a hairline crack and filled with petrol thus rendering it useless as it could no longer float due to the weight of the fuel. Effectively all I could do in an attempt to dry it out was to shake it vigorously until I had all the fuel out.

I reassembled the carburettor and after a few turns on the starter motor, she fired up and ran beautifully all the way back to the lodge. The only two methods of a permanent repair where soldering the hairline crack closed or fitting a new float. Neither option was available to us, so rather than possibly cause further damage trying to close off the crack on such an important and intricate item, decided to live with the problem.

My plan was to strip the carb each night that we returned from fishing, shake it out, then prior to leaving for Kasaba Bay in the morning, reassemble it and go through the same procedure on our return. This worked well for the following few days and I felt if push came to shove, I could manage it blindfolded. However, on Christmas Eve of all days, this little problem gave us a huge scare!

Chapter 44

John and Mavis had decided to have a rest day and were going to relax around the lodge. It had been extremely hot and with the fishing continuing to be poorly it sounded like a good idea.

"Trevor, why don't you guys do the same, I'm sure we could all do with a break?" said John, immediately supported by Mavis.

"John, you are probably right, but we only have a few more days here and I really need one of us to catch a perch." I have never been good at sitting around reading books or whatever when there is a lake out there teaming with fish waiting for us to hook them. "Les, how do you and the kids feel, are you happy to go out or should we stay?"

"I know you won't be happy and will be moping around with ants in your pants wanting to go out. As you said, maybe today is the day for the big one?" The kids agreed we should go. Sometimes things happen for a reason and that day was no exception, I most certainly should have taken John's advice.

I assembled the carb whilst Les, Darrin and Dion loaded the boat with fishing tackle and cool box. With a wave good-bye to John and Mavis, we set off for an interesting day on the lake. As usual, on arrival at the bay, I set up all the rods for trawling. I rigged the lure differently to the norm whereby you would have the deep diving lure attached directly to the line. With the use of a three-way swivel, I ran a separate trace with spinner bait attached. The lure was on a slightly longer trace and effectively would dive deeply taking the spinner bait with it. Prior to releasing the newly tied trace set-up, I checked that they were operating correctly in the water. This gave us a second chance on each line sent out for a fish strike.

After trawling for about twenty minutes Dion's line went tight and immediately he struck hard to set the hook. Amazingly, the rod never jerked, but remained motionless bent over in a bow. This gave rise to our assuming he was stuck due to the lure hooking onto a structure near the bottom of the lake. I stopped the boat and apart from Dion, we all reeled in lines. Dion's problem suddenly turned to sheer excitement, up to this point he had calmly sat holding his rod with the tip bent over. The next thing, out of nowhere, there was an almighty tug on his line. He had to immediately lift his leg and support himself with his foot pushed hard against the rail on the boat.

"Dad, I have caught a fish and boy oh boy is it a big one!" he shouted excitedly as the line peeled from his reel. Then as suddenly as the action had started, so the run stopped. Keeping the line tight, he slowly managed to reel the fish in by pulling back with the rod doubled over and then reeling back down again.

We all felt possibly the fish had gone and he was now pulling in a log or something. It was most strange how there was just this dead weight on the end of his line. The excitement had waned to some extent and the disappointment and confusion as to what had happened had him relaxing a little. His reel was almost full of line by this stage so we would shortly find out what had actually taken place. *'Bang'*, almost pulling Dion off the boat once more, there was an almighty pull on the line as the fish was close enough to see the boat. Quite how he managed to stay aboard and not lose his rod we will never know. The mysterious fish took off on another run peeling line from the reel.

"Dad, you will have to bring it in this time, my arms are tired from pulling and pulling. I didn't even think the fish was still on the line and now look at him run!"

"Hey my boy, I think you have a perch on the end of your line. We have not even seen one never mind catch one; you are going to have to hang in there. Imagine being the only one to land one."

Although early morning, excitement mixed with the oppressive heat had sweat pouring from his face. Fifteen minutes later, he landed a six-kilogram Nile perch and was extremely proud of himself and so should he have been.

"Well done, my boy, that was truly exciting for all of us watching you fight that fish. Catching one of those is the reason for coming on this long trip. From what we have seen of the fishing so far it could be the only one," I said elated with his catch.

We continued fishing through to 3pm with only a couple of smaller bream caught that were beautifully coloured in various shades of greens, silver and reds. Darrin was complaining bitterly, he was hot and wanted to go for a swim. We warned him of possibly being eaten by a croc if he jumped into the water and pointed to the ones sunbathing some two hundred metres off on the lakeshore. Shame he was so uncomfortably hot and in desperate need of a swim that he was not deterred in any way by this theat.

"Please Mom, the water's so clear around the boat and yet we haven't seen one swimming in all the time we have been here. I just need to go in for a minute to cool down."

Having a good look around Les and I eventually capitulated and let him jump over the side. In less than a minute we had pulled him back onto the boat looking much happier and certainly cooler than when he went in.

We then asked Dion if he also needed to go in and he was adamant he did not intend to play with crocs. He pointed down into the water and to our utter shock, there were two huge crocodiles swimming along the bottom directly under the boat!

"Now do you see why we didn't want you going in?" shouted Les. "Had we left you in there a few more seconds those crocs would have taken you!" Shame, she was actually shaking in her state of shock.

"Gee, Mom, they swam very quickly to get here so fast; I'm sorry I thought it was fine and I promise you I'll never do that again!"

"Well its fine now," I said, "we were extremely lucky my boy and I think let's learn from this experience and restrict our cooling off to the swimming pool back at the lodge, the crocs aren't as big in there!" This eased the tension to some extent and we all burst into nervous laughter.

Chapter 45

We fished on for a while in bright sunshine when suddenly it became darker. I looked up to the sky and instantly a chill ran down my back. We were well into the bay, lined with high beautiful mountains on the western side. To my horror, rolling over them looking like massive wads of darkened cotton wool were cumulous storm clouds now blocking out the sun.

"Hey guys, we need to leave now!" I shouted urgently. "Please start packing everything into the hold. Already we could be too late to make it back to the lodge with that storm coming in!" I had an intense feeling of foreboding that we were in serious trouble and should get to shore immediately. Funny how often in my life I have ignored these mental warnings, mostly to my detriment and this time was no exception!

We had been warned the western entrance to the bay named Nundu Head was notoriously dangerous and to stay well clear of the shore when in the area. Apparently there were many submerged rocks that in the past had smashed and sunken numerous boats sadly with all aboard becoming croc food!

A strong westerly wind had picked up that had not affected us whilst in the bay due to being on the lee side of the mountains. This became evident as we rounded Nundu Head to enter the lake and travel west back to camp. Periodically over the past few days we had had a little wind and the waters became choppy, but of no real concern to me. Having never fished there before I had no idea what the lake could turn into when hit by a huge storm with high winds.

I continued on, ensuring I keep clear of the rocks, but having seen the massive waves building up further out in the lake, kept a far tighter line than normal. The reckless side of my brain was telling me to get home as soon as possible, yet on the logical side something was screaming for me to turn around and head for safety.

Seemingly, out of nowhere, I had recklessly managed to place us at the point of no return in a raging, angry sea. The waves had to be close to three metres in height with steep banks immediately followed by another and then another that just kept coming at us relentlessly.

Immediately I knew I should have stayed in the bay. Regardless as to the personal difficulties this would have caused, it was our only form of protection. Had I stayed in there we would have had to spend an uncomfortable night on the boat, yet we would survive! Nevertheless, knowing if I attempted to turn the boat it would most certainly capsize, I continued on keeping the bow directly into the waves.

"Trevor, you are going to crash into those rocks, you must go further out into the lake!" shouted Les in a total panic.

"Doll, I know we are far too close, but if I change the angle of the boat even slightly we are going to go over and I don't need to remind you what will be swimming around under the boat." I have been fortunate in life to have the ability to stay calm in stressful situations, yet I was terrified way beyond anything I had ever experienced before! My mind took me back a few years, when I came within a hair's breathe of a charging elephant trampling me to death. At that time I only had myself to protect, here through my total lack of experience, coupled with stupidity, I now had my whole family with me!

We were in desperate trouble, completely on our own at the mercy of the raging storm. Even had there been another boat close by they would not have been able to get to us. I had been out deep sea fishing many times, but never seen anything as violent as this!

The gaps separating each wave were perilously close. With the use of gentle throttle control, I was managing to keep the boat in a straight line. I was sure if I put on too much power we would have flipped over backwards. As each wave hit, it had us looking up into the sky, it then disappeared leaving us airborne to come crashing back down on the other side with a tremendous thud. Then immediately once I had control again the next wave hit, bursting over us like a waterfall. The rain was lashing down in torrents yet was hardly noticeable with all the excitement.

The lake riddled with leeches covered all of us from head to toe including our face and hair, from the waves breaking over us. These little blood-sucking creatures were quite revolting. I seriously believed our chances of survival were extremely bleak at best. The hull of the little craft, subjected to an enormous pounding wave after wave, had to at some stage break up, assuming we had not already been smashed to pieces from hitting a rock before that!

I had to stay calm and in control, but knew it was not going to be easy. Over the years, living in the bush, I had gone through many scary and distinctly life threatening experiences; yet all these happened on land where the leopard or elephants and I were in our natural surroundings. Out here in the raging waters, with submerged rocks and hundreds of crocodiles, the experience presented a unique scenario that was terrifying beyond words. Knowing I irresponsibly had no life jackets on board, I shouted for Les and the kids to empty the jerry cans of fuel into the water without falling overboard. My plan being we would need them to hang onto for buoyancy, as once empty with the spout tightly sealed they would float freely. Our chances of making the shore, our bodies constantly smashed from rock to rock in these waves without some assistance were slim in the extreme. Worse still were my terrifying thoughts of the possibility of storm surge washing us out into the middle of the lake whilst clinging desperately to our petrol cans. I quickly dismissed these from my mind as were too horrendous to contemplate.

The direction the waves moved and having to keep the bow of the boat at 90 degrees to each as it crashed over us forced me to navigate exceedingly close to the rocks.

Keeping the boat upright was my primary concern. We were making extremely slow progress, yet with the use of landmarks and rocks in the water, I could see we were in fact moving forward.

Then the next terrifying thought struck me, in my haste to get out of the bay I had not given the leaking float in the carburettor a thought! Would the engine now give trouble and cut out. If this were to happen we were most definitely doomed, we would be totally at the mercy of the raging waves.

Les and the kids were sitting on the floor and all three were shaking with a combination of cold and shear panic, understandably terrified out of their wits! They had given up on their futile attempts at brushing the leeches off, there were just too many. Instead, and wisely so, they used their hands to hang on for dear life.

I kept mentally admonishing myself for getting us into this mess, how could I be that stupid. Gladly I would have sold all I owned to pay any amount of cash to turn the clock back an hour, but realistically this was not going to happen! I never mentioned my thoughts of the motor cutting out to the three of them. They were terrified to their limits already. With each wave, we shot up and then crashed down. When I changed the throttle settings, I felt sure I heard a misfire simply because I was now fully aware this could happen. Amazing what such horrific circumstances do to the mind.

Somehow, I managed to keep it all together and an hour later eventually managed to get us safely beyond the beckoning rocks of Nundu Head. Fortunately, the boat had a self-drain deck, which worked well. If not, with the combination of heavy rain and waves bursting into the boat, we surely would have sunk a long time ago.

Visibility was not good as steadily it became darker and darker. Normally at this time of day from our current location, there would be the most stunning sunset. Different shades of magnificent mixtures of oranges and yellows painted onto the clouds then reflected spectacularly off the water. Sadly, due to the dark storm clouds there was no sign of the sun.

Ever searching for a way out of our life-threatening predicament, I noticed a small bay to our left. The waves had eased marginally so I decided to take the plunge and head slowly in that direction, yet, keeping in mind the possibility of capsizing. Immediately Les shouted,

"Why on earth are you turning that way, now we will surely be smashed up in the rocks?"

"Relax doll, if I can ease the boat into that bay we might get out of this mess. I really must go for it," I said pointing to the left. "I made the mistake of getting us into trouble so most certainly don't want to miss the chance of making it to possible safety."

"Okay, well you normally know what you are doing, just please end this nightmare, we cannot take any more of it!"

Chapter 46

More by good luck than good judgment I managed to ease the boat into the bay. Waves continued pounding the boat, which under normal circumstances would be extremely dangerous, but after what we had just endured, was a pleasure. Approximately thirty metres from the shore I threw the anchor over board. Les was surprised as she badly wanted to get her feet back on solid ground and now here I was anchoring us out in the lake and waves.

I put her mind at ease telling her I was afraid of unknown rocks or dead submerged trees causing possible disastrous results. We were for the moment safe and I believed the storm had passed through and things would now start to improve. The boat was pushed back until the anchor found a firm grip leaving the bow still facing the oncoming waves, which for safety reasons was a good thing.

"I didn't want to tell you guys out there, but in my rush to beat the storm I had not cleaned the float in the carb so added to all else happening around us I was terrified the motor would cut out which would effectively have been the end of us!"

"Gee Dad, that was lucky for us as it doesn't normally last that long, now what are we going to do?" said Dion, naturally most concerned as to what was going to happen next.

" Well guys, I think before it gets too dark I should strip and clean the fuel out of the leaking float, hopefully by then the waves would have calmed down somewhat and we can head off home." Almost in unison, both Dion and Les said that as long as we were safe where we were they weren't prepared to go anywhere. Even if we had to stay for a few days, it would be better than what we had just endured.

"Listen guys, it is Christmas Eve and I'm sure we'd all like to be back at the lodge for Christmas Day. Let me get started on the repairs required whilst you all de-leech yourselves. I'll then see how things look wave wise and we can have a vote as to what we should then do."

I set about doing the repairs and by the time I was ready the waves had died down significantly. The revolting leeches had been dealt with, jerry cans, fishing tackle etcetera displaced in the storm were tidied up and safely secured where they belonged.

"Right guys, it is really getting dark, I need to know now if we are going or not?" Les and Dion were still undecided, but Darrin and I desperately wanted to get home to a dry and warm bed. We were all freezing cold and uncomfortable by this stage. With gentle coaxing from Darrin and me, we all agreed to take the chance and head back to Ndoli Bay.

Immediately, I fired the engine into life, wound the anchor in and once safely stored, headed off towards the lights of the Kapenta harbour a long way off in the distance. On leaving the bay, the waves were large, but manageable being more like rolling swells with deep troughs as opposed to the monstrous crashing waves earlier. I could now also make out the lights off to the left of the Kapenta harbour, knowing they belonged to the lodge was most comforting to all of us.

Eventually after a most exciting day, we pulled up to the jetty, cold, wet and tired, but happy. John and Mavis had been extremely concerned and were waiting for us down by the water's edge. We arrived just in time, as they were about to head out to look for us. Standing in the hot shower that night felt about as good as any shower could ever feel. Christmas Day was spent relaxing around the lodge and happily so. I never touched a fishing rod the whole day or for that matter ventured anywhere near the boat.

We continued fishing hard for the last few days of our holiday, but once again with disappointing results. Soon after docking at the lodge late one afternoon, we were highly entertained on seeing a waterspout. We had returned to camp early that day and were having a drink on the balcony at the lodge watching a storm building up in the distance over the lake.

Out of nowhere, what initially looked like the beginnings of a small whirlwind suddenly grew into a massive waterspout; fascinated we all leaped up for a better view as none of us had ever witnessed one before. We had all seen the smaller one on land pulling dust high into the sky, yet here we were experiencing something quite exceptional. Although we were at least twenty kilometres away, the spout looked huge and powerful so we could just imagine all the water, boats and fish being sucked up into the sky. I joked with Les and the kids, "Just imagine the fun we would have had contending with one of those as well as the waves on Christmas Eve!"

The time came for the trip to end and we packed up and drove all the way back to Ndola to off load the boats. It is quite incredible how the drive always seems further when going home. It took us three days to get to Kasane where we planned to spend a few more days fishing.

On arrival at the Kasane Safari Lodge, there was water everywhere. They had experienced a tremendous storm that day with the whole town flooded. The rain was so severe that all that was visible of the five boats moored to the lodge's jetty were stiff ropes pointing down into the water where each one had sunk after filling with water from the deluge. I had been fortunate in that I had removed my boat from the water prior to going up to Zambia, if not it would have joined the rest sitting on the bottom of the river!

We decided there was no point in trying to fish in the muddied water and left for home early the following morning arriving safely late that afternoon. This gave us a few days rest after a round trip of approximately seven thousand kilometres. Would I undertake the same trip again, most probably not!

Chapter 47

A large percentage of Botswana is covered by Kalahari Desert and largely uninhabited by humans. All major centres from Lobatse through Gaborone, Mahalapye, Palapye, Selebi-Phikwe and Francistown are situated along the peripheral edge of the country starting in the south west, running east along the northern border of South Africa then turn up north along the western border of Zimbabwe. To some extent, it reminds me of Australia in that it is a huge country with a massive void in the centre. The obvious difference of course being size, population and the fact that Botswana is completely land locked.

To the south west, into the Kalahari are the Molopo Farms, essentially one of the most productive cattle ranching areas in the country. The climate during the months of August through to April, as is the case throughout the country, varies from hot to exceptionally hot with low annual rainfall. Although rare, they have experienced exceptionally wet seasons over the years. Historically the farms in general pass on from one generation to the next and are run by hard, tough men who give it everything and refuse to buckle down to anyone.

During the day, pleasant temperatures are the norm through the remaining winter months; however, the temperatures plummet dramatically as the sun sinks its head in the west. So much so that a two-litre bottle of water left in the open will freeze solid. Needles to say the severe cold makes camping somewhat uncomfortable at this time of year as I discovered on many occasions.

John Coetzee, a farm owner, was no exception to the Botswana norm as I discovered on our first meeting. A contract to drill exploration holes on his farm went out to tender and I was successful in my bid. At that stage, I had never worked in the real Kalahari or had the displeasure of experiencing just how thick, difficult and soft the sand really was. John's farm is located two hundred kilometres directly west from the most southerly Botswana town of Lobatse. The initial forty kilometres consisted of reasonably firm dirt roads; however these steadily transformed into deep rutted sandy tracks with a high middle "mannetjie " (centre portion of track) for the remainder of the journey.

It was quite an experience how kilometre after kilometre the vehicles were forced to struggle their way through a never-ending bottomless sandpit. There was an overwhelming impression of going uphill all the time. Not only due to the soft sand, but also for whatever reason the horizon ahead of us remained closer than one would normally expect. In flat terrain as in the Kalahari Desert, theoretically I felt we should be able to see for kilometres all the way around us, but the impression of being in what felt like the centre of a massive hollow never left me. We never reached the summit where I was planning to stop and give the vehicles a rest from tortured and screaming engines.

Finally, after having been stuck in the sand many times, we managed to reach what I believed to be John's farm gate. I opened it and drove through, then with a little effort pulled my 4x4 out of the deep sandy ruts to allow the entire vehicle convoy to pass and keep going whilst I closed the gate.

I instructed the driver of the truck carrying the drill rig to keep going until he sees a track leading off in any direction and then to stop and wait for me. With engines screaming all the trucks managed to move off. I closed the gate securely and proceeded to follow slowly at the rear. We had possibly only travelled ten kilometres when the leading truck came to an abrupt halt.

' Oh no, what has happened now? ' I thought to myself as I climbed out and walked past the other vehicles. When approaching the truck, a white middle-aged man in khaki clothes was standing next to the driver's door throwing his hands in the air. As I ran up to him, he pulled the driver's door open shouting for him to get out. Then seeing me re-directed his fury at me.

"Who the bloody hell do you think you are and who gave you permission to drive through my farm and bugger up my roads like this?" Surprised as I had no idea what he was going on about, but seeing he was already way beyond angry I extended my hand in an attempt to introduce myself. "Don't think you can soften me up with a handshake, now turn around and take your bloody equipment back to wherever you come from!" As it had been a long, frustrating and exhausting day, I certainly was not in the mood for this drivel.

"Trust me, the only place I'm taking my equipment is to the first drill site. If you have any issues with that you can take it up with the mining house. We are both well aware this has been cleared with a signed acceptance by yourself to mobilise to your farm." I paused for a breath and before he could respond continued, "Shit, I'm sorry, I have no idea what your problem is and certainly haven't come all this way to argue with you. But believe me after the long grind and having to dig ourselves out on numerous occasions trying to get here we aren't going anywhere!" He glared at me for a second or two then let fly again.

"Listen to me you little townie, I don't give a shit who you are contracting to. Quite obviously, the minute you leave the luxury of tar roads you are lost, clueless and out of your depth. How the hell can you come into this area with double wheels on your trucks?" Still confused I replied.

"Well, the drill is really heavy and as I'm sure you are aware these 1517 Merc's come out standard with dual wheels on the rear." Once again, he glared at me as if I had possibly arrived from another planet. "I'm sorry, but I really cannot see your problem," I said.

"You can't see my problem!" he shouted. "Let me tell you something as you have made it quite obvious you have no experience driving through the Kalahari. Those bloody double wheels of yours are stuffing up my standard spoor. We live and work here and daily drive these sand tracks, which are fine until someone like you arrives. It is obvious no-one has ever advised you regarding soft sand driving. How can you attempt driving through the sand with your tyres pumped so hard? It is no wonder you've had to dig yourselves out many times. Hell, I have seen some greenies come through here, but must say you really take the cake!"

This is one hell of a welcome I thought to myself, but figured it can only get better, if not this will turn into a long and tedious contract. Sure, I was on his land and he had the right to tell me to take my stuff and get out of there immediately. Nevertheless, I seriously didn't need this right now and especially not in front of my staff. Knowing we were going to be operating in the area for at least a year I felt sure we could resolve this little misunderstanding without exchanging blows! To prevent myself from doing or saying something I might regret at a later stage, I again extended my hand toward him in a bid to introduce myself. "Hi, I'm Trevor and have to assume you must be John Coetzee? If not, I'm not only lost, but I'm also being soundly shat on by the wrong guy!" Somehow, this seemed to ease the situation somewhat and I detected the faintest of smiles on his deeply sunburned face.

"Funny you should ask, but yes I'm he and this is my farm so you aren't lost and believe me you are certainly not being shat on by the wrong guy!" He then extended a firm strong handshake. "I imagine my bearded friend Ivo Chunnett sent you down here, how is the old bugger?"

As suddenly as our problem started so it evaporated into thin air just as quickly. We both apologised, but to have the last word he told me he was going to have to teach me a lot about life in the Kalahari if I was going to have any chance of successfully completing the drilling contract. He had us follow him to the designated drilling area and pointed out where we should set up camp.

Whilst the crew unloaded the truck, John took me off in his Land Cruiser to a borehole where we could draw water, both for drilling and drinking. He stressed I should keep accurate records of water usage as Ivo and himself had come to an arrangement on charging for this most precious commodity. We then went to his home some five kilometres from the drill sites. There he introduced me to his wonderful wife Wilma with the opening phrase,

"Wilma, I would like you to meet Trevor, someone who has never ventured off a tar road before in his life." We shook hands and she smiled sweetly saying,

"Pleased to meet you Trevor, take no notice of my old man as he goes out of his way to give everyone who comes to the farm a hard time even if you haven't put a foot wrong. I'm sure you would enjoy a cup of tea?" She was a pleasant woman and I had to wonder how John had managed to get her to marry him! Certainly not through his kind friendly manner, I thought to myself with a quiet chuckle. "Yes, thank you, and if I may be honest it's certainly been far nicer meeting you than John and would appreciate it if you could please tell me how a woman as lovely as yourself could finish up with a guy like John. I have to assume you were the unfortunate one who drew the short straw?" With that, we all burst out laughing and a solid friendship formed from that moment on.

Chapter 48

Alan Longstaff had managed to find a drilling operator called Willie who would run the percussion drill rig operating on John's farm. Willie and his wife Elsa were arriving the following day with one of Alan's Company caravans in tow. Our only caravan was out being utilised on one of the drill sites. Leaving directly from Johannesburg they would travel on well-maintained South African roads to the Bray Border Post leaving them only ten kilometres of soft sand to contend with on the Botswana side. Through consultation with John, we found a suitable spot for them to set the caravan on, close to the main road and central to the drill sites. Essentially the road through John's farm was also the main road out to the north for the farmers in the area. It extended all the way up through the village of Khakhea on to Ghanzi five hundred kilometres to the north. Ghanzi also known for being an extremely successful beef ranching area had many large cattle ranches in the surrounding area. Top grade beef exports at that time were the largest forex earner for Botswana and the bulk came from these ranches. Albeit being the main road, essentially it was a 4x4 sand track with little traffic.

It was late afternoon by the time we had organised the staff camp and rigged the machine over the hole ready to commence drilling first thing the following morning. I set my little two-man tent up on my proposed caravan site to bed in for the night. Having had a long hard day in every respect I sat on my fold-up camp chair with Coke in hand, taking in the sheer beauty as the sun slowly settled down in the western horizon producing a magnificent African sunset. I had hoped to go over the border to the small town of Bray to purchase a few supplies for the night, but had simply run out of time.

Thankfully, I had picked up thirty-five kilograms of ration meat for the staff in Lobatse on the way through and we always carried ample maize meal. I had given my tin plate to one of the crew asking him to dish up some of their stew, sudza and gravy for my dinner that night. Similar to running out of cigarettes when any brand then tastes good, so it is when you have no supplies of your own. The meal tastes like the best you have eaten in your life, but certainly requires washing down with a Coke or two.

Once darkness descended, followed by crisp cold air, the feeling of peacefulness was overwhelming, almost as if the world was void of humans, barring us. There being no false lighting to distort the effect, the stars in the sky appeared twice their normal size. It might sound crazy, but the Kalahari stars seem to twinkle far more than elsewhere, mingling with the night bush sounds. It felt surreal, special and a reason to be on earth. I must have sat in my own little world of wonderland for an hour or so when I eventually shook myself back into reality as I needed to get some sleep. I stripped off and washed in cold water from the built-in water tank I had fitted to my vehicle in our workshops for just such an occasion. Eventually, on hands and knees I crawled into my tiny tent in which there was hardly enough room to sit up yet alone stand up. Within five minutes of my head hitting the pillow I fell into a deep sleep.

The cold woke me, it was shortly before 2am and I was absolutely frozen stiff. I fumbled around in the dark for my clothes bag and pulled a pair of overalls over the tracksuit I was wearing. My feet felt like they were about to explode from the cold. I pulled on two pairs of long socks and to finish off also added a jersey over the overalls. With nothing else to add for warmth I snuggled down into my sleeping bag trying to get some sleep.

The cold persisted; I had never experienced anything like it. The thought crossed my mind that freezing to death has to be a terrible way to die and it felt like I was shortly going to experience this. I wondered how the crew were getting on, as they had to be in the same predicament. I even contemplated leaving the tent and sleeping in the car with engine running and heater set full blast, but was too cold to move. That had to be the longest night of my life and quite how I made it through to the morning I will never know! I made a mental note that when speaking to my wife Les on the radio scheduled for 7am to ask her to buy me the warmest, most expensive sleeping bag she could find or possibly even two.

I was up well before sunrise, but it was light enough to see. Stiffly crawling out of the tent I noticed a fire burning close to the staff camp. I immediately wondered off to join them, thawing out with the heat from the flames. It was a weird feeling, when facing the fire you were warm in the front and freezing on your back and vice versa when turning around, the warm side immediately turned cold. How could the Kalahari get this cold, it was after all a desert well known for extremely hot climates, yet here we were feeling like a bunch of Eskimos.

My right hand man Tips had warmed water on the fire in a twenty-litre container and poured some into a bowl for me to wash my face. At last, I felt almost human again and once I had cleaned my teeth, had a cup of coffee followed by a cigarette was ready to face the day.

Due to the remoteness of the contract, I handpicked the crew personally. When enquiring how they had coped with the cold they said the only way they managed was by keeping the fire going throughout the night. I assured them I would purchase as many blankets as the little town could supply when going into collect Willie. None of us ever wanted a night from hell like that again. A daunting thought, being mid-June meant we had another possible six weeks of winter before it started warming up.

By 6.30am after going through all the pre-start checks, I began drilling the first hole. I was strict on mobilising taking place on or before the due date stated on my tender document. This contract was no exception; we were actually three days ahead of schedule.

By lunchtime, I managed to drill down to thirty metres and insert surface casing before heading off for Bray to collect Willie and his wife. Bray is a small border town servicing the local farmers. There are a few shops, a garage and a hotel. Fortunately, the general dealer stocked blankets of all sizes; allowing for two each, I purchased twelve of the warmest he had.

Chapter 49

A nice old man named Fanie Eloff owned the garage. He had been there many years, hence well known and loved by all. Regardless of the problem, he was always willing to help. I opened a fuel and general repairs and spares account with him, which helped tremendously. I was only able to spend a limited time on each site throughout the country before moving onto the next. Having this facility gave me the confidence that in my absence any possible minor breakdowns Willie was unable to deal with, Fanie's mechanics would attend to the problem. It felt strange to have a feeling of total isolation whilst on site and yet within thirty minutes help was at hand. In general, this was not the norm when operating in the Kalahari with having to drive many hours to reach any form of civilisation.

Willie had worked for me for approximately six weeks and I was impressed, he appeared to be honest, hard working and a non-drinker. His good wife Elsa handled bush life extremely well and generally, the entire situation was stable. In a bid to maintain maximum production, I made a point of visiting each site as often as possible.

Prior to each visit to site I spoke to Willie on the radio which was scheduled at 7am each morning to inform him of my intentions over the next few days and made notes of all requirements needed on site. Everything always seemed in order and I had few complaints from my staff regarding his treatment of them.

Elsa was wonderful and treated me like a king. Whilst spending a few days there she went out of her way to ensure I was as comfortable and well fed as possible. Initially I set my tent up some fifty metres from their caravan, but eventually she insisted I placed my thin foam mattress in the awning and slept there to be more comfortable. It was late July and winter had arrived in full Kalahari tradition. It was freezing cold at night and early morning. Climbing out of bed first thing was a real struggle. Stripping off your warm tracksuit used as pyjamas to get dressed in overalls ready for work was a daunting thought to say the least. I have always enjoyed the heat and admit I am a total wimp when it comes to cold; I hate it with a passion.

Funnily enough, it was never as bad as the mind conjured up. I was sure the only reason for this was when stripping naked to change your body goes numb due to the extreme cold air hence there was no feeling. I always placed my pair of overalls under my mattress prior to climbing into my sleeping bag in a bid to keep them as warm as possible for the morning. Once dressed I immediately went outside to stand and thaw out by the fire made by one of the staff.

I can remember my toes inside the safety boots felt like they had swollen to the point of bursting so held the base of each boot in turn over the flames, which undoubtedly helped. Amazingly, by 9am the sun had risen high enough in the east to send wonderfully warm rays back to earth and the temperature remained comfortable for the rest of the day. Then around 5.30pm sank back down on the western horizon in an orange ball delivering one of the renowned and outstanding Kalahari sunsets. This instantly sent temperatures plummeting, setting the trend for another freezing night.

Then everything changed, the peace and stability I felt was there in the work place instantly disappeared. Tips approached me prior to my leaving for home.

"I'm sorry my boss, but I must report a problem with Mr. Willie. When you are not here, he is drinking too much and is away from the machine sometimes for a few days. When he is drunk he is shouting and swearing at us all the time, but is too drunk to operate the machine!" His statement astounded me; I had never known him to have a drink yet alone get drunk and go on a binge for a few days.

"Tips, I have always trusted you, but feel you might be telling stories this time. I have never on all my site visits seen him have a single drink. He always only asks for Cokes!"

"Yes, my boss, you are right, but it is only because you are here. Within an hour of you leaving he will go off and start drinking again, the same problem we had with Johnny in Orapa." He was not happy telling me this, but felt it his duty to do so. He had to be the most honest, hard working and certainly one of the most productive operators I have ever employed. "He knows when you are coming down because of your radio schedules, if you come without calling you will find I'm not telling stories." I was absolutely shattered, as a non-drinker I would normally pick up immediately on anyone with a drinking problem. "I'm sorry Sir, but the crews are not prepared to continue working with him unless you sort the problem out soon."

"Okay Tips, you have never lied to me before, I have to go for meetings in Gaborone and then onto another drill site for a few days." I paused still contemplating my next move. "I will then return here unannounced and see what happens. Please tell your guys I will sort it out and for them not to do anything rash whilst I'm away."

Chapter 50

One of the crew having been instructed to do so had rolled my sleeping bag and mattress up tightly, ready to pack behind my seat together with my little tent, a permanent fixture in my vehicle. I was never sure on my travels around the rigs as to where I would be required to spend the night. I said my good-byes to all and left on the long and hard two hundred-kilometre slog through the soft sand to Lobatse.

Although having a successful four days on site with Willie and Tips I now had an empty feeling in the pit of my stomach thinking of the information Tips had passed onto me. One and a half hours after leaving site I arrived at the veterinary fence and was surprised to see a grader in the middle of the road on the far side of the gate. I climbed out my vehicle, opened the gate and drove through, once again getting out and closing the gate behind me. I had to pull out of the sand tracks to get around the grader and noticed someone sitting in the shade under a tree. Intrigued and assuming he was the driver of the grader I walked over to him to see if he was okay.

He was fast asleep and to all intents and purposes appeared dead. He looked terrible having extremely parched lips and flies buzzing around his head. When giving his shoulder a little shake he opened his eyes and was quite obviously surprised to see a white man standing there above him.

"Sorry, but I see your grader is in the middle of the road so came to see if you had a problem?"

He looked at me seemingly in a trance.

"Ah the grader she is buggered," he said and attempted to stand up. As he was struggling, I helped him to his feet where he stood on shaking legs. Sounding a little slurred through his parched lips he told me what had happened. "I have to take the grader to the Molopo Farms area and when I stopped and walked over to open the gate the engine she cut out. When trying to start it again the starter motor was dead. That was three days ago and I only had one bottle of water with me which I drank the first day!" The thought went through my mind that he was lucky to be alive, due to not only the fact he had nothing

164

to eat or drink, but also having to endure the cold nights! Immediately I ran over to my vehicle and brought him a cold Coke to drink. Shame, it never touched sides he drank it so fast and followed it up with another one. I also had a lunch pack that Elsa had kindly made for me, which I gave to him and said he should take his time eating, I was concerned he might choke.

I wandered over to the grader and attempted to start the engine, but sure enough, it proved to be dead. Climbing back down from the cab, I checked the battery terminals. I found them fastened securely and they appeared in good condition. Then checking for flat batteries found when shorting across the terminals there was a huge spark indicating otherwise. All the external wires both on the starter switch and starter motor also proved well connected. The only other possibility had to be the starter motor itself; I always carried a full and well-equipped toolbox mainly for use on site, but also for such emergencies.

With some difficulty, I removed and stripped the starter motor. I found one of the wires had burned through and was not making a connection. Fortunately, I carried some spare electrical wires in the vehicle and with the use of my 12-volt soldering gun managed to replace the cable. Using insulation tape, I ensured there were no exposed wires. Everything else appeared to be fine so I reassembled and installed the starter back into the grader engine. After double checking the wire connections I once again climbed into the cab and turned the starter key, to my total surprise the engine cranked over a couple of times and burst into life.

As weak and wobbly as my friend the driver was, it was obvious the food and drinks combined with the excitement of the engine starting had produced amazing medicinal powers. He was leaping around with his hands in the air and shouting something in the local Motswana language.

As I climbed back down to the ground, he ran up and gave me a hug.

"Hey, my boss, you have saved my life, may God be with you always!" The thought crossed my mind that possibly had I not travelled back today he could well have died as who knows when the next vehicle would pass this way! I must be honest I felt good and privileged to have been the one able to assist him.

He could not stop shaking my hand and insisting I was to accept one of his prime cattle from his cattle post as appreciation for saving his life. I told him I was glad I could help and said he better climb up there and go before the engine cuts out again. I took his empty bottle, filled it with water from my tank on the back of my truck and handed it up to him. Before driving off through the open gate he shouted down to me.

"Hey Sir, the next time I have to come through this way again I'm not going to stop, I'll just drive straight through the gate." He then burst out laughing and with a huge puff of black smoke from the exhaust pipe headed off down the sand track waving madly.

Chapter 51

I had been away from Bray site for a week and decided that it was time for me to head off back there on my surprise visit to see how Willie was shaping up. I hated the thought of driving all that way not knowing what might be required on site. To this end, I loaded as many spares as possible just in case. I had drill bits, shells, core springs, baskets, oil filters and a couple of DTH (down the hole) drill bits for the air rig.

On my way through from Lobatse, I was half expecting to see my grader friend along the way. I needn't have worried, as apart from one Toyota Land Cruiser travelling in the opposite direction the trip was void of any traffic whatsoever. Willie's caravan was on the eastern side of the drill site meaning I arrived there first. As I pulled up Elsa came running out and I could clearly see she had been crying and was sporting a black eye!

"What on earth has happened to you? Shame you look terrible, did you have an accident or something?" I said shocked to see her in this state. Only a week ago, when I left she was looking gorgeous, radiant and happy.

She gave me a hug and between sobs said, "Willie started drinking within an hour of your leaving and went out of his way to make up for lost time. He has always pretended to be a non-drinker whilst you were here." She was in a far more serious state than I first thought and wondered what else had happened. She then continued saying, "Three days ago he was very drunk and I was trying to reason with him, telling him he would lose his job if you were to find out what he was doing." Once again, she paused to steady her emotions before continuing. "I'm so sorry I didn't speak to you about it earlier, but he had threatened to beat me up if I had done so. Well it turns out that before I even had a chance of telling you Trevor, in a drunken rage he punched me in the eye. He then ran into the caravan where he collected a few clothes and whilst using the most abusive language possible started his vehicle and left. He has not been seen since so to be frank I really don't give a shit if the bastard loses his job or not, because this time we are finished. I have said this before, but this time believe me, I'm serious!"

My blood was boiling by this stage and I was ready to kill him. How he could leave his wife on her own on a cattle track route where she could have been gang raped and murdered was beyond comprehension. My anger already fuelled by his clear disregard for my instruction of zero tolerance for drinking on site never came close to what I felt about his punching Elsa and then leaving her on her own!

"Elsa, I'm terribly sorry for what you have been through and believe me he is going to pay for his actions. Please pack your things as best you can, I'm going to the rig quickly to have a word with Tips and will be back shortly to take you to John's house where you will be safe."

"Trevor, please, I don't want to get them involved in our problems. They have been wonderful to us and I will feel terribly embarrassed with the situation. Please can't we sort this out some other way?" I felt sorry for her; she was a special girl, even after going through this trauma she was still concerned about causing problems for other people.

"Listen to me Elsa, they would be terribly hurt and annoyed if they weren't able to help and I know they would insist you stayed with them, now please go and pack." With that, I drove off to the rig, spoke to Tips about Willie, and wanted to know if he had any idea where he might have gone. Unfortunately, he had no idea, but knew where he had driven off into the bush veld for his drinking binge previously. He joined me in the front of my vehicle, but alas, on arrival he was not there.

I dropped Tips off back at the rig and after verifying all was in order on site I drove back to collect Elsa. Once her bags were loaded, we set off for John and Wilma's house. When I related what had taken place they were shattered and asked her, why hadn't she come to see them for help? Whilst Wilma ushered Elsa into the house I asked John if he had seen anything of Willie. He said he had been out in the back end of the farm for the last few days so had no idea where he could be.

Prior to wasting my time running around the bush veld in Botswana I drove to the South African border post to check if he had not possibly gone through. It happened that he had, two days previously and had not returned. Immediately I cleared myself through and headed for the garage to see Fanie and question him regarding Willie's possible whereabouts. He had seen him a few days earlier in an extremely inebriated state. He felt he could be at the construction camp just out of town. He was last seen at the hotel with one of the contractors from there.

Thanking him, I drove off to the camp and on arrival saw a guy near one of the caravans so drove over asking the same question. He informed me he was there in the caravan at the top of the rise. I drove straight over there and sure enough, there was Willie sitting inside the awning of the caravan. His eyes were badly bloodshot and clothes extremely scruffy. He looked an absolute wreck and initially seemed not to recognise me in his drunken stupor.

"Come outside here you little shit, I have something to settle with you!" I said. He replied telling me clearly to go and screw myself! "Willie, I'm not asking you again, if you don't come out here right now I'll be more than happy to come in there and knock the shit out of you. Beating your wife up and then leaving her out in the bush for a few days is lower than shark shit!" Receiving a similar response from him, I flew into the awning and punched him hard in the face knocking him clean off his chair. I was so tempted to use the boot and break his ribs, but fortunately, sense prevailed. He lay there motionless, I assumed unconscious from the hefty blow I had delivered to his jaw and to be honest right there and then felt even if he was dead I couldn't care. His mate whom I had spoken to earlier had seen the commotion and came running up.

"What the hell is going on, you can't just come into our camp and start fighting with people. Now listen to me, if you want to stay healthy you had better piss off out of here right now before I throw you out!" he shouted.

"If beating his wife up and leaving her out in the bush for three days gives you a reason to fight his battles then give it your best shot, believe me if ever I was ready for a good punch up now is the time." I was extremely angry and prepared to fight anyone who backed Willie.

"Hey, I know nothing of his wife, he told me he was on his own doing some drilling on the Botswana side. We met a few weeks back and he has been visiting regularly on drinking binges ever since." Suddenly he was concerned and quite obviously the thoughts of throwing me out had disappeared. "Had I known he had his wife with him over there I would not have allowed the situation to get to this stage, believe me I'm really sorry."

"Well unfortunately sorry doesn't cut it for his wife, so you tell this piece of low life, if and when he wakes up, he will find his belongings at the police station and his wife and job gone forever. Also tell him if I ever see him again, regardless of where or when, I certainly won't be as lenient as I have been today." With that, I turned and headed off to my vehicle.

To this day, I have never seen or heard from him again, not even a phone call asking for his money. John arranged a lift for Elsa back to Johannesburg the following day and I gave her five hundred rand, which was all I had on me to help see her through the tough times ahead. She said she was going to be staying with her parents and immediately commence divorce proceedings. In the drilling game you get to meet many strange characters, Willie certainly ranked high up on that list!

Chapter 52

We continued with the drilling contract in the Molopo farms for a further eight months. Ivo Chunnett, the Chief Geologist for Gold Fields at the time and based in Gaborone, made regular visits to site, monitoring progress and results and ensuring the correct location for the start of each new hole. We had become good friends and he and his good wife Eve had been kind in offering me accommodation at their home when I passed through Gaborone.

By this stage, John and Wilma had also opened their home to Ivo and me, which was most appreciated. It was amazingly convenient to go to site without worrying about camping equipment each time. I was a non-drinker and although John gave it his best shot to teach me the art, he failed. However, poor old Ivo did indulge from time to time and John made the most of it. After a wonderfully tasty meal provided by Wilma we'd adjourn to their sitting room to talk about the day's events and have a few drinks. I always had my usual Coke, but when it came to Ivo, it was a completely different story and certainly not instigated by himself.

John would pull out a new bottle of whisky from his well-stocked booze cabinet, unscrew the cap, crumple it in his hand and send it flying into the dustbin. Thereafter John ensured poor old Ivo could not go to bed until the two of them had consumed the whole bottle together. Clearly, Ivo could not match John's resilience in this activity!

Ivo has always been an early riser and yet trying to get him up and out to site after a night with John was most challenging. Once eventually up and successful in clearing his head of cobwebs I was convinced it had to be physically impossible to see clearly through his bloodshot eyes until around mid-day. Added to his dilemma was the guarantee of a pounding headache that always accompanied such behaviour. I always felt sorry for him as it most certainly was not the norm, yet John was well known for being sociable, insistent and extremely talented in this regard. We enjoyed many good laughs together over this for many years to come.

On one of these evenings, a huge rain spider appeared in the sitting room and ran along the wooden skirting board. All in the room including Wilma wanted to immediately kill the spider, but I persuaded them to leave it alone as although they give off the appearance of being vicious they are in fact totally harmless. John was not going to listen to me and insisted we should kill it before it bites someone. I pleaded with him saying that we regularly had them in our lounge in Phikwe and never once had there been a problem so should let it be to get on and do its own thing.

Although not happy, he decided to leave it alone and we continued discussing the day's events. We talked for a few minutes when I felt something crawl onto the back of my head. Immediately I lifted my hand, but before I could swipe it off the rain spider sank its fangs into my head. I threw it off, in a panic leapt up, and squashed it with my boot.

John was in hysterics, I have never seen him laugh so much and Ivo and Wilma joined in, thoroughly enjoying the comedy show. In between fits of laughter with tears flowing from his eyes John said,

"Shame Trevor, how can you do that to a poor defenceless spider that doesn't bite? That is just so cruel and I believe he will be back from wherever to haunt you." Everyone was laughing so much that I received no sympathy whatsoever. I on the other hand was rubbing my head wondering if I was going to die or not.

"Why is it that I save the bastard's life yet it comes and bites me?" Well by this stage, John was almost rolling on the floor with laughter. Ultimately, I was partially right in saying they weren't poisonous. After rubbing my head for a few minutes, it was fine with no ill effects. However, at the same time I learned a good lesson on just how powerful their pinches are.

My upbringing was living in the bush with elephants, leopards and hippo wandering around my tent at night without being overly concerned. Yet I have always had issues with spiders and detest them immensely. Why oh why I ever tried to save this guy's life I will never know?

Chapter 53

John was a top rate farmer; he knew cattle ranching as well as any man. He was also extremely experienced in mechanics and, as in my case, completely self-taught through circumstances. When problems arise out in the middle of nowhere you have no one to call on so through trial and error you learn how mechanical equipment works and how to repair it. He would see to any breakdowns on the farm immediately and spent much time in his workshop when not out in the veld checking on his cattle and fences whilst always keeping eyes open looking for snares.

Unfortunately, this is a serious problem throughout Southern Africa. To try to explain the suffering of a defenceless animal when caught in one of these wire snares is beyond understanding. We have found animals long dead with the wire cut deeply into their legs and sometimes the neck. It could take many days of excruciating pain and suffering before the animal dies from stress, heat exhaustion and dehydration.

Firstly, laying the snare on a known animal path attached to a tree trunk was bad enough, but not going to check them on a regular basis is a criminal act beyond comprehension in my book. The bastard that laid the snare should suffer the same fate and be hung by the neck until dead. Although an enormous effort in a bid to eradicate this dreadful practice is in force, as is the case with corruption, I doubt it will ever stop mainly due to a combination of both desperation and greed!

Talking of desperation, another one of John's talents was the art of divining for underground water. The scorched sands of the Kalahari Desert devoid of rivers or dams cover his farm from one end to the next. The only possible source of water for the animals and of course the homestead was through the drilling of boreholes. Not only is this expensive, but extremely risky, yet John excelled in his talent of successfully divining for this most precious commodity.

The art of water divining can be discussed for hours, as there are many methods used, some more successful than others. Some of these methods are highly technical and expensive as in the use of geophysics that can pick up fault zones below the earth's surface. Then there are the traditional methods as in bottles balanced on the hand, forked sticks that bend dramatically towards the ground, wires bent into an L-shape that turn and cross each other and many other similar techniques.

John was a master with the two wires bent into the L-shape. He had successfully divined many boreholes on his and surrounding farms. My father had been a successful diviner and on many occasions tried to teach me the art using a forked stick. For whatever reason regardless how hard I tried, the stick method never worked with me.

However, I had witnessed my Dad walking over what is generally referred to as a fault or water strike and the stick bent to such an extent it actually cracked in front of his hands. Physically it is impossible to manipulate a forked stick to do this, therefore from a young age I was brought up believing in traditional divining even though at the time, for me it never worked.

After a scrumptious meal served up by Wilma the one evening, John talked of water divining asking if I believed in it. I explained about my Dad's efforts and how successful he had been finding water, yet I obviously never had what it took to emulate him in that respect.

"That's a load of crap!" said John, well known not to mince his words. "Most people have the gift, but just have no idea how to apply it. Not sure what your plans were for tomorrow, but whatever they are cancel them. I'm taking you out and it will be my pleasure to teach you how to find water."

The following day he arrived at my drill site and said if I had an hour or two spare to come with him into the veld. My guys on site knew what they were doing, the drill hole was progressing well so I climbed into his Land Cruiser and off we went some five kilometres away. Once we had climbed out the truck John pulled his pair of brazing wires from behind his seat and so started my career in water divining.

He showed me how he held them with the long side of the 'L' pointing forward and parallel to the ground. He explained how you were never to have the ends pointing up as they could, due to the natural force of gravity, swing on their own. If anything, it was better to have the ends pointing ever so slightly down.

Holding both wires with hands 20cm apart he slowly walked forward. After some twenty or so paces both wires turned slightly to the left. He followed them and continued walking until they were both facing straight ahead again. He explained that we were close to a fault zone and the wires attracted to the magnetic pull turned us in the right direction.

Yeah sure, I thought to myself, as if I am supposed to believe that. Seeing the doubt in my facial expression, he said he wanted me to try to do it myself. We went back to where we started from and off I went wires held at the ready. To my astonishment, at the same point they distinctly turned in unison to the left. Still dubious I was sure I must have turned them unconsciously with my fingers.

"Hey John, I'm glad we're out here in the middle of nowhere so that my mates cannot see what an ass we are making of ourselves," I said with a laugh.

John with a smirk on his face said, "Believe me young man, by the time I'm finished with you today you will realise what a clever ass you actually are! I want you to keep walking slowly in whatever direction they lead you, keeping the wires as steady as possible."

I walked on for a few more paces and unbelievably both wires swung in, crossing completely over each other. As instructed, I continued walking and within a couple of metres, the wires swung back facing forward once again. John explained that now we had discovered a fault we needed to know in what direction it ran underground. To achieve this we needed to move in a circle away from the spot we had crossed and keep going around until the wires once again crossed each other. At that point, we made another X in the sand indicating the spot.

Each cross was constantly on the same line heading south westerly. Yes, there seemed to be a definite pull on the wires each time, nonetheless, I was still sceptical as could not understand how this could possibly work.

"Okay clever boy, we are confident we have the line trend. We now need to walk parallel and some six metres away to check for the possibility of a second independent strike that with a little luck could cross over this one. This being the case it would obviously then give us two chances of finding water, or better still the chance of intersecting two separate strikes in one single hole," said John.

Obediently, as instructed, I walked slowly parallel to the direction of the strike. Initially the wires kept turning to the right towards the original strike so I moved further away from it. This worked and the wires remained constantly pointing forwards. I must have walked about forty metres when again the wires turned in crossing over each other, then within a few more paces swung back to facing forward again. This was starting to freak me out a little as there was no doubt the wires moved with absolutely no input my side.

"Right, now move to your left away from the original strike in a large circle until the wires cross again," said John, excited by what was happening. Sure enough, I eventually had another reading and mentally joining the two marks up was pleased to see it was heading towards the original strike. With much criss-crossing over this strike together with doing the same on the original, I found exactly where they intersected each other.

I was astounded to find a small pile of rocks placed right in the centre of where the two strikes crossed! I had managed to find the exact spot John had surveyed in some weeks before. I was completely overwhelmed and just stood there shaking my head.

There was John looking at me with an '*I told you so*' look on his face.

"I think you have just become a believer and you will find it to be of tremendous help to you in the future especially in your business. I now need to teach you how to determine the depth of the water strikes." I honestly thought he had to be kidding, but by the time he had finished demonstrating and having me go through the same procedure I steadily became a believer.

Initially the hand holding the wire is resting on the ground, slowly and as steadily as possible, it's lifted up ensuring the wire remains parallel facing away from the wind. Once it starts swinging left and right the distance in centimetres lifted relates to metres down in depth. (E.g. 100cm when lifting the wire relates to 100m of drill hole depth required to reach to water.)

I am sure you as the reader must believe I require help from a psychiatrist to believe in such nonsense! Well believe me, at the time I felt the same about John. Some weeks later, he had me testing this method on a couple of his producing boreholes. Without giving away any known information, he asked me to check the depth of the water strikes and to my astonishment, I was within a few metres of the known water strike depth. Had I become a believer and did it help me in later years? Most definitely, it gave me a completely new dimension to my operations much of which I will go into more thoroughly at a later stage in the book. I cannot thank John enough for passing on the art of water divining to me.

Chapter 54

The recession in the early 1980's drastically affected business throughout most parts of the world. Exploration drilling companies were no exception as sadly the first thing the Mining Houses cut immediately in their budget is exploration projects. Reason being generally exploration work is to determine ore reserves over the next ten years or more to enable mine planning. Deep into a recession knowing and controlling the now as opposed to the future is far more important to the mining sector.

Fortunately, in our case we had four drill rigs busy on deep holes in Phikwe at the time. The results from the current holes were critical to the planning of operations within the mine. Mine management made the decision to suspend all drilling apart from those four rigs. Drilling was to continue to completion of the current holes, giving me some leeway on deciding our way forward with only gloom and doom lying ahead. The writing was clearly on the wall, we were in for an extremely tough and lean period.

The initial signed contract with BCL was for up to eight drill rigs, depending on production, for two years. I had worked exceedingly hard to be in a position to tender for such work. My successful bid for the drilling contract involved a huge outlay of capital on our part to ensure we had the machines and equipment on hand to cope. Suddenly it felt the world had collapsed around us! I was shocked at the news knowing it would drastically affect us financially, not to mention the likelihood of having to lay off staff.

Not only was the future looking bleak, but I also could not think of any remedial action to alleviate the problem. Looking for work with other Mining Houses was not an option as they were all under the same financial squeeze. To all intents and purposes once the four current holes were complete, I would have no work!

Being predominantly a diamond drilling company we had little to do with percussion work. Some years previously, I had purchased a decidedly old and pensioned off Halco Tiger air rig from the mine. This I used for drilling and casing shallow pre-collar holes for the diamond rigs to move onto and complete at Bushman Mine. There was a need to increase production and although the rig was antiquated, to some extent it proved to be useful.

Some months after the Bushman contract was completed a friend of mine offered to buy the Halco Tiger rig from me. Only having minimal finance at his disposal he planned to go into the drilling of shallow water holes. To be honest I saw no future in the rig for us, not only was it old, but also extremely restrictive in its performance. Gladly, I sold it for the price I had purchased it for some years previously.

During this period Alan, Gus and Mr. Longstaff registered a drilling company in South Africa. Due to license restrictions on attempting to name the company R. A. Longstaff as in Zimbabwe and Botswana, they shortened it to Raldrill. The idea was for Alan and his good wife Jo to move down from Rhodesia permanently to manage the new company. They had been operating for approximately a year and as is the case in most new ventures things were tough in the beginning. Alan and the late Rob Brown, who with his good wife Glynis had also moved down from their home in Rhodesia, worked their butts off, which clearly showed as they were slowly, but surely managing to get on their feet.

Complete control and management of the new company was from a smallholding in Honeydew, Johannesburg where they both lived and worked. There was the master house where Alan and family stayed and a neat cottage where Rob and family lived. Also on the property was a moderate workshop which had been up-graded to suit their needs. Rob undertook all the repair work required, and shared his invaluable on-site drilling experience while travelling extensively throughout South Africa ensuring the chucks were spinning.

Drilling is a tough business for a family man and far better suited to the single person. When living in the bush on the drill site with the family it is really taxing, mainly on the woman folk. Seldom are there any fancy amenities such as flush toilets, water on tap and nice kitchens. Nor for that matter, any shops nearby. Alternatively, on a managerial, supervisor level living in town the same applied. Only this time the problem being separated on a regular basis with the husband clocking up huge distances checking on all the rigs spread everywhere throughout the country.

At the time, coal became the mineral of the day. Exploration throughout South Africa, Botswana and Rhodesia looked like picking up with talk of large contracts coming up for tender. The most popular and financially efficient means for the Mining House to drill for coal was with 412 Air-Flush methods.

It certainly sounded simple enough as did many things in life. Effectively, it was providing you had the equipment, machines required and the experienced staff to handle this kind of work.

The overburden generally consists of sand stone and clay layers. The 'open holed' drilling method is preferred for the following reasons. It is exceptionally cost effective with remarkably high penetration rates utilising tri-cone drill bits. The chip samples collected on surface into plastic bags through a cyclone are expelled from the hole by high-pressure air from the compressor. Closely monitoring the chips is the site geologist and once he feels we are about to intersect the coal seam instructs the drilling crew to change over to the 412 Air-Flush coring system. As is the case in diamond drilling this consists of attaching a three metre core barrel to the bottom of the rod string with a diameter of 4 ½". The inner and outer-tube are manufactured from cold drawn steel with a very high tensile strength and straightness. The head assembly is manufactured from heat-treated alloy steel to ensure long life. The inner tube for collection of the core sample is attached to the head via a roller bearing. They are simple, but rugged core barrels popular for site investigation, geotechnical coring and coal exploration. The tubes are thicker than the equivalent metric core barrels (T2 and T6 series) and thus less prone to damage when handling on site. Unfortunately due to the thicker cutting face of the core bits, marginally lower rates of penetration are experienced. However not requiring water, air-flush completely outweighs this problem.

A massive advantage is not requiring substantial water carting equipment for drilling purposes and for personnel consumption the use of 200 litre drums proved sufficient. Nor is there the need to negotiate with what at times were extremely difficult farmers, and understandably so, for the use of their precious water. There was also no need to dig and prepare water sumps with each move. It was a case of complete your current hole, rig down, move to the new site and drill. Production of two hundred metres plus per day was possible in certain formations.

These core barrels are used in conjunction with face-discharge core bits. They are specially designed for air-flush, having a relatively large annulus between the inner and outer tube allowing high-pressure air supplied by a portable compressor to flow freely through the system.

Being face discharge bits the air pressure has no detrimental effect with the formation being drilled. This minimises core erosion in soft, unconsolidated formations resulting in excellent core recoveries, an absolute requisite in coal drilling. The 412 Air Flush is widely used for opencast coal exploration and for general site investigation work when water flush is not permitted.

We had never drilled with this method before, plain and simply we were not equipped for it; I felt the time had arrived to expand our company to give ourselves a fighting chance. Shell coal had already approached me about tendering for a massive contract. This was to take place in the Serome Valley area some thirty-five kilometres south-west of Mahalapye on the main road to Gaborone.

Hearing of the possible potential for such contracts, I spoke to Alan and Gus in connection with the need to buy a rig capable of the work. I felt by not doing so would be extremely detrimental to the company as we would be left behind and stagnate in the drilling game. We needed to show that we were pro-active and not afraid to move with the times.

There are always highs and lows in the drilling business, some good some not, as I am sure is the case in most other businesses. We always said and believed when one door closed another would open and in many cases we were right. Here we were with a door opening up for us to march through and sadly, our hands were tied simply due to being under-equipped!

After lengthy discussions both Gus and Alan were agreeable in principal to the idea, albeit concerned firstly at the impending cash outlay and secondly as to who would operate the new rigs. I assured them that would not be a major issue and we should focus on acquiring the machines and then worry about work force.

Not really knowing what rig to buy, I put the word out around my suppliers for advice. Mr. Jock Dewar from MDS had been our number one supplier for many years. A more honest and down to earth salesman would not be found anywhere. His service and prices were legendary, when he told you your order would be arriving on a certain date, you acted on that information knowing it would happen. He just happened to have secured the agency for the Dando 250 drill rig designed and built in the United Kingdom.

He said they had proved to be extremely reliable overseas. Coupled to an Atlas Copco 750/350 he felt it would be the perfect combination for our requirements. The down side being there wasn't one in South Africa for us to look at. Jock however supplied me with comprehensive pamphlets giving us the full specifications and capabilities.

We discussed the rig at great length and ultimately decided ordering one without actually seeing it in operation was not the way to go.

After extensive negotiations between Jock, the overseas supplier and ourselves, we arrived at an arrangement amicable to all parties. Dinky Brown (Rob's brother), who worked for Alan in South Africa with some experience on air rigs, and I were to fly over to the UK and see the rigs firsthand in operation. The understanding being that if after our visit and inspection were we to order three new rigs, one for each country, Botswana, Zimbabwe and South Africa, our travel expenses including full board and accommodation would be deducted from the price.

Our flight bookings to the UK confirmed, we boarded the aircraft a week later heading off for an interesting trip. Our hosts proved well schooled on how to look after and satisfy the customer, even down to letting me win a game of squash whilst over there. More importantly, they knew the product and a guided tour of the factory was most impressive.

Having been amazed at how beautifully green the fields in the UK had been, we were shattered to find Ireland even more so. It was too beautiful for words, the fields out in the countryside were a deeper green than I had ever seen and then surrounded by an even deeper green hedge. Living in Botswana this was unique for me and would remain in photo form in my memory bank for all time.

The obvious reason behind the fertile and beautiful lands was rain, lots and lots of rain. On visiting the first rig busy drilling on a water hole, we talked at length with the operator. He was most accommodating and went through the rig thoroughly with us pointing out the good and not so good points. Fortunately, the positive points completely outweighed the bad at around 95% good, to 5% bad.

The last rig visited was up to the north in Belfast. Our tour guide Robert wasn't happy going there, it was shortly after the terrible Maize Prison fasting episode and historically there was extreme tension between the North and the South anyway. Our vehicle was carrying southern registration plates and he felt this could cause problems and serious ones at that.

Dinky and I on the other hand were keen to see the rig as it was a track-mounted configuration as opposed to the truck mounts already seen. Apparently it was busy working on a road construction site in the city. Whilst travelling and enjoying the magnificent scenery I asked,

"Seeing that we are going there anyway, would it be possible to visit the Maize Prison and Falls Road area?" Both had been much publicised over the last few months in the news media and were obviously points of interest to Dinky and I.

"I have to assume you are joking, we will be staying well clear of those areas. I enjoy my life, love my family, my job and so would dearly love to live a few more years!" said Rob our host salesman making it clear it was non-negotiable.

"Oh come on Robert, we just drive past and I'll take a few pictures as we go, you don't even need to stop."

"You quite obviously haven't any idea how dangerous it is to venture anywhere near either place", now there was distinct concern written all over his face. "Just thinking of taking pictures clearly proves your ignorance of what happens in Belfast!" Taking another deep breath, he continued, "Believe me, if the wrong guy see's your camera pointing where it shouldn't be you could instantly be killed by a gunshot through the head in a flash. Trust me, Trevor, these guys don't play!"

"I think you are grossly over exaggerating." I said and winked at Dinky then jokingly continued. "We have travelled a long distance to get here with the distinct possibility of never coming back again. We feel being denied the opportunity to visit those two areas because of something that happened quite some time ago is just not acceptable," once again after a short hesitation, I continued trying my utmost to keep a straight face. "I would hate for a small incident like this to be included in my final report to your Company directors, possibly blowing the whole deal!" This seemed to get his attention fully.

"Well, can we go and see the rig before having our heads blown off, like you I would hate to have come all this way to die for nothing. A least I could tell someone in heaven that I was just being forced to do my job!" We all found this rather amusing and eventually arrived at the rig.

To our utter disappointment the machine was standing, for that matter there was nothing happening on site at all. We located the security guy sitting around the back of one of the cement structures having a smoke. On enquiring what was going on, he said the site was closed pending an inspection and had no idea when they would commence work again.

We explained the point of our visit and he was more than happy for us to look around, to be honest he found his cigarette far more interesting than he found the three of us. Although the rig was not operational, it proved a worthwhile visit to see firsthand the modification and design to suit a track mounted rig. Both Dinky and I were most impressed and managed to take a few photos without anyone shooting us. Within half-an-hour of our arrival, we felt we had covered everything and were ready to go sightseeing.

"Right Rob, thank you so much, we are pleased to have been given the opportunity of seeing the rig and the beautiful country. Now which of our two tourist spots do we visit first?"

Hoping we might have forgotten about it Rob now resigned himself to the fact that the sooner he gets it over with the better. Firstly, we drove past the prison and I managed to get a few photos. Rob had said only one of us was allowed to take pictures to lessen the chance of someone seeing us. As is the case with tourist spots, generally your mind conjures up these wild images and it often turns into an anti-climax. This was no different; it just looked like a prison anywhere in the world, yet somehow portrayed the feeling of danger and had the hairs on our arms standing up due to its terrible history.

Driving through the Falls Road area I kept the camera hidden and when required lifted it quickly, took the shot and immediately brought it down again. Poor old Rob was particularly nervous, essentially in a state of panic. He kept telling me that I should stop as I had taken quite enough. All the blood had drained from his face and he was extremely pale and sweating. He strongly advised me not to push my luck any further.

Like the prison, the streets were quiet but the deserted atmosphere produced the same feeling of danger. There was graffiti painted all over the walls, windows boarded up and generally, it looked like a scene from a movie of where the baddies would hang out. Eventually there was a huge sigh of relief from Rob as we drove out of the city area and into the safety of the countryside again. I was pleased to have seen it, but must admit was also pleased to get the hell out of there.

The day before flying back, we had our final meeting with the supply company who were thrilled when I confirmed the official order for three complete units to be shipped as soon as possible to our three Southern African companies

Chapter 55

I informed all our clients of our new acquisitions and felt good to be in a position to submit an offer for our first 412 Air Flush contract up in the Makgadikgadi Pans district.

Once all new equipment was loaded, we headed off with our little wagon train of three trucks and my Land Cruiser for our first ever such drilling contract. Not having an experienced operator, I had no option but to operate the machine myself. To be honest, I had little experience in this particular method of drilling and needed to learn fast!

To keep me company in my little tent was my ever-faithful dog 'Titch'. She was a small Jack Russell we had fallen in love with when visiting a pet shop in South Africa. There was this tiny little puppy only six weeks old with the most pleading eyes you have ever seen saying "*take me please take me.*" We were unable to resist and so started a long and extremely close bonded relationship between 'Titch' and myself. From that time on, we were inseparable, regardless where or by what means I travelled she had become my shadow.

The drilling progressed particularly well, especially when taking into account it was the first time we had used the 412 Air Flush methods. Using a try-cone drill bit I open holed down to the black shale laying just above the coal seam.

The bit is manufactured with three rollers (hence the tri) in steel or tungsten tipped configuration for drilling hard or soft rock. These attach to the face of the bit on roller bearings facing each other at the precise angle required. The bit attached directly onto the drill rod. With rotation down in the hole, the cones spin independently and with weight generated through the drill string, they cut into the formation and grind it into small chips.

These are then expelled from the hole by either your mud pump mix, or if using air by the pressure from the compressor. Essentially all you get are chip cuttings as opposed to core samples. However, penetration rates are extremely high in soft material providing you with a cheap, fast and effective means of achieving an open hole down to the point you are required to start coring.

Jock Dewar from MDS, the company that had supplied the equipment, had advised me to allow the air flush core bit of the 412 to penetrate as fast as possible without forcing or adding excessive weight.

Having spent years diamond drilling generally in hard solid formation at slow penetration rates, I was amazed at the speed I was able to cut the coal. Our contract stipulated 100% core recovery rates through the coal seam were mandatory. On my first few runs with the new system, I was concerned and nervous about what condition we would find the core. How would it be possible to achieve such core recoveries at the speed I was drilling?

Once the full core run was complete, I pulled all the rods from the hole to remove the core. A stand provided for this purpose is utilised to strip the core-barrel. The drill bit is removed to ensure all the face flush holes are open as there are times small grains of formation can block off a couple of the airways, effecting performance of the bit.

The core barrelhead is loosened and unscrewed to allow the removal of the inner tube. A rubber plunger located inside the top of the inner tube allows with the use of a high-pressure hose to pump the core smoothly from the inner tube.

Prior to pumping the core, a perfectly sized plastic sleeve is installed over the front outer side. As the core pushes out of the tube, immediately it is encased inside the plastic sleeve. This ensures competency of the core as coal can prove extremely fractured in areas. The on-site geologist would log and measure the core once neatly placed in the core trays.

My first day went well with us managing to complete two holes to the final depth of eighty metres including the twelve metres of coring required on each. Concentrating so intently on the new coring system I had not given much thought to what Titch had been up to since feeding her after completing the first hole.

I looked around feeling confident she would be lying in the shade of one of the vehicles or the Mopani trees, which were in abundance in the area. Not seeing her, I walked around the drill site calling, but nothing, not a sign of her anywhere! I wondered if being our first day on site the sound of the compressor screaming sent her running off in a panic into the surrounding bush. Shame, she was still so young and not

accustomed to all the noise and this had me feeling a little panic setting in.

It was late afternoon; I had to find her before nightfall. The area is remote with much wildlife and once darkness descends there were any number of jackals, hyena and lion all of which could kill her effortlessly. All I could do was set off in ever-increasing circles calling constantly. Throughout my life, I have had an incredible affection for animals and believed they think and feel the same as we humans do and still believe that today.

Therefore, I had to wonder what would be going through her mind. Here she was kilometres away from home, lost not having the faintest idea where she was. Would I be looking for her? Should she lie down and wait for me? Alternatively, should she keep running in a vain effort to find me? I believed she had all these concerns running through her little mind. I felt like I had abandoned her and blamed myself fully for not checking on her during the afternoon.

Shortly before the sun disappeared, I heard the faintest of barks far away off to the north of my position. Could it have been from her or was it a call from a wild animal? I stood motionless listening and willing her to bark again assuming it had been her. My stationary position only lasted a couple of minutes. I had to find her and could not waste any more time as darkness was approaching fast. I set off running in the direction I felt the sound had come from.

Approximately fifty metres further on the bark came again and this time I was certain it was Titch. I knew distinctly what direction I needed to go in. Again I started running and calling at the same time, my brain worked overtime. Was she trapped in an ant bear burrow, was she barking at a snake or could she just be calling for me to come to her?

Tearing recklessly through the bush I inadvertently surprised a massive kudu bull. He took off ahead of me leaping effortlessly over the bushes showing off his white tail. The kudu has always been my favourite buck and as always, I was in awe of its elegant manoeuvring through the bush. Living out in the wilds is what gets my adrenaline going; it makes me feel alive and happy. The feeling of freedom is awesome.

The barking became louder, indicating I was getting closer, also she had to be staying put in one spot. The area was full of spiders, huge black and yellow fellows. To this day, I am still not sure if they are poisonous or not, or for that matter what exactly their purpose in life on earth could be. What I am sure of is the strength of the web fibres.

Accidentally running into one stretched between the bushes was akin to running into a net. The fibres were extremely resilient and took some effort to remove from your body, face and hair. Having spent the better part of my life in the veld, I had learned to live with what the wild sometimes throws at you, but with spiders, I have always had a major problem and hated them intensely. I would not go out of my way to kill them, quite the opposite; there were times I actually protected them against others wanting them dead. However, wherever possible I stayed well clear of them.

In my panic of running fast through the bush, I ran into a second web and completely entangled myself. Instantly I looked for the spider convinced I was about to be bitten for annihilating his masterpiece. Fortunately for me, he was hanging onto the remains of what had most likely taken him many hours to build. His body language and the extremely grumpy look on his face told me not to stay around to apologise. I ran on trying to untangle myself from the web for a short way and suddenly there she was, bouncing on her back legs with the front legs stretching as high up a tree as possible. She was so intent on what was up above her she had not even noticed my arrival. When I called to her, she leaped around and came running up to me, jumped up a few times on my leg asking 'where the hell have you been all this time' and then ran excitedly back to her tree.

Cautiously I wondered over to see just what was causing all the fuss. I was flabbergasted. Here I had been worried sick about the dangerous situation in which she found herself. To my utter astonishment the only dangerous animal anywhere to be seen was a tiny squirrel looking back down at us from high up in the tree, twitching its tail each time it squeaked. Titch's passion to chase these little critters had begun and continued throughout her life.

We drilled ten holes in the area all intersecting coal, which was however, of poor quality and of no use for the soda ash plant.

Whilst we had the machine in the area the geologist decided to drill a further four holes, much closer to the planned production plant location. Operating in such close proximity to the pans, large herds of zebra and wildebeest roamed freely through the area and were not concerned regarding our intrusion into their domain. Again, we found coal in the area, but also of low grade. The client was not prepared to continue with the project and we demobilised back to Phikwe.

Although disappointed in not being successful in finding a coalmine I found the exercise extremely productive in that our first air flush contract had gone off really well. The client was more than happy with our performance and excellent core recoveries. Fortunately the mining world is small and news travels fast ultimately opening the door to many more such operations.

Chapter 56

By this stage, Darrin and Dion had reached their mid teens. From Grade 4 they had been attending CBC (Christian Brothers College) boarding school in Pretoria. Our decision to go this route was most certainly not a negative reflection on the actual schooling in Phikwe, but simply due to lack of sporting facilities available at that time.

We owned a Mazda 626 as our personal vehicle, which proved extremely reliable. Due to my work commitments, Les ferried the boys to school and back at the beginning and end of each term, not to mention mid-term breaks. The one-hundred and five-kilometre road to the Zanzibar border post was gravelled. Thereafter fifteen kilometres of an extremely corrugated gravel road required negotiating before reaching the tar section. Well, both Les and the car took this in their stride as if a short trip into town. From home, the school was a round trip of over eleven-hundred kilometres. Back then, it was part of life. Today however, I would most certainly think twice about sending a woman with two young children in a saloon car on such a long trip. Especially when considering the state of the roads, not to mention the minimal traffic in the case of a mechanical problem. There were no such luxuries as cell phones or any other form of communications! However, Les handled the trips well, which allowed me to focus on the business.

Darrin hated school intensely. I hate to admit it, but quite obviously a chip off the old block as it were. Neither of us achieved in academics, I do not believe for a second because we were not capable, it was simply through total lack of interest. Eventually after professional advice, we switched him from CBC to Settlers' Agricultural School. Instantly things changed with him showing more promising results and not just scraping through exams.

Dion on the other hand, academically obviously following his Mom's example, excelled in school through hard work, grit and determination. He also proved extremely talented when it came to sport. He captained the first teams in cricket, rugby and hockey. Once again, because of my intense workloads in Botswana I missed much of his sporting achievements, sadly something I cannot take back or change. I have deeply regretted ever since this misjudgement on my part in not finding the time to have been there on the sidelines supporting him in these events.

As is generally the norm at that age, due to the added maturity both mentally and physically both our boys found girls terribly intriguing. Certainly, they found them far more desirable than they had a few years previously.

The town was small and during school holidays, the teenagers organised parties and gatherings at the Matloutse River or at the gigantic hollow baobab tree behind the golf course and other such locations. It was a wonderful and safe place for a child to grow up in, away from the real city stresses of drug abuse etcetera.

During this period, Darrin met and fell in love with a lovely and extremely attractive young girl called Sharon. They made a great couple and became closer as time went on. She certainly was not his first girlfriend, but this time it was for real, they had become an 'item' as was the term back then.

After being together for some time, an amusing situation developed. I was sound asleep one Saturday evening when at around 1am I wokeup with a start by the sound of the phone ringing. A call at that time of night is foreboding, accompanied by a feeling of dread, as it is usually bad news.

"Hello," I said in an extremely tired voice.

"Hi Trevor, this is Jim, Sharon's Dad!" came back the disgruntled voice through the earpiece.

"Hi Jim, I don't want to be funny, but have you any idea what time it is!"

"Yes, I know exactly what time it is, but I'm afraid your son quite obviously doesn't or probably doesn't care! We caught him and Sharon in her bedroom and believe me they weren't exactly fully dressed!" It was extremely clear by the tone of his voice he had been terribly upset by the situation, then continued saying, "Please can you come and pick him up immediately and take him home, this just isn't on!"

"Hell, Jim, I'm really sorry about what's happened, but you need to settle down and remember we were once young as well. Now please do me a favour and tell him to get out of there, he is quite big enough to walk home. Maybe we can all get together in the morning to discuss the situation." I hate to admit it, but having managed to get myself into many such situations, and possibly worse, back in my wild days as a teenager, was more amused than surprised by his actions.

"Well okay I'll do so, but please have a really serious talk to him when he arrives; I cannot believe how he is leading my daughter astray!" Anyway, I thanked him, apologised once more, placed the hand piece back in its cradle and after a brief discussion with Les to calm her down fell soundly asleep.

An hour later, the phone once again woke me. It was my friend Jim. He was in a real state and I had to ask him to speak more slowly as he was having a full go at me. My half-asleep and befuddled brain found it difficult to understand everything he was saying.

It turns out that some time after Darrin left, Pat, Jim's wife, went through to the kitchen to have a drink of water from the fridge. As she walked past Sharon's room, she noticed her door closed. Quietly she pushed the handle down to open it, only to find it locked! Immediately alarm bells rang in her head, she went back to her bedroom and woke poor old Jim up from his deep sleep.

Muttering to himself, he stumbled down the passage and started banging on the door, yelling for her to open it. After a few minutes the door lock clicked and Sharon opened it asking,

"Oh come on Dad, what is your problem now, I'm really tired and need some sleep?"

"You know very well what my problem is young girl, I know Darrin is back in there! How on earth can you do this to us after all that has already happened tonight?" He then burst through past her to confront Darrin. The room had burglar bars on all the windows, so there was no escape, he just had to be in there, yet the room was empty!

"Sharon, what is going on, where is Darrin?" shouted Jim and proceeded to look under the bed, behind the curtains and then opened the dressing room cupboard on the side where you would hang your clothes, it was the only other place he could possibly have been, yet once again, empty!

By this stage completely bewildered, he looked up at the ceiling checking for an inspection trap door that Darrin might have climbed through into the roof. In desperation, he then opened the other door of the cupboard knowing there was no chance of him being able to fit in there and to his utter astonishment, there was Darrin. He had somehow curled himself into a ball and squashed himself into the small space on the shelf!

Flabbergasted Jim was speechless; he just stood there glaring in total disbelief at this nervous face staring up at him from within! Darrin, on the other hand, in his terribly embarrassed state curled up like a contortionist on the shelf said the only thing that came to mind, "Good evening Sir…!"

When hearing this it was all I could do not to burst out laughing. I found it terribly amusing and was impressed he could think of being so polite under the circumstances. It so turns out they had made themselves a duplicate key for the back door, which Sharon kept and would let Darrin in at night after the old folks had gone to bed. I knew he wasn't going to live this one down and his mates would not only rag him forever about being caught twice the same night in his chick's bedroom by her folks, but be amused that he had managed to get into the cupboard on his second attempt to escape. I also believed they would be extremely envious and impressed by his and Sharon's perseverance in their quest to be together.

Once I had put the phone down and told Les the whole story, unlike my finding it terribly amusing she was beside herself, how could her son do such a thing? She said he had to be mixing with the wrong crowd to get himself into such a mess. I tried diluting his sex exploits by telling her it was far safer than taking drugs. For some reason this did not help the situation in any way.

Les was educated at the Convent School and brought up under strict supervision. There is nothing wrong with this, however in our teens we would joke about girls attending the Convent school saying they would become nuns so not to bother wasting any time with them as the chances of getting lucky were not good! She quite obviously had not become a nun and, to be honest, the thing I found most attractive about her when we first met was her natural innocence.

I drove around to Jim's house and we all sat in his lounge to discuss the problem. By the time I left approximately thirty minutes later, Jim had calmed down to some extent. Poor Sharon, in her terribly embarrassed state, had gone off to bed having had her key confiscated. Darrin and I eventually managed to get back into bed around 2am and I immediately dropped off into a deep sleep. Some years later when making my speech at his 21st birthday party I related the whole story and had the crowd in fits of laughter, much to Darrin's embarrassment.

Sharon and her folks eventually moved back to the United Kingdom and sadly the two of them lost contact. Purely by chance some seventeen years later, Darrin obtained her contact details. Thereafter one thing led to another via e-mails etcetera; Sharon ultimately moved back to Botswana to be with Darrin, and they have been extremely happily married for some six years now. I have always believed everything happens for a reason and they were just destined to be together and I am so happy for them.

So to all parents reading this, do not despair when finding your daughter's boyfriend in her bedroom cupboard, it all turns out for the best in the end.

Chapter 57

I received notification to submit a quote for a drilling contract at Turk Mine located to the northeast of Bulawayo. Our sister company in Zimbabwe would normally handle such tenders in that country, but being fully committed elsewhere were unable to submit a price for the work.

Successful in my tender I arranged for temporary export of the equipment to Zimbabwe. Our passage through the Plum Tree border post turned into more of a nightmare than I had anticipated. It took two full and frustrating days to complete. Eventually we set off directly to Bulawayo and onto Turk mine. I had a good idea of the rock formations to expect having drilled there some years previously when living in that beautiful country. This was of huge advantage as I was able to arrange for the correct matrix mix of diamond-impregnated bits now universally used by drilling companies throughout the world.

In a short time, the contract was going well with excellent results coming via the Hobic impregnated bits I had imported from Canada. They were brilliant in that not only were the penetration rates excellent, but the life of the bit was exceptional, reducing our bit cost per metre substantially. I sent my right hand man Tips Koketso to manage the contract as being in another country required top supervision. I had also employed Oletetse Koketso, his nephew, who had his uncle's genes and was proving himself as a top drill operator.

On the Wednesday prior to the end of the first month I made a trip through Plum Tree border post with a few thousand pula in hard cash. I intended changing this at the bank in Bulawayo for Zimbabwe dollars thus giving me local currency to pay the Zimbabwe staff at Turk mine on the Friday. I parked across the road from the bank and walked over to the entrance.

As I was about to enter a local Zimbabwean approached asking if I wanted to change pula. I was not sure what to say wondering if this was a set up and that possibly I could run into trouble exchanging forex. He said he could significantly improve on the exchange rate.

Being my first time through to Bulawayo needing to change money I thought 'why not' and took him up on his offer. The rate he quoted would save me a fair amount of money, how could I go wrong. We walked back to my vehicle and he and his friend joined me in the front. They asked how much I wanted to change and said I should drive off to a safer area as the police could be watching.

I drove off following their instructions and eventually pulled up and parked a few blocks from the bank. There were houses on both sides of the road, but otherwise it was quiet without a human in sight. They handed over a huge wad of one hundred Zimbabwe dollar notes for me to check for both quantity and to satisfy myself they were not counterfeit! This I did and satisfied gave them the pula equivalent for the exchange rate quoted. Quickly they counted this and said they should roll the Zimbabwe notes into a tight bundle to make it easier for me to hide lest pulled over at a police roadblock.

This made sense and I sat watching as the person sitting right next to me rolled them into a tight ball and secured them with an elastic band. I was thinking to myself that in the future I would go this route as it would save a significant amount of money and had been a simple and straightforward transaction.

Suddenly, as he handed the roll of bank notes to me they acted extremely panicked, looking out through the rear window saying the police were coming and I should leave immediately. They in turn jumped out the car and walked off at a fast pace. Concerned about the police I started the engine and drove off having tucked the roll of money into a safe hiding place under the seat. I honestly don't know if the police were coming or not as I never bothered to look back. I had just managed to pull off a great deal and needed to get out of there smartly before trouble arrived.

My heart quickened a touch when approaching the turn off to the Bulawayo Airport some ten kilometres out of town. A police roadblock closed the road and immediately the brain sent messages that I had been set up for illegal forex exchange! I thought to myself that if this were the case and they had managed to act that quickly then the police force here were far more efficient than anywhere else I had travelled in Africa!

The road leading to the police block was dead straight so I knew they could see me coming from far away. Trying to turn around and run would look so obviously suspicious and compound what was already possibly a serious problem so I drove on. The brain however was working overtime and rationally enough to tell me I never had my seat belt fastened, which I immediately rectified.

I also realised the people I exchanged the money with had no idea where I was going so this had to be a standard roadblock. On arrival, I managed to put on the most honest looking face I could muster and was ever so polite. Fortunately, it turned out to be a complete anti-climax. They were interested only in checking my driver's licence and enquired about my future travel plans in Zimbabwe. Satisfied they waved me on wishing me a safe trip. I must say the relief was immense and I left the checkpoint slowly not wanting to cause any suspicion.

It was nice to see the rigs running smoothly and after saying hello to my drilling manager, faithful friend and without doubt top operator, Tips, he disappeared off to his camp. A few minutes later, he returned with some tea and biscuits for us to enjoy together. The bond and trust between the two of us grew stronger by the day.

By mid afternoon, I left the site heading for Harare after a short meeting with the site geologist and a full list of spares required by Tips; Les had given me a parcel of goodies, foodstuffs unobtainable in Zimbabwe for her parents who lived there. I had also planned to see Gus in the morning at his office in Massa. There were a few things to discuss regarding the work at Turk mine and I would be able to update him on the Botswana operations. I arrived early evening and drove straight to my in-laws flat located in Avondale where I planned to spend the night.

They were thrilled with their parcel and we spoke late into the night, me giving them all the news of Les and the kids. Not really thinking it would be a problem I mentioned the great deal I had made in Bulawayo changing money. Les's Dad was a top and well-respected anaesthetist in Harare and as straight as they come doing everything strictly by the book. He sat there dumbfounded shaking his head.

"Trevor, how you could be so stupid is beyond me. Have you any idea how illegal it is to do that not to mention being robbed at knife point or killed for that matter considering the amount of money you changed?"

"Oh, Dad, don't worry, it was no problem and as I said I managed to get a great deal more for my pula than originally expected. Anyway, I can see your concern so will be more careful in future." What I actually meant was I would not tell him the next time!

"Well, all I can say is you have been really lucky so please think carefully before contemplating anything so stupid again." By the look on his face, that was the end of that discussion.

The following morning I left early for the office and Gus was there waiting for me. It was great to see him again and we talked for some time. He eventually asked if I had made any arrangement regarding the paying of wages. I told him what I had done and he too was surprised it had all gone so well. I asked him if he could please pull ten pay envelopes out of the filing cabinet whilst I went to get the roll of money from under my seat. I had not given it another thought after hiding it there in Bulawayo.

Within minutes I was back and once done with writing the relevant information on the envelopes I removed the elastic band from the money roll and opened the notes out to count and insert into each packet. Initially, to my astonishment which quickly changed to horror, I saw that all the notes inside were two dollar bills! The only one hundred dollar bill evident was around the outside. I was speechless as I felt the blood drain from my face! Gus looked up from what he was busy with on his desk and said with concern,

"Hell, Trevor, what is wrong, you have lost all colour in your face, are you okay?" All I could do was point to the problem lying on the desk in front of me. It also took Gus a second or two to register; it was too unbelievable for words. My money changing friends had duped me for thousands of pula. Essentially, I had not enough money to cover a few days work by one of the employees on site, never mind a full month's pay for ten people!

Yes, there is no question losing the money was a huge blow, however the embarrassment of being conned so easily felt tenfold worse. The first thought that shot through my mind was trying to imagine what Les's Dad would say about his ever so clever son-in-law!

All my life I have unfortunately possessed an extremely trusting nature, I say unfortunately, as at times it has been to my detriment. Even with this disposition, I generally picked up immediately on con tricks thrown at me over the years and yet completely failed in this instance. To say I felt like a right old fool would be a gross understatement, I am sure I have never felt like such an idiot in all my life.

I was extremely fortunate in having Gus there to help me out and was able to pay all the staff on the Friday. I left from the site at Turk mine at around midday and headed straight for Bulawayo on a mission. On arrival, I found a parking spot away from the bank, but with an unobstructed view of the entrance. At that moment in time, there was nothing more important than finding the culprit who stole from me. I wanted to get my hands on him and hurt him so badly that he would never think of doing the same to any other unsuspecting idiot.

I sat there for over an hour and there was no sign of him or his accomplice. Eventually I had to leave as I still had a long drive home, not to mention having to go through the Plum Tree border post, which could be extremely frustrating and time-consuming.

I went through similar procedures on the following three trips trying to find the highly accomplished con artists, but there was never a sign of them. Begrudgingly I eventually had to write it off to experience, a bad one, but vowed to learn from it!

Chapter 58

At the time, we also had a contract to the west of Francistown and I had Oletetse operating one of the rigs on that project. Six weeks after the start of the Turk mine contract I received a radio message that Oletctse had collapsed and was extremely ill. I told them to make him as comfortable as possible and immediately left after filling the vehicle with fuel.

I arrived on site two hours later shocked to see how seriously ill he had become. I was informed he had not been well for a few days, suffering from severe constipation. I enquired as to why he had not taken one of the Brooklax tablets included in the First Aid kit supplied on site. This had always proven extremely effective for constipation, yet for some reason beyond my comprehension, he had sought help from a traditional healer/witch doctor in the area. After paying the standard bush consultation fee of P75.00 for such service, the witch doctor presented him with a concoction to drink. Assured his problem would be cured by the following day, he drank the liquid and returned to site. Sadly, within two hours he started having convulsions and became gravely ill.

With assistance from of one of my staff, we helped him into my vehicle. Immediately I rushed him through to the hospital in Francistown where he was whisked away to be checked by the attending doctor. At reception I was required to give full details of their new patient including my contact phone numbers and told they would keep me informed. Knowing he was safe and there being nothing further I could do I left for home. I phoned the hospital first thing the following morning to be informed he was in a critical state after ingesting what was essentially poison which clearly showed up in the blood test results! Asking what the prognosis was they replied that only time would tell, but they felt I should inform the family as soon as possible. I thanked them and knowing that Tips up in Zimbabwe was his closest family I radioed through to inform him of the problem and suggested he came through immediately.

He was truly shocked to hear the news, but typical of his loyal work ethic replied saying that as Oletetse was in hospital there was nothing more he could do for him by coming through immediately. He went on to inform me they had just completed the current hole at 225 metres and as soon as he had moved the rig and set it up ready to commence the next hole he would come through. I told him I felt Oletetse was far more important than moving the rig and that the operator should be capable of moving the rig on his own anyway. He responded by telling me he would have the rig moved by that night and would leave first thing the following morning.

Shortly after 10 am, I received the call. "Hello, this is the Francistown hospital, could I please speak with Mr. Frost?" For some reason I experienced a terrible feeling in the pit of my stomach, almost as if I knew what was to follow.

"Yes, this is Mr. Frost, please tell me what news you have of Oletetse?"

"I'm sorry Sir, we did all we could, but he passed away an hour ago, his body has been placed in the mortuary. We will undertake to perform a post-mortem as soon as possible."
I immediately had a lump in my throat and found it difficult to speak; he was not just an excellent drill supervisor, but also a hell of a nice person.

"Well, I don't know what to say, but I appreciate your call, thank you. I'll get in touch once more with his uncle who is in Zimbabwe." With nothing else to add, I replaced the receiver on the cradle. Once again, I radioed through and was fortunate in having Tips come on almost immediately. It was so difficult to tell him over the air that his nephew had died; I could just imagine how he felt hearing the news that way. After a lengthy pause, his voice crackled through the speaker once more thanking me for the message and telling me he was going to check out the new site with the geologist and would leave thereafter.

In a state of shock and disbelief, I went through to Les's office and told her the sad news. Colour drained from her face as she just sat there staring at me with a look of disbelief in her eyes. My receptionist having overheard the radio message ensured the news had filtered through to my staff in the workshops and a sombre mood descended on the premises. I could not help thinking to myself that had he just taken one of the tablets I had supplied he would still be alive. It felt like a day from hell and then became dramatically worse when receiving another phone call just after 11 am, this time from the geologist at Turk mine.

"Hi Trevor, I'm sorry, but I have some shocking news for you. Your drill foreman has just passed away!" I replied saying,

"Yes, I know, sadly he died early this morning in the Francistown hospital. I have spoken to Tips on the radio and he will be coming back tonight to make arrangements for the funeral as it was his nephew who died."

"Sorry Trevor, but I don't think you understand, it is Tips I'm actually talking about. He's just had a massive heart attack and died." This was not possible, it had to be a joke.

"Listen, I have really had a bad day. His nephew has died and we are all in a state of shock, so I'm afraid I don't find your joke funny at all!" I was surprised at how he could say such a thing under the circumstances.

"Hey, Trevor, you know me a lot better than that, I would never make a joke of something so tragic. Please listen to me now, as I am being deadly serious. I took Tips in my truck to show him the new site. As we arrived, I climbed out the car with him sitting in the passenger seat, walked to the peg surveyed in for the new hole and turned to see if he had followed. I was surprised to see him still sitting in the truck with his head slumped over to one side. I waved for him to come on over, but received no response. There was a short pause and then he continued. "Obviously he had told me the sad news of his nephew and I thought he was in shock and didn't want to get out of the vehicle. Anyway, I went back and opened his door and found he had gone, there was no pulse whatsoever. Incredibly it happened that suddenly; I really am sorry and if there is anything we can do to help from this side please don't hesitate to ask." I apologised for my earlier remark, thanked him for the call and said I would phone back shortly once I managed to get my head around all that was happening.

If I was dumbfounded at my previous call an hour earlier, it was nothing like I felt now. Over the years, Tips and I had become good friends. He was a black man and I was a white man and yet this had never been an issue, we had this amazing bond. We had not only worked hand in hand for years, but also on countless occasions sat around the fire at night talking for hours. We would be in a remote area of the Kalahari, mostly with only the drill crews within a fifty-kilometre radius, sharing experiences and a good meal, which always included sudza, a porridge made from maize, to soak up all the gravy.

As I replaced the receiver once more the emotional strain of the day's events were just too much for me. Please could someone wake me from my nightmare, sitting in my office I broke down and sobbed with genuine large tears rolling down my face. Les walked into the office and stunned at my state asked what had happened. It was a good few minutes before I was able to relate, between sobs, the story to her whereby she also broke down. I had said many times in conversation that Tips as a person and work colleague was one in a million in the drilling world. I knew of no one to replace him, including white drill supervisors, anywhere in the world.

We had not only lost two of my top men in one tragic day, but had lost two close friends. Les had befriended Tip's wife over the years, a wonderful, pleasant and intelligent woman. They lived out at Mmadinare, a small village nestled along the banks of the Motloutse River some twenty kilometres north-west of Phikwe. Whenever she came into town, she never failed to pop in and say hello. They were an extremely close- knit family. She and Tips had been married for eighteen years and had one child, an 18 year -old son, and to break the news to them was not going to be easy. Tips had not only been her beloved and faithful husband, but also the breadwinner and his death would place huge stain on them financially.

As soon as we were able to control our emotions to some extent, I walked out my office into the courtyard and called my staff together. Finding it terribly difficult to relate the tragic events, I eventually managed to tell them the full story. Tips possessed a natural talent both in his profession and as a person, in gaining respect by all, almost to the extent of being their second father and the feeling was similar for his nephew Oletetse. Initially there was a stunned silence, the shocked look on the faces told the whole story.

Then Judith, my receptionist, started singing and one by one, the rest joined in. Their bereaved feelings expressed so powerfully in song and the harmony made the hairs on my arm stand up in admiration. These were special people mourning the tragic and sad loss of two loved ones in an incredible and meaningful way. Once the singing died down, I asked them to clear up the tools and equipment used in the workshops and to go home for the day.

It was a terribly sad time, which stretched over the following ten days due to extensive funeral arrangements. Les was amazing in that she went out and spent time giving her support to the family each day leading up to the funeral. Word went out by bush telegraph. Amazingly, mourners continued to file in joining many celebrating the lives of the deceased at Tip's house in Mmadinare with singing, eating and drinking. Two special people highly respected and loved by many, tragically and unnecessarily lost their lives.

I felt privileged when asked by the family to speak at the funeral and found it incredibly emotional. Then humbled when it came time to fill in the graves to be handed the shovel to start the process; it has to rate as one of the saddest and most traumatic periods of my life up to that time. Their loss largely affected the Company for many years to come and even today, some twenty-five years later, I've failed to find equal replacements.

Chapter 59

The ore body in Phikwe continued dipping in a south-westerly direction proving it was far deeper than first anticipated. The completion depth of the most recently developed number three shaft in Phikwe was eight hundred metres. Quite obviously, this was not going to be deep enough through positive results at depth achieved through our drilling.

Rod Jones was chief geologist at the time and had been so for the past few years. He was extremely efficient and knew the ore structure and behaviour intimately. Generally, the drill holes produced a constant deflection of approximately one and a half degrees per one hundred metres through formational pull. Taking this into account Rod designed and marked out new holes accordingly.

However, there was strong opposition at the time to drilling deeper as management felt the ore body would pinch out. The exploration costs involved to prove this at depth were incredibly high not to mention the astronomical cost of mining to those depths. Extensive infill drilling continued in known positive areas to prove continuation of ore. This is an essential side of a drilling project for mining houses and many have suffered through under drilling in a bid to save capital outlay. Only to lose tenfold when mining operations prove the original strike represented pockets with barren to low grade ore in between. In the case of Phikwe, great excitement was building as borehole after borehole proved high-grade copper/nickel ore zones.

Rod at the time had spent a huge chunk of his life in Phikwe and most certainly contributed enormously in the geological planning of the mine. Nonetheless, the time comes when enough is enough and his time had arrived. He had handed in his notice and a certain Martin Gallon would be taking over the position as chief geologist at BCL mine.

Martin proved to be an extremely confident and positive man settling quickly into the running of the mine on the geological side. He had big plans and was not afraid to be outspoken regarding new ideas either of his own or coming from the competent team of geologists under him.

He arranged for a farewell party at his home for Rod who would be moving to Australia. It was going to be sad to see him go as I had worked with him for many years. We had our moments, as is the norm with contractor/client relationships, but generally got on extremely well. Purely as a joke at the party, I presented Rod with a miniature steel wedge that I had manufactured in my workshops as a going away gift. This was due to a hole he had marked out in the Selebi area estimated to intersect at plus minus 1,000m in depth.

Initially the hole had progressed extremely well when at 385m there was a distinct change in colour to a much darker grey in the recycled water whilst drilling. After winching the inner tube from the rods, clearly the core proved we had intersected dolerites! This was bad news and after drilling a further six metres only to find the same formation I stopped the hole and went into see Rod at his office. Immediately concern showed on his face, but after a brief discussion, he suggested we drill a further twelve metres and see if there was a change. Unfortunately, as expected, there was no change in formation and a decision on further action required.

Essentially, he had erred badly and positioned the hole in extremely close proximity to a major dolerite dyke clearly visible on the geological map. Somehow, this slipped through undetected by the geologists and we now sat with what could become a substantially expensive problem. Rod, obviously dejected, felt almost four hundred metres of drilling could not be wasted nor the cost thereof and told me I would need to insert a directional wedge. He wanted to check the core prior to giving me specifications on bearing deflection he felt would produce the most positive results. He suggested I go to my workshops and sort out the equipment required to save time.

Seeing the extent of the dyke on the map, I advised that the mine needed to cut its losses and move the rig to a new site. My concern being even if we were successful at wedging out of the dyke the chances were high, in the positive, we would re-intersect the dreaded formation thus adding to the wasted costs already known. Rod would hear nothing of this and sent me on my way to sort out the equipment required and leave the technical data and decisions for the geologists to sort out.

Six directional wedges later, including heated exchanges at production meetings between Rod and I, the hole terminated at 685m. We had drilled a further 300m of wasted core as we were in and out of dyke all the way down. The overall cost of the hole had now doubled as each wedge was not only costly, but time consuming. There was also a high risk of the drill rods jamming due to the six steel wedges placed permanently in the hole. The relief was immense for all concerned when eventually given the go ahead to pull all casings from the hole and move to the new site. This having been carefully surveyed in by Norbet Webster some three hundred metres clear of the dyke. The new hole was eventually completed producing an extremely high-grade ore intersection.

Rod accepted my gift graciously telling me sarcastically with a wry smile how he would cherish it for all time. Realistically I felt sure he would rightfully drop it into the dustbin on the way out! A week later, he left for Australia and we have had little contact since, but I have heard he and his good wife are happy over there and they deserve it.

Martin now firmly in the chair as Chief Geologist and through researching the geological database for the mine came up with some new ideas. Geologically it was believed the magnificent granite koppies stretching over a wide area had separated the ore body between Phikwe and Selebi North. There had never been any exploration drilling in this section due to the above belief.

Martin however had other thoughts and firmly believed the koppies had effected the ore body, but not by splitting it in half with barren rock. He advocated that due to the occurrence of the koppies the ore zone had not split at all, it had simply pushed it down to greater depths. During his first few months in the hot seat, we had undertaken extensive drilling down to depths of 1,200m plus in the town area. We had five drill rigs operating twenty-four hours a day, not only in close vicinity of the houses, but literally from their backyards. The noise resonating from our machines rotating the drill rods at 1,000rpm at depth was quite something.

I received numerous phone calls through the night with complaints and insisting I shut the rigs down immediately. I could fully understand the reasoning and frustration behind their complaints. Where we lived we were no better off and suffered many sleepless nights due to the noise from our drill rigs. Due to estimated completion depths of +- one thousand two hundred metres the machines could be operating for up to two months within metres from their houses! However, it is a small mining town and regardless where you lived the sound emanating from the rigs made sleeping extremely difficult. My answer was always the same in that they should contact mine management as it was through their instruction we worked these hours. The mine was bound to tight schedules and results had to be forthcoming on planned dates for mine planning and budgetary purposes. Relentlessly we continued drilling starting up at 6am Monday and continued non-stop through to 6pm on the Saturday. On a few occasions drill sites were marked out close to people's swimming pools and strangely enough, they were not amused when I suggested, in jest, the use of their pools for my water/mud mix recycling sumps.

Martin really pushed for and eventually received the go ahead to drill a deeper (+- 1,400m) hole in the parking lot of the Sports Club in close proximity to the koppies. Management were not happy and threatened severe consequences if the hole proved to be blank as the cost involved to that depth would be a massive strain on the annual drilling budget. Management called me into a meeting to determine if in fact I was equipped to drill a hole to that depth. To be honest, up to that stage and with equipment on hand we had never drilled beyond 1,250m. However, I having had experience on deep hole drilling in South Africa assured them it would not be a problem and if necessary would arrange to bring a Sullivan 45 drill rig down from Zimbabwe if we ran into trouble with our current machines. This I had already discussed with Gus who kindly offered to send the machine down when required. Martin was so upbeat and confident I fully backed and believed in his new theories, confident the hole would not fail.

Ultimately, the hole terminated at 1,460m producing a high-grade intersection amazingly close to what Martin had predicted. Essentially this opened a completely new chapter as to just how extensive the ore body could be. There was great excitement knowing if confirmation through in-fill drilling was successful, it would extend the life of the mine by many years. This hole gave rise to increased confidence in Management who gave the go ahead for drilling in the housing area to continue at full pace.

Martin had an uncanny sixth sense, he always managed to arrange for investors from head office to come to Botswana shortly before intersecting ore on one of the sites. I would ring him once I knew we had intersected and he arranged for a site visit to that particular rig with his distinguished guests. Timing was important; I had to ensure the six-metre inner tube containing the ore had not yet been extracted from the hole prior to their arrival. Once my lookout sitting twelve metres up in the drill mast signalled their imminent approach we would commence pulling again and would generally have the core out within fifteen minutes of their arrival. This gave all concerned a chance to witness firsthand what essentially resembled beautiful round copper bars of massive sulphide being placed in the core trays. If there was ever a sure way of increasing investor confidence this had to be a winner.

By this stage thousands of tons of added ore reserves had been positively proven through our drilling and Martin was back on a mission to produce more evidence of the ore body being pushed down to far greater depths. Through thorough logging of the core, Martin produced a formational map joining all the grey/pink gneisses, quartz veins, amphibolites the host formation for the ore zones and all other formations involved at the exact depths intersected. Clearly, this exercise proved a constant increase in depth all the way through the various strata as we moved closer to the koppies. His theory was beginning to take shape, in his mind there had to be ore far deeper down before working its way back up to shallower depths in the Selebi North basin.

Once again he pushed for the authorisation to drill a hole he anticipated to intersect ore around the 1,700m mark located some four hundred metres south of the Sports Club hole. If there was resistance before on his theories, they were now even greater, Management felt possibly the sun affected his judgment and he was calling for the impossible. However, when Martin believed in something he was like a bulldog and not prepared to let go due to nervous management. Totally convinced he had done his homework he continued in his quest to obtain the go ahead. Already by this stage, I had imported from Zimbabwe the Sullivan 45 deep hole rig. Also on Martin's request, I had supplied a comprehensive quotation to drill down to 1,800m and assured him I was ready to drill the hole when given the nod.

Finally, through continued pressure from Martin and with great reluctance and little faith, Management gave the green light to go ahead. Immediately I pulled the trailer-mounted rig out to site and rigged up. My top two drill operators, White Koonyatse and James Botsobela, were to operate twelve hour cross shifts for the duration of the hole. There was great excitement and so there should have been. We were about to drill the deepest hole ever in Botswana at that time. I had purchased a brand new string of BQ drill rods at huge expense especially for this hole, not wanting to leave anything to chance.

The hole progressed really well with minimum stoppage time and soon after exceeding the 1,500m mark Management once again became edgy. They felt if the ore were to be there, we should have intersected by this time. Martin assured them, by correlating geological information comparisons with the current hole to the Sports Club hole, the minimum expected intersection depth would be 1,650m plus. Our production rate of drilling due to depth of hole had slowed considerably. Pulling rods to change bits or reaming shells became extremely lengthy exercises with added cable sheaving required due to the weight of the drill string. This most certainly lessened the load and stress on the mast and hoist drum, but also slowed the rate of pull dramatically.

Drilling to these depths can be extremely dangerous to both the drilling crew and in-hole equipment. Even with my two top operators doing a great job I spent as much time as possible supervising and ensuring correct procedures and safety precautions were strictly adhered to at all times.

Eventually we reached the 1,675m mark and Management were at their wits end. The cost per metre at this depth was exceedingly high and they felt they were throwing good money after bad. Yet both Martin and I had full faith it had to come shortly after seventeen hundred metres. We kept a close eye on the geology coming from the core samples and essentially everything tied in perfectly with the 1,460m hole at the club, only much deeper. It took all of Martin's persuasive skills to keep Management happy; assuring them if there was no intersection by 1,730m, he would call it quits and terminate the hole.

Bingo! At 1,704m we intersected two and a half metres of high-grade massive sulphides. Finally, with the formation clearly showing footwall in the core samples at 1,709m we were informed to stop the hole and get ready for the final Sperry-sun camera survey. If the excitement at the commencement of the hole was high, it did not come close to what was felt by all concerned now that Martin had proved his theory. As to mining ever taking place to that depth was another story altogether and something that would need thorough investigation at a later stage. Whatever was to happen we had managed to drill a successful hole to that depth and were proud of ourselves.

There was no doubt in the two years Martin, as chief geologist, had proved a tremendous asset to BCL Mine for many reasons. He and I built a wonderful personal and working relationship and through diligent work from Martin and his accomplished team of geologists' enormous strides forward were realised regarding extra tonnage achieved. Sadly, the time eventually arrived when Martin had completed his contract and he his good wife Caroline and lovely daughter Michelle moved onto greener pastures.

During this time, we were not only working colleagues, but became good friends having played golf and squash together on a regular basis. Although sad to see them leave, we maintained contact. He had really moved up in the world, involved internationally in geological and mine management consulting. I received many calls from him enquiring if I were interested in large drilling contacts in Ethiopia and similar North-African areas. I took these as a massive compliment coming from technically one of the top geological engineers I ever had the pleasure of meeting and working together with on the same project. As tempting as the contracts sounded I knew deep down I was fully committed in Botswana both work and family wise and sadly declined the generous offers.

Chapter 60

Colin Bird was mine manager at the BCL Mine in Phikwe for many years. He enjoyed his golf and played regularly. I will always remember a game I had with him one Sunday morning. He had obviously enjoyed a good party the previous night and to be honest the wear and tear on the body resulting from this clearly showed. Likewise, he was not playing his normal steady game; essentially, he was hitting the ball all over the place. We had just teed off on the short fifth and found the bunker next to the green. Immediately he turned to me and said, "You know, Trevor, I really feel sorry for you." Surprised by the spontaneous comment asked,

"Why is it you would feel sorry for me Colin?"

"By not partaking in the pleasures of alcohol you must understand when you wake up in the morning it's as good as you are going to feel all day. I on the other hand know full well I'll improve throughout the day!" Mike, Herman and I had a good laugh about that.

A couple of years later Colin accepted a managerial position in the UK. He packed up and left and I never heard a word from him for years. Then one day unexpectedly mid-morning my secretary put a call through to me. Yes, it was Colin phoning, but not from the UK, from Saudi Arabia! It was great hearing from him; after the standard niceties, he dropped the bombshell. He asked if I would consider going to Saudi to do some work for him on an interesting gold project. Taken back I asked him what he had been drinking and jokingly added that I hoped his day would improve. He laughed knowing immediately what I was referring to.

I must be honest, I thought it would be totally out of the question, yet the longer we spoke the more exciting the contract sounded. Initially it would be reverse circulation (RC) and the location was a hilly area where rig moves would be challenging. Colin explained that we would require small compact rigs due to the terrain.

Depending on the results of the RC drilling programme, there was a possibility of follow up work with diamond drilling. He stressed that we should quote in US$ and was an opportunity to make some good money. I eventually agreed to discuss the offer with both Gus and

Alan. I made him fully aware that were we to come over it was not a firm commitment, simply an exploratory site visit. The only thing I knew about Saudi Arabia was its location on the world map and that it was an extremely oil rich country.

Gus and Alan, the majority share holders, although reluctant initially, finally agreed that it might be worth looking at. We then brought Dinky Brown into the picture. He was single, knew his drilling, liked adventure and worked for Alan in South Africa. He was agreeable to join us on the site visit and thereafter decide what he wanted to do regarding managing a company over there.

Colin phoned back a few days later and was most excited to hear we were coming over. Two weeks later Gus, Dinky and I flew into Jeddah to commence what proved to be a hectic, but most interesting ten days in Saudi Arabia. Colin worked on a mine some distance from Jeddah and being the organised person he was, everything just fell into place. Our chauffeur was waiting at the airport ready to transport us once complete with customs and immigration to the beautiful city of Jeddah where we spent the night. Again punctually, first thing the following morning he was waiting to transport the three of us out to the mine to meet with Colin.

Quite incredible to witness, everybody in the city drove around with his hand pressed firmly on the hooter. The noise vibrating through the buildings from this was incredible; how anyone was able to carry out a conversation or even think was beyond me. When asking our local Saudi driver as to why he and all other drivers do that all I received was a thumbs up, once out in the open we discovered he could hardly speak a word of English. For all we knew he might not even have been transporting us out to meet Colin as we had no means of communication!

Our relief once arriving at the mine and being ushered into Colin's office was immense. It was good to see him again after the prolonged period of no contact and was surprised how well he looked and had not really aged. Knowing how he enjoyed partying I figured he would look a little rough around the edges, but this was not the case at all. After catching up on news over the last few years, he led us through to the Managing Director's plush office. He was a full on Saudi dressed in flowing white robes complete with headdress, undoubtedly an impressive looking man. He spoke well and explained what their future drilling requirements were for the following few years.

After a comfortable evening on the mine, Colin introduced us to Khalifa, our Saudi driver and guide for the duration of our tour. I was pleasantly surprised; we were to be chauffeured around Saudi in a new Land Cruiser VX station wagon. Over the following few days, we got to know Khalifa fairly well having spent many hours together in the vehicle and enjoyed his sense of humour.

When stopping for fuel I happened to be standing on the concourse enjoying a cool drink. Suddenly Dinky shouted for me to get out of the way. Not questioning the urgency in his voice I leaped up onto the pavement just in time as a local Saudi came screeching into the garage. I was annoyed and wanted to go and vent my rage on the idiot. Khalifa however grabbed me by the arm to stop me.

He went on saying that it would have been entirely my fault had he run me over. Immediately I refuted his allegation saying the person was a danger to others and a reprimand was in order, if not for me, but for the safety of others. Khalifa reminded us we were tourists so to all intents and purposes had no say whatsoever. I certainly was not happy about it, but decided to cool it and take his advice.

Further into our travels en-route to one of the mines where drilling was taking place we stopped in at a small gold shop. Previously informed of the beautiful gold products produced in the country I must say we were all most impressed. Whilst in the shop a Saudi woman entered wearing the traditional black attire with the only body part visible being her eyes. Carrying with her in her arms was a young child possibly two years old. I have always had a problem with children and animals. I cannot resist from saying hello to them. She came up to the counter and stood close to me. Without thinking, I lifted my left arm and rubbed the little boy on the head saying hi. To my astonishment, she clutched onto the child and shot out of the shop!

"What on earth is her problem?" I asked Khalifa.

"Well, you can count yourself as being extremely lucky her husband wasn't with her, he would have been quite entitled to shoot you where you stood!" I was now even more flabbergasted than I was at the filling station.

"Are you smoking something or what? What on earth are you talking about that he would have been within his rights to shoot me?"

"Well what you did would have been perceived to be trying to take her to bed."

"Firstly, I'm almost killed by a crazy driver and it's my fault, now I say hello to a young child and I'm chatting up the mother?" I paused for a breath as was quite taken aback and then continued, "Why on earth would I chat up a woman when I have no idea what she looks like as all you can see are her eyes, what kind of country is this?" Annoyed I walked out the shop saying that I felt before anything else happened that we should head off to the mine. *'Hell, what a fun trip this is turning out to be'* I thought to myself.

Driving through the country was most interesting, wide-open flat terrain with large areas of flat rock. It was incredibly hot, well into the 40 degree C mark so apart from heat haze, visibility in any direction was endless. Having lived in Botswana for many years I was accustomed to flat desert terrain, yet it was much like I would imagine the moon to be, but without the heat.

On arrival at the drill site I was interested to see the operators and crew on the drill rigs were all Filipinos. They certainly knew what they were doing and proved not only to be excellent operators, but top class people. After spending that day and evening with them talking around a fire, I felt like I had known them for years. You would have to go a long way to find more down to earth, hard working and honest people.

On leaving their site the following day to continue our tour, four of them handed me an envelope with all their particulars saying they would dearly love to come and work for me in Botswana. One of the biggest mistakes I ever made was not following up on their requests and have deeply regretted it ever since. Sadly, somewhere along the line I misplaced their CV's. To this day, I firmly believe they would have been great assets to our Company.

Chapter 61

Winding our way through the desert heading off to yet another mine where apparently some underground drill rigs were operating, we came across a Bedouin. It consists of a large tent housing nomadic herders. Due to the extreme lack of water and vegetation, they are continually on the move for greener pastures. Generally, they are also private people and discourage unknown intruders.

I could not resist asking Khalifa if it were possible for us to stop in for a visit. It was a unique opportunity, one that might never present itself again in our lifetime. Obviously, we had all heard and read of them, but this was the first actual encounter. He kindly agreed to go in to discuss it with them, but stressed if they were not agreeable to our intrusion on their privacy it was non- negotiable and we would be obliged to move on. Fortunately, he was quite persuasive in that the woman in the tent agreed to our visit, but it would need to be on our return through the area the following day, as she wanted to prepare for us.

Mid afternoon, we eventually arrived at the mine having travelled through various countryside conditions. As we drew closer to the mine we passed through magnificent valleys and passes, not particularly high or deep, but incredibly different with amazing rock structures rising out of the desert with a unique rugged beauty of their own.

We were met once again by a friendly Filipino who kindly led us off to our accommodation for the night, fundamentally a small shack, but quite adequate for our needs. Once our bags had been dropped off we were taken across to the somewhat basic mine offices and issued with hard hats and lights to enable us to go underground via an inclined shaft, followed by a tunnelling system. Unfortunately, there were only three hard hats and four of us. I volunteered to be the one to go in without one. I hated wearing them at the best of times and only did so when duty bound by safety regulations. Here however, this was not an issue and like a bunch of puppies, we followed our Filipino friend down the incline shaft.

Once again, I was most impressed how well acquainted and efficiently they handled their drill rigs. On seeing that I had no headgear, the operator immediately came over offering me his hard hat. I declined as politely as possible saying he needed it far more than I did. Reluctantly he returned to the rig shaking his head and continued working the various levers smoothly and efficiently giving the impression he was a born driller. The drive space where they had the rig operating was exceedingly restrictive, yet somehow they had managed to get all the equipment in and operating at excellent production levels. I cannot adequately stress as to how impressed I was with their effortless handling of the drilling equipment.

Ultimately, they completed their shift and we all filed out the shaft with Gus, Dinky and I breathing hard by the time we completed the long climb back up to the entrance. To the contrary, our Filipino friends still looked fresh and were breathing quite normally, obviously fit from having to go in and out to the working area on a daily basis.

Once again we spent many hours sitting around together that evening talking to them about how long they had worked in Saudi, what experiences good or bad had they been through and their reasons for being there. The simple answer being there was little work back home. They went on to say they would jump at the chance of working for us in Africa if offered a position.

The following morning we left early for our trip back as we had to catch a plane to Riyadh and find time to stop in at the Bedouin. Both drill operators made sure we left with their particulars, reiterating how much they would love to come and work for us. We had only spent a short time with them yet we were sad at leaving; it was like saying goodbye to good friends. Within a few hours of driving, we arrived at the Bedouin and asked to wait in the vehicle whilst Khalifa went in to confirm our acceptance. The three of us were then ushered into the large tent. Everything was neat with carpets everywhere. It felt good knowing this was the real thing, not some set up camp near the cities to impress tourists. These people actually lived here, this was their home and to all intents and purposes, the only life they knew. The woman of the house was dressed in full traditional dress, with only her beautiful dark eyes being visible. They were so striking it immediately made me wonder just how much beauty was hidden beneath the robes.

She ushered us through to the middle of the tent indicating for us to sit on cushions already laid out on the carpet for the occasion. She also indicated that she would like to prepare a drink for us by lifting her hand up towards her covered mouth. Not being sure what to expect I looked over to Khalifa who confirmed she wanted to make coffee. I then turned back to our host giving a thumbs up sign and said "Thank you". Although only her eyes were visible, it was quite clear she smiled and I imagined it to be a pretty smile.

She wondered off to the one side of the tent, sat down and proceeded to drop coffee beans into a small steel pot. Thereafter she pounded the beans, shells and all, into a pulp with a wooden shaped tool obviously specifically designed for the task. The three of us sat there obediently behaving ourselves waiting for our special Bedouin treat. Eventually the strongest and most awful coffee ever was served in small tin cups. Not only was it extremely bitter, but also full of ground-up shell. Not often have I required a tooth pick after drinking coffee, but certainly needed one in this instance. However, as bad as it was, Khalifa insisted we firstly had to drink it all and secondly, regardless of how much of an act was required, needed to make out that we had thoroughly enjoyed it.

As if this was not bad enough, there was worse to come. After we had all managed the impossible in somehow forcing the coffee down, our gracious host with outstretched arms approached me offering a large tin bowl. Peering in, all that was visible were flies, literally thousands of them! I had seen many beehives in the past, but this was my first fly hive. Once again, in a bid to enlist some help I looked over to Khalifa for advice.

I could find nothing particularly funny yet he sat there with this huge smile on his face. He could clearly see sheer revulsion in my eyes and in his sordid little mind found this most amusing! He told me she was offering us dates from the date palm trees that abound in that particular location. As was the case with the coffee, we were committed to eating some; not accepting her offer of food would be a massive affront to their hospitality and we'd be told to leave immediately.

Why oh why did she have to approach me first, why couldn't she start with Gus or Dinky? As it was, the terrible taste from the coffee was still evident in our mouths so we all felt a touch nauseous. Knowing how honoured we were having been allowed to visit, I took the plunge and waved my hand vigorously over the flies which had them rising up in a black cloud. In seconds they had settled, but done so on our heads, faces and arms.

Sure enough to my surprise, the dates were now visible in the bowl, but there was still evidence of the sticky fingered flies wondering around on the top few pieces. All I could think of doing was to force my fingers down through the top layer and pull a few from within.

The other two had no option, but to follow suit. Trying to keep the dates down took some effort, but fortunately, we managed. I wondered what might have happened had we vomited! Possibly, strung out to dry and then eaten by the flies in the desert surrounding us. To be honest, if you could ignore the obviously filthy fly contamination they didn't taste that bad and to some degree masked the terrible coffee taste. It was certainly disappointing not being allowed to take any photos, but felt honoured for having the opportunity to enjoy the experience. Something that came to mind immediately, I most certainly would not be taking up residence in a Bedouin on a permanent basis, well certainly not in this lifetime anyway.

Thereafter in the few short days left to us we travelled extensively, including a flight up to Ryhad to visit other mines in the area. Throughout this time, I talked at length to our friendly guide. He was quite open to any discussion. Intrigued with some of their more personal life, I asked him the one day,

"How on earth does a Saudi pick a wife when he has no way of knowing what she looks like as all he ever sees are the eyes?" He found this question most amusing and gave me his version of how it was achieved.

"If you are lucky and have more than one sister, the odds of finding the girl of your dreams are increased." He said still laughing. "Essentially you ask your mother and sisters to go around the neighbourhood in your area and look for a suitable partner for you."

"Well surely that is of no help as they also won't know what they look like," I replied.

"The woman folk whilst at home don't have to wear the traditional headdress covering their faces. Once they find a girl whom they feel could be the right one for you, a meeting is arranged between the two parties. You are given an hour on your own to talk and meet each other. Once the meeting is concluded and the couple have unanimously decided to be together you arrange to get married."

Obviously surprised I enquired, "Are you telling me getting married has nothing to do with falling in love? What happens when finding within a few months you aren't suited living together?" "Oh, that is no problem as you are allowed to have three wives, but trying to satisfy all them in bed is difficult and extremely exhausting!" He then managed between hysterical outbursts of laughter to confirm it was a true story.

Chapter 62

Last, but no means least we visited the location of the initial drilling project we were to price, assuming we were still interested. Colin had given an accurate description of the topography; mountainous involving some extremely challenging rig moves. With this in mind prior to flying over I had travelled through to South Africa to investigate the availability of the most compact drill rig with the depth capabilities required in the unlikely event of our coming over.

Smith Mining based in Johannesburg had such a machine with impressive specs. It was light, compact, easily hitched to and pulled with a Toyota Land Cruiser. Talking to Gus and Dinky on site we all felt the South African rig would certainly have been ideal for the contract.

Dinky however had shown some reservations during our travels and rightfully so. There is a ban on drinking, coupled with extremely harsh penalties. Khalifa had told us a story of a Filipino, who somehow had managed to get hold of some booze. He drank far too much and in his inebriated state unsuccessfully chased the nurses around in the hospital. He was arrested immediately for what's perceived to be a heinous crime in Saudi Arabia and locked up in prison approximately a month prior to our arrival. Thereafter, on a daily basis he was publicly subjected to severe lashings ensuring future compliance by all concerned regarding liquor laws in the country! Shocked at hearing this I asked.

"How long could this go on for considering it is such a minor offence, back home this takes place all the time with little consequence?" It was Khalifa who was now shocked.

"Well I don't know anything of the laws in South Africa, but if lucky he would eventually be sent home in disgrace. The other possibility being the authorities could continue with the beatings until he eventually dies!"

This really got Dinky's attention. Now I do not think he intended getting drunk and chasing nurses around, certainly no more than he would under normal circumstances. However, like most hot-blooded men he enjoyed a few beers after work. Essentially, he had already made a decision not to come over regardless of what package we offered him.

To highlight the strict laws of Saudi our informative guide told us of the penalties of theft, if caught you would have a hand cut off. If caught a second time the other hand is also removed! He said this proved extremely effective, as there was little crime in the country; hardly surprising, rarely is there ever a case of theft anywhere. Made me wonder why similar penalties in Southern Africa where not enforced as crime has sadly become rampant and part of everyday life.

Infidelity is another major crime in the eyes of the authorities with extreme penalties. The guilty woman concerned would customarily be stoned to death in public to ensure the message is sent out loud and clear to all. The man, and most likely the instigator of the transgression, jailed for life, assuming he survived daily lashings administered with vigour and intent. We as foreigners began feeling the intense and violent discipline that prevailed freely throughout the country. Did we want to live under these conditions? I certainly didn't, nor was I prepared to send crews in to work in a place I would not come to myself!

That evening we drove through to Zalim to spend the night en-route to Jeddah. We booked into a modest hotel, showered, dressed and were ready to go out for a traditional meal in a Saudi restaurant. Khalifa said he knew the perfect place and would treat us.

The three of us followed our host to a restaurant within walking distance from the hotel. None of us had any expectations of what the evening might bring, we had tried the coffee and fly infested dates at the Bedouin so what could be worse than that. On entering the restaurant, we found ourselves in what we believed to be the entrance hall. It was a large room empty of furniture of any description.

Immediately a local Saudi person approached us and spoke with Khalifa in what I assumed was Arabic, we could not understand a word spoken.

Khalifa turned to me asking where we would like to sit.

"Well, I suppose in the restaurant would be nice," I said, a little confused by the silly question.

"You are in the restaurant so once again where would you like to sit?" Now feeling a little sheepish not being sure if he was pulling my leg or not and getting no assistance from neither Gus nor Dinky I replied,

"I guess in that case why don't we sit right here where we are standing." I honestly expected Khalifa to burst out laughing; it would be something that would appeal to his sense of humour. To our astonishment, he seated himself down on the hard floor. Reluctantly and still unsure if it were a joke or not the three of us sat down. I thought to myself at least at the Bedouin our gracious host provided cushions!

There was further discussion with whom we presumed to be our waiter who then disappeared through a closed door. Khalifa seeing the confusion on our faces said he had ordered food. He apologised for not discussing the order, but felt being a traditional meal he should do it all on his own. In a short while, our waiter returned into the spacious uncluttered dining room.

He had two medium sized pots full of meat of some description in what looked to be a thick gravy mix. This he dumped on the floor between the four of us. Scuttling off once again he returned with a similar sized pot full of rice. I thought to myself that we had to look ridiculous sitting on the floor with these three pots of food placed before us; there was not another soul in sight and why should there have been when forced to sit on the floor to eat your dinner! Khalifa indicated we should eat before the food gets cold. The three of us just sat there with puzzled looks clearly showing on our faces.

"Listen to me Khalifa, I really don't want to be funny or appear to be rude, but where are the plates and eating utensils?" I asked.

He found this terribly amusing and said, "No, no, no we don't use those here, we eat with the utensils we were born with, our hands."

"How on earth is that possible? How do you eat stew and rice by hand with no plates, not even a spoon?" This was becoming a little bizarre.

"Please watch and learn from a master." Using just the right hand, he made three fast scoops one in each pot and scraped the resulting food mix into his mouth without even dropping one piece of rice.

The three of us sat there stunned.

"Okay, well done, and yes we were most impressed with your trick, now when do we gets plates and spoons so that we can also have some?"

"No Trevor, you called for traditional and now that is what you're getting, so please once again before everything loses its flavour, please get stuck in."

We had a lot of fun and laughs throughout the unusual meal and the three of us looked like we had been dropped head first into the pots. We had rice, meat and gravy all over us not to mention the immediate floor area. Khalifa I am sure had eaten twice what we had and yet had hardly made a mess at all.

Even the waiter was in fits of laughter at these foreigners looking like three naughty little schoolchildren. None of us had any idea what the meat was nor was our guide giving anything away and possibly just as well. We all had fun, a wonderful new experience eating a tasty Saudi meal by hand in the traditional fashion. Earlier, on our arrival in Zalim, covered in dust we needed a shower before going out for a meal. Now we were even more desperate for a shower after the messy meal!

The following morning we drove our last leg of the trip through to Jeddah. There we met with Colin who was extremely disappointed with our decision to refrain from tendering. However, he said he could understand our reservations and thanked us for coming over, adding if we were to change our minds to contact him immediately. We thanked him sincerely for the incredible experiences he had afforded us. After a tour around Jeddah he dropped us off at the airport and we flew home having thoroughly enjoyed these most wonderful and unique experiences.

Chapter 63

Some months after our whirlwind trip to Saudi, I employed a youngster named Hennie. He was a white man born and bred in Botswana who had a few years of experience drilling water boreholes. His parents owned farms in the Tuli Block, an extremely successful ranching area. The farms were located some thirty kilometres east of the international border post separating Botswana and South Africa named Grobler's Bridge (more popularly known as Martins Drift). However, he had no experience whatsoever in core drilling and I was yet to find out what he was like on the percussion rigs. As they say, time will tell.

As the core drilling contracts had all but dried up due to the current world recession I had decided to register as a water-drilling contractor with The Department of Water Affairs (DWA), a governmental department. Their head offices were, as was the case with all other government departments, located in Gaborone the capital city of Botswana.

This involved a few trips of four hundred and thirty kilometres one way from our home base in Phikwe to finalise paperwork. DWA had a commendable operation in progress drilling for water in villages spread throughout Botswana. An enormous budget had been set aside in a bid to alleviate the desperate water shortage experienced by many. This included, but certainly was not restricted to, extremely remote areas way out in the Kalahari Desert, areas not normally, if ever frequented by even the most adventurous traveller. To this end, the drilling contractor had to ensure he was well equipped as in 4x4 and 6x6 trucks to enable mobilisation to such locations.

Prior to hiring Hennie, I had purchased a rig through a Mr. Renier Jooste. It was a used Super Rock (SR) 1000 air rig designed and built by the company Super Rock based in Pretoria and owned by Renier. A 1517 Mercedes–Benz 4x4 was the truck selected for mounting purposes together with the old Atlas Copco 750cfm/ 350 psi compressor mounted on a similar vehicle.

His company manufactured drill rigs designed for Southern African conditions. Not only was the design perfect, but the quality of work was exceptional. He was a great guy, a man's man and we clicked from the first day we met. In the following years I gladly gave him all my business. He was also involved in off-road racing and we raced against each other many times and became good friends.

Eventually I managed to get my registration through with the DWA and issued with my first water drilling contract of five holes to the southeast of Mahalapye. I was thrilled and found it to be exciting knowing I had once again diversified into a new phase of operation for the Company.

Yes, I had drilled many *private* water holes with the Dando 250 air rig. However, it had always been a sideline, only doing so when the rig was available and if I could afford the time to get out there and look after the drilling. Effectively it was more as a help and assistance to the community than a financially viable drilling operation.

I have always had a problem of being too soft, many times to my detriment. This applies especially to the possibility of animals suffering in any way or form. Without water to drink animals will die a slow and agonising death.

Mentally I tried to imagine myself being in their predicament. We humans have all been in situations where we get thirsty at times and yet are generally in a position to resolve the problem by opening a tap or going to the fridge to drink water. Conversely, these animals are completely reliant on either rain or man to provide this precious liquid. Added to this, the loss of cattle experienced by the farmers who have struggled through life, is devastating in that it is often his only form of income. How do you not feel sorry for them when you have the means to help?

Due to this, there were numerous occasions where I, the drilling contractor going out of my way to help, lost money with customers simply not paying once the hole was complete. Another problem involved the amount of my time required on site. Firstly, in having to drive out and divine for water to ascertain if it could be found or not in their particular area then select the best site to drill. It was not financially viable and certainly needed addressing!

If approached to drill a hole further than two hundred kilometres from our home base in Phikwe, where possible, in a bid to save the client money, I would give them the contact details of a drilling contractor closer at hand. Mobilisation costs were high and an added expense covered by the client over and above the drilling costs.

There were instances when divining I could not find any evidence of water and in such cases was not prepared to drill knowing I would be wasting their money. On other occasions, the client might have engaged and paid for the services of a private diviner. I would check the spot selected on site and if not happy of there being water there, would walk the immediate area with my wires to see if there was a more positive reading close by. Assuming I found a positive site I would advise the client accordingly and leave the final decision for him to make. However, in such cases, if the client insisted I drilled the original site which proved to be dry, I was not prepared to drill my surveyed position until cash settlement in full for the original hole had been received, especially after advising against drilling that particular site in the first place.

Sadly, I drilled many dry holes as a result of this at a great and needless expense to the client. I have always believed and found success in drilling for production, results and client satisfaction. If a profit through this thought process is achieved it is a bonus.

Most businesses are able to repossess equipment or materials not paid for. In my case repossessing a hole in the ground was a little more complicated! I received many requests for a discount or worse still, the client stating they were not prepared to pay for dry holes at all. Unfortunately, I was not able to provide either as regardless to the hole being wet or dry, my direct drilling cost such as wages, diesel, bits, mobilisation etcetera remained the same. Even when surveying with the latest high-tech geophysical equipment available today, there is not one method or individual that can guarantee the rig intersecting a water strike. Only the drill rig can prove or disprove water exists. Yes, thorough divining utilising the latest equipment, not to mention the correct interpretation of the results (always a grey area), can possibly produce the most likely area to drill. Yet to pinpoint and intersect the exact spot with the drill bit was to some extent a lottery. For an example, missing the water strike in granite formation by a metre is all that is required to produce a dry hole.

The feeling of accomplishment and help provided to the client when divining and drilling a wet hole is immense. I found it to be extremely special seeing the cattle post owners' faces light up, as the life saving water gushes from the drill hole.

It was plain in many cases that this was one of the biggest and most exciting events in their lives. It meant far more to me on a personal level than striking a massive new ore body of gold, copper, coal or the like for a huge mining corporate company with extensive financial resources at their disposal anyway.

I certainly do not want that statement misinterpreted by the reader. Naturally, I find the ore body strike incredibly exciting for both our company and the mining house concerned. It would mean far more holes would be required and at times leading into possibly a few years of continuous drilling. The project could, and has done on many occasions in the past, become a profitable mine. Knowing we, the drilling company had some input into this was extremely satisfying.

Nevertheless having personally divined and drilled a wet hole for a desperate farmer and helping to eliminate his suffering, including all the animals involved, is an incredible feeling of personal accomplishment every time. Possibly this has a lot to do with surveying and finding the water myself, as opposed to exploration whereby you drill where instructed by the client.

The little farmer no one ever cared for or wanted to help, suddenly has a complete life changing experience with just the one wet production hole. I believe there were times I made a difference for the betterment of many lives, both human and animal and was a most rewarding feeling each time.

Chapter 64

Our first contract with the DWA was successful in that we completed the contract well ahead of the time schedule allowed. We were also successful to some extent with three production holes (two thousand plus litres/hour of water) of the five holes drilled. Unfortunately, the other two were dry.

This was the start of an interesting association with the DWA drilling water holes throughout Botswana. In a short while and largely due to the help of having Hennie on board, we became so busy that I was forced into looking at a new rig, then another and then another. Over the following year, I increased our air rigs by four, not counting our Dando 250. The first two were the Super Rock 1000 and then I decided to go all out and purchase two new Super Rock 5000's.

The SR 1000 was a brilliant and reliable rig and yet the extra torque and pull back power of thirty-two tons produced by the SR 5000 was enormous. I purchased all the rigs through my good friend Renier who specifically built each to suit our purposes. The two 5000's were certainly impressive rigs with extremely well constructed telescopic masts. Due to the added size of the rig, the ex-army 6x6 Magirus Deutz trucks with air-cooled V8 engines was the mounting choice. My new compressors were two Ingersoll-Rand 900cfm/350psi mounted onto 4x4 ex-army trucks and a new Sullair 900cfm/350pri mounted on a robust trailer. All three could push out 900cfm at a pressure of 24 bars. We had become a recognised water-well drilling company and were well equipped to drill anywhere to any depth at any size.

I briefly discussed water divining earlier in the book. I discovered utilising the basics taught by my good friend John Coetzee I steadily became more proficient at the art of finding water over time with lots of practice. Slowly the call for my services in this regard increased over the years. I would like to relate a few such instances.

Tati Ranching, a massive cattle ranch to the south east of Francistown, called me regarding finding water for them. They explained difficulties experienced with many dry holes after using numerous diviners and drilling companies. Notoriously it is extremely difficult to pinpoint water strikes in granites. Unfortunately, for the ranching company this just happened to be their predominant formation.

After arriving on site Mark, the ranch manager, took me to the area they had previously drilled, but with minimal success, meaning there had been evidence of water as in plus minus five hundred litres/hr (1/2 a cube/hr), but not sufficient to pump. He explained how desperate they were to have water in that particular part of the ranch.

Armed with my trusty pair of bent brazing rods I set about firstly checking the actual site drilled and found no indication of water. Then walking out from the hole I picked up a positive pull some ten metres off to the east. I then checked in what direction the strike ran and surprisingly passed within three metres of the originally drilled hole.

I continued my investigation looking for another strike that might cross over this one, giving us a second chance of finding the precious liquid. Once again, I had a positive result and ultimately marked, with the use of a pile of rocks, where I believed we should drill and was only approximately fifteen metres from the original site.

Having only heard of me through the grape vine as such, Mark was extremely sceptical and deservedly so, considering his past disappointing and costly experiences. I then checked the depth I felt we should intersect water and passed this information on to Mark. By the look on his face, I could clearly see him thinking that now he had heard it all! However right there and then I was all he had and they were desperate.

"Okay Trevor, I find it hard to believe you can predict depths, but having been informed of your many success stories feel I have no other options left to me, go ahead and start drilling." He certainly had a sparkle of excitement in his eyes and then asked, "What happens in the case of your hole being dry, will I get a discount?"

"Sorry Mark, whether the hole is wet or dry, my costs remain the same. However, I will give a guarantee by offering you a 20% reduction in price if my hole doesn't produce more water than the site you previously drilled.."

By the following evening, Mark called an end to the hole at seventy-five metres. Two intersections within a couple of metres of my original predictions producing an exciting productive hole of four and a half cubes/hour of sweet water! Mark was both surprised and elated at the same time; he ran over to where the water flowing from the hole had built up into a large puddle. Happily, he jumped around in it with muddy water splashing all over him and anyone else within reach. I felt sure, had he just won the state lottery he would not have been nearly as excited. He was a true cattleman and water for his animals was far more important than money.

I drilled many holes for them over the following years. Admittedly, there were a few dry holes, but generally, we were successful in varying degrees. They were quite adamant that they would only use me. Even on occasions when telling them to find another contractor as I was fully committed with all my rigs, they said they would wait until I could get there.

In another dry area on their farm, I found what felt like a massive fault zone, it was wide and continued for a long way in each direction. Regardless how tightly I squeezed on the wires they pulled and crossed.

Excited with what I had found yet at the same time feeling a little pensive I wondered if what felt extraordinarily strong might have a simple explanation like a large pipeline coming through there from the Shashe Dam. With this in mind, I decided to take co-ordinates with my GPS. I then drove off to visit my good friend Charles Byron, an authority on the local geology of the area and check the co -ordinates on one of his geological maps. We were both amazed to see it plotted out right in the centre of one of the known major fault zones in the area and running in the exact direction I had indicated!

When checking depth I told Mark to expect water no deeper than twenty metres, which surprised him. After drilling the hole and striking twelve cubes/hour of fresh water at eighteen metres had him dancing in the resulting out flow from the hole again. This had now become a ritual with him, except this time he was also screaming in delight and clapping his hands above his head. Seeing a client act that way, makes you realise just how desperate they were and makes it all worthwhile.

I could write a completely new book on this subject, but will relate just a few such finds. One that comes to mind immediately had nothing to do with divining for water. We were diamond drilling to the south east of Selkirk Copper Mine when we intersected a zone of dolerite at eighty-five metres. These dykes, prevalent over a large proportion within the area of interest, are expected, but certainly not what the mining house needs or is looking for. At approximately the half way stage of the hole, around one-hundred and twenty metres down we intersected and drilled into twelve metres of solid dolerite. I stopped the hole and made a quick survey with my wires in the hope of mapping out the dykes. Within an hour, I had completed what I believed to represent the dykes and marked out a hole where I felt we could drill without intersecting the dreaded dark grey to black formation.

I told the drilling crew to service the machine and pump whilst I shot off into Francistown to discuss the problem with Jerry Sharrock the geologist responsible for the surveying and drilling of the holes. On arrival, although understandably not happy with my news, he was not overly surprised either. He said he would arrange for a full magnetometer survey, results of which would determine the site for the new hole.

Naturally, he chose to ignore the information my investigation and mapping of the dykes produced. To be honest if I were in his shoes I would have felt the same way. Diamond drilling is a highly expensive operation and to site a new hole from results obtained by a pair of brazing rods in the hands of a driller would certainly be most questionable.

He informed me the rig would be down for approximately three days whilst doing the survey. Once again, I pushed my luck telling him I had the perfect site we could move onto immediately and would save him three days of standing time on his bill and the cost of the survey. All I achieved by this was receiving that Jerry look I had learned to read so well over the years of working together. There being no point in further discussion I left for site to let my staff know our way forward. I told them whilst waiting they were to close up all the old water sumps in the area excavated by us to ensure some poor animal would not fall into any of them. This being mandatory on all drilling contracts, so would save much time later on.

A few days later Jerry phoned saying he had marked out the new drill site. On my way through Francistown, I popped in to see him to collect the map made up from the magnetometer survey. I had kept mine in my diary which travelled everywhere with me. I pulled it out and placed the two together on his desk. Amazingly the similarity and new drill hole location were all but exact between the two of them. I am at a loss trying to explain the working mechanism of my faithful wires, but such instances as these help to increase my already bubbling confidence in them.

In a completely different and highly unproductive area north of Matsitama the water survey company contracted to site the boreholes for DWA had after undertaking extensive work in the area marked out twelve holes. I was thrilled when allocated the contract to drill these sites.

True to form for that area, all twelve holes were dry! In desperation the geophysicist responsible for sighting phoned, asking if I would go out and check the sites with my antiquated method using the wires. I willingly obliged and to the astonishment of all discovered not a single one of the sites gave me any reading whatsoever! I continued my investigation checking the immediate vicinity of each site. All twelve produced a positive pull on the wires within ten metres of the original site. I marked out each new site by driving a 200mm steel peg into the ground and for ease of visibility, placed rocks in a circle around the peg.

Of the twelve re-drills, only four were dry, but within metres of my original depth estimate produced badly fractured and discoloured rock formation. This clearly indicated the presence of a fault zone that at some time in the past possibly held water, but had since dried up. All others produced low yielding holes ranging between five hundred to two thousand litres/hour. This proved the survey company had successfully found the most promising areas. However, pin pointing the exact spot for drilling involves accurate and precise interpretation of all survey results concluded. Unfortunately, this can vary from one person to another.

Some months later, DWA contracted our company to re-drill four holes in the Kalahari some eighty kilometres north west of Mahalapye. The original holes were well marked out and produced between fourteen to sixteen cubes/hour. Sadly, as far as casing design of the holes was concerned the consultants at that time erred badly. Three years later, all four holes collapsed and became unusable in an area desperate for water.

The original completion certificates issued gave us an indication at what depth to expect water, together with incorrect casing design applied at the time. Due to known water strike depths and quantity, instructions given were to complete the holes at 10" size as opposed to 6 1/2" as originally drilled. This would allow the installation of 6mm wall thickness x 8" casing, screens and gravel packing to bottom. Also being a known high yielding area, DWA felt there was no need for surveying the new sites and simply marked each new hole with a mark on the ground some two metres from each of the original holes.

I sent Darrin, my eldest son, out to site with a tent for his accommodation to run the contract. After drilling the first hole, he radioed back telling me that the hole was successful and with the use of a 90-degree' V' notch system showed fourteen cubes/hour. Once complete with casing, screen, gravel pack and hole development he moved the rig to the next site.

This proved to be dry which was astounding considering the information at hand on the completion certificate! Darrin, whom by that stage I had taught the art of divining with the wires, said that having checked the site found they had actually marked the hole off the strike.

I immediately phoned DWA in Gaborone explaining the problem and asked if we could drill the site Darrin had marked out. They were just as surprised as we were that the hole was dry, but found it terribly amusing us wanting to drill our hole marked out with a pair of brazing rods! They said to just move onto and drill the third site whilst they discuss a way forward on the second hole. Having also checked the new hole Darrin predicted correctly the marked hole was off the strike. We had the same disappointing result in drilling another dry hole. Once more Darrin, extremely frustrated by this time, was quite adamant if they moved to his site only two metres from the original they would get water.

Again, I phoned DWA, eventually after a lengthy discussion they informed me that seeing two of the holes had now proved dry, in desperation, we could go ahead and drill Darrin's sites. They insisted I was present on site and they would be sending a DWA official to monitor the progress. Early the following morning I drove through and met with the DWA representative. He wanted to see firsthand our method of divining with the wires. When checking Darrin's survey myself I confirmed his site was positive.

Ultimately, he gave us the go ahead to drill. This we did and all four sites produced the full yield as per the original completion certificate. Once again, our antiquated wires proved themselves admirably reliable. I told the official that I had no idea why they wasted enormous sums of money employing a geophysical water surveying company that often produced dry holes. I went on to say I would be more than happy to do the surveys at one thousand Pula/cube of water produced if in excess of two cubes/hour. If the hole proved to be dry there would be no charge.

This would literally save millions, money that could be utilised on extra village drilling throughout the country. He was not entirely opposed to my offer, but asked how would he ever be in a position to submit the extensive mandatory report required by DWA on my surveying results provided through the wires? My reply being that people and animals do not eat or drink reports, it's water they need to keep them alive! I was fully aware my idea was a pipe dream, something that would never come about; however, there were many instances where highly experienced geophysicists called me in for confirmation of their drill sites, armed with my trusty wires.

Chapter 65

A contract to drill for Kimberlite (diamond bearing formation) came out for tender in the Central Kalahari. Due to the inaccessibility to the area, as important as the price, so was the section of the tender process relating to the contractor's availability of 6x6 trucks and equipment to enable mobilisation to facilitate and complete the challenging work in the time schedule stipulated.

The terrain, as throughout most of the Kalahari is dominated by soft Kalahari sand with narrow deeply rutted small tracks, in some areas, challenging for a 4x4 pick-up. Yet the contractor had to mobilise with fully loaded sixteen ton trucks carrying the drill rig, compressor, water tanker, drilling rods and equipment in extremely high ambient temperatures reaching the mid to high 40deg C mark!.

The bush-veld is extremely sparse with the dunes covered in light, but tough shrub, ever ready to strip your vehicle of paint, and dry grass for literally miles around in any direction. I was reasonably busy at the time, but had trucks and one complete machine with compressors capable and available for the work. Fortunately as one of the five selected contractors invited to do so, I submitted a tender. During the two week period the tenders were being assessed I received continuous phone calls from one the contractors in Gaborone (for the sake of the book will name him Terry) fishing to find out my bottom line figure on the work. Naturally, I was not willing to pass on this information and told him to relax until officially the client awarded the contract. A week later, I received a further call from him, informing me he had it from good authority I was successful with my tender, this even before I had received the news from the client.

"Trevor, you have a few rigs out working at the moment, taking much of your time having to run around ensuring they are all running efficiently." He paused for a second or two, I remained silent not knowing what he was going on about. "We are quiet with no work, what I would like to propose to you is for me to undertake the drilling and management of the complete operation utilising our staff and equipment. I will report to you directly on a daily basis on production etcetera, you won't even need to go to site." Once again, I waited for the next incredible narrative to his unique offer. "I have obtained your prices through my contact and would be willing to drill for you at 15% under your rates. You invoice the client your full tendered rate and we invoice you less the 15%. Essentially you make a good profit without having to do anything, no worries of breakdowns, drilling problems, inaccessibility of sites and regular visits?"

"Well Terry, thanks for the call, but no thanks. I only tender for work I feel confident I can complete, regardless of other work ongoing. I have a machine equipped and ready to go out tomorrow if necessary."

"Yes Trevor, I'm quite sure you do have, but think of the distance from Phikwe, whereas from Gaborone for us it really isn't a problem. We can mobilise to site in a couple of days and the control thereafter will be so much easier," said Terry confidently.

"Listen pal, I have never in all the years I've been in the drilling game sub-contracted work out in any way or form, so certainly see no reason to start now. To be brutally honest with you, due to the location of the contract I don't feel you guys have enough experience for the work required. I keep a close eye on drilling carried out throughout Botswana and to my knowledge you have drilled little under the harsh conditions that will prevail. At the end of the day it will be my name on the line, so sorry, but I'm not interested. To change the subject, how is your weather down there?"

Terry, desperate for the work continued his appeal until I, as I have been known to do often, allowed my feelings of being sorry for him, to cloud my judgement and eventually I agreed, under one condition. I would contact and let the client know what we intend to do, then only with their blessing will I go ahead with it.

Rightfully so, they weren't too happy with the idea, but I convinced them that I would be monitoring the contract with the same intensity as if we were doing the drilling ourselves and would be personally held responsible for everything that took place on site.

Within the week, I arranged for Terry to commence mobilisation on the following Saturday morning first light, explaining to him my strict obsession on mobilising on or before the due date. I would then follow, leaving Phikwe early the Sunday morning, giving them a complete day and a bit ahead of me, to meet on the first site Sunday evening, ready to commence operations on the Monday morning as per tender.

Driving my Ford Courier 4x4, the trip to Gaborone went well arriving there soon after 11am. After finding something to eat and ensuring the main and spare petrol tanks were full as was my twenty-litre stainless steel fresh water tank, I left for Salajwe. Although easily navigable, the roads to this small village being the last town of any significance before heading into the real Kalahari had deteriorated significantly. Here I was fortunate in finding a few more cold drinks to fill my cool box and left for what turned into a nightmare and frighteningly close to a complete disaster.

Within thirty kilometres, my heart sank to find the complete convoy of trucks carrying the drilling equipment stuck in the sand. Terry having heard my vehicle approaching was standing behind the last truck to greet me. I leaped from my car almost with the feeling of going through a bad dream and walked briskly over to him.

"Terry, I felt sure you guys were on site by now and yet here you are still hours away, what the hell is going on?"

"I'm terribly sorry, but I was leading the way in my Hilux when the engine stopped. After checking everything, it appears that the ignition coil has packed in and I don't have a spare one. We have been sitting here since yesterday afternoon waiting for you as there have been no other vehicles." I always carried a spare coil, in case of such an incident. As luck would have it, the week before we had the same problem with one of our vehicles and I had removed and installed it into the pick-up to get it going again.

"Okay, but then why didn't you let the trucks continue to site, there really is basically only one road in and out?"

"Sorry, but with no engine power I couldn't get my vehicle out of the tracks, I need you to pull me out with your vehicle. The trucks trying to drive around me all became stuck in this bottomless sand and we have sat here ever since."

Why oh why did I let him talk me into this crazy idea, we have yet to go through the gate of the Khutse Game Reserve where the sand becomes progressively worse and here we are already stuck! Far too angry and disheartened to talk to him I pushed my way past to check the trucks and was shattered to find all the tyres were pumped hard, there wasn't the slightest hint of a bulge on the bottom of any one tyre. I made this same mistake myself the first time I ventured into the real Kalahari, but learned what to do from my good friend John Coetzee. Terry on the other hand had convinced me of his endless experience working in these conditions!

I immediately rounded his guys up and stationed them as best I could to start letting air from the tyres of all the vehicles. Some one and a half hours later, firstly after pulling Terry's Hilux off the road, I believed we now were close to the correct pressure required to give a flat section at the base of each tyre. I called the leading truck driver up and instructed him to get into his vehicle and drive off. All standing around they obviously felt that I had possibly gone mad, they had been stuck for the remainder of yesterday, last night, most of today and I tell him to drive off!

With a look of disdain on his face, he selected first gear, eased the clutch off and applying throttle power drove off with little effort. There was much shouting, clapping and celebrating once each truck in turn followed suit.

"Okay Terry, now that we know I grossly underestimated my assumption of your lack of experience as obviously you know less than I first imagined, now please tell me how do we solve your coil problem?"

"Hey, I feel like a real arsehole and I promise things will improve. I did manage to get a call through on my sat-phone to the site geologist who is in Orapa and driving through to site tomorrow, he will bring me a new coil." As I looked over towards his forlorn vehicle, he continued saying, "Your vehicle has a really powerful engine, can you not pull me to site. To leave it here will be risky; being a Toyota it will be completely stripped down to the chassis by the time we return."

"Shit Terry, have you the remotest idea as to how far we still need to travel, but yes you are right for the first time today, your vehicle will be stripped." I, by then was resigned to the fact that it was the only way out for him.

I always carry towropes in the tool trunk of my Ford, so hitched him up. As the sun was setting fast on the western horizon darkness would soon descend upon this desolate landscape. I told him not to turn his lights on after dark, being concerned for his battery going flat without any charge going in. I said I would keep my hazard lights flashing to give him some visual aspect of the situation.

Hour after hour, we ground our way through the Kalahari sands, the spoor so deep in the track there was no need to steer the vehicle, and the tyres held in there until I forced them out of the spoor.

As we mounted one of the many grass-covered dunes, to my surprise there were two massive male lions with impressive soft manes, seemingly wafting back and forth as they walked. They always appear larger at night, but the Kalahari lion is well known to be larger than most others are. They looked very confident and proud of themselves and never appeared terribly concerned with us in anyway, wandering off to our right and eventually disappearing out of sight into the darkness. I thought to myself that after all we had been through at least we had a great sighting of the two lions. There were no visual signs of the trucks, but they had left obvious spoor letting me know they had not somehow taken a wrong turn and become lost, which was comforting.

It was now late into the night and just passed the five hour mark of pulling Terry's stricken vehicle through the Kalahari with my radio blaring away to keep me awake. I clearly saw, but through sheer exhaustion took little notice of the orange hazard lights getting brighter. Thinking my eyes were playing tricks I rubbed them in a bid to clear my imagination of the growing light. Then clearly I smelt smoke, instantly I was wide awake, jammed on brakes and rolled from the car to see the underside.

To my horror, there were open flames by the transfer gearbox. In total panic, I clawed feverishly at the burning grass scorching my bare hand badly. Not only did I try pulling the burning grass away, but threw sand onto the flames at the same time, all with my right hand as there was only space to get one arm under the vehicle.

Thoughts were flying around my head; the one-hundred-litre additional petrol tank was mounted directly above the fire. Do I continue pulling at the grass in a bid to extinguish the flames? If the fuel tank blows, that would mean certain and terrible death, do I get up and run away before this takes place? Why is it Terry is not laying under the left side of the vehicle helping to avert the disaster, instead he's running around and around the car like a headless chicken? Although my hand was burnt, I could feel no pain due to the adrenaline flowing through my veins. With another handful of sand scooped into the flame thankfully, so it was gone, there was just complete darkness.

I continued pulling all the grass jammed between the protection plate, transfer case and prop shaft to ensure it would not re-ignite; I had seriously had enough fun for one day. Somehow, I found no appeal being stranded out in the Kalahari with two burnt out vehicles and the odd lion roaming around to add to the excitement. Eventually, satisfied there was absolutely no further danger of fire I wriggled out from beneath the vehicle.

"What the hell is wrong with you? Firstly, you must have seen the fire when I was pulling you and you did nothing to warn me earlier. Secondly, and even more of a cock-up as far as I'm concerned, you run around and around the car, shouting for me to put the fire out, whilst I'm burning the shit out of my hand trying to extinguish the flames to save us and the vehicles. Why didn't you get under the other side and help me put the fire out?" I was angry beyond words and out of breath from the frantic work carried out under the car in the sand.

"I tried to warn you and get your attention by hooting and couldn't understand why you took no notice.".

"Well the reason I never heard your hooter was because I had my music on loudly in the car to keep me awake. Why didn't you just apply brakes to stop us and flash your lights? I would then have known immediately there was a problem! Shit Terry, you could easily have killed both of us with your stupidity." I could not believe his irresponsible behaviour, not only was I angry, but badly shaken by the ordeal.

"You called yourself an arsehole earlier with no prompt from me, well I now totally agree with you and as far as I'm concerned you can stay out here all night and play with the lion! Believe me they will pick up your scent and come to investigate."

With that I walked to the back of my vehicle and as I started removing the tow rope he ran and pushed me. Without thinking, only reacting spontaneously, I punched him hard in the jaw knocking him to the ground. He lay there muttering something I could not hear, so I removed the rope, climbed into my car and drove off over the rise in front and down the other side. There I stopped, climbed out and listened to him screaming like a baby for me to please come back. I was so angry knowing I was seconds away from dying out here in the desert and had no help from him whatsoever so figured I should just leave him there for the night. He would be safe locked in the car, but certainly terrified out of his wits. After a kilometre or so I had time to cool down a little so turned around to go back and hook him up again.

I was surprised to see Terry remain inside his vehicle as I drove up so with the use of a little engine power coaxed my vehicle out the spoor and turned around. Only once I had reversed up to his vehicle, climbed out ready to secure the towrope once more, did he come out. "Hey Trevor, I'm so sorry for everything and the reason I never got out immediately as you arrived was because there are lion close-by. I heard them clearly as they must be close by, so please let's get out of here fast." He then held his hand up to his jaw and rubbing it said with a smile on his face, "I truly don't want to make you angry again and have apologised so please, if possible, can we just move on and get to site?" We shook hands. "Okay let's get away before your bogus lions come and eat us," I said laughing climbing back into my driver's seat.

"Oh, you are so funny, they are definitely out there," he shouted back. Within minutes of leaving three lionesses ran past the front of my vehicle! Wow, I thought to myself, what a day this has been and we haven't even started drilling yet and I held my arm out the window with the thumbs up sign. He flashed his lights saying *'I told you so.'* Tired and desperate for sleep we arrived on site just after midnight.

There were a few teething problems on the first couple of holes, necessitating my driving all the way out there three times in the first two weeks to deliver drilling spares! Once they got into the swing of things the contract progressed well, often the case after a bad start. Whilst drilling the sixth hole I picked up a nice contract for my rig earmarked for this contract. Due to the added commitment with my rigs drilling all over Botswana, felt I was unable to find time to focus on what Terry was up to on the Kalahari contract. With this in mind, through consolation with the client, I handed the contract over to Terry whereby he could deal directly with the client. He was obviously happy with the idea as were the client who was able to continue the exploration project at reduced rates.

Chapter 66

In the past, I had surveyed and drilled a few water holes for my good friend and top geologist Charles Byron on his farm, fortunately with a high success rate. Many years later, he sold his farm and bought a new one, which desperately required water. I was not living in Botswana at the time so was not available to survey his holes for him. Darrin was running the company in my absence and Charles not having had any experience working with him in this regard decided to have an independent company come in and survey a site.

He phoned Darrin asking if he had a machine available as he had a hole marked out ready for drilling. Charles had been good to us over the years allocating many diamond drilling contracts and became a good friend. Due to this, we would go out of our way to service his needs wherever possible.

This time was no different and Darrin mobilised a rig immediately to his farm. Knowing how many holes I had sighted for Charles over the years, Darrin decided to double check his positioning of the hole. Walking with the wires over the peg marking the site he had no reaction. He then continued walking the immediate vicinity eventually picking up a strong positive pull. Thoroughly checking his spot, including depth predictions indicating a water strike at about thirty five metres. Confidently he advised Charles to drill his site not drill the original one.

Charles told him that until he had some form of a success rate in divining under his belt he was to do as he was told. His other reasoning regarding the drilling of that site was financial; it had cost him ten thousand Pula to have that peg sited in! Darrin responded telling him that regardless how much he paid for the survey there would be no water. He emphasised he didn't want to drill the hole, feeling he would be partly responsible for Charles wasting more money Charles, determined and eager to have his hole drilled, told Darrin to stop wasting his time arguing and to start drilling the hole. At one hundred and twenty metres he stopped drilling, conceding that Darrin was right and there was in fact no water. After some serious discussion, he agreed to drill Darrin's site, adding he was not prepared to pay if the hole were to be dry.

The first thirty-seven metres only produced varying colours of dry dust with no sign of water. Charles' face was clearly showing concern when at thirty-eight metres the drill rods gave a little kick, the dust disappeared and seconds later to the relief of all, the life saving water came gushing from the hole only three metres beyond Darrin's original prediction! Some years later Charles called Darrin to drill a few more holes on the farm. With the use of his trusty brazing rods, Darrin confirmed the holes Jerry Sharrock had surveyed, saying he was quite happy to drill each site. Sadly two of the four holes were dry. Of the remaining two, one produced two cubes/hour and the other strong yielding with eight cubes/hour. Historically a difficult area for finding water it was most exciting for all concerned.

A separate story, a friend and successful rancher phoned me at the office one day. He asked if I had a few hours to come out with him to an eight-hectare smallholding. He was considering buying the property some fifteen kilometres out of town towards Sefophe. Concerned there may not be water as there was no evidence of any boreholes, he needed me to run a complete survey of the land. It just happened I had the time and we went out in his vehicle. I walked every inch of the property with no joy whatsoever. At one stage, I felt there was a promising area towards the centre of the plot due to vegetation change and large anthills, however regardless how many times I walked that section, it came up negative. Eventually I had no option but to inform Janie that the area was dry to the extent that regardless of what he offered me I would not consider drilling anywhere on the smallholding. To show the faith he had in my surveying abilities with the wires, he simply lost all interest in the smallholding and pulled out of the deal. Over the years I was involved with literally hundreds of water surveying projects in varying formations, some interesting with the most amazing and unexplainable results, yet with others it appeared to be straight forward, but generally producing positive results. I will be forever grateful to John Coetzee for his tuition in this regard.

Chapter 67

Driving long distances had become so much a part of my life. I was averaging one hundred thousand kilometres a year. Often I spent twelve to fourteen hours behind the wheel of my 4x4, many of these well into the hours of darkness yet constantly remained an essential and integral part of my job portfolio to ensure efficient management.

Driving after dark in Botswana was like taking your life in your hands. My family were not happy with this as I had many narrow escapes at night.

Coming across wild animals, kudu being the primary concern, plus donkeys and cattle, standing or jumping out into the road always posed a threat. To compound the problem, for whatever reason, the majority of people driving in Botswana at night had no idea of the important function of the headlights dipswitch in their vehicle. Your impaired vision due to this irresponsible behaviour was frustrating beyond words and extremely dangerous. Sadly I believe this, together with drinking and driving, played a huge contributing factor in the number of road deaths of both animals and people in that country. They not only refused to dip their lights on approaching you, but also, when overtaken, kept them on bright, blinding you in the rear view mirrors. For this reason many of us fitted spotlights facing both forward and backwards, thus allowing us to give the culprits a blast either way letting them know to dip their lights!

Physically, I had no problem with the excessive driving at all. I certainly felt frustrated by the unproductive time spent behind the wheel. Due to the spread of our drilling contracts throughout Botswana, I seemed to be spending more time driving than actually being on site or in the office. It was getting to the stage where I felt the dogs would soon be barking at me on my arrival home, not to mention leaving Les and the kids on their own for extended periods.

In general, the Company was going well, but admittedly, many facets of running a company had changed dramatically over time. Sadly, the handshake, a binding gentlemanly agreement a few years ago was long gone. When originally arriving in Botswana drilling tenders where a simple one page document and confirmation of award was via a handshake and to all intents and purposes, the process worked extremely well. Trust and honesty to the vast majority meant everything. However, this was now changing fast, largely due I believe to a minority of fly by night drilling companies not fulfilling their contractual commitments. Sadly, to some the handshake meant little.

Contractual documentation was not only here to stay, but steadily became more comprehensive. Tendering for work had become an incredibly tedious operation, but quite obviously an essential one. For the larger companies with departments and staff handling this side of the operation it had to be easier. Running a one-man show with the help of Les required slogging away for many hours late into the night, including weekends, to meet these deadlines.

Ideas as to a way around this problem were discussed between Alan, Gus and myself. One of these was to concentrate on work in our area only and possibly leave the remote work to other drilling contractors. I felt once word was out of our new selfish intentions of only selecting convenient contracts for ourselves, mining houses might not even consider us for future work in any location and honestly believed this could be extremely detrimental to the Company. To be successful we had to be prepared to take the good with the bad. I then dropped the bombshell to both Gus and Alan.

"Why don't we invest in a plane? I could go for my pilot's license and instead of spending all this wasted time driving, I could fly. This would allow far more productive time both on site and back in the office!" By the look on Alan and Gus's faces, they obviously felt the intense heat in Botswana had affected my brain and I had gone crazy.

"Shit, Trevor! Have you any idea what a plane costs and where would you land? The contracts we are talking about are really in remote areas, there are no cities and towns with fancy runways for miles in any direction!" said Gus with Alan just sitting there staring at me with his mouth ajar. Quite obviously, the shock to his system regarding the plane was so overwhelming he was speechless.

"One of our suppliers has a Cessna T210 for sale. They are upgrading to a bigger plane. The asking price is possibly twice that of a new 4x4 vehicle." Neither of them uttered a word, so I continued. "Time we would save, not to mention the advantage we could offer in our bids for the contracts, would pay for the plane in no time!" I paused for comment, but still nothing was forthcoming. "Having a plane at our disposal opens up the whole country to us and possibly further afield, who knows what opportunities lay in Zambia for example? I'm the one who needs to be at site visits and meetings, certainly throughout Botswana. As I would be flying the aircraft myself, a fully paid pilot would not be required!" Surely, it must be starting to make some sense; by the look on their faces this was not the case. "You haven't mentioned where you would land the plane or how you would travel to site from wherever that might be!" said Gus. I was thrilled he was at least asking questions, that was at least a start in the right direction. Certainly, the idea had not disappeared out the window without further discussion as I originally felt was a likelihood.

"You would be amazed just how many little dirt landing strips there are throughout Botswana, including isolated areas in the Kalahari. The Botswana Government has gone to great lengths to ensure access to these villages is possible." Gus and Alan looked on waiting for me to further explain my crazy idea. "This Cessna is turbo charged and equipped with what is called the Robinson Stall Conversion on the wings." Understandably, another blank look from my two bosses. Until informed I also had no idea what it meant either. "Basically the wings have a small extension running all the way along the leading edges. Coupled to this, with flaps engaged for landing or take-offs, the ailerons extend simultaneously producing a far larger wing area. This in turn dramatically improves landing and take-off performance due to increased lift." They were now completely at a loss for words, with no idea what I was talking about. I immediately continued saying, "Thus allowing for the safe use of these shorter strips, within reason of course!" I waited for a response.

"What size is it? I mean can you fit anything in the plane as in people, spares for the rigs and so on?" asked Alan at last and continued, "I don't like flying with commercial airlines so trust me I'd be damned if I would climb into a tiny little plane to go and land on an international tarred runway, never mind some rough little dirt strip in the bush!"

"It can take six people including the pilot carrying minimal baggage. Although at a tight fit, once you are in apparently it is quite comfortable. Granted you would not be able to get up and walk down the aisle to the toilet, as there isn't one, as is the case with the aisle." This caused some laughter and eased the tension a little.

Gus continued in a more positive frame of mind. "Thinking about it, the idea sounds good. We've had a great year financially and not only would it make us more efficient, but also reduce our profit for the year and therefore our tax!" Suddenly this pipe dream was possibly becoming a reality. "I have spoken to people in the know and they tell me purchasing the right aircraft can be one of the best investments you can make. Unlike cars they appreciate in value!" I felt that could get us a little closer to a positive decision. "I'm not saying I am, not by any means, but let's assume we agreed to go this route, when would you have time to go and train for your pilot's license and where?" asked Alan.

"Well Al, I have already looked into that. There is a flying school down in Port Alfred in the Eastern Cape with an excellent reputation. They have space for me in their December intake." I paused for a few minutes as Alan shaking his head stood up, wandered off to the kitchen returning with beers for the two of them and a Coke for me. After swallowing a few mouthfuls he asked,

"Firstly, why learn at the coast, surely there have to be flying schools in Johannesburg where there won't be any wind and secondly, what does it cost for the course?"

"You are right, the wind hardly ever blows in Johannesburg which is one of the main reasons I'd be far happier going to Port Alfred. If I had no experience learning to fly in windy conditions, what would I do if on my own and encountered strong winds?" Once again, I paused to take a sip of my drink. "The cost to take your PPL is around R85,000. This covers a forty-hour flying training course including full board on the base. If unable to complete it in that time there would obviously be extra charges. In the unlikely event that should happen I'd be more than happy to cover those personally as only I could be blamed for that failure!"

"Well Alan, I don't know about you, but I'm starting to like the idea?" said Gus.

The decision to go ahead and seriously look into the purchase of an aircraft had become a reality and to say I was thrilled would be an understatement.

First thing the following morning I contacted the supplier concerned and set up an appointment for them to fly the Cessna 210 up to Phikwe for a test flight. They arrived with the air worthy test certificate I had asked them to produce through an independent flight maintenance company in Johannesburg.

At the time, I had a good friend working for me by the name of Clinton Rice. He and his family had been living in Botswana for some time and not only knew the country well, but also like us had seen the tough side of living in rough conditions. He had a wide range of experience in various professions, but more importantly to me at the time, he was a licensed pilot with many hours of flying experience. The majority of these hours flown as a "bush pilot"; what a plus to our Company this turned out to be!

Taking the 210 for a test flight with him at the controls was a great experience. I was easily impressed with the plane and all the instruments as in dual ADF's, dual radios with VOR's, Robinson Stall Convention on the wings, turbo charged engine and so on and so on as I truly had no idea what all this meant.

Clinton on the other hand was most impressed. He put the aircraft through a rigorous test flight with tight turns, steep climbs and incredibly short take-offs and landings. He then surprised me by switching on the autopilot. It held the heading perfectly and the plane could be manoeuvred just by turning a dial. I was of the impression only the large commercial flights would have had this facility. Just goes to show that when it came to aircraft equipment I was ignorant and had lots to learn.

Wisely, although happy with the test flight and impressed with the aircraft, he insisted it went for a further air worthy test with someone he had dealt with previously. Once cleared the contract of sale could then go ahead. The Cessna passed with flying colours and ultimately the purchase went through. We were thrilled with our new and extremely high tech mode of transport and the seller went ahead upgrading to a King Air!

Clinton was going to be of great assistance. He was not only a good friend and work colleague, but also an extremely experienced and competent pilot. He had many flying hours logged on single and twin-engine aircraft.

Chapter 68

I booked to go for my PPL that December 1989 at 43 Air School in Port Alfred.

Any spare moment available leading up to that time we spent going through the pre-flight procedures and instruments acclimatisation. Although Clinton was not a qualified instructor, I was fortunate to have the opportunity of learning to fly.

He taught me how to fly a circuit doing touch and goes at our little airstrip in Selebi-Phikwe. His control of the aircraft was remarkable with not only pinpoint landing on the threshold, but also touching down so smoothly you hardly knew you were back on the ground. Methodically he took me through all the procedures of entering a circuit, altitude required, ensuring downwind procedures, brakes, undercarriage, mixture, flaps, propeller pitch and richer fuel mixture are checked and re-checked. Air speeds required on finals to maintain lift and all this together with radio procedures! The training I received from Clinton, albeit it being illegal, as officially he was not a qualified instructor, helped tremendously when eventually going for my Private Pilot's License.

The Air School is well known and located in the quaint town of Port Alfred in the Eastern Cape. From its simple beginnings in 1942, the 43 Air School has established a reputation within the SA aviation industry for providing a high standard flying training service.

I arrived at the air school on a Sunday afternoon. Our flight training was to start the following morning and there were eight prospective pilots enrolled of which Manfred, a friend of mine from Botswana, and I were the only two on the wrong side of forty.

As instructed, we all reported for breakfast at 5am followed by our first introductory lecture in the hall. Immediately the professionalism of the flight school was evident. Instantly the lecturer made us aware of the seriousness of flight and called for each one of us in turn to talk about why we wanted to fly. I was the only one who actually needed it for business purposes. The six youngsters had all been given the chance of flight by their parents either as a birthday present or for a similar reason. None owned or had parents who owned their own aircraft, nor were they sure quite what they would do with the PPL once qualified. Essentially, they had a dream to fly, their only reason for attending the school.

After a full session of the introductory lecture, we moved onto the office for issue of our overalls and flight books. There seemed to be a mountain of books and to be honest my heart sank realising just how much studying was going to be involved. As a youngster at school I struggled to get down to serious homework, now many years later it could only have become more difficult. On the physical side of flying I was bubbling with confidence, but not so with the theoretical side!

Initially Manfred and I paired off and together followed our instructor to the Piper Cherokee, being the standard school trainer aircraft. Methodically we went through the pre-flight checks and told regardless of circumstances to do so before every take-off. The instructor rightfully made it extremely clear how dangerous it would be if finding a problem whilst in flight Peter the instructor indicated I had the first run in the left-hand seat.

Once satisfied with engine and run-up procedures, he instructed me to line up for the take-off run and so the flight training started in earnest.

Having already had a fair amount of flight training in the Cessna 210 the lack of power and prop yaw delivered by the training aircraft surprised me. We joked that the only reason the Cherokee eventually became airborne was due to the curvature of the earth! Yet as a training aircraft, it proved to be ideal. Our allotted instructor was extremely proficient in all flight manoeuvres as in stalls, engine failure procedure or forced landing, tight turns and all other relevant flight instruction.

However when it came to punctuality he was abysmal. We, the pupils, were responsible for booking our aircraft for each training session. I always opted for the 5am slot, but disappointingly, he regularly arrived late for work. Initially I kind of accepted this, but informed him, making it quite clear, I only had this period in the year free. I was not prepared to lose flight time through his inability to arrive at the workplace on time.

On the positive side, when he was there he went out of his way to teach me all he knew about flying. One example of this, it was a blustery day with seriously strong winds; all planes were grounded until further notice. There would be no flights so we were advised to go and use the down time productively by studying.

I immediately approached my instructor and told him the reason I had chosen 43 Air School was to learn to fly in the wind so insisted he took me out. He most certainly was not happy, but after my insistence and eventually receiving the go ahead from management, we climbed into the aircraft and took off. The plan was to fly touch and go circuits.

After take-off, I banked off to the left and eventually joined what would normally be the downward leg of the circuit. However, for the sake of cross wind landings we were to use runway-heading one zero, as the wind was almost at right angles to our flight path. I was amazed at how the wind affected our flight. It felt like not only were we flying sideways and yet heading in a straight line, but also the wind was buffeting the plane excessively. Shortly prior to crossing the Kowie River, I noticed he gave me a glance to check my precautionary actions.

I was quite happy that I had full control of the aircraft and continued on my merry way. Well, as I crossed the river my heart almost leaped up into my throat as the aircraft tossed onto its side. Looking out of my side window, I was looking straight down into the river. I was sure we were going to crash and had no idea why this had happened. Then just as suddenly with no input from my side, we were back to normal. Peter just sat there with a smile on his face.

"Okay, what is so funny, we nearly crashed and died there and you are amused?" I was seriously concerned, as still had no idea why it happened, or for that matter if it would happen again, possibly with worse consequences?

"You have obviously not been concentrating at our lectures," he said and paused for a moment hoping to get some form of reaction from me; there was none! After what had just taken place, I was concentrating so hard on not crashing the plane, there was no time to think of lectures! "What have you been told about velocity of wind passing through a narrow space?" Once again, there was a questionable pause.

"It significantly increases in speed velocity, but what the hell has that got to do with our flight today?" For the life of me, I could not relate to what he was saying.

"Well, we have just flown over the river which has really steep sides increasing the wind speed and the effect of that up here is why the aircraft behaved like it did. We have to fly over it again on our final approach to one zero, I look forward to seeing what action, if any, is taken on your side to lessen the effect." My heart rate by this time had returned to just above normal and I was starting to feel more in control once again. Heading back on finals for runway one zero, just before I flew over the river, I went with opposite ailerons and rudder at the same time then back to normal as we crossed the far bank and hardly any effect was felt, the violent kick previously just never happened.

"Well done, you have learned something today that might ultimately save your life sometime in the future. Now let's do a touch and go followed by one more circuit then call it a day, we really should not spend any more time than necessary flying in this weather."

I appreciated his commitment to come out and fly with me in that dreadful weather, I felt sure there weren't any other instructors crazy enough to have agreed to my request. I had specifically come to this flight school to learn to fly in the wind and a more fruitful lesson could not be possible. Those two circuits, plus coming in sideways due to the cross wind on finals was a new experience for me, but having Peter talk me through it, I managed to grease both touch downs. This had given me confidence for future such landings of which there were to be many.

Sadly, due seeming to his lack of interest in reporting for work on time, management fired him and I had another instructor assigned to me. Prior to our first flight he took me through a pre-flight gruelling which also included questions on the Cessna 210 we owned up in Botswana.

He questioned me on flight manoeuvres completed with Peter and was surprised how advanced we were regarding the flight manual for the school. He was not impressed in the slightest insisting I was pushed excessively fast and would have to go through all the exercises again. He made it abundantly clear that to become proficient in the left-hand seat of an aircraft, the correct procedures and training had to be taught strictly by the book.

Eventually he sent me off to complete the pre-flight whilst he sorted out his papers etc. Immediately after take-off he told me to fly out to the training area to the north of the airport and commence right and left hand tight turns. Having studied all the procedures thoroughly from our flight manual and practiced them many times, I made sure I followed each step rigidly. This included making a complete observation in all directions to ensure there were no other aircraft in the immediate area prior to commencement of the turns.

Finally, having pulled each flight manoeuvre off perfectly, Alan, my new instructor, still supporting an attitude about me for whatever reason, said I should head back to the airstrip. Sure, Peter had me fairly well advanced, but simply through having confidence in my control of the aircraft. The reason was not that I was special or clever, but simply due to having had many hours of flying our Cessna under the instruction of Clinton Rice prior to coming down.

Once given clearance to join the downwind leg for one zero Alan said, "I want you to believe you are flying your 210 in Botswana and not this Cherokee! Now let's say an oil pipe in the engine has burst and it's pumping out all over the windscreen, what would you do to help your vision?"

"Well, I would need to sideslip the plane with opposite ailerons and rudder."

"Okay, so you better get it done as by now the windscreen is covered in oil and you are basically flying blind!" I immediately set the plane into a sideslip and thought to myself, well that was easy enough; little did I know we had only just started!

"Right, now you think you are so clever to have some vision back through the side window. However the oil is still pumping out and the engine is about to seize up solid, what are you going to do?"

"Shut the engine down and perform a forced landing."

Urgently he shouted, "Do it now, shut the engine off!" I immediately shut the throttle down to idle and commenced the procedures required for our forced landing. He shouted for me to turn the ignition off completely. Puzzled I looked over at him and he once again gave the same order, so I turned the key and shut the engine off. This was really happening fast and he was trying to put me under as much pressure as possible.

"Okay, you may have switched the engine off, but through the wind streaming over the prop it is still turning which means the oil is still pumping out and the engine is still in danger of seizing. Not sure if you have any idea of the cost of a new motor, but believe me it is mega bucks. How are you going to solve this new problem?" He was really pushing this to the limit.

"I would need to stall the prop by pulling back on the stick until such time as it comes to a standstill". I thought to myself surely that should cover the exercise and we could start the engine and land, but once again, to my surprise, this was not the case,

"So what are you waiting for? Kind of looks to me like you don't have a problem losing your motor." Slowly I pulled back on the stick and eventually the propeller came to a standstill.

Immediately I pushed the nose down again to increase air speed to prevent stalling the aircraft. I certainly had no intensions of falling out of the sky through a flight manoeuvre going wrong! I must be honest, sitting in an aircraft flying a thousand feet above the ground with the prop standing still was a daunting experience. I have always been keen to fly a glider, well to all intents and purposes I was doing so right now, but most definitely in the wrong aircraft.

"Right, so now you think you are very clever. Well, we need to start the engine and land, however, the starter motor has packed in. How are we going to start it?" We were already losing altitude so this time I didn't waste my time asking any questions. I immediately turned the ignition on then pushed the stick sharply forward and sent the plane hurtling down towards earth!

The prop spun a few times, but the engine failed to fire. Eventually it was becoming decidedly dangerous, as we weren't that high in the first place from when the oil pipe supposedly burst! Alan leaned over and spun the motor into life with the key. I immediately pulled the nose back to level flight.

"Okay, that should cover it for today, set yourself up to land on one-zero," said Alan.

After producing one of the best greasers of all time, he surprised me by telling me to take off again and join downwind for runway three six.

"You said we were finished for today?" I said.

"I'll decide when we are finished, now remember you are still flying the 210 so please take off and join the downwind run. I obliged and once on the downwind run I went through all the required checks. I was told to land as short as possible and ensure touch down on the tar section immediately short of the grassed strip threshold. There were some tall trees on the way in on short finals and I was so low over these I was sure the fixed undercarriage was going to brush through the leaves. I managed more by good luck than good judgement to land on the tar and then run onto the grass strip. Wow! That had to have impressed him immensely I thought to myself. "Totally unacceptable, please take off again and join downwind and see if this time around we can get the checks right, you forgot to lower your wheels and would have landed wheels up. Once again may I stress, you are flying your 210. I want you to think that way every time you fly to get into the routine of doing the checks you'll be required to go through on your Cessna." He paused and then with a smile on his face continued,

"The whole point of the pressure I put you through with the broken oil pipe etcetera was to firstly see if you had the balls to perform the required manoeuvres. In this respect you passed with flying colours. Secondly and equally as important, I wanted to see whilst under pressure if you would get the downward checks right. I'm sure you will never forget them again!" He was right, I never did make the error again, and thoroughly enjoyed the rest of my flying course with what I believe has to be one of the best instructors anywhere. I not only passed the final flight test, but also produced the highest pass mark in our intake on the theoretical side, simply through sheer hard work and determination late into the night.

Training for my PPL had been a wonderful experience for me. I learned a huge amount about flying and control of the aircraft. I learned to respect the safety that goes with all flight procedures, including knowing when to fly and when not to fly due to weather conditions. The general rule of thumb being, if unsure do not fly.

I had arranged for Les to come down from Botswana towards the end of the course so that we could spend a week together on holiday to help me wind down after the extensive training. It was then that we fell in love with the quaint little town of Port Alfred and made up our minds that ultimately, when the time came, we would retire down there.

Chapter 69

On my return I was required to write my Botswana air law having registered our Cessna in Botswana. It always has and always will amaze me that as a qualified pilot, rated on a particular aircraft, you are unable to fly that self same plane with the only difference being the registration markings. It is no different to driving a car registered in another country. All the controls and driving procedures are the same as is the case when flying.

However, it is a regulation so once passing my Botswana air law I was then required to undergo a few days flight familiarization on the Cessna. Yes, I had flown the plane and been a passenger observing firsthand the procedures, but was only rated to fly the Cherokee. This I enjoyed and learned a lot from my good friend Joubs, a top-flight instructor in Gaborone. Finally, I was at last qualified and could legally fly on my own in Botswana. I have to admit it felt quite special at the time. I suppose similar to the time I passed my driver's license way back as a sixteen-year-old kid in Rhodesia. Suddenly I was free to use the plane as I saw fit and over the next eleven years took full advantage of this.

Having the plane at my disposal most certainly opened many doors. Regardless where or how remote, it was no longer an issue quoting for contracts throughout the country. Added to this I could offer a fast and efficient service and believe this helped with the awarding of contracts. Even way out in the Kalahari there was always somewhere not too far from the sites I could use as a landing strip. These were not always registered, licensed or legal airfields, but provided a means.

The added lift from the Robinson Stall Convention combined with the power produced from the turbo charged engine provided amazing landing and take-off performance making it possible to land in these remote areas. In many cases, it would have been out of the question if utilizing the standard Cessna 210 wing configuration.

The location of one of these contracts was approximately one hundred and twenty kilometres south of Maun and close to the Ngwanalekau Hills. The area was desolate, featureless and extremely hot with temperatures in the high forties! The scorched sands of the

Kalahari reach temperatures where the heat burns through the soles of your safety boots. I felt sure if attempting to fry an egg on sand heat alone, you could be successful! This endless and seemingly bottomless sand was evident everywhere and could only be negotiated in four-wheel drive vehicles. The access track winds its way through the scrubby bushes that abound in the area. The branches were always ready and laying in wait to strip your vehicle of paint. Once your wheels were in the deep tracks of the soft sand, you stayed in them, bush scratching or not.

Another issue were the sharp stumps left by the mining house when preparing the road for access. Many expensive truck tyres were lost due to this and I believed the immense heat generated into them also contributed in a big way. The toll taken on our equipment was tremendous, causing many problematic and expensive mechanical problems. Transportation of spares or staff from our home base in Phikwe to site by vehicle was an extremely long hall of eight hundred kilometres, effectively being a full day of non-stop driving. In the summer temperatures soared into the mid forties, generally making it an inhospitable and unpleasant area to operate.

Yet as late afternoon arrived and the sun settled on the western horizon, it produced the most magnificent sunsets seen anywhere. I always feel there has to be a plus to everything in life, sadly that was the only one I could think of for the area.

Anglo American, one the biggest and best-known mining houses in Southern Africa just happened to be our client for the project. They had also contracted a company operating out of Maun with heavy-duty equipment to clear the area for the camp and cut all the roads to the various drill sites. Added to this they instructed the contractor to carve out a short narrow runway two hundred metres from camp.

Coming into land there for first time was daunting in that from a height it looked so narrow and short, almost as if being an impossible task. The thought crossed my mind the wings on landing would not fit through the bushes lining each side, not to mention how incredibly short the little dirt strip looked. Once coming in on short finals I was tempted to power up and fly around once more, but figured I had everything under control and set up perfectly for landing. To all intents and purposes, I was committed and possibly beyond the point of no return.

With full 30-degree flaps and carefully adjusting rate of descent with throttle control, I maintained air speed at just above stall as I entered short finals. I planned on touching ground, or more accurately in this case soft sand, as close to the threshold as possible as taught by

Clinton. Being fully focused and concentrating on the job at hand I greased the landing and taxied off to a graded section designated for parking the plane. It was a relief to pull off a tough landing and it gave me lots of confidence for many future such landings.

We operated in the area for close on a year. I was certainly spoilt having the aircraft at my disposal, without which, I am not sure how I would have managed. On many occasions, I received a message via the 4pm radio schedule that I was required to attend a meeting on site the following morning.

I was also supplied with a list of drilling supplies required on site. These I would immediately pull from my stores, drive down to the airstrip on the road out to the Selebi Mine shaft, load the plane and submit a flight plan for 6am the following morning. The air traffic controllers operating the tower were most obliging, I would be airborne on time, and two hours later, I touched down on the camp strip. This enabling me to attend the meeting in their site office and from there drive out to the drill sites to sort out whatever issues arose.

Normally by mid afternoon I had completed all that was required of me on the sites. Due to the incredible heat in the area and the short airstrip, it would be suicide to take off at midday. To be safe I would leave my take-off time as late as possible. Generally, being airborne by 4pm worked well and had me landing at 6pm in Phikwe just in time before the control tower shut down for the night. I made radio contact with the tower at least thirty minutes out of Phikwe. This ensured the air traffic controller did not depart and lock the gates leaving me stuck inside.

Once again, they were most accommodating and never made an issue if I was running a little late. The huge advantage for me flying was being back in the office first thing the following morning. Had I made the same trip by road, at best I would have been away for three days. It allowed me to be productive in the office and in the field.

I made a point of visiting each site, spread all over the country at least once a week when possible. Due to the remoteness of some areas, there were times I was forced to touch down where aircrafts rarely even flew over, never mind landed. Regularly, I was required to fly into the little Anglo strip twice a week. Without the aircraft, this intensity of supervision by me throughout the vast country would have been extremely challenging and certainly impossible to run efficiently.

Chapter 70

My close friend John Sweet who navigated for me in the 'Roof of Africa' and a few other off-road races had a son named Mark. He grew up with our kids so we had known him from a little boy. Often our two families would go on fishing trips to Deca Drum on the Zambezi River in Rhodesia and Mark never failed to amaze me with his obsession and incredible ability to consume loads and loads of food. Eight slices of toast following a large full English breakfast of two eggs, bacon, sausage, mushrooms and baked beans was common and then by lunchtime his hunger pains started again!

Considering all the food he consumed one would imagine he turned into a big fat boy. Well, the big part he got right, but as opposed to being fat, he became one of the strongest and most powerfully built youngsters around. He was a fitness freak and trained hard physically. To add to this he never smoked or touched alcohol in any form. A nicer, more genuine youngster would be extremely hard to find. As a compliment to his parents John and Mavis, he was a perfect mixture of both. I felt it then and still do believe I have never met a more genuine, honest and down to earth couple anywhere.

Once he had completed his schooling I employed him as a learner driller/fitter on the rigs. Finding youngsters interested in going into drilling was becoming difficult. There weren't too many willing to go out and live in the wilds, many times in extremely tough conditions having to rough it for extended periods with no modern comforts of any sort.

My eldest son, Darrin, had also joined me after completing his apprenticeship as a diesel mechanic. To this day, I am still not sure if it was a good idea having the two good friends working together on many projects out in the Kalahari Desert. They were naughty at times and I believe they egged each other on. Hey, we were all young once and I knew that when there was work that needed doing they gave it their all. Still, I felt them working together on the same site was not a good idea.

I had been successful tendering for a contract to drill some R/C (Reverse Circulation) exploration holes into some known kimberlitic formations in the Kakong area located well to the south west of Botswana and as such in the heart of the Kalahari. I was pleased about getting this contract and felt Mark would be the perfect person to have permanently on site to look after the drilling operations for me.

Jerry Sharrock, a good friend whom we had worked with on many other projects, happened to be the onsite project geologist. Mark had taken the big step of marriage by this time and decided his wife Maracel was to join him on site. Fortunately the better of my two caravans was available for them.

One of my concerns on this particular contract was that there had been a small landing strip approximately twenty kilometres from the drill site, but unfortunately was closed many years previously. Without the use of a grader, repair work to land an aircraft safely was completely out of the question. Mark being the resourceful man he was had discovered the answer to my prayers, or so he thought. On the Saturday, a couple of days after his arrival on site, his voice crackled excitedly over the radio in my office at 7am, the mandatory radio schedule for all the rigs.

"Morning Uncle Trevor, sorry, but the bad news is there are a few things we need desperately that I had not put on my original list. The good news is I think I've found the perfect place for you to land and it's only just over two kilometres from our first drill site, over!"

"Morning Mark, I'm all ears, but having checked with the guys in the know there are no other strips in the area, over."

"That's correct, but as a thought Jerry took me out to the Okwa Pan. Checking the length with my vehicle, it has about four hundred metres of landing area. It is really smooth if you stay exactly on the line of where you see my tyre tracks." He was most excited about his new find and assured me that apart from some holes the wild animals had dug in places on either side of where he would mark it out, I could not wish for a better surface for a landing strip. He went on to assure me it was better than most of the bush strips I had landed on when he had been with me. With all the excitement, I had not given a thought to why his vehicle had left distinguishable tracks, and I never gave a thought to the wide balloon tyres he had on his 4x4 compared to the Marie biscuit tyres on the plane!

"Okay Mark, well done, that is really good news. I'll get hold of Jerry's wife Martie who doesn't work weekends and together with Les the three of us will fly down first thing tomorrow morning with your spares. Seeing it will be Sunday, we will also bring some meat to braai to make a nice day out for all. Do you copy, over?" He confirmed he had copied the message and proceeded to give the list of spares required. I often wondered how I would ever have managed to run the company without radio communication.

I went on telling him to park his vehicle to the side of the pan with the bonnet pointing into the wind. This would help me for landing. Landing into the wind was a huge advantage in that you could maintain air speed due to the flow of wind over the wings yet at the same time reduce ground speed giving a shorter, safer run-off after touchdown.

Early morning flights are always a pleasure in that the air is thicker giving improved lift as heat and airwaves associated with it had not yet become a factor. With this in mind, we were up and packed early and in the air by 6.30am. We enjoyed a smooth and uneventful flight in stunning weather. Martie was excited to be unexpectedly on her way to spend the day with her husband out in the Kalahari. Although effectively heading off to one of the drill sites to deliver spares, the atmosphere in the aircraft was almost like going on holiday for some reason.

I must confess to having been naughty in that it is a requirement of air law to submit a flight plan on all flights. I complied fully with this in every respect apart from being truthful on final destination. The closest licensed Government airstrip to my actual destination of Okwa Pan was at a village called Hukunsi located some sixty kilometres north west of that position. By road, however, it had to be close to one hundred and fifty kilometres.

Knowing permission to land on the pan from ATC (Air Traffic Control) would be out of the question, I used Hukunsi as my final destination on the flight plan! It most certainly would not have looked out of order as I had flown in there many times recently when working in that area. The other plus being it is unmanned so effectively there were no records as to whether I actually landed there or not.

Flying with the help of my Garmin GPS on coordinates supplied by Mark of the exact location of the pan, maintaining our track was not a problem. Twenty minutes prior to my ETA (Estimated Time of Arrival), I called for and received clearance from ATC to commence my descent. By 7.45am I was able to point out to Les and Martie the Kokong Village off to the left and soon after flew directly over the old disused airstrip clearly seen from 1000' AGL, (Above Ground Level) our current altitude. Had I not personally inspected the strip on the ground myself, could have been led to believe it was safe, fortunately, I knew better.

A few minutes later Okwa Pan was clearly visible straight ahead of us and true to form Mark had his vehicle there pointing directly to the east where traditionally the prevailing wind comes from, indicating we would come in from the west on finals. Flying low over the pan, I could clearly see Mark's vehicle tracks running almost through the centre of the pan. Sitting in the cockpit up there above the pan, I had to agree with Mark that it looked a good surface. The holes dug by wild animals that he had mentioned were not noticeable at all, I wondered if he had possibly had them filled in.

Everything certainly looked in order to me, yet Les and Martie were terribly nervous about landing on this little pan, in hindsight I guess I should also have been a little more apprehensive myself. I have always been fortunate in that seldom do I become nervous about anything. Mostly this has been a good thing; other times, as in this case, it can cloud your judgement to some extent.

To ensure all checks were in place I flew around once more and joined left downwind leg to join finals on a 08 heading. I went through the standard downwind checks twice and then on short final once again made sure I had the green light indicating the undercarriage was down and locked in. I touched down directly in line with the tyre tracks a few metres onto the pan just as the stall warning went off, the perfect landing for a short strip.

Relief of being safely down on the ground was immense. However, on our roll out as we neared the centre of the pan I could feel the tyres were breaking through the surface. Immediately I pushed the throttle to full power and more by good luck than good judgement managed to power our way back onto solid pan away from the centre. Pans generally have a slight hollow so dry up from the outer edges and eventually work its way to the centre. This was certainly the case here where the centre was far softer than the outside.

Due to the balloon tyres on Mark's 4x4, this was insignificant and would not have been noticeable apart from the obvious tracks left on the softer surface. The narrow tyres on the aircraft broke through the upper crust and to be honest, we were extremely fortunate in managing to power our way through the centre of the pan. You often hear you cannot buy experience and you learn from your mistakes. Well this turned out to be a huge learning experience, something I would never forget!

I now sat with a major predicament of how would I be able to get out of here, not to mention how I would explain to DCA my reasoning for making an emergency landing on the pan in the first place, if we could not take off. We were flying a perfectly sound aircraft with plenty fuel only fifteen minutes away from where I had flight planned to land. I felt sure I would lose my pilot's license. 'Just how stupid can one be?' I thought to myself. I was fully responsible for my reckless actions and had only myself to blame.

Now that we were on the ground, the animal diggings were all over the place and most certainly not filled in. There was absolute silence in the plane, neither Les nor Martie said a word, but I felt quite sure similar thoughts were going through their minds! I taxied weaving my way around the holes and kept to the outer limits of the pan. When reaching the far side, where in effect we had touched down originally, I swung the plane around to face back into the wind. I left the motor running for the required time for the turbo to run down and eventually after shutting the engine down, there was silence in the desert. We climbed out, stretched what were now stressed muscles and waited for Mark and Jerry to drive around to meet us.

"Hi Uncle Trevor," said Mark with his infectious smile. "Well done, what a great landing, it was a good thing you had the plane in 4 wheel drive to get through the centre portion!" Everyone found this terribly amusing and it broke the pensive mood that had befallen us.

"Well Mark, I want to tell you something, never and I mean never again, will I take your advice on places to land!" This I also said with a smile on my face; we were here and I had to find a way out of our predicament without spoiling everyone's day. Fortunately Mark had a couple of his local staff with him, so with their help we managed with some difficulty to push the aircraft backwards as high up onto the bank of the pan as possible. I had seen a section going off at an angle when taxiing around that was free of animal holes and away from the centre. Realistically however it was extremely short and I seriously had my doubts as to our gaining enough air speed to become airborne. With the help from the steep downhill gradient on the commencement of our take-off run would certainly be an advantage, but would it be enough?

All the spares including the cool box with meat and drinks were loaded onto the vehicle. With the two girls sitting in front and the rest standing on the back, I drove off heading for the drill site. Mark had brought one of the staff to leave behind to guard the aircraft. Quite what he was guarding it from I am not sure as we were in an extremely remote area. There are lions scattered all over the Kalahari, but the chance of one of them coming to attack or damage the aircraft, especially during the day, were slim. Nonetheless, we had enough problems not knowing how we would get out of there without possibly adding to them.

Mark's wife Maracel had the kettle boiling on our arrival at the campsite, ready to welcome us with a cup of hot coffee. She was shocked to hear of the problem.

"I certainly hope you have brought blankets and tracksuits with you, because if you need to spend the night I must tell you it has been absolutely freezing. In the morning the inside of the caravan windows are iced up from our breathing and here you guys are in shorts and 'T' shirts!" Obviously, blankets to us had not been an issue as there was no thought of spending the night anywhere when leaving Phikwe.

Winters in Botswana are beautiful in that during the day you cannot wish for better weather, not hot or cold, generally clear skies and pleasant. Things change dramatically late in the afternoon. As the sun gently sinks over the western horizon in a magical orange glow, the temperatures plummet and it just gets colder and colder into the night, to the extent of freezing water into solid ice. It is impossible for anyone who has not experienced these temperatures living in a tent in the Kalahari to appreciate just how cold it becomes.

"Right come on Mark, I don't want to be rude, but there is no time to waste. Let's head off and repair those problems on the rig you mentioned and check out the other drill sites whilst the women make salads for the braai. We need to be back at the pan by three this afternoon." I felt rather get back there too early than too late. We completed the repair work required and returned back to camp at 1pm feeling famished. Jerry had the fire going and the woman had made a great salad. All that remained was for us to cook the meat. By 2.30pm we bade farewell to Maracel and the staff, having satisfied our hunger pains with a great meal including sudza with tomato and onion sauce, my personnel favourite. Bidding fair well to Maracel and the staff in camp we headed off to the pan. The mood by all in the vehicle was pensive wondering if we were going to be able to fly out of there or not!

Once there and having loaded the cool box back into the plane I took a walk on the line I was going to use for my take-off run. Generally, apart from the length or lack thereof it wasn't too bad, however, under foot felt softer than I would have liked. I also checked out the area beyond the edge of the pan and was relieved to see there was room, assuming we managed to become airborne, to put the nose down and use the layer of thick ground haze (ground effect) to help build speed before pulling back on the stick and climbing out. I came back to the plane and carefully went through the pre-flight checks. As requested the guard had thoroughly cleaned the mud off all the tyres and with everything else checking out, I asked the girls to jump in and make sure they fastened their seat belts. Jerry thanked me for bringing Martie down to see him, we then shook hands and I climbed up into the left seat in the cockpit.

With a few spins of the propeller, the engine fired into life. Methodically I went through all the pre-flight checks and run-ups. Once satisfied I waved to Mark and Jerry and with pressure on the brakes, built the revs up to max, engaged ten degree flap, released the brakes and set the aircraft off down the slope onto the pan. The magic number for lift-off is sixty knots. Initially, I felt sure we were fine as I had the speed up to fifty knots well before my planned take-off point. However, due to the friction on the tyres through the semi- soft surface the air speed indicator (ASI) hovered just above that point. I was tempted to gently pull back on the stick and attempt take-off. Had I been on my own I might well have gone for it, but I was responsible for my two passengers, one being my wife Les.

Sense prevailed and immediately I made the decision to abort pulling back on the throttle, eventually safely coming to a standstill some twenty metres from the far edge of the pan. "I'm sorry girls, but the ASI was just too low to safely get ourselves airborne, I'm afraid it's not looking good at all." Once again we all piled out and stood on the pan, I was now feeling seriously concerned. "If I cannot get us out of here and we're forced to spend the night we'll freeze to death!" I had to find a way to get airborne without killing us, although I must confess it flashed through my mind that it could be far less painful than freezing to death slowly!

I waved to Mark to bring his vehicle over. I climbed into the back to improve my vision and asked him to drive as slowly as I instructed. Using this method, I managed to map out a possible route to try, in between the animal holes and away from the muddy centre. It meant going all out at full throttle, approximately one hundred and fifty metres, firstly in a northerly direction, then with the use of the left brake turn, sharply onto a westerly, heading where there was approximately three hundred metres of similar consistency of flat pan as we had on the first attempt, but in the opposite direction. There being no wind to talk of, it made no difference as to what heading we were on for take-off.

We drove back in the reverse direction to make the tracks more visible therefore easier for me to follow. I then had Jerry stand as a marker at the point I would need to turn. There was a definite track through there, but the close proximity of the animal holes left no room for error. The position I had so recklessly managed to get us into was hard to believe. Using one of those easy *'in hindsight theories'* regretted terribly making the decision to land.

"Okay, I'm going to give it one last try, so let's jump back in and get ready to leave," I told the girls as I jumped off the back of the vehicle.

"Are you sure this is going to work this time, I'm not too happy getting back into the plane, I really don't want to die out here!" said Les, and Martie fully backed her on this.

"You know I would never let that happen, come on now, jump in and let's go home."

After firing up, I went through the pre-flight checks once again. It was now 3.45pm; even if successful with this attempt, we would only just make it home in time before they closed the airfield. I built up the revs, released the brakes and off we went. Within seconds, I had Jerry right in front and hit the left brake hard, shortly shutting the throttle. The plane spun left and immediately I was back up to maximum power. Slowly, ever so slowly, the ASI climbed toward the magic sixty knots. It just wasn't quite getting there and I was again tempted to shut off, but being aware of a safer run-off area on this side of the pan kept the throttle fully open.

Within metres of the edge of the pan, I gentle pulled back on the stick. The wheels lifted off the ground and immediately I eased the stick forward again. We were skimming along metres above the ground in a bid to extract all the help possible from ground effect. It must have looked disastrous from where Mark and Jerry stood, but I was confident the crisis was over with air speed increasing rapidly and once satisfied, eased the aircraft into a full climb turning out to the right. With the use of the ailerons, I waved the wings to all watching from the ground to let them know we were safe and everything was now under control.

We touched down at our home airstrip with ten minutes to spare. It had been a long, stressful, but also successful day and apart from our few hiccups experienced in our attempts to take-off, we all thoroughly enjoyed the days outing. Getting into a warm bed that night was sheer bliss and I instantly fell into a deep sleep and remained in that state through to 5am the following morning. I am sure that I walked through for my morning shower still wearing the smile I had gone to bed with, we really were extremely lucky.

Chapter 71

Khakhea district in central Kalahari is located some two hundred and eighty-five kilometres west of Gaborone. We had drilled in the area some time back and had returned to drill a few more exploration holes. The area consists of scrubby bush and sand, lots of sand making site moves difficult. A 4x4 vehicle was essential for the personnel together with four and six wheel-drive trucks for transporting equipment. Our first hole was nearing expected target depth and Simon Bear the consulting geologist for the project wanted to be there to check the cores himself. Based in Johannesburg, he was an extremely busy man, thinly spread between his office duties and mandatory site visits on numerous drilling projects in both South Africa and Botswana.

He phoned me shortly after 3pm on the Wednesday to find out how long it would take him to drive to site from Gaborone in a hired vehicle. Although desperate to study core samples, time was not on his side as he had an important board meeting back in Johannesburg on Friday morning.

Darrin, who was running the contract for me and living on site in a caravan, had radioed through the previous afternoon excited to let me know he had found an airstrip only fifteen kilometres from the drill site, albeit a sandy one. It was just long enough and fully fenced so animals should not be an issue on landing and take-off. This can and has been a notorious problem on many of the isolated airstrips due to wild life grazing on them. This being the case, it necessitates 'buzzing' the strip in an attempt to clear and make safe for landing your aircraft.

"Simon, I possibly have some good news for you. Darrin has discovered an airstrip close to site that sounds useable." I paused for a reaction, but there was none forthcoming. "If you can somehow get yourself to Gaborone, I'll fly down too, first thing tomorrow morning, pick you up and we can fly to site, do what is required and have you back in Gabs the same afternoon." Hell, if that does not impress him nothing will. Once again I was thinking to myself what an incredible asset the aircraft was proving to be.

"Well Trevor, that sounds interesting, but are you quite sure it is safe to land there?"

"Hey Simon, I would not suggest it if I felt it weren't safe, believe me it will be fine."

"Well if you are absolutely sure about this I'll catch the first flight out and see you in Gabs tomorrow morning."

"Yes, that should not be a problem at all. I look forward to seeing you in the morning, have a good flight!" Darrin required a few spares on site which I took down to our airstrip and loaded onto the plane submitting my flight plan at the same time. All that was required the following morning was pre-flight and run-up procedures allowing me to get airborne by 6.30am and touchdown in Gaborone at 7.15am.

Simon had managed to catch the early flight in, so we were able to take off and head for the newly discovered strip in Khakhea immediately after submitting a new flight plan, giving the control tower my intentions for the flights ahead of us. Being early morning the flight was smooth and within twenty minutes I had the field in sight.

"Wow Simon, that looks like a really nice strip and will be useful for the duration of the contract now that I know it's here," I said, whilst systematically going through the downwind checks.

With a concerned look on his face he responded by saying, "Shit Trevor, it looks really small to me, are you sure it's safe to land here?"

"Yes relax, Darrin checked the length and it's plenty long enough for this plane as landing and take-off performance is exceptionally impressive. That's his vehicle parked next to those bushes waiting for us."

Coming in on finals when landing on a short strip I kept the air speed just above stall. Clinton always told me to come in as slowly and as safely as possible to enable touch down on the numbers so to speak, never land deep, but also remember landing short might not be a healthy option either. The landing was perfect and initially the run off felt fine, but this unfortunately was only due to our initial ground speed after touchdown. As our speed bled off so the evidence of soft sand gripping our wheels became plainly evident. In trying to turn and get back to the threshold, we totally lost momentum and became stuck! So much for my believing landing here was not a problem and then to add to my predicament, having my distinguished passenger on board simply didn't help matters!

"Well that's great, how the hell are we going to get out of here now?" said Simon now extremely unhappy with the situation, to be honest so was I.

"Don't worry," I said, "you should know that a driller always makes a plan, but first things first. We must get the plane back to that side of the strip to enable our take-off being into the wind later."

Darrin drove over in his Toyota and fortunately had a shovel attached permanently to his roll bars with the use of wing nuts. Also fortunate was he had brought two of his staff with him. After some spadework and lots of pushing and swearing, we managed to get the plane back to and facing the right direction. I didn't want to say too much, but concerned that take-off was going to be a problem, knew I needed to make a plan and quickly.

I spoke with Darrin's staff asking them to shovel off the top soft sand in the centre of the airstrip and keep going until we returned from the site. I explained the problem to them and they understood perfectly and immediately set to the task. I felt if I could manage to get a decent speed going initially on a firmer base, we might just get out of here.

We left them with a few cool drinks and headed off grinding our way through the soft Kalahari sand to site. Within half an hour we arrived at the rig and watched as they drilled down another three metres. The hole, currently at two hundred metres, was in fact twenty metres beyond the expected intersection depth. Simon painstakingly went through the core samples.

There was most certainly a formational alteration within metres of the expected intersection, but I must add it didn't look too interesting to me. Simon agreed they were disappointing results, but nonetheless was encouraged by the mineralization evident. Pulling a few plastic bags from his briefcase, he filled them with samples from that section of drill hole and felt we should drill to two hundred and ten metres. If there was no change in formation, we should stop the hole and move to the next site previously marked out some three hundred metres north of our current hole.

Les had included some boerewors in my cooler bag; I suggested we cook it for breakfast. With all the digging required to clear the airstrip of soft sand we had time on our hands. Once the bellies were full and Simon was happy he had all he needed regarding results of the current hole, we drove off back to the strip.

I was impressed by all the work achieved with the shovel whilst away on site, clearly the crew had worked hard. They had cleared about one hundred and fifty metres. Sadly however, not only had the wind strengthened, but had completely changed direction 180 degrees! Trying to take off downwind was simply not an option.

"Sorry Simon, but I cannot consider risking our lives. We are going to have to wait until it rains or the wind changes!"

"What the hell do you mean wait for the rains? I have a plane to catch to Johannesburg this afternoon; we have an important board meeting first thing in the morning. It's not going to rain for months and what difference would it make anyway?" He was genuinely agitated and quite obviously regretted flying out with me in the first place.

"Well the rain solidifies the surface sand and we would have no problem getting out of here in either direction depending on wind of course." Keeping as straight a face as possible I continued, "No, I'm pulling your leg Simon! We actually have three options available to us, two of which might get you to Gaborone on time. We can sit tight for a while to see if there is any wind change and give the guys a bit longer to clear the problem. Alternatively Darrin could drive you to Gaborone, but unfortunately you would miss your flight time as it's a long slow drive." Simon, looking extremely stressed with the situation he now found himself in, asked,

"So mister clever bush pilot, I dread to think, but what is the third option as I really don't have time for either of the first two?" He was clearly and understandably pissed off!

"The wind has picked up nicely. I believe if I can taxi the 210 to the other side of the runway without getting stuck using lots of power, spin it around on its tail keeping the power wide open for the take-off run, we just might make it out of here!" Taking a breath then continued, "I can guarantee it will be a hair raising experience, but to be honest cannot guarantee it will work. However, knowing firsthand the impressive take-off performance of this aircraft I would be willing to give it a try."

"Trevor, this is a serious situation and becomes more bizarre by the minute, are you saying we could die?"

"Simon, we are all going to die one day, but I promise you it won't be today. If I feel there is a chance of not making it I'll abort and you would have to go in with Darrin."

"As I have already told you I cannot miss the meeting in the morning and have a plane to catch so what are we waiting for?" After a thorough pre-flight inspection, we loaded the sample bags, said farewell to Darrin and his crew and climbed into the plane strapping ourselves in tight.

When starting the engine hot, you need to prime the fuel more than normal, which I was never happy doing as always worried about fire. Our motor had been standing for a few hours by this stage so I performed the standard starting procedure and she immediately fired into life. An exceptionally useful and important exercise I learned from Clinton for use on dirt strips was to perform all pre-take-off engine run-ups on the move. To some extent, this eliminates the possibility of having sand pulled up into the engine from prop wash if conducted in the normal manner at a standstill.

Everything checked out and in a short time I managed to taxi to the far end of the strip holding the stick right back in a bid to lessen the weight on the front wheel. Utilizing every inch of the sandy strip available to me and with engine power far higher than normal for taxiing, moved the aircraft off to the right with the gentle use of the brake pedal. Immediately, I then hit the left brake pedal hard and held it there until we had spun one hundred and eighty degrees. Elated we were not yet stuck, without hesitation I pushed the throttle fully open and effectively commenced our take-off run. The sand being soft severely hindered our advancement.

With the engine turbocharged we certainly were not lacking in power. Take-off performance on a normal hard strip was most impressive with a distinct surge felt once releasing the brakes. In our current situation, this simply was not happening! My brain worked overtime, not just on controlling the aircraft, but with the question '*do I go, or don't I go?*' It is always more difficult making a quick decision when another life is involved. Yet there was a definite increase in speed so felt I had to push on. Suddenly we were on the section cleared of soft sand by the crew's hard work and instantly there was a notable increase in acceleration.

The end of the airstrip was coming up far too quickly, but so fortunately was the ASI. I was now at the point of no return and eased back on the stick just in time to climb over the fences surrounding the airfield. Still at critical minimal air speed, I eased the nose down in the hope of assistance from ground effect. I had the aircraft flying level and could not have been more than six metres above the ground. With extreme restraint, I resisted the temptation to retract the landing gear in a bid to lessen the wind resistance caused from the gear hanging out below the plane. There's no question it would make it a 'cleaner plane' with less drag, however, this was not the time to do so.

'Joubs', my instructor for my conversion onto the Cessna 210, had schooled me well. He had thousands of both flying/instruction hours behind him. There were no airs and graces, a down to earth nice person and top rate instructor. I found him to instil absolute confidence in you as his pupil in a relaxed manner. When he tells you what works and what doesn't, you do not think of questioning him, as

99.9% of the time he is right. He had trained me and gone through actual exercises proving that in a case such as this retraction of the undercarriage would cause added wind drag as the gear folds, with possible disastrous results.

There were no large trees, hills or for that matter anything much higher than Darrin's vehicle which was a blessing. The ASI shot up to eighty miles an hour and climbing fast. Somehow I had pulled off the impossible and felt relief flowing through my veins together with sweat pouring into my eyes which was not only caused by the excessive heat. I commenced the climb out turning off to the right, retracting the undercarriage at the same time. Darrin standing on his vehicle gave me thumbs up and waved madly. Not sure if he was excited about our successful take-off or that he would not need to drive all the way to Gaborone and back to drop Simon at the airport!

Simon on the other hand had not said a word through this rather stressful period. Initially climbing into the plane he buckled up, crossed his arm over his lap and held onto the door rest with his left hand as extra security. Then looked out through his side window and never moved from this position and even now we were safely in the air he maintained his pose. I thought maybe through all the excitement he had suffered a heart attack and died on me!

"Hey Simon, welcome to Frost airlines, we hope you have enjoyed your flight and will you consider us for any future travel arrangements!" I said with a laugh. "Hey, are you still with me as you haven't moved since we got into the plane?" With a broad smile, he turned to face me saying,

"Shit, this is one hell of an aircraft. I must be honest I have never been so terrified in all my life." Shame, he was actually shaking having just been through a defining life threatening experience. "Quite how you managed to get us safely into the air from that sand pit I'll never know, but you've convinced me you certainly know what you're doing and will gladly fly anywhere with you."

"Well, the main thing is we are safe and you will be home sleeping in your own bed tonight and not in the awning of the caravan. Shit Simon, I know you would never let me live that one down!" We both laughed, which was a great ending to an eventful day.

Landing safely in Gaborone some twenty minutes later, we shook hands saying farewell. Simon was well in time to board his flight to Johannesburg and I, having fuelled the plane, flew back to Phikwe. Although a hectic and stressful day, I would never have managed without the aircraft and essentially felt like just another day in the office.

Chapter 72

As previously mentioned we were fortunate in having the opportunity to drill for water in areas where wild game abounds, including the *"big five"*. One particularly interesting contract comes to mind.

This took place eighty-five kilometres out from Nata on the national road to Zambia. DWA in this instance were admirably financing a water-drilling project for game in the Ngwasha Pan area, although their primary objective being to fill water holes for the elephant prevalent throughout the region.

Not having drilled the area previously, I decided to drive up on a site visit to acquaint myself with the conditions. Immediately leaving the tar road, you entered soft Kalahari sandy tracks. Approximately four kilometres in from the main road, a government game control camp had been set up some years previously primarily for the control of the dreaded foot-and-mouth disease, mainly carried by buffalo. Although deep rutted tracks led to the camp, due to constant use by government officials in Toyota Land-Cruisers, the centre portion was void of grass. However, immediately continuing past the camp east towards the Zimbabwe International boundary, due to good rains that year, not only was the grass long, but unfortunately full of seed. For the sake of sustaining future grazing for the game, this was a positive, for driving a disaster.

To the uninitiated, this might sound somewhat trivial and insignificant. However, as you negotiate the narrow track, constantly brushing the grass down in front of you, so the seeds efficiently pulled in by the engine fan stuck in the radiator. Within a kilometre the lack of airflow through the radiator-core increased the engine temperature considerably necessitating remedial attention. You have to stop, climb out and with difficulty due to the inaccessibility of the core, brush the offending seeds away. Generally burning your arm and hand on the hot radiator, turning the process into a slow, laborious and painful operation.

Determined to reach our operational area, I pressed on, but it was slow and frustrating beyond words. Traversing south along the

Zimbabwean fence line separating the two countries, I came across a large water hole in the road. There was no way to continue, but to go through the middle due to the fence line to the left and thick bushes on the right. I drew closer in a bid to determine the depth, but from the steep slope on the left side next to the fence, it appeared significantly deep. I was about to climb out from the vehicle to poke a stick into the water hole when from approximately eight-metres from my vehicle there was a slight movement behind the bush that caught my eye.

It happened to be a massive bull elephant that, I assumed had just quenched his thirst in the water hole. Seemingly, not that interested in me at that moment, but standing within two metres of where I planned to drive through the water hole, had me seriously in two minds as to what to do next. From many years ago when I came extremely close to being trampled to death by one of the magnificent creatures, I have certainly afforded them far more respect ever since.

The road was exceptionally narrow, even reversing back for kilometres would be difficult to find a place to turn. Moreover, I needed to go forwards, not backwards to reach my destination in the first place. I turned the engine on my 4-wheel-drive Ford Courier off to save it over-heating and sat there in the oppressive heat and total silence. I pondered as to how long he would stand there for; surely he had far more interesting things to do elsewhere, thinking to myself it was certainly so in my case.

Eventually after what felt like hours, but in reality was only about fifteen-minutes, he took a few paces off into the bush and again stopped. He had that look in his eye of hey, come on I dare you to try your luck. As it was now becoming late afternoon, I needed to either go or abort the trip and reverse until I could find a place to turn around and head off home. Feeling this would prove an absolute waste of a trip and possibly being more fool-hardy than most, I decided to go for it and started the engine, as this caused no real concern to my friend and ensuring I was in 4-wheel-drive, eased the front wheels into the water. It felt fine and not too deep, so I continued more confidently, suddenly the left wheel dropped into a hole and forced me to accelerate marginally. The extra engine sound together with the splash of the water gained the elephant's attention and he swung around with a loud bellow and ears flapping, from this close he looked like a double-storey building! Using gentle throttle control up to that point, it ceased immediately and I floored it to push through; plainly my friend was now not happy with my intrusion into his day's events.

I felt the vehicle sink slightly and almost become stuck with the wheel spin caused by the added RPM of the engine. 'Oh come on' I thought to myself. 'You cannot get yourself stuck right here with this guy boring down on you.' Although on the fringes of total panic, fortunately, sense prevailed and immediately I eased back on throttle power and to some extent, gained more traction. With full concentration on my driving and the rear end slipping and sliding around, somehow I managed to climb the far bank to dry land.

When checking the rear-view mirror, a chill ran down my spine, he was standing in the middle of the water hole where I had just driven through. Quite obviously and rightfully so, satisfied he had frightened the hell out of me, he fortunately remained where he stood, possibly enjoying the cooling effect of the muddy water. I hoped that he wasn't enjoying it too much as I would be returning this way within the hour and needed him to be long gone by that stage.

I continued on my way, still needing to clean the radiator at regular intervals, when eventually I arrived at the GPS cords for our first drill hole site. The thick bush had thinned out allowing me to drive out of the sand ruts and turn through the long grass lining the side of the road. Halfway through the turn with the grass reaching window height, I noticed the engine temperature rising fast and switched off instantly.

After surviving the water hole problem, I had been fortunate in seeing three giraffe, two magnificent sable antelope and a small group of five kudu. These wonderful wild game sightings had dispelled any further negative thoughts of elephant from my mind. Knowing what was required to rectify the heating problem, I pulled the bonnet catch and confidently opened my driver's door and climbed out. Just as I unlatched and opened the bonnet, I heard or more accurately felt a rumble through my feet. I swung around to see a female elephant charging me!

In a split second, I leaped back into the vehicle slamming the door closed and at the same time trying to convince myself that it would only be a mock-charge. It so turned out that this was the case and she turned and wandered off back to her baby that I had not previously seen, due to the long grass. Like the bull elephant, she was not moving from her position. After ten-minutes, I figured she might possibly believe I was not the threat she first thought and would allow me to climb out again. Instantly this theory proved to be incorrect and once again she charged, this time I was sure it was the real thing as she only aborted metres from the vehicle. For those never having seen this behaviour from an elephant in a situation of mercy as I was in at the time, believe me it is a frightening experience in the extreme. Although I felt some security being inside the vehicle, knew she was big, strong and heavy enough to squash my truck like a paper bag with me trapped inside!

I could not fire-up the motor and drive off in fear of engine damage due to over-heating. The last thing I needed was to be stranded out here in the Kalahari with no transport and many kilometres from help. I tried to phone my office on my cell to inform them of my situation and location in case things became worse. This was futile as there was no cell-coverage, I was completely on my own. By this stage, the sun was setting closer and closer to the western horizon and I knew within a couple of hours darkness would descend on the Kalahari bush-veld. In desperation in a final last bid to communicate, I typed a sms in the hope it might just go through somehow. Hell, I would hate to die out here and only have my remains discovered weeks later!

I found it strange that both elephants were so unusually agro, yet thinking about it, the bull at the water hole was obviously in musth. Bull-elephants between the ages of fifteen to twenty years old go through this once a year and it can last approximately six weeks. Their temporal glands swell and release a strong smelling fluid rich in testosterone that runs down their cheeks. During this period they become sexually active and extremely aggressive. She, on the other hand through incredible protective instincts naturally possessed by elephants, was going to ensure the safety of her little one. This is highly commendable, no doubt. However, believe me, right there and then sitting trapped in my car, hours away from help I found it difficult to be impressed by it all.

Almost an hour later to my utter relief, she eventually turned and slowly wandered away with the baby submissively following like a little puppy, miraculously disappearing from sight in the long grass, bushes and dusk setting in. To ensure I was safe I waited a further five-minutes then climbed out and as quickly as possible cleaned the seeds from the radiator. Eventually satisfied and vowing to install seed deflectors made from netting to all vehicles involved with this contract, I started the motor and drove off. My only concern now was the thought of the aggressive bull-elephant at the waterhole. I shouldn't have worried and once through the waterhole had a uneventful trip home. Having disturbed most of the grass seeds on my way in, driving out was far easier with fewer stops. Although I arrived home late that night, I was happy, extremely pleased to be alive and safely back with the family.

The drilling contract progressed really well and produced a few reasonable fresh boreholes for the game. I mention fresh boreholes as although striking high yields on other holes the Total Dissolved Solids

(TDS), essentially salt, was far too high even for the game and had to be abandoned.

Once we started pumping water from these holes into the dry pans in the area, elephants started arriving seemingly from no-where. It was amazing lying in my little tent at night hearing the joyful sounds of these majestic animals, mingling with all the other beautiful night sounds of the Kalahari bush-veld. During our time in the area game was plentiful, including three separate lion sightings, a wonderful area to visit on holiday and to think we were paid to be there.

Chapter 73

I made many trips to my favourite fishing area at Motopi, only now being far better equipped. A good friend of mine was leaving Phikwe and had advertised his little rubber duck boat and motor for sale. The minute I heard about the deal I went to his house to check it out.

Most certainly, it was a small boat and powered by a fifteen-horse engine. I was excited about it and bought it from him for next to nothing. I now had the perfect boat for such trips.

On my first trip out there with my newly acquired form of water transport I found the fifteen horse powered motor rather heavy and bulky to carry and attach to the boat. It was certainly an over kill for the size of the boat. The other drawback was the fuel tank being independent, restricted the tiny floor space even more.

Floor space was minimal when empty, yet with the fuel tank, fishing boxes and gear and cooler box, there was little room left for your feet. Seating was by means of the rubber floats on each side and was quite comfortable. The power to weight ratio with two people on board was most impressive, but I believed for my requirements was not ideal.

I was fortunate in that I managed to sell the second hand bigger motor for more than the cost of a brand new five horse Yamaha with fuel tank incorporated in the engine cover. It was light in weight and easy to carry. Designed as a two man dingy the rubber duck proved ideal for my requirements.

Frank Hendricks worked for a drilling supply company in Bulawayo called BOART, mainly servicing the mines and drilling contractors in Rhodesia. He also supplied the BCL Mine so drove through to Phikwe on a regular basis, more to supply the mine than myself, but always popped into the office to say hi. We hit it off really well and in time, I felt it might be a good idea to talk to him in connection with running MTS (Mining & Technical Services) for us.

Gus, Alan and I had equal shares in the business run from my offices in Phikwe. Licensed to supply drilling and mining equipment throughout Southern Africa there was certainly good potential for an independent manager to control and market the products for us. Being committed to running the drilling company I had little time to focus on MTS. Borehole pumps had become a big seller, but even there, Les completely on her own, handled that side. We also manufactured through our workshops general add-on 4x4 accessories as in bull bars, tow bars, railings, long range fuel tanks and stainless steel water tanks.

With Frank joining us, it opened the door for me to purchase the extensive equipment owned by a local engineering company that was closing. Part of the deal consisted of high-pressure hose repair machines and boxes and boxes of various sized fittings. This proved to be popular and we supplied all the contractors and the BCL Mine with new hoses when required.

Frank proved to be a huge boost to the Company and was not only extremely efficient at his job, but was also a dedicated and excellent angler. My hearing this in our final interview sealed the appointment for him.

He was meticulous to the extreme in everything he did. To be honest there were many times when he drove me crazy with the time it took him to ensure a perfect job, yet worth it as a perfect job was always guaranteed. We worked and fished extremely well together.

On the first trip up to Motopi with the rubber duck, we had an interesting first days fishing. I found it highly amusing and yet Frank failed to appreciate the humour in what transpired.

Our problem started on the way up, having forgotten to load a braai grid. It only struck me some one hundred and twenty kilometres after leaving Nata. There were no shops until Maun and we were turning off some forty kilometres before there so I needed to improvise and did. Sometime after realizing the problem, I noticed a fence on the side of the road in disrepair. I pulled off the road, climbed out and pulled a pair of pliers from my toolbox.

"Is there a problem with the vehicle?" asked Frank.

"No, I've just remembered that we forgot to load a braai grid so just going in there to get one," I replied.

"You going in where to get one?" he asked looking out into the barren Kalahari sand veld with a puzzled look on his face.

"I'm going to cut off a few pieces of wire from that fence over there and we can make one when we arrive, hey we can't go fishing without a braai grid."

"What do they say? A good driller always makes a plan,'" said Frank and we both laughed.

We arrived at my fishing spot as it was getting dark. Frank was amazed just how large the trees were. If ever there was proof of the need of water for growth it was here. Some two hundred metres from the river we were driving through normal Kalahari terrain of long wispy dry grass with open plains interspersed with small bushes and the occasional medium sized tree. Suddenly as you arrive at the river, you enter this impregnable forest. The trees are huge and the foliage surrounding them extremely dense with vines growing down everywhere. It gives the feeling of a hi-tech hand built monkey pen. We wound our way in for about a hundred metres on an extremely narrow disused track to what had become, in my mind, my own personal campsite. There was a special feel to this place, a feeling of wonder and excitement of what the weekend would bring.

In a short time between Jacob, Frank and I we had offloaded the vehicle and set the camp up with three small tents. For me it was exciting to have Frank with me. I loved taking people on fishing trips and knowing Frank's obsession to have a fish fighting on the end of his line added to the excitement.

I had made up two trunks large enough to house the folded inflatable boat and the second one for the little outboard engine. I made these from 1.5 mm galvanized iron so they were not particularly robust. However, they efficiently achieved my objective of hiding the boat and motor. This helped in totally alleviating my concerns when passing through the veterinary control gates on the way up. If the officer controlling passage through, saw the boat, he would certainly ask for a boat permit that I never had.

In an attempt to control the dreaded Kariba weed you were required to apply for a permit for either Maun or the Kasane area, but not for both. My wanting to use the rubber duck in either fishing area I had only applied to get a permit for Kasane. Doing it this way lessened my chances of being caught without one in the Boteti area, as it is extremely remote, seldom did we see anyone there. Yet in Kasane, boat checks took place on a regular basis and my little boat was legal there. I felt I had it all covered and to ensure compliance to some extent, apart from not having a permit for the Maun area, I had the boat sprayed each time on my return from a fishing weekend.

Putting the boat together took about twenty minutes. It had to be rolled out neatly, floorboards fitted, secured, and then pumped up using a foot pump. Obviously thereafter, with motor securely fastened to the back, you were ready to go fishing once fuelled up.

"Frank, is this place heaven or what?" I asked.

"Shit, it really is something else, I had no idea there were trees this size anywhere in Botswana, never mind out here in the middle of the Kalahari Dessert!" He was like a little boy going on his first fishing trip. "Now show me how we make the boat up, we aren't going to have time to do it in the morning, we need to get out there first thing and start catching fish!"

"Come on Frank, it's getting late, it's dark and I'm hungry and tired after the long drive. Let's get the fire going, make the braai grid, cook some meat, relax with a drink and get some sleep." I was not joking; it had been a long six and a half hour drive from Phikwe, the last three hours on dirt road. "Tomorrow is another day, Boet, so come on just relax, those fish out there aren't going anywhere, that river just happens to be their home, they live there."

"I really don't give a shit where they live, all I care about is going out there at first light, we're only here for a day and a half! Either you help me or between Jacob and me I'm going to sort the boat out, one way or another it will be assembled tonight!" Clearly, I was not going to win the argument so whilst Jacob went off collecting wood for the fire we set about putting the boat together. Once complete I suggested Frank made up his fishing tackle ready for the morning whilst I roughly bound a braai grid together from the pieces of wire sponsored by the broken fence on the road in. Eventually at 10pm I climbed into my tent and instantly fell into a deep sleep.

At 4.30am, a strange sound woke me. Firstly, waking from such a deep sleep I wasn't even sure where I was. When it dawned on me, I immediately thought it had to be a hippo making the sound as it was extremely vocal! As I lay there intently listening I thought to myself that there was too much of a constant rhythm to it.

My only other conclusion being, was it Frank snoring? His wife Bron had warned me of his expertise in this department, but surely any human snoring that loudly has to wake themselves. Sticking my head out I peeped at his tent approximately ten metres away. There was no doubt in my mind, the sound came directly from there. With a half moon shedding sparse light and looking into the gloom I imagined the tent bulging as he exhaled and sucked back in again as he took the next deep breath. Strange how often the mind conjures up visions that appear to be real and not just a figment of imagination. The sound however was real. I smiled as I thought to myself that I hoped it was not similar to the mating call of the hippo or Frank was going to be in for a huge surprise.

Suddenly there was a loud gulping sound, a cough, then silence, absolute silence. I felt sure anything for miles around would be too scared to make a sound after listening to Frank. Was he alive or dead? The silence was so deep that I wondered if the gulp and cough had been his last breath. Should I rush over there and perform CPR? I shouldn't have worried as to my complete relief after making a few more grunting sounds to kick start himself he once again settled into his earth shattering crescendo.

Jacob had the fire going with the lid of the tin kettle rattling away telling us it was boiling. It was just before 6am, with the fish eagle calling for us to go and catch some food for him.

Frank stumbled out his tent, stretched himself, farted loudly then sauntered over to Jacob and me sitting next to the fire.

"Hell, I must have been really tired last night as I slept right through. I expected to hear all kinds of bush sounds, but it was dead quiet!" said Frank.

"Well firstly, good morning to you too, secondly, there was no chance of your hearing any bush sounds. You chased everything within a ten kilometre radius of our camp scurrying away looking for refuge!" I said laughing, then continued, "Shit Frank, Bron had warned me of your snoring, but hey she never told me you were the 8th wonder of the world in that department. Hell, I have never heard anything quite like it. I'm not sure if you realise just how talented you are!" By this stage, even Jacob was laughing and shaking his head from side to side.

"Hey Boss Frank, even the lion, she ran away from the noise from your tent. Now the fish I'm sure have also run away to another river, you won't catch fish today my Boss." Listening to the humour coming from Jacob, levelled at Frank, I found it hilarious and by this stage, I had tears coming out of my eyes from laughter.

"Now listen nicely Jacob," I said managing to stifle my laughter for a minute, "today when we go out fishing I need you to move Mr. Frank's tent to a nice shady place, but it must be very far away from here. Tonight you, I and the hippo need to get some sleep." Jacob found this so funny he was hitting his hands on his knees whilst laughing. "Jacob, it might sound funny, but I'm serious, I don't want to see his tent within one hundred metres of here!"

Jacob replied, "No problem, my Boss, when you come back it will be gone."

"You guys are so full of shit!" said Frank. "I really don't believe it could have been that bad. Just you wait until we go out fishing, if you want to joke about my talent of snoring, wait until you see my talent with the rod in my hand. I'm going to teach you a thing or two about fishing today." He rubbed his hands together and continued saying, "Also I don't see why my tent should be moved far away on its own, what happens if a lion comes visiting me during the night, are you guys going to come and save me?"

"Trust me Frank, there is no creature on earth that would come anywhere near you with the kind of noise you make at night and further more neither Jacob nor I are the problem here."

Eventually, we managed to get the rubber duck onto the water and the little five-horse Yamaha engine fired into life with only four pulls. This, after standing for some four months safely in its tin trunk, was impressive.

Chapter 74

The excitement and anticipation from both of us with each cast was extremely high. When the three spot bream strikes, he does so with vigour. The incredible jerk on the fishing rod followed immediately by line peeling off your screaming reel from the strong run from the fish is indescribable. To the non-angler, this most probably sounds crazy, but I would often jokingly say 'it almost feels better than sex!' and hey at worst it has to be a close second!

By 8am Frank began muttering much better, neither of us had a touch on our rods, it had been completely dead. Although hoping the fish would be on the bite early, I was not surprised; having been there a few times, I half expected this. For some reason the bream only appear to get hungry from 8am onwards. I felt this could be because the sun was not yet bright enough to reflect the spinner to any extent in the water, enticing the fish to eat it, or the water was far too still as at that time of day there is little to no wind. I strongly believed through previous personal experience that fish are more active with wind ripples on the surface of the water.

"Trevor, I appreciate you bringing me fishing and you are 100% correct the place is beautiful. But from what you have told me about the actual fishing your stories were obviously exaggerated somewhat!" The excitement in Frank had waned noticeably and I could understand his anxiety. When I fish, I never stop. From sun up to sun down, I work the water and try everything I know. Drifting down the river for an hour with both of us continually casting in all directions without any luck, it is natural for a keen angler to feel this way.

"Trust me Frank, when they start you will be sorry you never loosened up with a few press-ups this morning. Your arms will be tired by the end of the day with keep nets full of fish." I really believed that this was the best fishing spot I had experienced anywhere. The words had hardly left my mouth when with an almighty bang the line started peeling off my reel. "There you go Frank, what did I tell you, shit this is a really strong fish, just check how my reel is peeling line!" After a good few minutes of tremendous fight, I landed a beautiful bream with the landing net. Frank's mood changed instantly due to witnessing the size of the fish. That look of despair a few minutes ago transformed immediately into excitement and concentration personified.

I slipped the bream into the landing net that Frank had recently purchased and never used. He said it would be a lucky net and insisted we should use it as opposed to my very old faithful lucky net. For ease of access, I always used a partially inflated 10" mini tube around the neck of the net to enable it to float next to us in the water with securing rope attached. I had done the same with this new one of Frank's.

Four casts later I was into another fish and shortly after landing it caught another one. "Hey Frank, have you remembered to fasten a lure onto the end of your line as you appear to be struggling there my mate?" I said sarcastically as the fish pulled line from my reel. I found my little joke funny and laughed with excitement, yet Frank failed to see the humour in it at all.

He responded sounding a touch disgruntled, "Oh you are so funny, just you wait and see when I get going. You have been here before so know the trick about catching these fish."

"Come on, Frank, what is there to learn, we're both sitting two metres apart in the same boat with the same tackle fishing in the same water, either you know how to fish or you don't. You accused me of telling stories, I'm beginning to wonder about all the fish you claim to have caught over the years!" I was having fun and thoroughly enjoying myself as I always did on these fishing trips. We had drifted well away from where I had hooked the first one and the action had stopped completely. I assumed we had drifted over the shoal and were in barren water.

"Frank, please will you pull the net onto the boat whilst I start the engine and go back to my spot." After reeling in and carefully placing his rod down he leaned over and pulled the net in, to our utter amazement it was empty!

"Hell Trevor, I can't believe you could have missed the net with all four of your fish. Here you are catching when I'm not and then to add insult to injury you just let them go again!" he said. "Come to think of it I'm not too sure you haven't been catching the same fish over and over just to make me look stupid."

"Frank, trust me, I never miss when it comes to fish, now let me have a look at this new hi tech quick release keep net you have bought for yourself."

The landing net has a spring-loaded flap on the top and bottom to help remove fish from either end if required. Both flaps are mounted inside and slightly larger than the accompanying hole to ensure a seal. For some reason Frank had probably bought the only one in the world where the flap on the bottom had inadvertently been attached to the outside.

He obviously had not checked this at the time, but there again who would check such an obvious thing. Each fish I dropped into the net obviously swam down, bumped the flap open and took off to tell all its mates how lucky it was. To put into print the language that came from Frank's mouth could not be possible without having the book banned! Had his mother been there she would have forced him to eat a bar of soap a day for a full week to wash his mouth out!

"Okay, so now I see what is going on, you were sure I would catch more than you so to save yourself embarrassment you made sure my fish swim away. Then, if and when you ever catch one you would tie the bottom flap." I was pulling his leg and we both knew it and laughed. We had a great relationship with this kind of banter flowing freely between us constantly.

I powered the boat back up stream into the wind beyond my first strike and once again drifted back with the wind. To the utter astonishment of us both I landed five more bream and then had a barbel take the lure with poor old Frank still fish-less! Counting the ones that I lost in the famous flap-less net our score was ten zero in my favour!

Immediately feeling the change in the strike on my rod, I complained saying, "Shit Frank, I can't believe I have hooked a bloody mermaid." This comment under the circumstances did not go down well with Frank. He totally threw his toys out the cot so to speak.

"You have nailed ten fish and have the cheek to bitch about the last one being a barbel, how the hell do you think I feel. To be honest, I have never and I mean never in my whole life been out fished like this. I'm not sure what you're doing, but Jacob certainly got it right this morning saying I would not catch any fish today. It's like he has put a curse on me or something."

"I believe if you sit up all night and don't go to sleep ensuring you won't snore you could do well tomorrow, the wild life might even start returning to the area!"

I, still fighting the barbel, laughed and told him there was no way Jacob could have put a spell on him. Before I could land my fish Frank's rod almost jerked from his hand with the reel screaming for the first time. This was followed immediately by an even more vocal scream of excitement from Frank. Thereafter and without changing his method of fishing, he began hauling the bream in one for one with me. We had a great weekend and caught enough to keep us in fish fillets for months. I told Frank on the way home he had now qualified to join the Ziz Ziz Ziz club, this being the sound of the drag as the bream take off with your lure. Once again, the Botetle River had not failed us with a great fishing weekend enjoyed by all.

Chapter 75

There were other trips when four of us standing back to back would fish off the tiny craft, in which case extreme care when casting was paramount. With only one up, I could get the boat to plane without a problem. With two or more it progressively became slower and took forever to make our way upwind to the top of the pool. I use the word forever only because we were all so keen to cast our lines into the water. In reality, it would not take much longer than fifteen minutes to get there

Once there, I shut the engine, allowing the wind to drift us slowly back to where we started. With all aboard constantly spinning in all directions, we covered a large area. Once we got into a shoal of fish, we drifted through the spot repeatedly until it went quiet again. Our constant hungry companion the fish eagle followed us flying from tree to tree, as we drifted. Pike are plentiful in these waters and great fish to catch, but being full of bones, not good eating. Once we landed one we pushed a dry reed through the gills and threw it into the water a few metres from the boat. Immediately the magnificent eagle majestically flew down and without ever missing, grasped the hapless fish, then retreated into his tree to enjoy fresh fish for breakfast.

This pattern continued from sun up to sun down and proved to be most productive with up to one hundred and fifty bream caught over the Saturday and Sunday. Some found this to be hard work, we on the other hand relished it, loving every minute out there. My staff, although having to work late into the night, constantly filleting the fish, loved being there. Financially it was a boost for him as I paid him the overtime rate and always gave him at least two large catfish (barbel) to take home to feed his family. If given the choice the Motswana would always opt for the barbel over the bream. Essentially, it is a fresh-water kingklip, with no small bones to worry about and an abundance of meat. One of these catfish was generally equivalent in size to six bream!

On one of these trips, my good friends John Sweet and Frank Hendricks joined me. Although hooking a few bream, the fishing for whatever reason was not as active as normal. A pod of five hippos some three hundred metres away made themselves conspicuous with that unique grunting sound. It sounds like it starts from the tail, works its way through the stomach into the throat and eventually comes out through the huge mouth. Visually of course, their blowing a spray of water in the shape of a fan and spinning their ears like a propeller each time they surfaced was unmistakable.

"Hey guys, I'm sure the fishing will pick up the closer we fish to the hippo. They churn up the bottom and the fish come in to eat the resulting suspended matter." I always believed this theory to be accurate and enjoyed success many times to prove it.

"Well, so long as we don't get too close to them, I don't need to tell you how dangerous they can be and what makes it worse is they have a young one with them!" said John, not at all happy with my idea.

"Come on John, you know us, we don't take unnecessary chances. Not even when trying to get the fish going," said Frank with a smile. John immediately retorted, "Yeah sure! That is exactly why I am bringing it up, trust me I know the two of you too well! The hippo might get the fish biting, but believe me one bite from the hippo and he will swallow the complete boat!"

I assured John not to worry and eased the boat as close to the hippo as I felt was safe. I was encouraged to see there was a section right there where the lily pads had encroached well out into the river. "There you go John, from here we can all keep an eye on the hippo and it's an excellent spot as the fish always hide and feed near these lily pads."

There was little to no wind so decided not to drop anchor. That way we could start the engine and move off immediately in the event our big friends decided to visit. By this stage, John's nervousness had diminished somewhat and more importantly the bream were back on the bite instantly. There were times when all three reels were screaming with the gamely fighting fish. As it was my boat, I felt responsible for the other two so kept a close watch on hippo.

Chapter 76

Frank having executed another pinpoint accurate cast between two lilies started reeling in slowly. We never really found the fool proof speed to retrieve the lure through the water. There were times when fast seemed to be the answer and other times slow to medium worked better. One of the joys of fishing was trying to outsmart the fish. Any angler telling you he succeeded with this would have to be pushing the truth to the limit.

Just as the lure came spinning out of the lily pads into the open water it moved off at a tangent, almost as if being caught on a small floating reed and was pulling Frank's line off to the right. Being an extremely capable angler Frank flicked the rod a few times to pull it away from the obstruction. Instantly his rod gave an almighty jerk and the line pulled down under the boat. Without warning, the water began boiling up around us with unbelievably large swirls and bubbles. In all my years of fishing, I had never seen anything quite like it. I must say with the three of us sitting in such a tiny boat with hippo close by the whole episode felt a touch disconcerting to say the least.

Meanwhile John was pulling frantically on the engine pull rope to get the motor started. "There now, you guys are always far too clever to listen to me. You have hooked a hippo and by the water churning up so violently he has to be seriously mad!" Initially when pulling up at this spot I had inadvertently left the engine in gear when I shut it down. With John, tugging away with all his might on the pull rope the boat was actually moving even though the engine had not fired up.

"Hey John, you are going to have the boat plane just now without even starting the engine," I joked and then clicking the lever back to neutral, the engine burst into life on the next pull. Frank still fighting the unknown quarry on his bream rod shouted to John,

"Calm down, pal, there is no possibility that I could have hooked a hippo with the tiny three pronged Mepps3-spinner, just relax and watch a master at work." Having nothing to do with it, John held the throttle wide-open heading for the safety of the riverbank. Before the bow of the boat had touched ground he leaped off and ran up to a safe distance shouting,

"You guys are out of your minds fishing amongst the hippo like that, I hope you realise the danger you placed our lives in for the sake of catching a few bream!"
Frank still on the boat with rod bent right over and line streaming from his reel as the mysterious quarry headed up stream called to me asking what he should do. I said it had to be a huge barbel and there was no chance of bringing it in so to rather snap the line before losing all of it. This he did by tightening his drag and the line parted with a loud snap.

Whilst Frank sorted out his rod with some more line and another Mepps, John wandered up and down the bank desperately looking for the hippo. One by one, they all popped their heads up out of the water as if nothing had happened and looked as peaceful as they had before the drama started.

"There you go „John," I said continuing, "There is nothing to worry about as Frank's punch up had to have been a large barbel, let's get back there and catch some more fish." It took a fair amount of persuasion, but eventually we had John back on board and fishing in the same spot eager to fill the keep net with bream. John standing at the front of the boat facing the lily pads had just cast in. I could not resist my spontaneous temptation. Tapping Frank on the arm with my finger in front of my mouth for him to be quiet, I carefully lifted the heavy keep net and dropped it into the water with a huge splash.

John in one movement threw his rod towards the bank some three metres away, leaped off the boat into the lily pads, and pushed his way through up onto the bank. Frank and I were rolling around the boat in fits of laughter with tears streaming down our faces. John failed to find the joke even remotely funny and uttered a few choice words, which coming from him was extremely unusual. He also told us clearly that regardless of where or how, he would never go fishing with us again, ever!

"Come on John, hey I'm sorry it just seemed like a good idea, I promise it won't happen again! Now let us get you on board and head back away from your friendly hippo. After dropping this full keep net off with Simon to fillet, we will continue fishing closer to the campsite. Now please, I have apologised so just settle down, we don't need you having a heart attack out here in the middle of nowhere. It would spoil the fishing trip!" John had that look of not knowing if he should laugh or cry.

Just to complete his day's excitement, after dropping the keep net off and loading a new one, he hooked a nice sized pike. As in the case with all others caught, this one was extremely active. It leaped out the water shaking its head repeatedly in a bid to free itself from the hook. Throughout the day, the resident fish eagle had followed us from tree to tree waiting for our offerings to him for allowing us to fish in his waters. This was too much a temptation for him and he swooped down in a flash firmly gripping John's fish in his massive claws as it broke the surface, then turned and immediately flew back to his tree with water streaming from the gyrating fish.

John's line was now peeling off the reel as was Franks some thirty minutes before, but now due to a fish eagle and not a fish/hippo! Incredibly, after settling into the tree, the eagle carefully studied the fish, bent over, with his impressively huge beak pulled the lure from the pike's mouth and dropped it back to the water from the overhanging branch. John was able to retrieve his line including the attached lure.

"There you go, John," I said with a smile on my face. "Surely that makes up for all the drama you have been through. That really was special and together with your earlier excitement with the illusive hippo can you imagine what a great video your eventful day would have made." Frank was in hysterics by this stage and even John, trying not to let it show, had a hint of a smile on his stern face; slowly this changed into a definite smile followed by excited laughter. He seemed to have completely settled down and admitted he just might come with us again, if asked.

Chapter 77

Frank and I had many further memorable trips up there; however, for him these became extremely painful under strange circumstances. Not because he did not enjoy them, it was quite the opposite. I generally informed him of my intentions to go a week before the time assuming all was in order work wise. His uncontrolled excitement of knowing we were going brought on the onset of gout! It was strange that under normal working conditions he would go for months without a problem.

The first time it happened, he mentioned his foot was a little painful before leaving Phikwe, but quickly added that he was quite confident it would be fine by the time we arrived at our destination. Having never experienced the dreaded gout myself, I was only remotely aware of the severely painful effects it produced. I asked him if he was sure, adding that we could always change the weekend to another time. He knew under the extremely hectic schedule we worked it would unlikely happen in the near future. He assured me he would be fine and ultimately we set off arriving late into the night.

By the following morning his right foot looked like a balloon, the skin tone was actually shiny and he was barely able to walk.

"Frank, I told you we could have come another weekend and now look at your foot, we will just have to pack up and head on home. Shame it looks terribly painful!"

"Trevor, if you think we are going to drive six hundred kilometres, camp one night in the bush then turn around and go home without wetting our lines then you have to be crazy!" He said this while trying his utmost not to show the pain in his eyes radiating from his swollen foot. "I'm sure if I keep it as cool as possible it will be fine."

"Frank, you are forever telling me you'll be fine and how do you propose to keep it cool, it is already stinking hot and it's only 6am. Who knows what the temperature is going to be out on the water during the day." I was stunned he could even contemplate going out into that heat with his foot looking like it was about to burst open.

"Yes, I have thought about that and figured if I were to hang my leg over the side of the boat, keeping the silly foot under water all day it would help tremendously. Therefore, if you think we are going home due to my problem you can think again, because I am not going anywhere until tomorrow, regardless. If you want to go, do so, but just leave me here on my own!"

I knew how badly he wanted to stay on and fish, he used to so enjoy these fishing trips I could swear he lost five years in age each time out. I also knew he did not want to be the cause of cancelling our trip, but he was in serious pain.

" Now you are really being silly, Frank, and I believe the only result you'll achieve by hanging your foot in the water all day will be having it bitten off by a croc!"

He burst out laughing saying,

"Come on Trevor, be serious, what croc would want to eat a foot that looks like this, if anything it would most probably scare them way. Even if I agreed to go home now, do you honestly think my foot will feel better? Because if anything it would be more painful knowing I was the cause of neither of us fishing! Let's not waste time talking crap and go fishing!"

Knowing how stubborn he could be, I made him sit on a chair whilst Jacob and I sorted the boat out and carried it down to the water's edge. Eventually with a little effort, I managed to get Frank to hobble down and get into the boat. I then fetched the fishing rods, fishing boxes together with my five-litre Colman's water dispenser. This I filled with iced water to ensure hydration throughout the day's fishing. Lastly, I asked Jacob to have the fire ready for me to cook breakfast by 10am.

After a few pulls on the cord I fired the engine into life and off we went fishing. Frank either was a good actor or was genuinely more comfortable and relaxed with his foot constantly held under the cool water. Never once did he complain of pain, concerned I'm sure, that had he done so I might have taken him back to camp to start packing to leave for home.

As always we had an amazingly successful day catching fish. The abundance of bream and pike in those waters never failed to amaze me. I was also surprised to see at the end of a hard day's fishing Frank's foot was still attached to his leg and hadn't been removed by one of the massive crocs that frequent the waters.

"You were quite correct in saying the crocs wouldn't bother with a foot that looked like that!" I said in a joking manner.

I made it abundantly clear to Frank whilst fishing that we would be packing up and leaving for home first thing the following morning. He started saying that he was okay for one more day's fishing, but I held up my hand telling him it was not negotiable. We had enjoyed a great day's fishing and although he never complained, I knew he was suffering incredible pain.

Confirming my theory of his excitement being the root cause of the gout, the same thing happened on our next trip. Thereafter, when I had decided to take him on a fishing trip to Motopi I would only tell him about it the morning that I was leaving.

On a permanent basis we both kept our fishing rods and tackle, together with all our camping gear and grocery box, ready to load into the car at a moment's notice. So apart from packing a small bag with clothes, buy some meat and drinks, we could leave at short notice.

This worked like a dream as far as his gout was concerned. At no stage thereafter did he have a similar problem. It actually became a private joke between us and we were fortunate in thoroughly enjoying many more trips. This included fishing the Caltex Bass Classic held at Inyankuni Dam some forty minutes drive south-east of Bulawayo in Zimbabwe on a few occasions. He was a great fishing partner and friend who taught me a tremendous amount regarding bass fishing, something he was rated highly for by his peers.

Chapter 78

Chobe National Park, in northern Botswana, boasts one of the largest concentrations of game in Africa. It is the third largest park in the country, after the Central Kalahari Game Reserve and the Gemsbok National Park, and is the most diverse. It is also the country's first national park.

The Chobe River, which flows along the north east border of the park, is a major watering spot, especially in the dry season (May through October) for large breeding herds of elephants, giraffe, zebra, kudu, sable and Cape buffalo.

Birding is also excellent here. Large numbers of carmine bee-eaters are common when in season. When in flood various species of stork, ibis, spoonbills, duck and other waterfowl frequent the area. This is probably the most visited section of park, partly due to its proximity to the Victoria Falls. The town of Kasane, situated just downstream, is the most important town of the region and serves as the northern entrance to the park.

The Serondela area, essentially the Chobe River front, situated in the extreme north east of the park, has as it's main geographical features lush floodplains and dense woodland of teak, mahogany and other hardwoods. Sadly heavy elephant pressure is largely responsible for the reduction in numbers of these amazing woodlands..

Frank and I fished there on many occasions including some big tiger fishing tournaments. On a few of our trips, equipped with our tiny two–man tents we spent the weekend at the Serondela camp site located inside the Chobe National Game Park overlooking the Chobe River. Firstly, it is a wonderful drive into the park of approximately fifteen kilometres along the Chobe River. Secondly, the area is teaming with game, which gives rise to the possibility of sharing the campsite with one or more of the ever-impressive 'big five.' (lion, elephant, leopard, rhino and buffalo)

On two separate trips, we managed to select a weekend that produced the worst thunderstorms of all time, especially noticeable when housed in a tiny and paper-thin material tent. Both storms were at night, the brightness magnified through the material from the lightning was both blinding and to be brutally honest, scary. The feeling of vulnerability was immense with little respite and effectively nowhere to go for safety. With low and saturated cumulous clouds lashing rain down on us mercilessly, coupled with thick bush surrounding our campsite, the sound of the immediately following thunder shook the ground where we lay.

Although shaken, we survived the storms and woke up to a wet, but clear day with bird life in the area devouring flying-ants in their thousands. They also proved to work well as bait for the bream that seemed to enjoy them. I joked with Frank that the only plus with the violent storms was by keeping him awake he never snored once.

On a few occasions when fishing off the bank of the river, although far smaller and certainly nowhere near as dangerous, a large group of banded mongoose honoured us with a visit. They are cute and amazingly bold for such small creatures, proving more than happy, with a little coaxing, to take and eat chips/crisps from our hands. Once just after I'd caught a small bream I offered it to one of these little guys with arm outstretched. Immediately he came up and snatched it from my hand then wandered off a couple of metres from where I sat. The next thing he stretched up as high as he could with fish firmly held wriggling in his mouth, then slammed the hapless bream onto a rock. He duplicated this action a couple of times and once satisfied it was dead commenced devouring it like it was his last meal. Up to that point, I had no idea they even ate fish and always associated them with snakes. For me it was a wonderful interaction with wild animals knowing they could have complete trust in us. This together with warthogs, front legs bent up backwards towards their stomachs, grazing on their knees within metres of where we sat fishing, felt surreal, something that would remain fondly locked in the memory bank.

During the winter months, May to August, in and around the park, as is the case throughout Botswana, becomes extremely dry and desolate. Hence game of all species and size converge on the river for food and water. Viewing game at this time of year in massive herds, free to wander for hundreds of kilometres, is amazing. It is most definitely the high season for tourists visiting the area. This is due to not only the incredible game viewing opportunities, but also the weather. The days are warm, but without the suicidal summer heat and the nights are cool to cold allowing for excellent sleeping conditions. The town of Kasane is not only the northern entrance to the park, but the gateway to Zambia, Namibia and Zimbabwe. Tourists from all over the world flock to the little town at this time.

The Chobe National Park has been considered for inclusion in the five nation Kavango-Zambezi Transfrontier Conservation Area.

The Linyanti River situated to the west of Kasane, but essentially a section of the park, again is well known, particularly in the dry season, with the tourists for enjoying the often unique and incredible experiences of wildlife sightings. For the more adventurous, there are a couple of camping areas with ablution block provided throughout the region. However, for the faint-hearted and uninitiated I feel a warning is required as sharing these amenities with lion, elephant, hyena, wild dog or any other game prevalent in the area at the time is certainly a possibility.

Then there are a few expensive lodges for those who are more comfortable with every luxury available, one that comes to mind is Kings Pool Lodge. It was still in it's infancy at the time and over-looked the picturesque oxbow lagoon on the Linyanti River. Quite magnificently designed and built with wonderful views of the lagoon and as far as location was concerned, would be hard to improve on.

Our company now well known in the water drilling business throughout Botswana, were fortunate in the successful awarding of the contract by management of Kings Pool Lodge to drill for water in their immediate vicinity. Their intention was to pump water into pans that dried up in the winter months, to enable watering the vast herds of game that abound. Mark Sweet was ear marked to run the contract and being the adventurous guy he was, looked forward to the challenge.

The following is Marks story version of events:

Linyanti

Not sure of the year but there was plenty rain, we mobilised to Kings pool with the Super Rock 1000, Mercedes water bowser and the 6x6 Deutz with the XRH350 also loaded with drill rods and casing.

At the Savuti Gate, we met up with Tony from Pony Transport; fortunately, he was taking supplies up to Kings Pool and knew the way in. The rain lashed down endlessly, trying to following the narrow tracks with standing water everywhere and knee high grass was at times challenging in the extreme.

Our 4x4 truck eventually became stuck on the left of a large waterhole; we tried to pull him out but failed. Our only option left was to drive around it with the 6x6 and with some luck pull the 4x4 out. This proved even more disastrous as all we achieved was getting it bogged right down to the chassis on the right of the pool.

We left the trucks there and headed off to Kings Pool Lodge to met Roy Rivers, a retired driller who happened to be the brother in-law of

Fred Keeley who owns the Lodge. He was our contact and responsible for divining the drill sites prior to our arrival.

Our first and most desperately important operation was getting the trucks out of the quagmire, failing which we would be unable to do any drilling. Initially we built mud walls around the trucks and began pumping the water out with centrifugal pumps to enable us to get in there a dig around the differentials and wheels.

Although expecting him, to my horror, whilst busy with this exercise, my boss Uncle Trevor arrived. To say he appeared a touch peeved with the situation doesn't come close. I will never forget the look on his face and sag in his shoulders, however, once the shock had diminished to some extent we all set about getting the trucks un-stuck. We off-loaded all casing, drill rods and equipment in a bid to lessen the weight. Eventually after two days of exhausting, muddy and frustrating work, we managed to remove the trucks from the mud's desperate grasp..

Thereafter having seen a few of the drill sites, Uncle Trevor left for home as there was little he could help with until things dried out. This turned out to be extremely fortunate for him as the following day a dam wall in Zimbabwe burst and the resulting floodwater completely washed a bridge away between Kasane and Nata totally isolating the towns. Waiting for the waters to subside to enable the contractor access to build a temporary bypass took a full three weeks. This caused major disruption in the cartage of goods into North Africa as this was the predominate route used by the transporting Companies, all traffic had to be diverted through Zimbabwe.

As we were unable to mobilise to any of the drill sites due to all the mud, which in places was like quick sand. Nor due to the bridge, were we able to go home until things dried up. Therefore, as we were trapped there, where possible, we spent this time productively using the 6x6 to assist the lodge still in the process of building, move materials around where required. Even the front-end loader succumbed to the bottomless mud.

After a few days, we managed with some difficulty, to get to the first drill site not far from the camp. We completed this hole at +- 35m cased, screened, gravel packed and v-notch tested the yields that were excellent with sweet water. It was a further two weeks before we could move to the chosen sites Uncle Roy had marked out. The primary objective for the drilling project was to source a reliable water supply for the fly camps and scattered drinking holes for the animals over the dry months. Water required for our drilling foam tanks was readily available with every depression in the area filled with water. Using the Honda centrifugal pumps utilized for the trucks that were stuck and strainer attached to the suction we pumped directly to the water bowser tanks. Holes were between 33m-45m in depth, sandy over burden and clay layers being the general formation drilled. We broke camp and moved everything to the new site on the longer rig moves between holes. The long grass full of seed caused havoc with blocking the radiators causing over-heating problems and required constant cleaning from the core. However, as with many things in life there is always a plus factor when working in the bush. On this particular occasion, the beautiful carmine bee-eaters flew next to the vehicles, expertly plucking insects from the air as they were flushed from the grass.

The Savuti Channel, well known for the amazing game that abound including, but not restricted to large herds of elephants with newborn calves that miraculously disappear in the long grass, wild dogs, giraffe and lions galore. Sadly, on the one day, we just missed a pride of lions take down a giraffe; they had ambushed it on an embankment with what had to be amazing teamwork. Seeing the result the following day with fourteen lion, bellies full, lazing around the carcass was a remarkable sight.

On a separate evening on the way back from site driving along the river, I was surprised with loud banging on the side of the bakkie and the guys in the back shouting, "go, go, go." Unbeknown to me, a mother hippo having been grazing on the bank was enraged having been separated from her baby in the water by our vehicle, chased the Hilux at full speed! Often I wonder what she would have done with it and us had she caught it!

One of the funniest experiences that come to mind, also returning to camp one evening in the dark, as always, the back of my vehicle filled with my staff, we passed a pride of lion. Shortly thereafter, an unbelievably large python crossing the track forced me to stop dead in my tracks. So large was the python that Uncle Roy got out, having a good look because it was as thick as a 6" casing and longer than the track was wide! Instantly the back of the bakkie emptied with my guys running away back toward the lion! It took some coaxing to get Molete the drill-rig operator and crew to return, I asked if they were not scared of the lions and they said the lions weren't the problem but the snake most certainly was!

Overall, it took approximately six weeks to complete the six holes. Funnily enough the most difficult and time-consuming operation was getting the equipment from A to B. Uncle Trevor's son, Darrin came up on completion of the contract to help me demobilize. More rain fell on our way out and as always, the two of us had many a good laugh and lots of fun when being together, seventeen years later this relationship has not changed!

Chapter 79

I lived for sport in one discipline or another, thanks to the grounding and encouragement stemming from my upbringing in Zimbabwe. Although Phikwe is a small town we were well looked after in this regard. The BCL Mine owned Makubu Sports Club and was well suited to all tastes. I had played a lot of cricket in Messina prior to moving up to Botswana and especially enjoyed opening the bowling for the small club.

On moving back to Phikwe, I was thrilled when the cricket season opened. During the following years I played regularly and enjoyed every moment of it, once again opening the bowling for the club.

Norbert Webster was a prime mover in the history and development of the cricket club. I honestly believe without his valuable input, possibly cricket might not have continued successfully year after year as it has done. He would selflessly give up weekend after weekend building and improving the facilities. To add to this he was a fine cricketer in his own right with both bat and ball, and an invaluable team member.

We played on a regular basis throughout the season with matches against our main rivals Serowe and Francistown. Both small towns producing fine players, although very competitive on the field, the matches were played in a wonderful spirit.

The cricket club held wild parties on the Saturday night after the first day's play. Braai fires were always on the go with lots of ice-cold beer available to wash the food down. As a non-drinker it never failed to amaze me as to just how many people could consume so much liquid and yet were able to remain in a vertical position!

Music played continuously with people dancing wherever they chose, some inside the clubhouse others on the veranda and even on the cricket field. Allowed to let your hair down, it was a fun weekend shared with special people and a perfect means of de-stressing yourself and others from the week's hard work. Sport of any kind is important. Stress is a killer, something I learned the hard way many years later.

There was a badminton court housed in the main hall of the club. More often than not, we played mixed badminton. This proved popular being well supported on Wednesday and Friday evenings, the scheduled nights of play. We played late into the night constantly mixing players by drawing partners from a bag. I would say the standard of play generally was reasonably good, resulting in close and hard fought matches. I can remember how hot it would be in the hall. The sweat freely ran from every pore in your skin leaving you soaking wet at the end of each game. This never proved to be a deterrent as the regulars would pitch up week after week. What the heat most certainly did help with, however, were bar sales.

Directly across from the main clubhouse were the two squash courts. They were basic, but functional, with lights and a raised platform behind the courts with seating for spectators and officials in tournament play. A small well-stocked pub constructed to the side of the courts on the ground floor proved popular with a great atmosphere.

At the end of the day, it can become easy to find a pub and temporally drink your problems away. I and many others felt the better option was play sport first then enjoy a few cold ones. Due to the incredible heat in the summer, playing squash was more popular in the winter making the number of players fluctuate during the year. In general, the club was highly successful for a small town and produced some of Botswana's top players. When not out in the bush on the drill rigs I would play as often as possible, many times up to three days a week. I was never one of the top players, but gave all I had and thoroughly enjoyed every minute. I found the exercise wonderful and it certainly helped to keep me fit, not to mention the special camaraderie that existed.

Chapter 80

Through all my years of bodily wear and tear, especially from racing off-road motor bikes, I eventually developed problems in my left shoulder. I had all sorts of tests followed by cortisone injections yet nothing helped. The pain was excruciating at times and affected me in work and sport, both equally important to me. Eventually in 1988, I had no option but to have what would be my first operation ever.

Being in hospital for the first time, I had no idea of what to expect or what was required of me when coming around from the effects of the anaesthetics. This being the case, as I started coming around I found myself desperately needing the toilet as I was bursting. Without a thought of any possible consequences through my actions, I climbed out of bed.

I felt a little tug in my left shoulder, but thought nothing of it as I drunkenly staggered off on my way to the loo. I thought to myself at the time that if people drink alcohol to make themselves feel this way, I most certainly do not intend to change my non-drinker views in this regard. I felt truly awful. On my return to the bed the sister was waiting for me, even through my blurry vision I could clearly see I was in trouble by the stern look on her face.

"What on earth do you think you are doing, just look at this mess!" I was shocked to see blood all over the sheet and pillow where my left shoulder had been. I also then noticed I had blood covering my shoulder on those funny little back to front gowns they give you to wear.

"Hell I'm sorry, but I had nothing to do with bandaging the shoulder up, surely that has to be done properly by you guys. All I did was lay there fast asleep from the anaesthetic." I could not understand her problem as I was the one covered in blood not her!

"Where have you just been to and who gave you permission to get out of bed?" Her face extremely flushed confirmed her agitation through my actions. With all the commotion, I now had an attentive audience. Breaking their boredom, the other five people in the ward

301

were most intrigued with my little fiasco and eager to discover the outcome.

"Once again I'm sorry, but firstly there was nobody here in the ward to ask for permission, secondly, and more importantly, I desperately needed to go to the loo, so I still fail to see the problem."

"Your being such a clever boy and having total disregard for regulations by climbing out of bed have caused major problems. You have pulled out the drain pipe so painstakingly inserted to drain the excess blood from the wound!" Honestly not knowing it was forbidden to climb out of bed, I could not think of an immediate response.

The nursing sister certainly was not particularly cute looking I might add and a touch overweight, stood there glaring at me almost supporting an evil look in her eyes. Anxiously waiting for my reply were our audience of five who were thoroughly enjoying our little spectacle.

"Hey, once again I'm sorry and if necessary I'll buy you a box of chocolates to make it up to you. Surely, you can just push it back in again. The linen and my gown could be sent to the laundry and we'll all be back to normal?" Our audience burst out laughing which eased the situation to some extent and I felt sure even the sister wanted to smile, but didn't!

Sounding a little less agitated, she informed me it would involve my going back into surgery to have it re-inserted. She was going to discuss it with the doctor and come back to me; the final decision being to take a chance and leave as is. Three weeks later with excruciating pain in that shoulder, I was back in hospital for a second attempt by the surgeon to hopefully sort the problem out the second time around. I never did find out why the first one was a failure, but was told had nothing to do with the drain, which I ensured remained in my shoulder until removed by the nursing staff. However, as we are all aware doctors are never wrong. Nonetheless, I would have to endure a further six weeks with my arm in a sling, resulting in no sport for that period and possibly even longer!

I had played a lot of cricket with a guy by the name of Ray Mascarenhas, a Sri Lankan and nice cricketer who had lived in Africa for some time. He excelled and without doubt became the top lawn bowler in the country. Knowing my passion for playing sport, he approached me one day.

"Trevor, playing as much sport as you do and seeing you only have one arm of any use I think you should come down and learn how to play bowls."

"Ray, I think you can come and ask me that in ten years time, I'm nowhere near old enough to play 'old man's marbles'!" I said having never even considered playing the sport.

"Yes, everyone thinks that and yet once you start you'll be sorry you never started ten years earlier! Do yourself a favour and come down on Monday night just for fun and see where you go from there."

That was in 1988 and I started what was to become a long career in bowls. I discovered, as many others have, Ray was right in that I felt I should have started many years earlier. It became a passion and a wonderful way out, when eventually giving up golf due to the never-ending back problems. Some twenty-five years later, I am still thoroughly enjoying both social and competitive bowls up to provincial level and plan to do so for many more years.

I have played every sport there is and in most cases at high level and find the game of bowls a good rival to any of them. It has proved to be a game successfully played either socially or highly competitively at any level, anywhere and by anyone regardless of age or gender.

It also has to be right up there at the top of the list as one of the cheapest sports played anywhere in the world. Annual club fees are in most cases extremely low and green fees next to nothing when compared to golf for instance. The other plus is never will you lose one of your bowls during a game unlike golf! Essentially a set of bowls, as is the case with a parrot, will outlive the owner. They simply do not wear out, yes, when playing provincial or higher level there is a restriction of a ten-year size and bias test being required. The club bowler, however, need not worry and can play with the same old set for life.

I, as many other 'younger players', have had the privilege of playing with people well into their eighties. To me it is wonderful that someone so well advanced in age can still play a competitive sport and play it well. I often wonder if I will even make it to that age before moving on to wherever that might be when life stops, yet alone be fit enough to play good bowls.

The other huge advantage to the game is that visiting players to any club generally receive such a wonderful warm welcome that you almost feel like a member by teatime. Sadly, this is not always the case in many other sports. Also, unique to the game of bowls, a rank novice can play against or with a top bowler and both players can thoroughly enjoy their game. On the day, a talented new bowler could quite possibly cause an upset by beating an experienced bowler. It has happened before and will happen many more times in the future.

It is one of the few recreational sports where men can play against women competitively, in my eyes neither have the advantage. Possibly the male is more aggressive, but in general the women draw better than the men. I have always advocated that in mixed singles the reason a lot of men shy away from entering is the fear of losing to a woman!

Bowls is an extremely easy game to play in that all that is required of you is the capability of rolling your bowl from one side of the green to the other. Conversely it is also an incredibly difficult game to master and to be honest a game you never stop learning. There are the intricacies of building the head, what calls you should make to your players and why, when to be aggressive or conservative, how to conduct yourself etiquette wise. Knowing the rules intimately is imperative and can help your game. Likewise, constantly practising the many varied shots available to a player and learning when to play them. The list goes on and on and with experience and knowledge of the above the game steadily becomes more enjoyable.

Chapter 81

Bowls is predominantly a team sport and each player is equally important in his or her individual contribution to the success of the team. So often I hear players discussing promotion to a second or third and so on. Yes, with experience and after learning how to play the many different shots, reading the head etcetera, gradually you move up the ladder, so to speak. Eventually with practice, potentially you could make the back rank, however that does not necessarily indicate you are a better player than the rest of the team members.

I honestly believe a new player just starting out should play as a second and not be thrown into the deep end at lead. For a complete novice the pressures on them rolling the jack and setting up the end having to play the opening bowl are enormous and can possibly chase a potential new member away from the game.

How often have we bowlers heard the joke of a player hidden away as the second? In many cases this is true due to the aforementioned. However, I must stress the second, third and skip are equally important in their roll of building the head and ultimately contributing to the team on each end. We are all human and where one fails hopefully one or more of the remaining team members can cover for him or her.

Nine out of ten top skips when selecting players for their team will look to fill the position of lead first. A professional lead is such an asset and worth his weight in gold. A lead has the opportunity of placing immediate pressure on the opposition after delivering only two bowls. I know of a few top players who have played for many years and are capable of playing extremely well in any position, but have no desire other than to play lead. These are the players known as professional leads and highly sought after.

The game has many formats as in fours (two bowls per player), trips (three bowls per player) and pairs (four bowls per player, as is the case in singles). Even this is not a hard and fast rule in that the trips, pairs and singles can and are from time to time played in the two-bowl format. I personally enjoy the latter as there is far more pressure and skill required knowing you only have the two bowls that must count.

Strangely enough when I started playing the game back in 1988 I kept asking Ray the question as to why I had to buy a set of four bowls, as we always played fours (rinks) and only used two? He rightfully informed me that once I had played for a few years I would appreciate the skills required in the two-bowl format. Often that particular conversation comes to mind and I would like to thank Ray for his time and tutoring over the years whilst I was in Botswana. I had the pleasure of playing third for him when winning the Botswana Nationals on two occasions.

If there was ever a sport where one hundred percent focus to play the game successfully is required, it has to be the game of bowls. When one or more of the players in a team are really struggling and tell you they are trying their best, certainly, this may well be the case. Yet, tension generated through this is transferred to the muscles making them tense and jittery as opposed to smooth flowing when actually delivering. I always believe to perform at your highest level, stop trying and instead relax, focus and concentrate on the delivery and not the result and by doing this the desired result will be there far more often.

Another major and common, and to be honest natural, fault being players are so afraid of playing a bad shot for their team and/or skip. This is the worst thing to think about as it distracts your focus on what actually gets that bowl close to the elusive jack, being the delivery.

Likewise how often do you hear from a skip, 'Oh you can't play this hand as this bowl behind is an opposition bowl.' Firstly, if you were to play a little heavy and pick the jack up you would follow it to some degree. Secondly, playing the same weight and just missing the jack instantly gives you great cover with the offending bowl. Thirdly, you should not give the opposition's bowl a thought as you are supposed to be focussing on drawing to the jack! Often this negative call from the skip results in the player's bowl finishing two or more metres short for fear of moving the jack!

Negatives in any sport, or in life for that matter, need controlling by turning them into positives! If for example as skip, you call your player to draw to the jack on the backhand, do just that, call the shot only. Don't kill their confidence and direction of focus away from what you have asked him or her to do.

By this I mean don't walk into the head telling the player not to hit this bowl or that bowl or move the jack and so on. You, as skip should know the possible dangers in the head together with the quality of your players, so just call for the shot you require. The chance of your player pulling the shot off by concentrating on the delivery rather than endless instruction as to what not do would be far greater! Any good skip would concentrate and take note of each bowl played from all the players including the opposition. Mentally, he should take note of where each bowl finishes. Where are the dangers? Should I call for a cover shot in case the jack is trailed? Always try to out think the opposition skip, what shot will he most likely call for from his player, then work out a strategy to counteract his thinking. Try building the head to allow you, as skip, to have the best chance of contributing to or saving the end.

Assuming you train your mind to at all times read heads in this manner, your chances are greatly increased of maintaining full concentration and focus on your up-coming delivery. You know, or certainly should do, where the important bowls are in the head so visualize your shot and play it with a positive mind. Do not leave the head, get to the mat to play and then start asking questions of your third as to whose bowls are where! You as skip having just come from there should know exactly what is going on! Asking questions breaks your focus and often results in a poor shot, regularly finishing short and narrow. I am sure there are bowlers reading this who are dubious of this statement. All I can suggest is please in the future take note of where the bowl finishes after excessive chatter between skip and third.

As I stated earlier, 100% focus is required for the few seconds it takes to deliver the bowl. Is my grip correct? Are my feet aligned with the direction I want to bowl? I must have a controlled back swing, not too fast, as my delivery will start before the backswing is complete resulting in loss of rhythm and poor shot. I must follow through on line and not pull across my body. Most importantly stay down in your follow through position for a minimum of three seconds.

Chapter 82

The Phikwe golf course was approximately two kilometres out of town and set out amongst large granite koppies. Had there been money for permanent water reticulation, it would undoubtedly have been the top course in Botswana, the actual layout and design was great.

It was a challenging eighteen hole course with a par 72 layout. The back nine in particular is exceptionally interesting with the koppies coming into play on the twelfth, thirteenth and fifteenth. The twelfth and thirteenth both being tight dog legs to the left giving you the option of hitting five iron to the right of the koppies followed by a seven iron to the green, but the more popular option by the bigger hitters being a three wood over the top with a flick wedge to the green. Hitting the perfect tee shot on the risk and reward line almost guaranteed a birdie, getting it wrong could easily result in disaster.

As with the other sports' facilities available golf proved to be popular. The greens were made of oiled sand whereby a steel scraper was necessary for each hole. Effectively to mark your ball on the green, a line was scribed approximately one metre wide through the position of where it finished on approach and parallel to the hole. The scraper then came into play. Placed just beyond your line and pulled through to a minimum of one-metre beyond the hole, performed either by one of the caddies or yourself. Some players insisted they scraped for themselves saying it helped them feel the consistency of the sand. I personally took note of the build up of sand in front of the scraper as my caddy scraped for me. Either way you were left with a one-metre wide smooth line to the hole.

The men's and ladies tee boxes were similarly constructed, but with oiled soil as opposed to sand allowing compaction in an attempt to give a solid footing when swinging the club. Rocks cemented together built the outer wall in a 3 x 3 metre configuration approximately 40cm in height. Dark compacted soil filled the inside and to complete what became an attractive feature throughout the course, the rocks were whitewashed.

Many of the local contractors clubbed in to help with the construction of both the clubhouse and golf course. Without a doubt sitting right at the top of the list were C&H Builders owned by Mike Hare and Tony O'Connor. The money, effort and equipment selflessly put into the project by them are legendary.

They also sponsored what had to be one of the most popular golf tournaments in Botswana, the C&H trophy. It was unique in that booze was available throughout the course, starting with a mandatory glass, or six if so desired, of a mixture of 80% champagne and 20% orange juice on checking in.

'The Dew Drop Inn' a small and much frequented structure was constructed in a central position on the course. It was well situated and accessed on completion of the 7th hole on the front nine and basically half way up the par 5, 16th hole. Within the structure on the day of the tournament would be four large plastic bathtubs filled with ice-cold booze of every make.

A volunteer, or two, was always on hand as barman and drinks flowed freely. The barman asked you to produce a doctor's certificate if ordering a soft drink, letting your hair down and drinking as much booze as possible being the theme of the day. Both of Irish descent Mike and Tony encouraged participants to wear green as the dress theme for the prestigious event.

Coming through the Dew Drop, ensuring the thirst had been quenched, then onto the clubhouse for more drinks after nine holes, vision became blurred to some extent. Moving on to the second nine and eventually arriving back at the Dew Drop on the 16th, certain bodily functions were no longer operating normally. In many cases, clearly the legs of players were no longer connected to the brain. They seemed to be on a mission of their own wobbling around all over the place. Also obviously noticeable vocal octaves increased by 75% to 100%! It was extremely festive, always fun and there were never any issues. The dress theme being green was one thing, however, when the facial skin pigmentation on some passed from a reddish tinge to green, it generally meant enough was enough!

Each cubby of players leaving the 'Dew Drop Inn' the second time around to complete the last few holes were never sure of making it home. On a few occasions, a player executing a shot from a bunker promptly passed out cold where he stood. Often remaining motionless until someone revived him with cold water and transported him back to the clubhouse.

The late Jimmy Patterson most certainly comes to mind. A character of note, loved by all, he played a huge role in the Phikwe community in many respects. He was the Managing Director of Nata Quarries and always more than willing to help with his machinery when required.

On one occasion, he staggered his way out of the clubhouse in a completely inebriated state saying good-bye to all after the C&H competition. After continuing the party for a further hour, a few of us also left. We were surprised to find poor old Jimmy laying passed out in the gravelled car park before reaching his car.

We managed to get him back onto his feet offering to take him home. He would have no part in this and insisted he drove himself. Not happy with this, but knowing firstly how stubborn Jimmy could be, and to be honest not feeling much better ourselves, we loaded him into the driver's seat.

He fired the engine into life, pulled his door closed, then with a couple of grating sounds as he crunched first gear into place wound his way to the exit gate. Here he attempted to turn left to head off home, but not taking into account he had not fully closed his door. As he turned left, his weight shifted to the right pushing the door open. Almost as if in slow motion, he rolled out of the car like a sack of maize onto the road and once again lay motionless. The car continued on its merry way ultimately finishing nose first into the ditch and stalled.

We ran over and once again managed to get him to his feet and drove him home, this time not giving him the option of driving, especially seeing his car would have to sleep in the ditch for the night.

Chapter 83

Initially, playing golf in Phikwe was challenging for me. Firstly, I had not played for many years so long hours of hard practice were required in a bid to find my golf swing again. Secondly, learning to play on sand greens and using a little mat to play your ball from off the fairway due to there being little to no grass felt different.

Through sheer determination, I managed to get myself back down to a three handicap. I played on a regular basis and was fortunate in winning the club championships on a few occasions.

A couple of highlights stand out, but without a doubt, there is one far above the rest. In 1992, Dion my youngest and I had the unique honour of our both making selection to represent Botswana in the zone-six golf tournament. It meant a huge amount to me and I was extremely proud walking down the fairways side by side with my son in National colours. A special moment in life that is ingrained for all time in my memory bank.

Something else we achieved together, but at different times, are course records. Playing off a three handicap in our monthly medal stroke-play competition in March 1996 was quite interesting. Dion had completed his round and was standing on the eighteenth green waiting for me to come in as he often did. I was sure he would have checked our scores on the front nine. I made a mess of the two relatively easy par 5's making six on both to turn in 37. On the back nine, every shot I hit turned to gold. I had played my second shot onto the green on the par 4 eighteenth some three metres short of the hole. We were the last to come in and when walking onto the green I asked him how he had played.

"Well, unless you guys have done something special, I have won as had a really good day and shot a 74 gross giving me a nett 67!"

"Well done my boy, that's a great round, but I don't think it will be good enough as I need to hole this putt for a 67," I said as casually as possible.

"Wow Dad, you must have had a really good back nine to shoot 33! Good luck with the putt and if you manage to hole it we will have to play-off which could be fun."

"Well you see that's the thing, what I'm saying is if I hole this putt, it will give me my sixth birdie for the nine and a gross 67!" He looked at me in total disbelief; it was unheard of to shoot 30 on the back nine or any nine for that matter. Fortunately, the ball found the bottom of the cup setting a new course record beating the previous one by a clear four shots! He immediately came running onto the green to shake my hand and congratulate me. It was a very special moment in my life, especially having Dion there to watch me hole that last putt.

Many years later in 2009, Dion was playing exceptionally good golf at the time, to the extent I honestly believed had he turned pro he could have made a good living out of it. He was playing off scratch and considering he was playing weekends only, due to his heavy work schedule through the week running his construction company, was quite a feat on its own.

I was living in South Africa and he had phoned to say if he could enter one more card of 71 gross or better he would be cut to a plus one handicap. Well, the following week, playing the Monthly Medal on the Francistown course he also shot 67! If there was ever an ultra proud father that was how I felt and more. To my knowledge, neither record was broken at the time of writing the book in 2013!

Chapter 84

Needing a few things for my rigs out at the Golden Eagle Mine I pulled into Haskins, a major hardware store in Francistown, on my way through. I never considered going anywhere else as they were well organised, extremely well equipped and always managed to supply my needs. Due to my many visits to the shop, I had befriended Vic Walsingham, a major shareholder and managing director of the company.

"Hi Trevor, where are you heading off to today?" He continued before I could answer. "I'm pleased you have come in as I'd like to talk to you about something."

"Hi Vic, I'm good thanks and how are you keeping? I assume still busy making your millions?" I replied.

He burst out laughing and said, "Busy yes, but as to making my millions, you have to be joking, anyway come and have a cup of coffee in the office and we can talk."

"Okay, thanks Vic, let me just organise the things I have on my list whilst you boil the kettle, I'm in a rush to get out to site."

"Hell Trevor, you are always in such a rush, you must learn to relax a little or one of these days you'll give yourself a heart-attack."

"Yes sure Vic, like you don't stress over your business?" I said laughing as I walked off into the store to sort out my requirements.

Over our cup of coffee, he said he had some exciting news for me.

"Trevor, you have always been the first to try anything with setting up motocross racing and so on. Well, I have found something you will really enjoy!" He paused to take a sip of his coffee and then said, "Windsurfing," and sat looking at me for my response.

"Vic, I don't have the faintest clue about windsurfing, who on earth up here in Botswana can teach us how to do it?"

"Well you see that's where I come in. I have bought a windsurfer and had a great time out at Shashe Dam over the weekend." Taking another sip, he continued. "I thought of you immediately being sure you would really enjoy it."

That conversation started a new chapter in my life. We had booked a holiday to Mauritius that December. One of the activities advertised on the hotel brochure was windsurfing and so I wanted to learn to master the sport before going there.

On my next trip to Johannesburg, I purchased a complete set-up at a windsurfing shop. I was excited about the new activity and the first weekend back we loaded up and drove through to Shashe Dam some one hundred and twenty kilometres away.

I was fortunate in that I had a natural talent for most sports and was bubbling with confidence and enthusiasm. Clearly, I imagined myself flying through the water with wind blowing through my hair and a spray of water coming off the board keeping me cool. I was going to be able to sail all over the dam on free wind power as opposed to fuel sapping engine power on a motor boat. Once I had the hang of it, I would teach the rest of my family. This to me was exciting; at last, I had found a sport the whole family could participate in together.

Well, what a disaster that turned out to be! I spent the whole day falling off, climbing back on, lifting the sail out the water and in no time was back in the water with a splash. It was frustrating beyond words not to mention the physical effort exerted with absolutely no progress whatsoever! Each time after lifting the mast I tried to set myself up convinced I had it right and was about to sail off into the sunset. Somehow, the wind always managed to come in behind the sail resulting in another embarrassing swim. I was making no headway whatsoever. Although that is not quite true, as each time, and believe me there were many, that I pulled the sail from the water in an attempt to sail off I went sideways a few metres.

In my desperate bid not to look to stupid in front of my whole family, I stubbornly continued my vain effort repeatedly. The only result and advancement achieved was finishing some two-hundred metres downwind of where I had started. It was an extremely hot day so by my continually falling into the water my outer body kept cool, inside I was burning up in frustration and embarrassment.

At this stage, saying I was tired does not come close to how I felt, completely buggered would be more accurate! My forearms were cramping badly and my lower back was stiff and sore. Far worse than the physical pain, my ego and embarrassment at total failure reached an all time high. I had not given a thought to not being able to windsurf. I have always been confident of achieving anything, especially in sport, as far as I was concerned, I would hop on and sail off.

I had been so excited about coming through that day to have a full go at this new sport. Yet here I had to admit to complete and utter failure! Sheepishly I laid the mast and sail on top of the board, and slowly trudged my way back through the water pulling the board behind me. Waiting for me on the shore were Les and the boys doing their best not to burst out laughing! Clearly, I could see the warranted amused look on their faces by my vain and pathetic attempts at windsurfing.

"So you guys think it is funny? I must be honest standing on solid ground watching my comedian show must have been quite amusing!" I conceded, pulling the offending object onto the bank then continued by saying, "Well I think there is something wrong with this board. Each time I get the sail up and pull it in to get going the board swings its nose into the wind and instantly sends me back into the water again!" Les and the boys gave me their *'Yea sure Dad'* look on their faces. They then suggested seeing that my windsurfing performance was abysmal I should rather look into making a fire so that we could have a braai. Between little sniggers, they added they felt I was far more capable of getting that right than I probably ever would be at windsurfing.

Prior to the trip, I had tried to phone my good friend Vic to ask if he would be at the dam to teach us that weekend. However, we had problems with phone lines down so was unable to contact him. Ultimately Les, the boys and I were the only people there and with a huge expanse of water, a new windsurfer and not a clue how to sail the thing. I say thing, because right there and then in frustration felt like lighting the braai fire using the board as kindling. My family found it terribly amusing when I asked if any of them wanted to try.

"You are always able to do new things instantly yet you spent more time falling into the water than standing on the board and you expect us to try, you have got to be joking!" said Les.

Two weeks later, we left on our holiday to Mauritius with my windsurfing skills, or lack thereof, unchanged. On our first morning at the beautiful La Morne Lebrante Hotel, I was fortunate in that a couple were going through a coaching class on windsurfing on the lawn.

Obviously, this sounds strange, as it is a water sport; however I was impressed with the setup. They had attached a cut and shortened board to a swivel fixed to the ground. This enabled tourists to learn the art of windsurfing safely on land and not in the water, alleviating the problem of people blown away into the sea as I experienced at the dam!

I wandered over in the hope of picking up a few tips. I honestly felt having totally embarrassed myself making such a hash of my first attempt to windsurf at Shashe Dam, it just had to be complicated and extremely difficult.

Standing there listening to the instructor I was intrigued at how easy it sounded. He stressed how important the initial movement of the mast was when trying to get going for the first time. Immediately tilting the mast forward towards the front of the board was imperative. Effectively this moves the bow off the wind allowing wind to fill the sail as you pull the end of the wishbone towards you. Also important, keeping your front leg as stiff as possible gave you leverage to help pull against, saving an embarrassing swim when the sail overpowers you. Basically, the further you moved the sail forward the more you turned off the wind and vice-versa thus giving you controlled steering.

Having already changed into my swimming costume I wandered straight off to find one of the hotel supplied windsurfers. We had paid for an all-inclusive holiday with the hotel group. This included dinner, bed and breakfast and free use of all water sports equipment available.

The Mauritian guy in charge of the equipment had me sign for a complete setup and was most helpful in setting up the sail ready for me to make a second attempt at embarrassing myself, only this time it would not only be in front of my family, but everyone on the crowded beach.

Apprehensive, but also excited as I now had some idea as what to do, I pulled the board into the water. Once deep enough to ensure the fin was clear of possible obstructions, I climbed on and heaved the sail out of the water. Holding the front of the wishbone with my left hand, I tilted the mast forward, stiffened my left leg and ready to lean back pulled on the double-sided wishbone.

Instantly, I felt pressure on the sail, I leaned back a little, bent my back leg a bit more and sailed off out towards the reef. My family and I were amazed how effortlessly and smoothly I set off, it really was incredibly easy. What had made all the difference was tilting the sail forward immediately. Undoubtedly, this was the single biggest contributing factor for my embarrassing attempts at windsurfing in front of my family at the Shashe dam. I feel sure many others struggled when first trying it without some tuition.

By the afternoon on our first day, I had Les and the boys sailing as well. It most certainly added a new dimension to our holiday. Together with the golf, fishing and snorkelling we all had a wonderful time. On days when the wind speeds picked up, I sailed on my own right across the bay and back. It was exhilarating with the board skimming over the water with the reef clearly visible flashing by below me.

Mirroring flying fish are common in these waters and helped make my long ride so enjoyable. Having the honour of this beautiful fish accompany me all the way there and back, popping out of the water every so often was something to behold. Effortlessly, the fish floated through the air, almost as if in flight within a metre from the board. It was a special place to holiday.

We continued sailing for many years after that, mostly at Shashe Dam where wonderful weekends were thoroughly enjoyed camping out in our little tents with family and friends. Glynn and Sue Morris with their beautiful little girl, Melanie, always come to mind as they sailed at least three weekends a month. We became good friends.

Due to the interest shown Shashe Sailing Club was formed. The venue became popular for not only recreation and competitive regattas, with participants from Gaborone and Zimbabwe, but for the parties held in the little clubhouse. The atmosphere was always good and when considering we lived in a country covered in Kalahari Desert sands, given the opportunity to sail felt unique.

The famous Orapa Diamond Mine, the third largest in the world, was located two-hundred and forty kilometres west of Francistown, directly out into the desert. At that time, the Boteti River enjoyed strong in-flow from the mighty Okavango Delta and ran at varying degrees all year round. A dam wall built on the western side of the Mopipi pan for water storage proved successful. The Mopipi Dam had become a reality and replenished through constant pumping from the river with large centrifugal pumps.

A few keen sailors working at the mine formed a sailing club at the dam. On a couple of occasions, we drove through to sail with them in their arranged regattas. The total extent of the dam was possibly less than half the size of Shashe Dam. However, with constant prevailing desert winds blowing from an easterly direction it became a popular sailing venue. The camaraderie, fellowship, braaing and drinking experienced at these events was special making the long trip worthwhile for all.

Unfortunately, over the years the river dried up completely and what was once a beautiful little dam and essential water source for thousands of zebra, wildebeest and many other species of game turned into a dry pan with occasional water in the rainy season. It is so dry today that a first time visitor to the area would find it hard to comprehend there was ever a dam there, yet alone a sailing club!

Chapter 85

Having the Cessna 210 aircraft proved, over the years to be a wonderful acquisition for the efficient and speedy control of our company contracts spread everywhere. Also whenever possible, we flew clients and family into the Okavango Delta to an amazingly beautiful and popular camp named Guma Lagoon. It is located well into the north western side of the swamps. This helps make the flight there an unforgettable experience with amazing views of game and endless lagoons.

My primary objective for going there was to catch fish, not only for the bream that are plentiful in the lagoon, but also in the main channel for both bream and tiger fish. To the uninitiated in the swamps, the boat trip from the lagoon to the main channel is something quite unique. Once the boat exits the lagoon into the narrow hippo channel, lined with long papyrus grass, there is non-stop entertainment for what is generally a thirty minute trip. Seldom are there sections wide enough for two boats to pass each other. This certainly keeps the boat pilot on his toes, as there are a never-ending series of blind tight-turns, with the possibility of meeting another boat travelling in the opposite direction. One minute the sun is in front of you and the next minute it is behind you, and so this continues the whole trip. I used to joke with the crew asking if the sun was rising or setting as it appeared seemingly in the east then the west and back to the east. You have the feeling of going through a tunnel with zero depth of vision due to the wall on either side of the impenetrable papyrus grass.

Every so often, you break out of the papyrus into small lagoons that appear large in comparison to what you have just come through. Generally, they are lined with the most beautiful trees, often used as perches by the fish eagle that abound, ready to swoop down for any offering of a fish meal. Approximately half way between the lagoon and mainstream happens to be one of these small lagoons and we named it hippo corner. I have been up and down the channel many times and seldom have we not encountered hippo there. They are not only huge animals, but grow considerably in size, when meeting them in these tiny lagoons hardly big enough for both them and the boat.

We certainly had many narrow escapes at that particular location and to add to the excitement the resident large crocodile regularly sunned himself on the bank only meters from the boats passage through, this gave the feeling that if the hippo was unsuccessful in sorting you out, the crocodile would surely get you!

Certain sections of the channel were so narrow and closed up that we had to climb out physically onto the floating islands of papyrus grass, on which we were stuck and pull the boat over the obstruction. Many times, it looked like an impossible task, however, when on a mission to go fishing up into the main channel, you force yourself to make a plan and find a way through. On two occasions, almost laying flat on the floor whilst pushing our way through the overhanging grass we had a snake drop into the boat. Its incredible how this immediately gets everyone's attention and produces amazingly vocal screams from the woman folk. On both occasions, we managed to catch the reptile with the landing net and tossed it back over the side, giving them a chance to visit us again on our return trip.

Once breaking out of the hippo trail, you enter into the wide and magnificent main channel that flows though the entire length of the Delta. The fishing throughout can be fantastic, especially in late October early November when the barbel migrate up stream in their thousands. At this time, the tiger fish go on a feeding frenzy which for the fisherman is an amazing experience. Added to the excitement there are many crocodiles either sunning themselves on the banks and others hunting for food in the water and in some cases these are abnormally large. Sadly, there are a lot of local people collecting water or bathing through necessity, that are attacked and killed by these ancient reptiles.

Generally two to three wonderful days would be spent at the camp prior to flying out to the little town of Maun to re-fuel the air-craft and then on home to Selebi-Phikwe. On one of Alan Longstaff's many business trips up to Botswana, after a hectic week of running around the rigs, he suggested that Darrin, he and I fly up to Guma Lagoon for a few days fishing to unwind.

Our plane had just been through the mandatory annual C of A (Certificate of Airworthiness), meaning theoretically it should be in perfect condition. Darrin flew it back home from Gaborone and for a change after the major inspection, checks and required repairs, he had a good flight with no issues. It always amazed me how many times after delivering the aircraft for the inspection, everything was in order, yet after taking off and flying home on completion there was often a problem. Either the VOR, ADF, radio's and on occasion and even more seriously, the undercarriage would malfunction, requiring having to return to Gaborone for repair. During my flight training, we were warned by our instructor's that the most dangerous flight is the first one after the C of A. Although at the time we believed it to be a joke, after experiencing all these problems, I had certainly started taking this advice more seriously.

We phoned Nookie at the lodge, who informed us that due to a couple of cancellations the previous evening, had accommodation for us. We quickly packed, got our fishing gear sorted out and flew up on the Friday shortly after lunch. Darrin sat in the left hand seat flying the plane; I sat in the co-pilots right hand seat and Alan who had never really been too excited about flying of any sorts sat behind us. Again, the flight was smooth and two and a half hours after take-off Darrin made a safe landing on the dirt strip servicing the camp. The last thirty minutes of flight over the Delta, as always was amazing, with sightings of elephant, a large heard of buffalo, giraffe and lechwe. As always, our transport having heard the aircraft coming, were ready and waiting at the strip to take us to the lodge.

What Nookie and her late husband Geoff had managed to build, on what is essentially a small island, is quite amazing. All the luxury tents, walkways and lodge itself have been raised up on stilts from the ground, above the high water mark to allow the water to run freely below in the months of July and August. The effect and atmosphere produced from this is exceptional, together with the massive trees encompassing the area and overlooking the beautiful lagoon, to my mind, make it one of the top camps in the Delta. I'm not sure how many readers have had the privilege of visiting this exquisite lodge, but I feel sure there are those that have heard talk of Nookie's roast potatoes and hot sauces that she so expertly produces for meal times. Her full English breakfasts were to die for and kept the hunger pains at bay until dinner time.

Yet Nookie, efficient as always, insisted on giving us all lunch-packs when we went out fishing, not knowing what time we would be back. The late Geoff, Nookie and I go back a long way. I have been visiting their camps from their first site on the main channel many years ago, then to their second and rustic camp with a real fisherman's atmosphere on the western side of Guma Lagoon and now onto this stunning lodge.

Geoff and I spent many wonderful hours together on his boat, catching fish, he really was a man's man and a lot of fun to be around, both on the water fishing or sitting in the bar at night. I have many fond memories of our times together, one of these being his love for nature in all its forms. In a bid to save any further destruction of trees, he successfully designed and built Makoro replicas on site at the lodge from fibreglass. Initially marketed only in Botswana, due to popular demand, were later sold throughout Africa. I believe this to be a most commendable achievement from an extraordinarily special man who was loved and respected by all who were privileged enough to have know him personally.

This particular visit to the lagoon was no different from our previous experiences and on Sunday, around mid-morning, we were air-borne, heading for Maun after two relaxing days of great fishing. Again the aircraft behaved perfectly and after landing in Maun, re-fuelling, filling flight plans and buying a few ice-cold cokes, we were set to climb back into the plane and take off when suddenly Alan asked,

"Please guys, can I sit in the front right hand seat for the flight home, I would love to see what it is like from there?"

"Alan, I don't want to be funny, but I don't think it would be a good idea, your view if anything is better from where you have been sitting anyway. Furthermore, I feel that as we have two pilots looking after everything up front, it will be far safer to remain where you were, in the unlikely event of a problem."

"Oh thanks a lot, you have always convinced me that this is the safest form of travel, now you talk of problems that need two pilots to sort out. I'm not even sure if I should get in at all!"

"Alan we don't have time to stand here and discuss this, please believe me everything is fine, as you are aware the plane has just been fully checked over, but we insist for safety reasons that you sit in the back and enjoy the flight." With that, he begrudgingly climbed in, but admitted what I had said made sense.

After taxing to the holding point, completing run up procedures and given clearance from the tower, we set off on our take-off run. Darrin, once reaching sixty knots, gently pulled back on the yoke and climbed steadily to a cruise altitude of 9,500', thereafter maintaining track for Selebi-Phikwe that takes you directly over the Lake Makgadikgadi Salt Pans. Regardless of how many occasions I flew this route, I couldn't refrain from being in total awe of the vastness of this ancient inland sea, it stretched for as far as the eye could see in any direction. To think such an enormous landscape can be completely void of vegetation of any description and flat with negligible change in altitude for thousands of square kilometres, is difficult to comprehend.

Fifty nautical miles out of Selebi-Phikwe, Darrin radioed ATC information in Gaborone, informing them of our ETA (Estimated time of arrival) for Phikwe and requesting commencement of decent which was given and handed him over to Phikwe ATC who cleared us through to left base for runway 08. With the airfield in sight, Darrin pulled back on the yoke, effectively lifting the nose of the aircraft to slow our airspeed. Soon after the ASI (Air speed indicator) passed bellow 140 knots, he activated the lever to lower the landing gear. This went off without a hitch and confirmation of the green light ensured gear was down and locked in. I had previously installed a small round convex mirror on the right hand wing. This clearly produced visual confirmation for the pilot that the right hand main and front wheel were safely down. We made this an integral procedure on our downwind checks and this time was no different. The left main wheel was clearly visible from the pilots window.

Darrin was an excellent pilot and had many flying hours of experience on the plane. His touchdown on runway 08 was incredibly smooth, but soon after I felt the plane moving off to the right. I wasn't concerned as I knew Darrin would kick the rudder to straighten it out. I began to get a little more anxious when it got worse and the left wing starting tilting towards the ground. Not thinking, but working strictly on instinct I grabbed the controls and immediately went opposite ailerons and rudder, in a bid to correct the problem. Momentarily, I felt relieved as the left wing levelled off again and the plane turned back a little towards the centre of the runway.

To my horror, the plane suddenly swung left and we went careering off the runway onto the grassed and rough surrounds, heading for the trees. I tried the brakes and there was no response. Immediately, I pulled the yoke right back as far as it would go, to lighten the load on the front wheel. I visualized the wheel folding backwards with the propeller and frontend ploughing into the ground, possibly somersaulting the aircraft and bursting into flames! Everything was happening so fast, as was my brain. I couldn't for the life of me understand what was happening, but at the same time, shouted for Darrin to switch off the fuel, magnetos, ignition and open his door, something I had already done with mine. The trees were coming closer fast and we began hitting ridges across our track and then the inevitable happened. The front wheel broke off smashing the frontend into the ground lifting the back of the plane. In seconds, we were looking out the front window straight down into the ground. I was sure we were going to go over and land on our back, but she hovered there for a few terrifying seconds, then swivelled around and fell back onto the wheels again, but leaning over badly. Having already opened the latch on the doors ensuring we wouldn't be locked in after the crash, we were able to exit in seconds. As I climbed out, I pulled my seat forward and Alan leaped out, moving faster than I had ever seen him move. The three of us ran off a few metres, worrying about the plane bursting into fire. We turned around to see what damage there was and to try to ascertain what could possibly have gone wrong. Most certainly, we came within a hairs breath of being killed! Alan standing there shaking his head from side to side with arms folded said, "For shit sakes what happened? You know, I was just starting to get used to flying and now this happens!"

"Well Alan, you realise this is your fault for tempting fate before we left Maun wanting to sit up front. Had we allowed you to do so, we would all be dead right now, as it required both Darrin and I to save the situation."

"Come on Trevor, there is no way my wanting to sit in the front caused this accident."

"No, don't worry Alan, I'm pulling your leg about this being your fault, but it goes to show that it wouldn't have been a good idea with you sitting up front. Come on now, let's go and find out what happened." With that, I walked back to check out what could have caused our near disaster. The propeller was a right off bend beyond repair with cowling damage around the motor. The left wing showed serious damage after scraping on the ground many times, once leaving the tar strip. The right wheel appeared fine and still locked in place, yet the left wheel lay straight back causing the plane to lean over so badly. Immediately I knew something had failed on touchdown, folding the left wheel back, leaving only the right and front wheel, obviously an impossible situation to deal with unscathed. I walked all the way back to the runway and my thoughts were confirmed, clearly the intermittent black marks left by the rubber tyre bouncing, showed immediately after touchdown.

A full independent and lengthy investigation took place, as is the case with all aviation accidents. The results apparently proved the failure of a retaining pin on the locking mechanism of the left hand landing gear. Close on three months after the accident and R465,000 paid out in full by insurance, we were up and flying again. To be honest, I have always felt the results of the investigation were a little suspect and have had to wonder about the ever re-occurring post C of A problems. To this day, I wonder who really was to blame for almost killing the three of us.

Chapter 86

Charles Byron has been a close friend and client for many years. Together we have tackled numerous projects out in the bushveld, spent many hours sitting around fires next to our tents talking late into the night whilst scorpions scuttled in for the warmth of the fire.

I have always highly respected him as a pioneer and top authority on gold deposits in the Francistown area. On top of this, he is one of the nicest, down to earth people you could meet. However, as masterful and efficient that he proved to be as a geologist looking for gold, so was he equally, if not more, talented at providing the most inaccessible and seemingly impossible drill locations! I always joked with him saying I believed he achieved far more satisfaction in locating difficult drill sites than actually finding the highly sought after and precious yellow metal!

With the Mupane Mine project he excelled himself, exceeding all expectations in this regard. I strongly believe somewhere back in time with his ancestors there had to be strong mountaineering blood flowing. Hills and mountains obsessed him, not necessarily for climbing, but for laying out drilling programmes.

As is the norm prior to tendering for any drilling contract, I arranged with Charles to do a site visit. We met in Francistown and drove out together to the Mupanipani Hills. On arrival, I was not particularly surprised at how narrow the access roads were. Geologists are great at telling you they have cut access roads to the sites. What they fail to realise is that the drill rigs, compressors and water tankers are far bigger than their small 4x4 vehicles, always necessitating extra work for the drilling contractor!

On reaching the base of the hills Charles said, "Right Trevor, we will now have to continue on foot." We climbed or should I say stumbled our way over masses of large ironstone boulders up and up until we reached a spot where Charles eventually stopped and looked out over the Mopani bush to the west. I had noticed a sample trench dug all the way up the hill to this point, but dismissed my concern of this being a drill site as it was difficult for a mountain goat to get here yet alone my drill rigs!

"Wow, what a great view!" I said lighting a cigarette, then continued, "Now where will the first drill site be?" Charles just stood there looking down at a steel peg sticking up out of the ground at his feet, expertly maintaining that strange but telling expression on his face he had mastered over time. "Come on Charles, you have got to be joking. Even for you this is crazy and it's certainly not April fool's day so seriously where is the first site?"

"Don't worry we are bringing in a bulldozer to sort it out a little and you'll be fine." I was speechless, but he continued saying, "I felt I would start you off on one of the more accessible sites to get you going, as you'll see some of the others are seriously difficult!" His uncanny ability in finding such impossible drill sites never ceased to amaze me.

We then continued our mountaineering exercise climbing over every possible difficult outcrop formation he could find. Eventually we arrived on the crest of the hill and to be honest I was in awe of the view. Being predominately-flat country the view was quite stunning. You could see for miles around, clearly visible were the Francistown koppies to the north west. Then scanning around to the south east the tall smelter stack of the Phikwe mine could be seen, demarcated by highly sulphurous smoke continuously pumping out over the countryside mainly to the west of the mine due obviously to the easterly prevailing winds.

"Okay, Charles, seeing we have only just managed to climb and scramble our way over all these boulders and steep climbs on foot, how, please tell me, do I get my rig and equipment up here?" I paused to take a breath and continued jokingly saying, "My helicopter is in for a service so I'm not sure how I will manage?"

"Hell Trevor, I would dearly love to drill an exploratory angle hole from here down the side of the hill, but even I can see that won't be possible. However, I figured you would want to see the view, which I think is special. Plus if you need to call the office on your cell phone this is about the only place you'll have signal."

"Hell, I'm pleased to hear it has something going for it!" I said with a chuckle.

Feeling like a mountain goat on a bad day, we continued our exhausting site visit. It became abundantly obvious amongst these ironstone koppies that having worked for Charles on many occasions over the years he had excelled himself on this project. Regarding the severity of slope and the enormous ironstone rocks scattered everywhere, this had to rank as his number one masterpiece.

The preferred method of drilling the first exploratory stage was reverse circulation (R/C). It is a fast and cost effective means of obtaining uncontaminated chip samples from the formation. Effectively high-pressure air via large portable compressors blows down the annulus of the drill rod and inner tube to the drill hammer down the hole. The hammer, ported in such a way, sets off a hammering action via an internal-piston. The kinetic energy generated from the piston passes directly onto the back end of drill bit. Then in turn to the tungsten buttons mounted on the bit-face producing formational chip samples as the rig rotates the drill string penetrating into the rock.

A shroud manufactured close to the OD (outer diameter) of the bit size mounts directly above the drill bit. Air pressure over the bit and restricted from returning up the outer drill rod with the shroud causes a reverse suction effect sending the chip samples through the holes on the bit face. The samples are then blown up through the inner tubes into a cyclone on surface and bagged in clear plastic sleeves. My smallest R/C rig mounted neatly to a 4x4 and the other one on a 6x6 truck. Mounted on trailers and pulled behind the rig truck were the huge compressors required to accompany them. This system worked extremely well throughout Botswana, the only exception being when contracted to drill for Charles Byron!

Seeing firsthand the seemingly inaccessible drill sites, I was under no illusions these were certainly going to be the most challenging rig moves I had ever experienced anywhere! I could possibly get my current rigs to a few of the sites with the help of extensive work required by a bulldozer, but for successful completion of the project I would need to consider acquiring a track mounted drill rig with on-board compressor.

Charles was not only an excellent geologist, but always extremely positive in all he did. I respected him highly in this regard and considered him amongst the best geologists I had ever worked with. His enthusiasm for this particular project was highly infectious and I had no doubt in my mind the gold would be there culminating in an extensive drilling program and possibly a mine.

First thing the following morning I phoned a few contacts in Johannesburg with regard to the purchasing of a crawler R/C rig. I managed to obtain contact details of someone in the Johannesburg area. They designed and developed R/C drill rigs to the required spec including track mounts. Pushed for time, I immediately left after phoning Rudi the owner to ensure he would be available for an appointment.

Rudi has successfully designed a drill rig called a Thaw. It is a compact machine with a three-piece hydraulically extendable telescopic mast. It is most impressive how smoothly the one section slides into the other when drilling or pulling rods. Much like the Super Rocks I was currently utilising, it was a simple and highly efficient drill rig. There were no complicated hydraulic systems, just the basics required and therefore designed to suit African conditions.

He came up with what to me was a unique and wonderful idea. He would mount the rig on tracks as requested, but with a difference. Generally track rigs more commonly known as crawler rigs, require transporting on sturdy low bed trailers. Self-propelled they are capable of going up incredibly steep slopes and over rough terrain not accessible by standard four or six wheel drive trucks. However, progress is slow.

To counter this problem he had designed an extension piece at the rear of the chassis neatly housing four retractable truck wheels. Essentially, once the rig has completed drilling a hole, it is hydraulically jacked up on the four corners until the tracks are well clear of the ground. The truck wheels then extend firmly onto the ground and lock in place with 60mm steel pins. The four hydraulic rams then fully retract leaving the rear wheels carrying all the weight. The rig, then towed through a standard fifth wheel configuration, is pulled to the next site connected to the horse truck. An additional advantage if confronted with steep climbs between sites, the rear wheels on the rig are retracted. Using the tracks on the rig, it was possible to push the truck instead of it being pulled until clear of the obstacle.

I loved the concept and ordered one immediately. The machine arrived and we were able to access all the drill sites Charles could throw at us. To say your heart was in your throat on some of the more difficult climbs would be an understatement of note, yet we managed and managed well. Although it ranked as one of the most difficult contracts I had ever undertaken, including low penetration rates through the ironstones, I found it to be extremely satisfying on successful completion.

Achieving fantastic gold values through our drilling results and turning an initially basic exploration-drilling programme into a large gold mine is an amazing feeling of accomplishment. Most certainly clear proof of the experience and intimate knowledge Charles possessed in his specialised field. I believe we both experienced similar emotions to what the famous Dr. Livingstone felt when discovering Victoria Falls way back in 1855!

Right through to 2013 we drilled at the mine on separate contracts in a bid to prove or disprove that the gold continued to greater depths. Currently we are drilling holes close to the one thousand metre mark, far exceeding the original depth estimates.

Chapter 87

It was another one of those Monday mornings fast turning into a nightmare after pay weekend. I developed a system whereby, within reason, all the staff spread throughout Botswana were transported back to Phikwe. Generally, this happened on the last Thursday of the month. This gave them time to get money to their families to pay bills, schooling and so on for the following month. I honestly felt it was necessary due to essentially spending the rest of the month on site at the rigs.

It was an expensive and stressful undertaking, but it was fair on the staff. I was always amazed how quickly and efficiently they managed to get themselves to the office on the Thursday. There were seldom any breakdowns, not even a puncture, and they always managed to be packed and ready to leave before light.

Conversely, when Monday arrived they were equally inefficient in organising their lives. The wear and tear of heavy drinking was evident on most of them and the majority were always late. To say the least, these Mondays were my pet hate for the month! I tried many deterrent methods in my vain attempt of instilling some responsibility in their lives, but somehow each post pay Monday had me almost frothing at the mouth by 9am.

In many cases, I fired the inebriated staff with immediate effect, or docked money from the following month's pay for those who came late, yet month after month little changed. Although against labour law, I threatened to pay half their monthly salary to their wives and the other half to them on site. My hands were tied in this respect and I really had little option but to continue as is.

On one of these dreaded Mondays, my phone rang again for the umpteenth time whilst I was in the process of going through the monthly reports. All possibilities of my being in a reasonably good mood by this time were long gone. I snatched the phone from the cradle and in a rough voice asked my secretary why she was still sending calls through when I had explicitly asked her to hold all calls. "I'm sorry Sir, but this man has phoned three times this morning and insists he speaks to you, he says to tell you it is really important and that he is phoning from overseas."

Begrudgingly I told her to put the call through to me.

"Longstaff's, good morning," I replied after hearing the click on the line for connection.

"Good morning, is that Mr. Trevor Frost?" he asked in perfect English. "Yes, but today it's really busy, Trevor Frost, how may I help you?" As I said it, I realised just how bad that had to sound and mentally admonished myself.

"Well, I'm sorry to trouble you, but my name is Hugh MacKinnon and I'm phoning from Europe so if I could please have a minute of your time." This certainly threw me a little, why would anyone phone me from there.

"Well, good day, but I must add if this has anything to do with off-shore investments I'm not interested!"

"I suppose it is a form of investment that I would like to discuss with you, only instead of monetary, what we would like is you investing some of your time on a project we are going into in Russia." If I was surprised at the overseas call, I was even more so by his statement!

He went on and explained how his newly formed company was involved in a project prospecting for silver high up in the mountains in Kyrgyzstan. They were looking for an experienced drilling consultant to come over for a week on a site visit. Firstly, to advise on drilling methods and equipment required, then follow up with an on-site experienced drilling supervisor to oversee and train local drilling crews on the latest drilling equipment and methodology through to completion of contract.

"Hugh, I'm sorry, but you have to be joking. Firstly, there are many experienced drillers in Europe and secondly I am far too busy here in Botswana to consider such an offer. However I'm intrigued as to how you found me anyway?"

"Well Trevor, Southern Africa is well known for exploration drilling and we have decided to source from there. During our enquiries, your name kept cropping up repeatedly, hence my call to you. We are more than happy to compensate you generously if you agree to come over and help us in this exciting new venture."

"Once again Hugh, thank you for thinking of me, I appreciate the offer, but there is just no way of me having the time for such a venture, I'm really sorry," I said with some regret as the prospect of such an opportunity to see that part of the world sounded exciting.

"Well, Trevor, that is disappointing as I can promise you it will be an amazing experience, plus you'll make some really good money. However, I am not giving up just yet. I'll give you a couple of days to think about it and ring you back with a firm offer." I thanked him once again and replaced the receiver.

Speaking to Les she also felt as I did, that although an exciting prospect, taking into account my workload, finding the time to go flitting around the world was going to be out of the question. I found it terribly difficult to organise my crews off to their respective sites that Monday morning with Hugh's phone call weighing heavily on my mind.

Some two years previously my eldest son Darrin had left school, completed his apprenticeship and qualified as a diesel mechanic. He wanted to go into drilling and as I was always desperately in need of mechanics, I was thrilled at the prospect of our working together.

Over this period, he had gained valuable experience in drilling and after saving up a little money decided he wanted to go overseas and have a look around. Many youngsters of his age had done the same thing almost as if part of growing up. I liked the idea as believed once they had been over and seen what was on offer they generally came home and settled down. The nagging thought of fulfilling their ambition of doing the overseas bit is then out of their system.

Les and I supported him fully in his wish to go prior to settling full-time into a drilling career. At the time of the phone call, he had possibly a week left over there before flying back home.

Suddenly the thought crossed my mind that this would be a wonderful and certainly unique experience and opportunity for him to see that part of the world and make good money whilst there.

Once again, Les and I discussed this at length and unanimously decided to speak to him and see how he felt about spending time in Russia. After many attempts I eventually managed to get hold of him; he jumped at the opportunity.

Chapter 88

Hugh was most excited when phoning me back to hear I was happy to come on board with the follow-up work carried out by Darrin. After some serious negotiating on an extremely attractive package, an agreement was formed between us. Within a week I was on a plane bound for Tel Aviv in Israel to meet the principal shareholder who was resident there.

Hugh warned me of the highly efficient and strict security when entering the country. He stressed that regardless what questions were asked of me by immigration I was to tell the truth, *'never, and I mean NEVER, lie as they will catch you out'*. I had nothing to hide so after a lengthy grilling at immigration was cleared through into the terminal building. Here I found a driver holding a board with my name on it who transported me off to my hotel in the beautiful city. My return through the same airport some five days later was not quite as easy!

The following morning I met with Hugh's partner and once our lengthy meeting was over, he kindly gave me a tour of the city. I found it most interesting and certainly in general found it to be an extremely different lifestyle to ours in Southern Africa. For lunch, we sat out on a street corner and enjoyed a local meal of a dozen small fish each that were scrumptious and crispy. Eventually he dropped me off at the airport late afternoon to catch my flight onto Bishkek where I would meet up with Hugh and Darrin. I looked forward to it as I had not seen him for some time.

The flight went as well as any long distance flight can and on arrival in Bishkek, I was surprised to see Darrin had grown a beard, not just a little bum fluff, but a long beard. It was strange to see him that way, as it was the first time he had grown one. I joked saying he would probably need it to keep him warm up in the mountains. As it turned out, he needed far more than that to keep him warm.

We arrived in a small town at the base of the mountain range after a most interesting and beautiful drive of approximately three hours. The endless mountain ranges seemed to climb into the clouds. Also impressive was the massive Lake Issyk Kul. It has an impressive length of 182 kilometres and a width of up to 60 kilometres and covers an area of 6,236 square kilometres. It is located at an altitude of 1,607 metres, with a depth of 668 metres. This makes it the second largest mountain lake in the world behind Lake Titicaca in South America.

I was fascinated with the small quaint towns spread two houses deep along the main road for miles. In addition, there were many small one-man makeshift stores selling their goods, which included various food dishes freshly cooked while you wait. Surprisingly virtually each one openly displayed and sold Vodka! It most certainly did not take long to figure out the most popular alcoholic drink available.

During the following few days we were going to be extremely busy. Hugh arranged for a Toyota Land Cruiser station wagon as transport for our site visit up the mountain almost 10,000 feet above sea level! He warned us it was to be a full day's exercise and the evidence of this was soon apparent.

Never mind the long drive up a mountain that high I'm quite sure I had never before seen one that high. The narrow dirt track winding its way up seemed never ending, but nor did I want it to end. The scenery was breathtaking with the mountain ranges stretching as far as the eye could see, with most of the peaks covered in stunning white blankets of snow. To some extent, it reminded me of Lesotho when racing in the 'Roof of Africa'

It was quite clear by the condition of, or lack thereof, the road was seldom used. Over a long period, due to lack of maintenance, sections had eroded away badly, especially where streams had formed from melting snow running down the mountain. At two of the more serious areas we came across people busy repairing these sections. Not only were they working with the help of what had to be the oldest looking bulldozer in Kyrgyzstan if not the world, but also with hand picks and shovels. It was plain to see the locals were not afraid of hard work.

Quite obviously we could not understand a word anyone said, but it was pleasing to see the friendly banter with much laughter when our driver stopped and conversed in the local tongue with the working party. I thought to myself working up here in truly rough conditions with cold weather and living in makeshift camps cannot be easy, yet they all seemed happy. When questioning Hugh as we continued our ascent he explained that in general the people in Kyrgyzstan were friendly and as long as they had work and were earning their keep were happy.

The unemployment rate was high and the majority had to fend for themselves one way or another. It is strange how one tends to focus only on hard times experienced by many in our home country. The fact is that every country in the world has it's unique problems and due, I feel, to selfishness on our part we tend to dismiss these facts. *'Hey it doesn't concern me in any way so why should I worry about what happens over there'* is the norm. Yet to those people the problems and hardships are real in every respect.

It was comforting to see repair work undertaken in haste to ensure access for the trucks that would be transporting the rigs to site. Also going through my mind was the possibility of having to cart water up the treacherous mountain pass. We use water permanently when drilling to cool the bit and allow for the use of drilling mud mixtures. Depending on your water returns in the drill hole usage can be excessive. The requirement of daily carting loads of water in six wheel drive trucks was going to be challenging. This certainly was not going to be an easy contract by any means and was put into perspective by the generous package they offered to get us to come out here.

Chapter 89

Eventually we arrived at the top of the mountain and quite honestly, it felt like being on the top of the world, a new and beautiful world. The view in every direction was awe-inspiring, endless snow-covered mountain peaks stretched out for miles around us, some of which seemed to plunge down into bottomless valleys. The air, clean and crisp with a cold bite to it, and the skies a magnificent deep blue, was most refreshing. If there is such a thing as heaven, I firmly believed if we hadn't yet found it, it had to be close considering our current altitude.

What really excited me was a clear stream of water flowing strongly from melted snow-covered peaks even higher than our current position. I immediately discussed the possibility of damming the stream, with Hugh. He informed me earlier that the old grader once complete with the repairs to the road, would come up to level the drill sites. I felt as it would be available it would be a perfect opportunity to utilise it to build a temporary dam wall. He found this rather amusing as was confident the possibility of the stream remaining in fluid form was extremely remote. I honestly thought he had to be joking, in my mind there was no possibility of this gushing river icing up in a million years. Little did I know how wrong I could be or for that matter just how cold this mountain became once winter set in!

Due to the altitude and lack of oxygen, there was no growth of any kind. Although beautiful, the mountains surrounding us were totally devoid of trees, almost giving you the feeling of being on the moon. Whilst walking around I noticed a tunnel going into the mountain and enquired what it was for and if possible could we go inside. I was not quite sure why I needed to go in there, but something in the back of my mind was telling me to do so. Where they come from I am not sure, but all through life I have had many such flashes go through my mind and had to some extent learned to listen to them.

With the use of torches, we ventured in for about twenty metres and came across a strong flow of water coming from a fault zone in the sidewall. I said to Darrin that in the highly unlikely event the outside water was to freeze over this could possibly be a useful back up.

Some hours later, we concluded the site visit and headed off down the mountain to our accommodation for the night. The innkeeper, a woman in her mid-forties, welcomed us in and led us through to our rooms. Fortunately, our host spoke broken English so we were able to converse with each other to some extent. A local scrumptious meal for dinner ended a tiring, but interesting day and we retired to our rooms for a good night's sleep.

First thing the following morning we drove up the mountain again, only this time in a different direction on our way to visit a local diamond drill in operation. On arrival, I was surprised to see how basic and antiquated the rig design was. The finishes on the steel castings were rough and to be brutally honest I was not impressed at all. Yet standing there watching them operate, although not pretty, they were most certainly functional. The supervisor came over and spoke through our interpreter with us. He was happy to answer all my questions. I was staggered to learn drilling technology in that country had to be twenty years behind ours in Southern Africa. The locally manufactured drill bits were of poor quality in the extreme. They produced pathetic production both in penetration rates and bit life. I could not believe that in this modern day such equipment could still be in circulation. I felt the only rightful place for such antiquated drill bits would be on a shelf in a museum.

I also noticed the drill rods lying on the rack were of different lengths. When querying this, the operator informed me the damaged section of male or female ends are machined off and a new thread cut. The drill supervisor was surprised at my not knowing this obvious fact! It was the norm over there so why would it be any different from where I came from. Any damaged or worn out drill rod in our part of the world, and I would tend to believe in any other country, was discarded to be used as fencing poles or the like.

Drilling with old and damaged drill rods was not an option for us especially on the deeper holes; it was far too dangerous and asking for trouble. The resulting costs in time lost fishing for in-hole equipment and possible re-drills caused by a broken rod can far exceed the cost of the new rod string. Even more significant is the damage caused to your reputation in the eyes of the mining house to perform efficiently as a drilling contractor. Building your reputation takes lots of hard work, dedication and time and just a few in-hole disasters caused by inefficiency can throw that out the window in no time at all.

With the use of the latest drilling technology and equipment as in wire line drilling it was impractical to consider shortening or tampering in any way with the high spec drill rod. Another consideration was the different lengths of each rod when shortened. The standard drill rod comes in three-metre lengths. Depending on mast capacity, as the hole progresses so your rod string is made into six, nine, twelve or eighteen metre length rod stands for convenience when pulling and lowering. Due to this, calculating depth of the hole after pulling rods is a simple process.

You multiply the total number of joined lengths on your rod table by whatever length they made up. Then add any extra drill rods inserted whilst drilling that run. To this figure, add the length of quill rod and core barrel. From this, deduct the length of quill rod sticking out of the hole from the total giving the precise depth of hole at that point.

Example: 12-metre rods x 24 =   288.00 metres
6-metre odd rod   =   6.00 metres
                Length of core barrel   =   6.34 metres
                                                300.34 metres
                Less stick-up of quill rod   7.55 metres
                Total depth of hole   =   292.79 metres

On enquiring as to how they then measured their stick-up for an exact depth of hole, I was once again shattered by the answer. A lead weight attached to a long length of string is lowered down the hole to get the depth. Wow, I have to be dreaming, this cannot be real. These people have sent spaceships into orbit and I had always perceived them to be highly advanced! Obviously in space technology they had to be, yet were prehistoric in drilling techniques. Darrin and I just could not understand this at all.

When Hugh explained the dictatorship and control of organisations and businesses when under Russian rule pre 31 August 1991, only then did it start making sense.

Chapter 90

Hugh had arranged a time the following day for all drilling personnel in the district to attend a workshop. He wanted me to address a packed hall on the latest techniques utilised in the drilling game in South Africa. The supervisor and his crew would also be attending. We were most interested to learn of how they went about their work drilling through the icy winters. What methods were used to keep water from freezing not only in the water sumps, but whilst being pumped through the system? How were they able to keep themselves warm and the like? Darrin and I coming from the hot climate in Africa, had lots to learn in this regard. As far as daily production was concerned, assuming there were no major breakdowns, they were happy to advance the hole two/three metres per day on average (+ - 100 metres/month.) Back home any company with such low production would be struck from all tender lists. I am not in any way implying we are better drillers, simply our equipment is far more advanced than theirs. In certain formations, we can produce close to their monthly production in a 24-hour shift!

The following day was most interesting in that we visited a local drilling company's offices. They had a large stock of drilling equipment, but once again all out-dated. Scratching around I was surprised to find a few BQ wire line drill rods. How could this be possible, they have to have operated with them at some stage and yet had reverted to their standard antiquated set up? I spoke to their drilling manager and he had no idea what they were or how they got there.

Later that day we arrived for the drilling workshop arranged by Hugh. It was to take place in a large conference room and the number of people attending surprised me. After introductions to the captive audience through our interpreter, I presented my talk on Southern African drilling.

I went through the process of wire line drilling, how it worked, how it saved time not having to pull rods to remove core, how drill bits had changed from surface set to diamond dust impregnated design. When giving production figures achieved with the new technology in penetration rates and bit life it was obvious my audience believed I had to be from another planet. I was successful in achieving the same nonplussed look when giving details of depth ranges drilled from shallow to depths of 2,000 metres being common, especially in the gold fields. To these people drilling to such depths was simply unachievable.

I then moved onto direction drilling and explained in detail how the mother hole once complete could have many deflections made from it. Not only was it possible to drill a new hole wedging off at any depth, but also drill in the exact direction required to produce second, third and fourth intersections all from the mother hole.

I found it a little amusing to see the look of disbelief mixed with amazement on the faces of my audience. Quietly I pondered the fun and games Darrin was going to have to endure training them in these new techniques. I glanced over toward him and by his expression, I knew he was thinking along the same lines. He smiled back at me slowly shaking his head from side to side.

The following morning I sent an order I had compiled the previous evening, after discussions with the client, for all drilling equipment required. My suppliers in South Africa assured me they had stock and would arrange to have it shipped off immediately once export paper work was complete. I could picture Steve's eyes lighting up with the lucrative order just received. Eventually having completed all that I had come over for, I was booked to fly from Almaty a few hours' drive into Kazakstan back to Tel-Aviv late afternoon. We sat down to our final meeting and decided Darrin was going to stay on for one more day to go through last minute arrangements with Hugh At the conclusion of the meeting, I asked about an interpreter for him. Hugh assured me it was in hand and called for two people to come into the office. One was a young to middle-aged man, the other a cute young woman. Hugh asked Darrin which of the two he would like to go up the mountain with as they were both excellent interpreters. Darrin looked at me with a big smile and asked, "Hey Dad, if you had the choice what would you do?" I burst out laughing knowing exactly what his choice was going to be.

Chapter 91

I packed my bags and after shaking hands and saying goodbye to all, set off with a local driver and his friend for the airport. Neither spoke a word of English. I, having no idea as to what direction we were going, sat quietly in the back hoping for the best whilst they both ate sunflower seeds and talked non-stop the whole way. Finally, we arrived at the airport, the driver helped unload my bags. He climbed back into the car, waved and drove off..... I stood there for a few minutes not sure what to do or where to go. There were no signs in English and trying to speak to anyone was a total waste of time.

After some considerable time of wandering around trying to converse in sign language and showing all and sundry my air ticket, I was eventually ushered into a waiting room. I was astonished to see some of the passengers had animals. A man had a medium sized dog and a woman standing in front of me was holding a small bag with her cat's head clearly sticking out. This was a first for me and I was sure the two concerned could clearly see the puzzled look on my face. The man gave me a dirty look and then I got lucky and the woman smiled at me. I tried speaking to her, but to no avail, she had absolutely no idea what I was asking her.

I found a seat and as I made myself comfortable the doors opened and passengers starting filing through. Much like a lost puppy, I followed the crowd onto the aircraft. I was ushered to a seat in the aisle, two rows behind the man with the dog. Even the air-hostess, and not through lack of trying on her part, was unable to converse with me. I decided the only way forward was to sit back, relax and let whatever happens, happen.

I really was not sure as to the destination of the flight simply through not having any communication with anyone, but knew my ticket indicated a direct flight to Tel-Aviv. We taxied to the holding point just as it was getting dark and took off into the murky skies heading for who knows where. The dog was happy to wander up and down the aisle and looked far more in control of what was happening than I. He actually allowed me to stroke him and enjoyed it, which I might add was more than I got from the air-hostess. I felt sure, even though a dog, he could understand me better than anyone else could on the aircraft.

I managed to drop off to sleep. Sometime later, I woke with the feeling of our plane descending. I checked my watch and found that we still had a few hours of flight left. I looked out of the window and clearly, we were on descent, headed for what looked like a medium sized town by the number of lights visible through the little window. What was happening, was there a problem with the engines or flight controls necessitating a forced unplanned landing? The air-hostess could obviously see the concern on my face and waved her hands in a fashion that I read as sign language for do not worry, so I didn't.

We had a reasonable landing, meaning nothing broke or fell off that I knew about, and taxied safely to the terminal building. As we stopped I loosened my seat belt and stood up, but I had the air-hostess all over me again indicating I stay seated. Once again, I obliged and sat down watching as the man, his dog and a few others disembarked. Soon afterwards, a few new passengers arrived and to my knowledge had no animals. Hell, who am I going to talk to now that my friend the dog had left, I thought to myself? As to exactly where we were or what country we were in, I must confess I had no idea whatsoever. Within the hour, we were once again airborne and with any luck back on track for Tel-Aviv.

Again, I fell asleep and was woken by the air-hostess indicating to me, I think, that we were descending into Tel-Aviv. Just hearing the word Tel-Aviv was reassuring for me. After landing and disembarking, once again the security personnel at immigration grilled me. Remembering Hugh's stern warning I explained exactly what I had done the past few days and of my intention to fly back to South Africa the following evening. They seemed most agitated regarding my short visit to their country, but finally accepted what I had told them repeatedly and allowed me through. Hugh arranged for my collection from the airport; eventually after a long day I collapsed into my bed at the hotel around 01.30am

Something I have struggled with all my life is sleeping late in the mornings and yet with black out curtains on the windows and a late night, I slept through to 09.00am. I was quite shocked to see the time, not to mention requiring a few moments of deep thought to work out quite where I was. By the time I had showered and dressed, my hunger pains were well advanced having not had dinner the previous night. I went down to have breakfast after which I wandered around taking in the beautiful views of the sea. I was on my own yet felt completely safe, certainly more so than one would walking around

Johannesburg. No one bothered me in anyway and I thoroughly enjoyed my little excursion, arriving back at the hotel just before lunch.

On entering my room I noticed the red message button was flashing on the phone. I lifted the receiver and pressed the button. Answering immediately the operator informed me a call came through earlier and asked if they could put me through to the number. Thinking it had to be Hugh's partner, I agreed and was quite correct in that he wanted me to join him for lunch. Well that evening I was to find out what an innocent, but huge mistake I made asking them to place the call.

He picked me up at the entrance and we had a great lunch at a restaurant not far from the hotel whilst discussing my thoughts and ideas on their project in Kyrgyzstan.

Chapter 92

Later that afternoon the same driver who collected me the previous day dropped me off at the International Departures. Knowing that it would be busy, he dropped me off hours before normal checking-in time. Finally, I was about to catch my flight home. There were literally hundreds of people in the International Departures. The queues snaked their way back and forth like meandering streams. Looking out into the masses in front of me I felt I should have come here directly after breakfast!

I had purposely kept a fair sum of local money with the view of buying something nice for Les at the duty free shop. After queuing for hours, it became my turn to precede to one of the immigration checkpoints. I wasn't concerned in any way as I was leaving the country and should therefore not pose any security risk whatsoever. The woman security officer was most efficient and grilled me with question after question. She was convinced I was a problem as I had flown in five days earlier to Tel-Aviv, only spent one day there before flying off to Kyrgyzstan. Then returned last night and now flying out again within 24 hours. Not sure if this is what the baddies do, but I was just following the booking instructions made by my contacts.

At that stage, I wasn't concerned at all. I had not done anything wrong. I felt as long as I was careful to explain my movements exactly, with no deviation, I should be fine. The security woman was like a bulldog not letting go and continued asking the same questions repeatedly.

Then the punch line, she asked if I had made any phone calls that day and not thinking, I said no. She immediately asked for my hotel bill, which I was happy to hand over to her. In seconds her eyes lit up and she asked why I lied about making a call. I had totally forgotten about the return call I had made to my client and once again insisted I had not made any calls. She thrust the bill in front of me and with her finger pointing out the clearly marked charge for the call, once again asked if I had made any calls.

There were hundreds of people waiting behind me in the queue and, I am sure, getting as agitated as I was becoming embarrassed.

Apologising as politely as possible saying that it was such an insignificant call I had honestly forgotten all about it, which is the truth, I continued to tell her what the call was about, but she was not listening to my story. I had lied about the call, now how much truth was there in any of my movements over the last few days. We were back to square one and again I had a barrage of questions fired at me continuously. With the obvious hold up, a second security officer moved in as back up for my lady friend.

I kept thinking to myself *'if only I had done something wrong to deserve this';* it was now extremely tight for my boarding time. I have never wanted to climb into an aircraft so badly in all my life. Again, I apologised profusely with the most sincere look on my face that I could muster. I told them that I was about to miss my flight which neither of us could afford. Firstly, I desperately needed to get home and secondly if I missed the flight they would be stuck with me, funny how that never seemed to hit their funny spot in any way or form. The grilling continued relentlessly and the muttering became more vocal in the queue behind me.

Surprisingly I had not been marched off to a private room to continue the interrogation as we were holding up the other passengers. I could just imagine the annoyance, anger and stress the crowd behind me felt. They too were in the same position as I needing to catch their respective flights. We had now reached the stage where not only would I miss the duty free shop, but would be lucky to catch my flight at all.

Yes, I had made an innocent mistake in forgetting about the phone call, but they had phoned my contact who had verified my story. The thought crossed my mind as to how many real baddies had passed through here without a problem. Here I was, completely innocent of any crimes anywhere in the world, yet treated like a terrorist for making an innocent phone call!

Quite obviously, I was not the first to have had this problem. A woman representative from the airline arrived looking extremely flustered and demanding to know why I had not yet boarded the plane. After a heated discussion, my security friend eventually released me into her custody. She led me away through the crowds directly onto the aircraft.

I was so relieved to sit and buckle myself in ready for take-off; I felt the tension flow from my body. I thought to myself that even if I were on the wrong plane, going to who knows where, I was not bothered, I just wanted to be away from here. I was, however, on the correct flight and thankfully we landed safely in Johannesburg the following morning.

Some weeks later, I received a call from Hugh informing me the equipment had arrived on site and they were ready to start drilling. Immediately I made contact with Darrin and within three days he was on site high up in the mountains.

It was a demanding contract for him in that although he had the interpreter communication was difficult. In addition, the temperature plummeted varying between - 4C and - 40C. The river up the mountain that I had earmarked for his water supply froze solid. He sent me some pictures of a 6x6 water-truck carrying 10 tons of water aboard driving over the ice on the same stream!

Trying to keep warm was not easy, but somehow they managed. With the use of a crude, but effective wood fire system, heat passed through steel ducting to the inside of their caravans. Naturally the crew had been equipped with warm clothing especially for when working outside in the open.

The drilling crews, this included Darrin himself, consumed vast quantities of pure Vodka nightly that also helped tremendously in keeping warm. Vodka played an immensely important role in the lives of the locals and was not only readily available everywhere, but extremely affordable.

He recalls how highly offended they were if you refused to partake in the nightly drinking sessions. You were persuaded to consume sufficient quantities of their favourite liquid nightly to the stage of making your legs feel like they did not belong to you anymore and started doing their own thing. High levels of concentration were then required to negotiate the steps to his caravan door amid hilarious laughter from the instigators of his predicament.

After the first few times of having been subjected to these drinking binges he was convinced he would never be in any condition to work effectively the following day or ever for that matter! Amazingly enough, regardless how much was consumed he never suffered with a screaming headache or any other ill effects of a hangover. Another advantage of the pure clear liquid is that it efficiently warmed your insides and made sleeping pills redundant. By the time your head hit the pillow you were fast asleep or more accurately passed out, not aware of or even caring about the cold.

It turned out to be a fantastic experience for him and he learned a lot about survival under extremely harsh conditions completely alien to the norm, having lived in Africa all his life. He managed successfully to complete the work in six weeks and returned home with some amazing photos of drilling in the ice and snow. Most certainly, a time in his life that will live with him forever.

Chapter 93

A friend of mine arrived in the office one day with a newspaper clipping. It prominently displayed an advert calling for tender prices to drill and equip with hand pumps a thousand water holes throughout Zambia. Apparently, it was a massive initiative by the government of Zambia to supply water to the rural villages with funding from an undisclosed source in Europe. I was obviously interested as Zambia lies directly to the north east of Botswana making it easily accessible to us.

On 24 October 1964, Zambia, known as Northern Rhodesia at the time, was granted independence from the United Kingdom and Kenneth Kaunda became the inaugural president. Kaunda's socialist United National Independence Party (UNIP) maintained power from 1964 until 1991. From 1972 to 1991 Zambia was a single-party state with the UNIP as the sole legal political party, with the goal of uniting the nation under the banner of 'One Zambia, One Nation'. Frederick Chiluba of the social-democratic Movement for Multi-Party Democracy in 1991 succeeded Kaunda, during which time the country saw a rise in social-economic growth and increased decentralisation of government.

Word out was that President Chiluba had made huge improvements in many areas throughout Zambia and things were starting to look up again, a country with huge potential. New investment was welcomed and encouraged through application of investment licenses to operate freely in the country. Things had certainly quietened down drilling wise in Botswana. Here was a possible opportunity to get something up and running in Zambia.

Decidedly, the contract was far too big and spread out for any single drilling contractor. I started phoning around other trusted contractors in Botswana to see if any were interested in going in together with me. I also rang a good friend Mr. Bart Aarse from Water Ways Botswana regarding looking after the pump installation. Not only was he a nice guy with whom who I got on well, I really enjoyed his straight forward attitude in saying things as they were, although he had certainly ruffled a few feathers in his time. How often do you come across people trying to tell you what they believe you want to hear and are completely remiss in telling you how it really is? In addition, he had undoubtedly proved himself as one of the leading pump installation contractors in Botswana.

All those I spoke to, agreed it was potentially an interesting contract and worth looking into so a meeting in Gaborone was arranged by all interested parties. In the end, three drilling contractors and two pump installation companies were present at the meeting to discuss a way forward. At the end of the meeting, I volunteered to drive up to Lusaka, the capital city of Zambia. Someone had to go to pay the R1, 000.00 tendering fee and collect the final tender document from Water Affairs. Wanting to go and see what opportunities existed in Zambia, I was more than happy to make the trip.

Les and Darrin were happy and more than capable of looking after things whilst I was away so I packed my bags and left for Lusaka some one thousand five hundred kilometres away to the north. I made my overnight stop in one of my favourite spots in Chobe some ten kilometres from the Zambian border post. The following morning once cleared through customs and safely ferried across the Zambezi River I set off for Lusaka. I had seriously contemplated flying up in the Cessna, but was not sure firstly, of the availability of a hired vehicle and secondly, of my movements once there. It had been many years since I last entered Zambia.

Having absolutely no idea what to expect I was shocked at the condition of the main national road. The potholes never ended, not ever. They were so bad I felt the only purpose of the remaining original tar was to hold the potholes together! Any loss of concentration whilst weaving your way through could be a disaster, not to mention the police roadblocks. Like the potholes, they were never ending with officials openly asking for handouts, as they were hungry! Shelling out money to allow you to continue with your trip appeared to be the norm regardless of whether your car was brand new, in perfect working order or an old skorra-skorra with no lights or windscreen and smooth tyres. Water Affairs had closed by the time I arrived, having wasted a lot of time trying to find them.

I booked into the Holiday Inn for the night and was back at the Water Affairs offices first thing the following morning. All went to plan and I was pleasantly surprised at the efficiency in the main office block. I obtained the comprehensive document in a short time and paid the tender fee within an hour of entering the offices. As I walked out to my vehicle, I had one of my many spontaneous impulsive thoughts. Having driven all the way up to Zambia figured I should continue up to the Copper Belt and do some homework on registration with the mines as a drilling contractor. I always believed nothing ventured nothing gained so decided to go for it.

I set off travelling north for a further four hundred kilometres. After two days of rushing around from mine to mine I was successful in obtaining all the necessary registration paperwork required for the separate mines in the area. Zambia is extremely rich in copper ore spread over a vast region known as the Copper Belt and necessitating separate mining operations; Chingola, Mufalira, Ndola, Kitwe and Luanshya with Chingola having the largest operating open cast pit in Africa.

On my return through Lusaka, I stopped off at the governmental company's registration offices. There I obtained all the documentation required for a new initiative by the government to promote investment by foreign companies in the issuing of investment licences. A successful applicant would have many advantages as in help with wages for the first few years and no duties required on the importation of goods required to run the operation. There were also tax benefits, an extremely attractive offer to tempt one to come into the country and set up business. I collected all the application forms of which there were many, then headed off back to Botswana.

With help mainly from Alan Longstaff combined with many trips backwards and forwards to Lusaka, we managed to complete all requirements to the satisfaction of the licence board and be granted a full investment licence.

Strangely enough, the primary reason for my entering Zambia in the first instance was for collection of the water boring contract documentation. The tender documentation was eventually completed after a tremendous amount of time and effort put in by all contractors concerned. I personally hand delivered our documents a week ahead of the closing date, to Water Affairs in Lusaka.

Chapter 94

Some months later after endless attempts by me to obtain clarification of tender results, I discovered the contract had been postponed indefinitely; reason being all monies set aside for the operation had mysteriously vanished! That was it! There was no mention of compensation for the costly tendering exercise, not only in completing and putting the documents together, but also for all the unnecessary travel expenses incurred let alone the R1, 000.00 tender fees!

Although a huge set back to all concerned Alan, Gus and I decided to continue with the possibilities of our setting up a new drilling company in Zambia. Unanimously we decided to operate out of Kitwe. Fortunately, through a contact we managed to secure a long-term rental lease on a large house and a workshop/office block. Nothing fancy, but would adequately suit our purpose. Over the following six weeks we began importing drilling equipment from both Botswana and South Africa. Having secured and registered the investment licence with customs proved to be a huge advantage making passage through the Kazangula border post far less stressful. It most certainly proved to be worth its weight in gold.

Our first diamond-drilling contract in Zambia was up in the Solwezi area approximately two hundred kilometres west of Chingola. What impressed me about the area on my first trip was the density of the trees. After turning off onto a little dirt track leading to the drill site from the main road I stopped and climbed out to admire the intensely green canopy. I found it difficult to spot even the smallest area that was not completely shaded.

Despite the beauty there was something missing, a special something; bird life, there simply wasn't any. In fact the area was barren of any life whatsoever; it was surreal, not a sound or movement anywhere, not even a lizard could be seen. The explanation given to me by the geologist on site was that any animal, bird or otherwise that moved was either caught and eaten by the locals or sold to passing traffic. The unemployment rate of the area was extremely high and through this hunger and desperation sets in resulting in drastic measures to survive,

We were pleasantly surprised as to just what impressive drilling it turned out to be in the area. The formation was solid, yet produced great penetration rates and bit mileage. We could not have wished for a better kick-start to our Zambian drilling operations. Having done some homework on pricing, I felt we had gone in at a realistic rate per metre for Zambia, but must say it was significantly higher than our Botswana drilling prices. Any drilling company not making decent profits in these conditions should not be in the drilling game. This set us up nicely and encouraged the importation of more drill rigs for future work. Suddenly the nervous beginnings not knowing if we would make it in Zambia financially instantly faded into insignificance on completion of the Solwezi contract.

The following few years we managed to keep the company running with Danie Scheepers at the helm as MD of our Zambian operations. Having the luxury of our Cessna T210 aircraft at my disposal, I was in a position to fly up at a moment's notice when needed to help with drilling problems, or supply spares desperately required.

We successfully tendered for a large drilling project between Kitwe and Chingola for the Japanese, which turned into a most enjoyable contract. The chief geologist for the project, Mr. Shugawara, only spoke broken English making communication difficult, however, over time we all became good friends. He knew what he wanted and made sure he got it and yet was an absolute gentleman, had a wonderful sense of humour and was a pleasure to work with.

Due to the deeper holes, we had to import a few of our larger drilling rigs and the contract continued for several years helping to keep our nose above water. Due to the poor exchange rate of the local currency the Kwacha, there were piles and piles of cash required when drawing wages at the bank. So much so, we used a tin trunk to shovel the notes into, at the bank teller. When paying out huge bundles of cash in wages the employees accepted that it had to be right, there were just too many bundles of cash to count. The largest paper money denominations at that time were five hundred Kwacha notes.

As time went on, we were able to purchase the workshop/office property and began to feel at home in what is truly a beautiful country. Business, although experiencing many issues over the years, some good and some bad, had gone well. In the year 2000, we tendered for some deep hole work for ZCM (Zambian Copper Mines) to the north of Chililabombwe close to the Zaire border. The contract started fairly well, but as the holes became deeper, so the problems mounted.

The formation with badly faulted zones proved extremely difficult drilling conditions.

In a bid to speed up production we decided to upgrade to a new top drive machine locally manufactured and designed in South Africa. There are times in business where wise decisions are made and sometimes not. Test holes drilled within the manufacturer's plot in Johannesburg proved to be most impressive. The machine was easy to operate, handled the high rotation speeds smoothly and with a three-metre continuous top drive head went a long way in convincing us to go ahead with the purchase.

The rig and transportation thereof to Zambia was a massive drain on our financial resources. Added to this, serious problems on the rig surfaced from the first hole. The machine's hydraulic oil overheated excessively, the rod holder malfunctioned and the four-metre hydraulic chromed ramrod scored badly for no apparent reason, leaking oil everywhere. To add to what had now become a major setback on the contract, our site manager by sheer negligence on his part, managed grouting in a string of drill rods at depth.

I spent my life flying backwards and forwards between Botswana and Zambia sorting out problems. It was endless and slowly, but surely, the stress levels increased. A particular trip comes to mind. My operator was in the process of lowering the rod string to start the next drill run. Whist I had a spare moment I drove into town to collect rations for the staff. On my return as I pulled up under a tree close to the rig, I saw out of the corner of my eye something falling from the drill mast. It happened so quickly that I had not even turned the engine of my vehicle off. Realising it was one of the crew that had fallen, I raced across to the rig in the Land Cruiser.

As luck would have it or more accurately lack thereof, James fell with his head smashing onto the knife-edge of a 50mm steel angle iron stitch welded to the base plate of the rod stand, effectively splitting it open. Shocked by the extent of his injury, I thought surely he cannot have survived, yet there was a gurgling sound coming from his mouth. Without another thought, I stripped off my overall jacket and wrapped it tightly around his head in an attempt to stem the bleeding and hold his head together. With the help of my staff we loaded him onto the back of my vehicle. I called for two others to climb into the back to support him and raced off, headed for the clinic. I honestly felt the chances of his being alive on arrival were slim in the extreme.

I phoned in to alert the nursing staff and explained the severity of the injury. Immediately on arrival, they wheeled him inside and treatment commenced. As he was now in professional hands, with nothing further I could do for him, I raced back, still in a state of shock, to the rig to investigate what had caused the terrible accident.

It transpired the reason for James being up there was to join the last drill rod through the chuck. As he was tightening it in with a rod wrench, accidentally the operator leaned over to engage second gear and accidentally bumped the small air clutch plastic lever with his overall. The clutch engaged spinning the rod with wrench attached, knocking him clean off the side of the mast.

The offending switch is small and had been in the same position for as long as I could remember. To take immediate remedial action I loosened and turned the switch around to make it completely inaccessible to an accidental bump. It did not help James in hospital with his head split open, but ensured the incident could not be repeated.

Due to the extremely strict safety clauses, understandably, I was obliged to go into the mine offices and commence with accident reporting procedures. On arrival, the safety officer insisted I transport him back to site for a physical investigation, prior to completing the documentation. I pointed out that I had already taken remedial action and explained exactly what had taken place. Fortunately, as none of the other rigs operated with an air clutch I managed to convince him not to stop those machines as we were on a very tight schedule.

Adding to the drama, the new rig operating some five hundred metres away dropped the rods down the hole due to hydraulic failure! I was smoking at the time and it is amazing how consumption thereof increases with rising stress levels. When was this going to stop, I had been under huge stress for some months now and it seemed never ending. The following day I was required to attend a meeting at 4pm in the ZCCM head offices. Initially called for by ZCCM to discuss our poor performance over the last six months, but just to add a little more stress, the accident would most likely head the agenda.

I worked through the night firstly pulling the new rig off the hole and replacing it with the old one. I was then in a position to commence the fishing job with some confidence of rig reliability. Admittedly, a sad thing to say considering our massive outlay for the new rig that had as yet to complete its first deep hole, yet factual!

Eventually I was simply too tired to continue and managed to get into bed at 4am having been on the go from 6am the previous morning. I only spent three hours in bed and was back on site trying to sort things out. Many people had warned me of a possible break down, saying I could not keep going the way I was. I immediately dismissed this, saying I was fit and strong and believed myself to be infallible.

Chapter 95

I was making head way with the fishing of the dropped rods when at 11am I started experiencing chest pain. It was a strange kind of pain, but mentally I dismissed it as simply being a case of severe heartburn, something from which I normally don't suffer. I honestly felt if I were able to burp, it would go away. My primary concern was getting the rods free to enable myself to take something positive to the meeting.

To be frank, we certainly had under-performed and regardless as to whose fault it might have been, the responsibility lay squarely on my shoulders. However, throughout my drilling career never had I been kicked off a contract for any reason. I was most certainly trying my utmost to avoid that happening today. Knowing ninety percent of my problems up here were due to negligence on the part of our managers irked me in a big way. I spent my life trying to extinguish their fires and had dismissed the latest manager with immediate effect some weeks back telling him never to come anywhere near my rigs again.

The pain in my chest persisted, but so did my obsession to sort out the in-hole problem. I was quite obviously under extreme stress and not thinking rationally. One of my labourers approached me saying he was unable to start the mud pump that I needed desperately for circulation of drilling fluids. I wandered off to the pump, crouched down to check the battery connections and when trying to lift my left arm nothing happened, it just would not move! Wow, that is strange I thought to myself and using just the right arm managed to get the pump started. As I stood up to go back to the machine, the pain in my chest increased dramatically. I called for Kobus, our new manager that Alan had sent up. He came with a known working track record having being employed by Alan in South Africa at the time and had many years of drilling experience behind him.

"Listen, I have a terrible pain in my chest so I'm going to rest in the vehicle for a short while," I said and was surprised at how breathless I was.

"I think we should rush you through to the clinic and have you checked out."

"You know full well there is no time for that! We must have the rods out by this afternoon or we will all be looking for work, please could you continue with what I was doing." I then walked off and climbed into the driver's seat of my vehicle.

As I settled down, it felt like a bulldozer had just driven over my chest. I cannot find words to describe the pain, but it was nothing like I had ever experienced before. Richard happened to be standing next to the passenger window. He was the Zimbabwean companies' store-man who had lost his left arm in an accident some years back and had come up to help put our stores back in order.

"Richard, please jump in quickly!" I shouted.

"Why Trevor, what is wrong?" he rightfully enquired.

"Don't argue with me Richard, I could well need your help so please jump in quickly, I must get myself to medical help fast!" As he climbed in, I was already firing the engine into life and raced off in a cloud of dust before he had even closed his door. I was driving and changing gear with only the use of my right hand.

"Trevor, what the hell is going on, shit you are driving much too fast?"

"Sorry Richard, but it has at last struck me that I'm having a serious heart attack and need to get to the clinic as fast as possible!"

He held on for dear life as I went sliding through the corners on the winding little dirt road. After a few kilometres my vision became hazy, I started seeing different colours and then passed out! To this day, I have no recollection as to how Richard managed to not only stop the car, but manage with one arm to pull me out and get me into the passenger seat, but know I will be eternally grateful to him for saving my life.

I started coming around as Richard pulled into the clinic. I felt weak, the pain persisted and the sweat flowed freely from every pore in my body; *'when oh when is this nightmare going to end'* I thought to myself.

I knew then it was just a matter of time before my heart stopped beating! The thought crossed my mind that I would never see my family again to tell them I loved them or even be able to tell them what had happened to me, surely life isn't supposed to end this way. What was I thinking stressing over a drilling project to that extent when all I will get for my efforts will be to die of heart failure?

One of the medical staff came out to the car pushing a wheelchair and opened my door. I, feeling like death warmed up, was not in high spirits.

"If you think I'm going to get into that bloody thing you can just go to hell!" I shouted.

"Well sir, I'm just trying to help you, if you think you are able to walk into the clinic on your own then please do so."

Desperately wanting to prove I was capable, tried in vain with every bit of reserve I had left to get out of the car and as if paralysed, was unable to move any part of my body. This enhanced tenfold the feeling I now harboured of my imminent death.

"Now, sir, may I please help you into the chair and take you through to the emergency room?" I have to give him his due; I had been excessively abusive yet he had remained calm and polite. I apologised and was then physically removed from the vehicle like a sack of mealies and placed in the chair. Once inside the clinic the nursing staff helped me onto a bed where I lay flat on my back. The nurse said the doctor was on his way and would be there shortly.

"Listen to me sister, I'm having a serious heart attack and am about to die. I have seen on TV that people in this situation are given a pill to put under their tongue, please I need one of those now!" "Oh, aren't you such a clever fellow who believes in his abilities of self diagnosing! Now for the last time please try to relax and wait for the doctor."

"Well just remember when I die whose fault it is and to let the doctor know I asked for the pill." All I received in return was a smile or was it possibly a sneer; I really was not quite sure which? Clearly I was not going to get anywhere with her so I lay there quietly, as instructed, wondering how much longer I was going to last.

Within a short while, the doctor arrived and confirmed after a check over and ECG that I had in fact experienced a severe heart attack. He explained that he unfortunately never had the medication to inject into my heart to free the blood clot so was going to heavily sedate me and closely monitor my progress whilst arrangements were made for my emergency flight to Johannesburg.

Chapter 96

By this stage, Richard had phoned to let Alan, Gus and my family know what had transpired. Alan immediately booked a flight for Les to come up and she would arrive the following day. The nursing staff wheeled me off into a ward with only one other patient and left me to sleep off the effects of the sedation administered.

A few hours later, I woke to the sounds of people wailing. I looked around struggling to work out where I was. Slowly it dawned on me that I was in the clinic and discovered the reason for the wailing was due to the other patient having died! His whole family were there and understandably in an extremely traumatised state. Once again, the negative thoughts crossed my mind. Could this be a bad omen? Was I to be next? Would Les arrive in time just so I could see her before I go?

Eventually the room cleared leaving me completely on my own thinking how lonely my death would be. Shortly thereafter, the chief geologist who would have attended our scheduled meeting kindly popped in to see how I was feeling. I could not resist and joked with him saying that although I certainly had not been looking forward to the meeting, felt I had pushed it a little too far trying to get out of it. Anyway, he laughed and said it was fine and I should not worry about anything except getting well. The combined effects of the heart attack and the sedation had me passing in and out of sleep mode. I cannot remember him leaving.

The following afternoon I was thrilled when Les arrived. Initially I was not sure if I had died and she was an angel that had come down to take me away. How I had made it through the night was a miracle and proof of the fact only the good die young; I was obviously going to be around for some time!

The following day an ambulance, severely lacking working shock absorbers transported me from the hospital to Chingola airport. The ride was incredibly rough that even had I not been in the throes of having a heart attack, would most certainly have had one from the hairy ride! It felt almost like riding a bucking bronco.

Once there I was loaded into a light aircraft and flown to Lusaka. Being a hot afternoon the flight if anything was worse than the ambulance ride, the plane, due to heat waves bounced around terribly. Again I thought to myself, why oh why me? What is it I had done to deserve such agony?

From Lusaka, a Med-Rescue King Air aircraft flew us to Johannesburg with two medical personnel constantly on hand monitoring my vitals. It was a wonderful surprise to see my two sons Darrin and Dion, who had travelled down from Botswana to accompany us in the ambulance to the Morningside Hospital.

My heart was too weak to perform an angiogram immediately. Due to this, my cardiologist kept me heavily sedated in ICU for a few days until stable enough. Darrin, my eldest, had been working for me for seven years at this stage. Whilst standing at my bedside I told him he would have to take over and run the business until I could get back on my feet. Understandably, he felt he was not ready. I assured him he would manage just fine and to remember Alan or Gus would always be there if help were required.

Eventually my cardiologist felt he could go ahead and perform the angiogram. After pumping the ink into the artery and with the help of a large TV screen, he thoroughly explained and pointed out all the damage to not only arteries, but also the heart muscle. He also mentioned it was unbelievable any human being could have survived the severity of the attack, especially considering the remote location it took place.

Seeing the carnage concerning my heart on the screen, I jokingly asked if there was any way of changing channels to another program. Receiving a puzzled look from my cardiologist I verified my statement by telling him the channel we were watching really wasn't great. My cardiologist laughed saying he was impressed I was able to maintain a sense of humour under these conditions. The results of the angiogram were then saved to the hard drive on the computer. A meeting was then called to inform Les and I of the way forward.

Shame, when Les learned of the extent of the damage and serious heart surgery required she burst into tears, the whole episode had proved terribly traumatic for all. We were certainly in for a long haul; it would be quite some time before I'd be fully mobile once more. I say we, as I believe stress and pain for a loved one, if anything, could be greater than mine.

The day finally arrived for what turned out to be an extremely complicated procedure. Not only did I have to undergo triple by-pass heart surgery, but also and even more devastating, a large section of dead heart muscle was surgically removed off my left ventricular. Unfortunately, the cause of the dead heart muscle was the excessive time span between the actual heart attack and hospitalisation in Johannesburg. So much so, it reduced the total heart mass by 25%. I am informed, had the blockage taken place in the right ventricular heart muscle, the problem would have been far less devastating to my general health. I spent a further two weeks in hospital and lost ten kilograms in weight. Through either the heart trauma or the meds prescribed, I was unable to keep any food down. Effectively, my only nourishment was through the drip. Admittedly, it works wonders as a diet, but I seriously do not recommend it to anyone!

Chapter 97

My cardiologist, after releasing me from hospital, strongly advised that, if possible, I should retire. He felt going back into the same stressful situation I had been in could well kill me due to my weakened heart. I was extremely grateful to him for his professionalism and expertise from the day I arrived. Quite honestly, I believe if not for him I wouldn't be in a position to write this book. Two special friends, Mike and Mary Heir from Selebi-Phikwe, owned a townhouse within close proximity to the hospital they used when in Johannesburg. Mary kindly phoned Les offering their home to us for however long we it needed during my recuperation time prior to the long drive back home. It is at times like this you realise who your real friends are and we have been eternally grateful for their kindness.

We were desperate to continue working and living in Botswana, but also knew it would need to be at a far less involved pace. Les and I had lived for more than half our lives in that beautiful country; our boys were babies when we first came in and were now both grown up and qualified in their own right. Truly, Botswana to all intents and purposes had become home, we had made some wonderful friends and we were blissfully happy there.

I promised the family I would step back and leave all the drama and stress to Darrin and Alan. By the expression on their faces, clearly none of them believed a word I said. Initially, being weak from my ordeal and going out of my way to relax, through necessity I behaved reasonably well in that regard. However, having run the company for so many years my way, as I became stronger unintentionally I started forcing my way back in again. It had nothing to do whatsoever with Darrin's handling of things. He took to it like a duck to water and was doing a great job of running the company. Plain and simply I believe the only reason was my compulsive and highly competitive attitude; something I was born with, it was in my blood and not going anywhere.

I was not only getting in Darrin's hair and making life difficult for him, but also felt weak and out of breath when trying to be clever and overdo things. Eventually, through lengthy discussion with our boys, our two partners, Alan and Gus, both of whom played a massive role in our lives, we decided death at fifty-one years of age through heart failure due to stupidity was possibly not the right option. The extremely difficult and heart rendering decision was made for Les and I to pack up and move out of Botswana to the quaint little town of Port Alfred in the Eastern Cape of South Africa.

A year before all this drama began we were fortunate in purchasing a three bed roomed house with amazing sea views for a real bargain. Our initial thoughts were to use it as a holiday home with the intention of ultimately retiring to that beautiful part of the world. Little did we know at the time this would take place ten years before our envisaged retirement age!

Within a month of making the decision, we left the Martins Drift border post from Botswana into South Africa for early retirement. The tears rolling down Les's face as we drove away said it all. Sadly, once again, we were leaving a country we had permanently lived in for twenty-eight years and grown to love and felt was home.

Darrin continued from where I had left off running both the drilling and MTS (Mining and Technical Services) Supply Company and grew from strength to strength. He has built a wonderful reputation in the drilling world through hard honest work. Owing to the difficulties in exploration drilling due mainly to the 2008 recession, he successfully diversified in many areas, not only in the two businesses he now owns and controls, but also on managing a game farm in the Tuli Block.

Dion on the other hand, after qualifying as a civil engineer, spent a few years working for C&H Builders based in Phikwe. They were undoubtedly one of the biggest in Botswana and run hands on by the owners, our good friends Mike Heir and Tony O'Connell. The experience gained on large contracts whilst with them proved to be invaluable to him in later years.

A building contractor in Francistown happened to be leaving Botswana to move overseas and was in the process of wanting to sell his company. Dion, methodical in everything he ever undertook, was no different here. He knew the owner personally, but nonetheless closely studied everything there was to know about the company. Satisfied, but requiring every cent he could put together including the shirt off his back, he bravely dealt with the problem directly and bought them out. Aware this was a good opportunity, he also knew that unless applying himself one hundred percent, together with a little bit of good luck thrown in, this new venture could ruin him entirely.

He started small, accepting any work that came his way regardless how insignificant. Working long hours, month in month out, he slaved to find enough money to pay wages. Feeling sure he was on the brink of insolvency he somehow always managed to scrape through.

He wondered if the struggle would ever change. What about the future, was there one? Would all the effort put in only produce, at best, a break even set up? Working those long stressful hours and only turning over enough cash to pay debtors and wages had him wondering if leaving C&H was a good idea. If there was ever a youngster going through a desperate learning curve in both life and business, it was Dion.

Through necessity and sheer determination, he pushed on. Amazingly, within five years he managed to turn things around to such an extent that in 2012 his company, IP Investments, received the honour of the prestigious Building Contractor of the Year award for Botswana. With the award came a first prize of a brand-new seven-ton truck, a beautifully framed belt and certificate to hang on the wall of his office. Possibly worth far more financially, two massive billboards were erected, one in Gaborone and one in Francistown in prime location on the National road advertising, his company together with a picture of himself proudly holding the award.

To say I was a proud father of both our children and all they have achieved would be a gross understatement. Although extremely sceptical of our move to Botswana from South Africa way back in 1973, it proved to be everything and more to us. Too numerous to name individually, I would like to thank all who helped make our stay possible and who added to the unforgettable experience it turned out to be. We will dearly miss the working challenges, wonderful people and close friends made during our time in that beautiful country.

The End

About the Author

Trevor Frost was born in Harare Zimbabwe on the 21ˢᵗ September 1948. Schooled at Haig Park Junior and Ellis Robbins High schools, he left end of 1965.

Enlisted and completed army training with the Rhodesian Army in 1966.

By shear chance in September 1968, he found employment with R.A. Longstaff (Pvt) Ltd a well-known drilling company based in Harare as a learner diamond driller, this turned into a life-long career.

1972 the author, his wife Lesley and two boys Darrin and Dion left Rhodesia immigrating to South Africa.

August 1973 proved a major turning point in their lives when offered the position as Managing Director for R.A. Longstaff (Botswana) (Pty) Ltd based in Selebi-Phikwe, Botswana. The family were privileged to live through the transformation of Botswana, beginning in 1973 from what was essentially a land-locked desert to the fastest growing country in Africa after the discovery of diamonds at Orapa and Jwaneng, today two of the largest diamond mines in the world. In 2000, he experienced a serious heart attack in Zambia, followed by major heart surgery. Due to the extent of heart damage and muscle lost through his ordeal his cardiologist encouraged him to retire. Sadly, in 2001, he and his wife Lesley packed up and moved to Port Alfred in the Eastern Cape, where he now resides. His two son's stayed on in Botswana, Darrin running their drilling company and Dion running his own construction company.

With more time available to him his eldest sister Monica encouraged him to write about his amazing experiences whilst drilling and living in the wilds of the old Rhodesia. His first book 'Where Leopards Cough' was completed and self-published in March 2012. In August 2014, Partridge Publishing Africa a Random Penguin House Company have since published the book. The author's belief and success of his original book led him to write the sequel: 'Scorched Sands of the Kalahari'

Printed in Great Britain
by Amazon